History of the Improved Benevolent and Protective Order of Elks of the World

1898 1954

By

CHARLES H. WESLEY

THE ASSOCIATION FOR THE STUDY OF
NEGRO LIFE AND HISTORY, INC.
WASHINGTON, D. C.

Originally published by the Association for
the Study of Negro Life and History,
now known as the Association for the Study
of American American Life and History (ASALH).

Reprinted in 2010 by The ASALH Press
a program of ASALH.

“Keeping the Lamp of Learning Burning”

The Tri-States Association of Maryland, Delaware, and the District of Columbia Education Department of the Improved Benevolent Protective Order of the Elks of the World, takes great pride in the establishment of the reprint of this History authored by the fourteenth General President of the Alpha Phi Alpha Fraternity, Inc.

Presidents

Carlton Stanley Jean Russell

To Brothers, Daughters, Youths,
In Antlered Friendship fused,
Marching onward toward the Light,
Unawed by shadows in the Night;
Testing weakness with their strength;
Drawing *Charity* to its length;
Seeking *Justice* and not power;
Serving *Fidelity's* finest hour.
So was the *Love* of Elkdom born.
Can any afford this Past to scorn?
For surely in story and song
Elkdom will be remembered long.

BENJAMIN FRANKLIN HOWARD,
First Grand Exalted Ruler, 1899-1909;
Founder of the Order

Preface

Probably no organization, born within the borders of Negro life in the United States with the promise of a continuous expansion, has been more colorful in its leadership and extensive in the influences of its membership and their contacts than the Improved Benevolent and Protective Order of Elks of the World. In many ways the history of this Order has to do with the struggles for citizenship and an improved status for the Negro population in the United States. While its narration deals primarily with fraternal history, the related aspects of American life are noted throughout this historical era, for these events did not take place in a vacuum. The facts of this past have been centered briefly in major descriptive trends, and they have been presented with reference to their bearing on the pivotal fact of the development of Elkdom among Negroes. This book seeks to sketch the changes which took place in this development mainly during the first half of the twentieth century. Since there is fluidity in all historical events, the account will extend backward into the nineteenth century and forward into years beyond the mid-century. It will embrace specifically the period, 1898 to 1954.

It is impossible to list all the sources of information in materials and personal narration from which the following chapters have been derived. Dr. Robert H. Johnson, the Grand Exalted Ruler, gave full cooperation in this project and instructed all Grand Officers and subordinate lodge officers to cooperate in the furnishing of materials. The Annual Minutes of the Grand Lodges and related records were placed at my disposal by the Grand Secretary, Judge William C. Hueston. The author was able to use the files of the *Washington Eagle,* which Judge Hueston had assembled for this account. Libraries visited in search of materials were the Library of Congress, the New York City Libraries and the Library of the New York Historical Society. Reliance has been placed upon these sources, and in many instances, quotation marks will indicate that the author desires to permit the actors themselves in this historical drama to tell their story in their own words.

The chapters, one to three, were read first by Grand Exalted Ruler Johnson and Grand Secretary Hueston. I am grateful for the opportunities of discussing questions of fact and opinion with both of them. Mrs. Leah Wilson, widow of J. Finley Wilson, deceased Grand Exalted Ruler, sent materials dealing with his life and contributions. Past Grand Exalted Ruler T. G. Nutter sent copies of the Virginia Cases, which were most helpful in the establishment of the historical facts. He and Past Grand Exalted Ruler, Judge Armond W. Scott, read chapters in the account and gave their critical judgment upon them. Grand Exalted Ruler Johnson, Grand Secretary Hueston and Brother George B. Murphy, Jr., have been most generous with their time and thought in reading the manuscript and in giving valuable suggestions. My wife has shared in the tedious task of reading the somewhat chaotic manuscript in its first typing. The cover was designed by Jean Paul Hubbard, Professor of Art at Central State College. Brother Arthur Warren provided the opportunity for the author to peruse Meade Detweiler, *An Account of the Origin and Early History of the Benevolent and Protective Order of Elks of the U.S.A.* Additional material for Chapter I was obtained from James R. Nicholson, *History of the Order of Elks, 1868-1952,* secured through the offices of Grand Exalted Ruler Johnson and Grand Secretary Hueston.

The names of those who have helped have been numerous and the author offers all of the unnamed his cordial gratitude, for it is due to many of them that the book has its value.

This volume has been written chiefly because the author has derived interest and satisfaction in its preparation and completion, and it is his hope that its readers may receive some reflection of his endeavors. Service to Negro Elkdom has been also a main incentive in the preparation of this work. The author will be fully rewarded if those who read this book will learn to know the facts of the struggles of Negro life and organization in the face of opposition, exclusion and segregation and observe how, in spite of these, the American tradition continues to live and grow through their historic contributions.

CHARLES H. WESLEY

Central State College,
Wilberforce, Ohio,
June 1, 1955.

Table of Contents

List of Illustrations

Foreword

BY

DR. ROBERT H. JOHNSON,
Grand Exalted Ruler, I.B.P.O.E. of W.

There has been a long standing need for an historical account of The Improved Benevolent and Protective Order of Elks of the World. An interpretation of the past achievements and accomplishments of this great order has been long past due. Among the organizations which have served the social, moral and spiritual needs of the colored people of the world, and through them other people, none is more deserving of a permanent record than this order which God has blessed so abundantly through the years. The Centennial celebration in 1948 was a good period when we should have had such a history, but we were occupied with the solution of problems of organization and growth during this time. However, the years since then have furnished more color to the luster of the story now told so effectively for us by the great historian and Brother Elk, Dr. Charles H. Wesley.

Several feeble efforts have been made to tell our story, but no one has reached the highwater mark of the following chapters and pages. This task was more difficult than any of us had thought. Small pamphlets of several pages were written, read to the Grand Lodges and printed for distribution under the title of our history. But we knew all the time that our story awaited the mind and hand of Wesley, our Master Historian. Little pamphlets called histories of our Order were prepared by Brothers Arthur J. Riggs and R. M. S. Brown and Daughter Emma V. Kelley, First Grand Daughter Secretary of the Grand Temple. Brother James E. Kelley, one of our great Grand Secretaries, wrote a history of the Order as a part of his Eighth Report to the Grand Lodge. These pages in his report were not ever published in separate form. These efforts were worthy attempts, but they were feeble ones when placed beside this work by Brother Wesley, which is our pioneer endeavor in book form.

When I became Grand Exalted Ruler, the first report which I made to the Grand Lodge of 1952 contained a recommendation that "a Historian be appointed for the Grand Lodge to bring the record of the Grand Lodge from its institution to date." Another evidence of this interest was my recommendation that the three living Past Grand Exalted Rulers be cited and honored by the Grand Lodge of 1953 for their worthy contributions to our great order. In the meantime, I was thinking and planning for our history book and I got in touch with Dr. Charles H. Wesley, President of Central State College and President of the Association for the Study of Negro Life and History. He had been interested in Elkdom for years, had delivered addresses at several Grand Lodge sessions including the address at our historical session, the Centennial Grand Lodge at Cincinnati, Ohio in 1948. In response to my request, he agreed to undertake the writing and preparation of the history. I requested our Grand Secretary, Brother W. C. Hueston, and all Grand Lodge officers and subordinate officers and brothers to give him every cooperation in the completion of this great and difficult task.

Then, at the Mid-year Conference in January, 1954, Brother Wesley submitted the plan and the first report on the history. I reported to this conference in the following words. "The history of the Improved Benevolent and Protective Order of Elks of the World was submitted by Dr. Charles H. Wesley, who is a brother Elk, educator, and one of America's outstanding orators. As we have never had a complete history written for a number of years, I, as Grand Exalted Ruler of the I.B.P.O.E. of W., by the power vested in me, have authorized a committee to work with Brother Wesley to bring our history up to date from 1898 to 1953." We found later that it was not necessary for this committee to function, and that the year 1954 could be added to our history.

My authorization was unanimously approved at the 1954 Grand Lodge and in the midst of an enthusiastic demonstration was crowned by the vote of all delegates and visitors for Dr. Wesley to continue his work and bring it to full conclusion. The result is that we now have a great book of twenty chapters telling our story in well written words from 1898 to 1954.

It would be an impossible assignment to embrace all of our subordinate lodges and temples, numbering in the thousands, in a single book. It is hoped that this Grand Lodge History will stimulate each subordinate lodge and temple to write its own history, call the names of its heroes, heroines and sainted dead whose works now live in Elkdom today. There have been so many who have contributed to our achievements that the names and deeds of all of them could not possibly be recounted in one book, but a great story has been told by the author of these events and currents in our history.

Every Elk brother and sister should have a copy of his own. It should be read, kept at home and in the office for reference. There is a great pride which will come to Elks who read of the achievements of our Order and view the milestones along the highway of our history. Pride in being an Elk because one belongs to an organization with a worthy past is an important quality for all of our members to have. This can be a cause for greater achievement in the future. For upon the past, under God, we can build a greater future. Every community library should have a copy, for this account is of interest to all who read. It is a story which should be widely read. It records leadership, cooperation, service, assistance in education, health programs and civil rights. It will develop loyalty for the larger tasks which are before us. It will bring hope for the future because there has been hope in the past through which contributions have been made by our great Order to men and women of color and to all mankind in the parts of the world reached by our Elkdom. Upon this good past, let us build a more worthy future!

Introduction
The Historical Background

The organization of lodges, clubs and societies among Negroes was the result of the need and desire for fellowship, association and advanced status. These were to be derived through the power of association exemplified in group traditions, symbols, titles, ceremony and ritual which were the characteristics of fraternities through long years. These organizations were not representative of activities peculiar only to Negro-American life, for in the Eastern and Western worlds secret fraternal organizations have played important roles for many of their population groups. The American organizations have been different but in many respects they have had similarities, and the Negro organizations were often counterparts of the older ones.

These lodges, clubs and societies have also had historical backgrounds in the societies of peoples in the ancient and medieval periods. Fraternalism was an active force in the primitive societies in which the family and patriarchal government were characteristic of folk groupings. Ancient Greece had a varied assortment of organizations, and the peoples of the Middle Ages embodied ideas, loyalties, symbols and abstractions in organized groupings which contained aspects of religious faith, idealism, social and ethical conduct. Peoples in Europe, Asia, Africa and North America have had secret societies as typical institutions in their early historical life. There were secret societies, lodges, guilds, initiation groups, age groups, bush schools and totem organizations. There were religious fraternities as well as religious bases for others which were among the most influential of them. These organizations were important factors in the development of these cultures and were representative of group social and fraternal interests.

There are few historical connections between the associations of the Old World and those of the New World. The development of the frontier, the expansion into the West and the dominant growth of domestic problems removed the center of interest from Europe and the East, but the inherent desire for association was the same and continued to seek its goals. The development of urban life, the increased leisure for workers due to shorter work periods and the pressure of economic life led to the banding together of individuals who felt deeply the need of association. Out of this need came the ceremonials, initiatory rites and secret activities, the offices, parades and manifestations of membership relations, which are characteristics of the external relations of these organizations. Aid to members was fundamental in these friendly societies. Their fraternal ties bound the members in a firm union for mutual aid through small contributions to a common fund. Closely associated with these ideals was the concept of charitable assistance and benefits in times of need. Social and ritualistic ceremonies were associated with beneficial features. These features, however, were more often incidental in most of the secret societies which arose in American life.

The government of these fraternal associations had similar characteristics. There was a beginning in one lodge and then several lodges were established in other places. These lodges assembled in a representative body to create a Grand Lodge which in turn created other lodges. A constitution, a ritual and by-laws were adopted by the parent body, the Grand Lodge. This pattern was the usual one which was followed in the development of these national organizations in American life.

It has been remarked by James Bryce that "associations are created, extended and worked in the United States more quickly and effectively than in any other country." This idea is borne out in the vast number of organizations which have arisen in American life. This is especially a characteristic of the closing decades of the nineteenth century. Between 1880 and 1890, there were one hundred and twenty-four beneficial fraternal orders established and between 1890 and 1901 there were three hundred and sixty-six additional ones. This period was called the "Golden Age of Fraternity." It was at this time that the Improved Benevolent and Protective Order of Elks of the World was born.

Millions of people ultimately became joiners of American lodges, associations and clubs. These organizations grew in importance and became channels for aggressive individuals to rise to positions of leadership and influence among their followers. Men and women of ability and talent discovered that the lodges gave them opportunities to develop the types of public leadership needed in their communities. These lodges provided the experience in brotherhood and group allegiance which no other agency had supplied. The participants in the meetings had the pleasure of knowing that some of their number would be elevated to superior posts among them and that they would all have the satisfaction of belonging to an association of equals. These organizations have been regarded as normal expressions of American life and, in the case of Negro-Americans, as group expressions not too dissimilar in origins from the alignments of other members who make up the thousands and millions of joiners and belongers in the secret organizations of the nation.

During the period of slavery, Negro societies did not exist openly, as the laws during this period made it impossible for such public activities to develop without bad reactions upon the participants. It was unlawful for Negroes in the South to assemble for any such purpose during the period of slavery. However, there was usually a way found, even in slavery, to develop some of the elements of mutual protection through group associations.

The first of the formal societies which was developed among Negroes arose in Philadelphia in 1787. It was known as "The Free African Society" and had as its leaders, Absolom Jones and Richard Allen. It began with the idea "that a Society should be formed, without regard to religious tenets, provided the persons lived orderly and sober life, in order to support one another in sickness and for the benefit of their widows and fatherless children." This was the first beneficial society among Negroes. It does not appear, however, that there was any secrecy connected with the organization. Its program was one of charity and of social and individual improvement. Throughout the period prior to the Civil War similar group organizations for mutual purposes were organized.

With the close of the Civil War and the appearances of freedom for Negro-Americans, fraternalism and mutual protection hitherto fostered in secret, transformed themselves into positive and directive forces. Societies and associations for the protection of members were rapidly formed. These associations were similar, in some respects, to the earlier societies of slavery days. In their business methods, however, too often they confused fraternalism and insurance. There was also an indiscriminate admittance of members as well as the absence of the foresight and ability to handle accumulated funds. In spite of these weaknesses, these associations have filled an important place in the economic and social development of Negro-Americans. They offered an opportunity for friendly relationships, presented a field of political activity denied the majority in most of the states, and they had value for the spirit of cooperation and unity.

Various lodges and secret societies were organized among Negro-Americans. They developed not only among those in slavery but among free Negroes in the Northern states. These included such societies as the Prince Hall Lodge of Masons, organized in Boston in 1775 under Prince Hall who was made a Mason by a British Lodge. The members of the British Lodge were soldiers stationed near Boston. Hall obtained a charter for

African Lodge No. 1 and later became the First Grand Master of the First Grand Lodge of Free and Accepted Masons among Negroes. The Grand United Order of Odd Fellows, which grew out of the Philomathean Society of New York City, was another of these important societies. When this society applied for admission to the older Order of Odd Fellows in 1842, its application was refused. Peter Ogden who had been initiated in a lodge in Liverpool, England, applied for and was granted the permission to establish the Philomathean Lodge in New York City. This lodge was established in 1843. There were various secret orders among Negroes before the Civil War, such as the Galilean Fisherman, The Nazarites, The Samaritans, The Seven Wise Men and other similar societies.

During the second half of the nineteenth century and the beginning of the twentieth century there were several national secret societies which were established. There was the International Order of Twelve of the Knights and Daughters of Tabor, which was organized in 1871 by Moses Dickson of Cincinnati, Ohio. The Grand United Order of True Reformers was one of the largest of the secret societies among Negroes whose founder was Washington Browne who was born in Georgia as a slave. This organization developed into one of the most important groups from the point of view of resources and membership then existing in the United States. Its business organization marked one of the epochs in the development of Negro business. Other organizations were the Independent Order of Good Samaritans and Daughters of Samaria, the Knights of Pythias and many others which brought Negroes together in the spirit of brotherhood for aid against an environment which seemed to be hostile to them.

These organizations attracted Negroes for the same reason that similar organizations attracted other Americans. They gave aid to them in time of sickness and need. They gave opportunity for the support which seemed to be needed through their spirit of brotherhood as represented in their rituals and their distribution of charity. They gave a higher status through membership and offices in the societies, which seemed to be desirable additions in their restricted lives. The titles and uniforms served to produce an increasing respect not obtainable outside of the walls of the lodge rooms. It is of interest to observe that these fraternal organizations arose mainly in urban communities. For it was in these places that the Negro population was facing its most serious competition and opposition.

During the last decade of the nineteenth century there were

continuations of the migrations of the eighties when movements of the Negro population were taking place on large scales. Negroes flocked from the rural to the urban districts, North and South. Migrations also were from many Southern states to the largest cities of the North—Philadelphia, New York, Pittsburgh, Cincinnati, Detroit and Chicago. The migrants were from many groups. They were from the educated and the unlearned, the workers and the idlers, those with some means and those who were poorer. Many, finding that they could not locate work along their special lines of work, turned to such occupations as waiters, butlers, chauffeurs and pullman porters. They worked where they could and at any jobs which they could find. They were vendors, shoeblacks, porters, domestics and construction workers.

One of these cities, Cincinnati, was to be the birthplace of the Improved Benevolent and Protective Order of Elks of the World, the most extensive of the fraternal organizations for Negroes. Thousands of Negroes flocked to Cincinnati, since it was the gateway from the South to the Middle West and North. Negroes had made great progress in this city during the nineteenth century. Cincinnati was located in free territory but it was not a "free" city so far as Negroes were concerned. In the early years of the city's history, there were very small numbers. While no Negroes were reported in Cincinnati in 1800 there were only 337 in the entire state at this time. In 1816 there were 347 in a population of 6,493, and in 1820 they were two per cent of the total population. This slow growth had been motivated by the action of the Ohio General Assembly prohibiting any Negro from settling in the state unless he produced a certificate of freedom, was registered, and paid a fee. Later a bond of $500 was required.

In spite of this action, Negroes were increasing in number as a result of the location of the city on the Ohio River, one shore of which was slave territory, while the Northern shore was regarded as free territory. Runaway slaves and free Negroes leaving the South were harbored and welcomed by other Negroes as well as liberal whites who were opponents of slavery.

Gradually, as the decades passed, the census reports showed small population increases. Whites from the uplands of Virginia and Kentucky as well as Negroes came into the city in large numbers, although the latter often faced conditions which were more difficult. They obtained employment in not only the occupations previously mentioned but also on the steamboats plying the Ohio River and as mechanics and laborers. Some purchased real estate with their savings and went into small businesses. Some few were housed in good homes during the last decade of the last century, but the vast majority were living in delapidated shacks on poorly lighted streets and alleys. However, they joined with others, furnished educational facilities for their children and took advantage of the opportunities for the advancement of their cultural interests. Their interests in the schools were paralleled by their loyalty to their churches. The moral and religious welfare of their children was given attention along with their mental development.

By 1900, there were 14,482 Negroes, who were 4.4 per cent of the total population of Cincinnati, and by 1910 this number had increased to 19,639, or 5.4 per cent of the total population of 363,591. This was a 35.6 per cent increase in the Negro population during this decade. The foreign born population in Cincinnati in 1910 was larger than the Negro population and aggregated 15.6 per cent of the total population of the city.

The conditions facing the Negro population in Cincinnati at the opening of the twentieth century have been described by Frank W. Quillan in an article in the *Independent Weekly Magazine*. He stated that Negroes were not admitted to the medical college, the hospitals, except two small charity concerns, the fire department, the hotels, restaurants, theatres and the popular parks. Trains had "Jim Crow" coaches. Even the Y.M.C.A. refused to give them either active or associate memberships until the Walnut Street Branch was established.

Quillan wrote, "The colored man, in earning his living, is hampered on every side by race prejudice. The labor unions as a whole do not want him and will not have him, and their members will not work by the side of him. The result of this is that he is practically debarred from all mechanical pursuits requiring skill. He can join the hod carriers' union only, and this is due to the fact that not enough white men can be found to do the work. The bricklayers' union, the painters', the carpenters', the lathers', the plumbers', the barbers', the bartenders', the printers' union and many others deny him admission. . . . Besides being debarred from skilled labor, they are not employed as stenographers, bookkeepers, or office men in any capacity except that of janitor. No one is employed in the public schools, none are employed as clerks in stores or factories." It was not at all strange to learn that a Negro who came to the city said, "I though upon coming to a free state like Ohio that I would find every door thrown open to me, but from the treatment I received by the people generally, I found it little better than in Virginia."

This was the background for the organization of a lodge of Elks in Cincinnati. It was a city in which Negroes had a tough struggle for freedom and opportunity. For there were the characteristic aspects of segregation and exclusion on the one hand, and the beliefs and sentiments of democracy on the other. They were given the right to work at certain types of jobs but the privilege of acceptance in the organizational life even of the churches and religious organizations was denied to them unless they were developed on the segregated basis.

At the same time there was a trend toward the decline of the many local Negro secret societies which had developed in the latter part of the nineteenth century as defense against the impact of hostile forces. There had been a continuous dissolution of the number throughout this period. As the new century dawned, there was the larger development of a few organizations of major strength in membership and strong leadership. Among these organizations were the Masons, the Odd Fellows, The Pythians and the Elks.

With its emphasis on the value of Negro cooperation, ceremonials, uniforms, parades and race-conscious orators, the organization of Negro Elks developed into the largest of the mass fraternal movements in Negro life. With additional emphasis upon moral and ethical values, the transmission of the highest social ideals, the avoidance of alliances with radicalism, the value of patriotism and the high purpose of Charity, Justice, Brotherly Love and Fidelity, the Improved Benevolent and Protective Order of Elks of the World arose from a small fraternal society into one of the great organizations operating in Negro life. No other organization, except the church, could boast of reaching into the masses of the Negro population and at the same time into the middle class and the *intelligentsia* with its appeal and its leadership.

From an organization of small numbers in Cincinnati the Order of Elks among Negroes developed into a strong, widely spread organization of lodges in every state of the nation and in areas outside of the United States, thereby giving reality to their designation as being "of the World." The older American Order of Elks might confine its mission to white Americans and to those in the United States but the Negro Order would open its doors to admit the qualified of all groups and throughout the world. This Order was more than a protest against exclusion. It was planned as a positive good. It was not intended as a temporary expedient while the white Elks considered their admission. It was a permanent order with an invitation of welcome for all. It was not exclusively a counterpart or imitation of the white Order. It had a special mission and purpose. Its basic theory was the same but its expressions of its ideals, services and objectives were unique and created for it a distinctive place among American fraternal orders. Before beginning the discussion of the history of Negro Elkdom, it will be both necessary and desirable to give a summary presentation of the rise of Elkdom among white Americans of the Benevolent and Protective Order of Elks as a background for the subsequent study of the Improved Benevolent and Protective Order of Elks of the World.

Chapter I
The Rise of American Elkdom

American Elkdom had its rise in 1867 from an organization known as "The Jolly Corks." A small group of actors had met weekly for some time for social purposes and had selected this name for themselves. The desire for companionship and fraternal association, so common to groups of men through long periods, had brought these men together. The inspiration for the assembly of this group had come from Charles A. Vivian, an English singer and actor, who had arrived in New York from Southampton, England. He was a good entertainer and a man of pleasing personality, but he was without vision of the fraternity's tomorrow. While he was one of the forerunners of the Order of Elks, there is some question about his designation as a founder. Without doubt, he was at least a precursor, but M. D. Detweiler in his *Account of the Origin and Early History of the B.P.O.E. of U.S.A.* (1898) stated that the title of "Founder of the Elks" should be given to him.

Vivian met at the Star Hotel, Richard R. Steirly, a piano player, who was also a native of England. These two struck up a friendship and association. They joined in music and song. Other actors joined them. Their purpose was social and convivial at first. A fraternal purpose could not be discovered in the first meetings, except as these personal contacts provided. However, it has been out of such early meetings that fraternalism has developed.

They began to play games and among them was the game of Corks. This game consisted in the dropping of the cork on the bar and picking it up as rapidly as possible. The last man to pick up his cork would pay the bill for refreshments. There was considerable fun and by-play in this game and these young men found it to be an amusing and interesting pastime at a time when amusements for youth were all too few.

This period of the post-Civil War years had few recreations and sports for its young men. The growth of the population in New York City and the increase of leisure from shorter work days were responsible for the development for such games as the one played by the "Jolly Corks." Organized recreation represented in baseball, football and tennis had not been developed. It was not until more than a decade after the Civil War that these sports began to appear as national and municipal pastimes.

Cover Page of *An Account of the Origin and Early History, B.P.O. Elks, of the U.S.A., including Proceedings of Grand Lodge, 1871-1878*, by Meade D. Detweiler (1898).

In the meantime youth had to create its own ways of spending the leisure days or hours in satisfactory ways.

At the same time New York City had a Sabbath law which closed the theaters, saloons, and places of amusement on Sunday. As a result of this strict Sabbath law observance, forms of amusement were created by various groups. The "Jolly Corks" met first in 1867, played their little games and had their fun as a loosely unorganized group. They killed time with this amusement and furnished the association needed as a result of their enforced leisure.

The meetings grew rapidly in numbers as additional actors and theatrical persons came together with the original members. An initiation procedure was planned with the candidate playing the cork games. Pranks accompanied the play as corks were used in several ways by the members. These experiences seem rather silly to those of us today, but they were loads of fun to the people of the first decade after the Civil War.

Within the next year, 1868, the members of the "Jolly Corks" attended a funeral of one of their friends who was well known in local concert circles. After their return from this funeral the suggestion was made that they should change their social club into a protective and benevolent society. It was decided on February 2, 1868, that the "Jolly Corks" should organize as a lodge on a benevolent and fraternal plan with a ritual and a new name. A committee was appointed to draft a constitution. Some members came to the committee meeting at the appointed time. Others were late in arriving. While waiting for the tardy members to arrive the punctual members thought of the name "Buffalos" for the organization, and another suggested "Beavers," but the majority decided against these selections of names. Others saw the elk head and read subsequently a statement descriptive of the qualities which could be used as a basis for organizational work. The elk was the largest existing species of the deer family, found in Europe, Asia and America, and with its large antlers, weighing fifty to sixty pounds, appeared ready for the defense of itself, its young and its homely haunts on all occasions. They read the account of the elk in Buffon's *Natural History* as "fleet of foot, timorous of doing wrong, avoiding all combat except in fighting for the female and in defense of the young and helpless and weak." This description influenced the decision in favor of the elk name.

The formal change of name took place on February 16, when a committee made its report and the Benevolent and Protective Order of Elks was organized. Charles A. Vivian was chosen

AN ACCOUNT

—OF THE—

ORIGIN AND EARLY HISTORY

—OF THE—

BENEVOLENT AND PROTECTIVE ORDER OF ELKS OF THE U. S. A.

Together with

SKETCHES AND PORTRAITS OF THE FIRST MEMBERS OF THE ORDER, ALL PAST GRAND EXALTED RULERS, AND OTHER PROMINENT ELKS,

Containing also

THE GRAND LODGE PROCEEDINGS FOR THE YEARS 1871 TO 1878 INCLUSIVE.

By

MEADE D. DETWEILER,

Grand Exalted Ruler.

Published by the authority of the Board of Grand Trustees
as directed by the Grand Lodge, July, 1897.

Title Page of *An Account of the Origin and Early History of the Benevolent and Protective Order of Elks of the U.S.A.*, by Meade D. Detweiler.

Right Honorable Primo with other officers. Committees on constitution and by-laws were appointed and reported in March, providing for two degrees. By the month of May the ritualistic work was added.

Gradually two factions appeared in the organization. One group of the actors wanted the organization to develop as a benevolent and fraternal one, and to confine its membership to actors and literary men. Another group wanted to continue the convivial activities started by the "Jolly Corks." When Vivian and his friends of this point of view appeared at a subsequent meeting they were denied admission and Vivian was refused entrance to the ceremony of the second degree. His connection with the organization was then terminated. Some of his associates on this occasion were later reinstated and became members of the Order. Neither Vivian nor they seemed to realize the future possibilities of the organization as the Benevolent and Protective Order of Elks, while they sought to maintain the carefree hours of play which characterized the "Jolly Corks." However, Vivian was the first presiding officer of the Order under the title of *Right Honorable Primo* from February 18 to May 24, 1868.

On the latter date an election was held with the following being elected to the offices of the Order: George W. Thompson, Right Honorable Primo and Exalted Ruler; James W. Glenn, First Assistant Primo and Esteemed Leading Knight; William Lloyd Bowron, Second Assistant Primo and Esteemed Loyal Knight; George F. McDonald, Third Assistant Primo and Esteemed Lecturing Knight; William Sheppard, Secretary; Henry Vandemark, Treasurer and Albert Hall, Tiler.

The Order grew rapidly. The increase in numbers led to a change of location from its Delancy Street location to larger quarters at Military Hall on Bowery Street. The initiation fee was at first two dollars but was increased to five dollars on the occasion of the change to larger quarters. The first Exalted Ruler, George W. Thompson, continued in office from 1868 to 1870, when he was succeeded by George J. Green who served as Exalted Ruler until 1871.

During this period a movement for a lodge in Philadelphia had arisen. It was then inevitable that plans should be made to hold a Grand Lodge so that the subordinate lodges could have a parent body. A resolution was passed in the New York Lodge on January 1, 1871, providing for the Grand Lodge to consist of the original founders of the Order, with the present and past officers of the first and second degrees and in good standing with the Order. On February 12, 1871, the dispensation was received from the Grand Lodge for New York Lodge No. 1, which was now upon firm foundations and the second dispensation went to Philadelphia Lodge No. 2, on March 12, 1871.

The years 1868-1871, had been formative ones but with the Grand Lodge in position to issue dispensations to lodges for permanent organization the way was opened for a development and expansion which would carry the influence of the Order into the important communities of America. The charter for the Grand Lodge was obtained from the New York Legislature on March 10, 1871, and the legal existence of New York Lodge No. 1 is dated from this beginning. Other lodges were established at San Francisco, No. 3; Chicago, No. 4; Cincinnati, No. 5; Sacramento, No. 6; Baltimore, No. 7; Louisville, No. 8; St. Louis, No. 9; Boston, No. 10; and Pittsburgh, No. 11. The membership in these lodges in 1878 was 820.

The first constitution adopted on May 17, 1868, contained the following preamble which showed the background and origin of the special membership character of the organization. Its Preamble was:

> "The undersigned members of the Theatrical, Minstrel, Musical, Equestrian, and Literary Professions and others who sympathize with and approve of the object in view (hereinafter stated in the Constitution), do hereby organize an order to promote, protect and enhance the welfare and happiness of each other."

The Order thus had its beginnings among men of the theatrical and literary professions. The main purpose was to "bring the two professions into a closer union of good fellowship." Resentment was expressed at first by the actors for other professions and derision was cast at "the members of the Sororis reading art essays, the drug clerk selling pills and dry goods clerk selling tape." It was not long before other professions and occupations were well represented in those who were sympathetic with these professions, and finally this membership restriction was removed. The interest of theatrical persons continued to be active in Elkdom all over the country where lodges were located in large cities. Members of road companies frequently appeared at banquets and socials of lodges in cities where they were billed for theatrical appearances. There were intimate relationships between the stage and the elk fraternity for many decades.

Several efforts were made to revise and rewrite the ritual of the Order. In 1896 complaint was made by the Grand Exalted Ruler that the practice of having a new ritual every two or three years would not give stability to the ritual. In 1897 and 1898 a uniform ritual was adopted by the Grand Lodge and there were no alterations in it from 1899 to 1904. The sole membership requirement of this period was "no person shall be admitted to this Order under twenty-one years of age."

One of the historic milestones in Elk history was the meeting in New York City of the First Grand Lodge on February 12, 1871. There were ten members present with G. J. Green presiding and E. G. Brown as secretary. A committee on the organization of the Grand Lodge was appointed. Positions in the Grand Lodge were filled by election and the officers were installed.

Another historic milestone was the national incorporation of the Grand Lodge of the "Benevolent and Protective Order of Elks of the United States of America." Its objects were "benevolent, social and altruistic; to promote and encourage manly fellowship and kindly intercourse; and to aid, protect and assist its members and their families." Through the years, in pursuit of the tenets of the Order, millions of dollars were spent on scholarships in education, crippled children, cerebral palsey, hospitals, youth activities, flood disaster and infantile paralysis. The salute to the flag was required at each meeting and patriotic demonstrations were common practices. The flower chosen for the Order was the Forget-me-not, and the colors were purple and white. Emphasis was placed upon *white* for it was regarded as "the symbol of innocence and is the raiment of angels and of the glorified saints of joy and of victory."

These features were exemplified and adopted in the Grand Lodge sessions. These sessions were held in different parts of the nation as the years passed. From the year of organization in 1871 until 1889 with the exception of the session of 1877 in Philadelphia, the Grand Lodge sessions had been held in New York City. Beginning in 1890 to 1899 the cities serving as hosts were Cleveland, Louisville, Buffalo, Detroit, Atlantic City, Cincinnati, Minneapolis, New Orleans and St. Louis. Charters were granted to lodges at each of these sessions so that by 1898 there were 44,252 members in 442 lodges; in 1899 this membership had increased to 60,129 in 514 lodges and in 1910 there were 1,155 lodges with a membership of 304,899.

The fundamental workings of the Order were being developed in these years and also the ceremonials, regalia, the question of Sunday meetings, mutual benefit activities, state Grand Lodges, and provisions for the selection of members. In 1892 the names of the Grand Officers were changed to Grand Exalted Ruler from Exalted Grand Ruler; Grand Esteemed Leading Knight to Grand Esteemed Loyal Knight; Grand Esteemed Lecturing Knight and the Grand Trustees were changed from five in number to three. The unity of the Order was broken by a division between the Grand Exalted Ruler and the Board of Trustees. After two years of division, unity was restored by the Grand Lodge in 1895. An associate organization with its emphasis upon an insurance feature was started in the Elks Mutual Benefit Association which had a brief existence. The Grand Lodge history shows no information about the creation of this association but it seems to have been established about 1878. By 1881 there were only 117 members, with a membership fee of three dollars and an assessment of $1.10 upon the death of a member. In 1886 a committee to examine the books of the Elks Mutual Benefit Association reported that the books were correct and that the receipts of the Association were $2,884.30 and the expenditures were $2,371.87. Finally, a committee reported on the impracticability of associating the Order with any insurance or benefit association, and in 1893 the Grand Lodge adopted the report that no system of insurance was endorsed or adopted by it.

There were originally no requirements by the Grand Lodge for membership in the Order except that the applicant was required to be over twenty-one years of age. Other requirements were that he should state his name, age, business, birthplace, residence and personal references. A definite restriction in membership was made in 1890 in the following:

> "Any *white* male citizen of the United States, of sound mind and body and good reputation, over twenty-one years of age, who desires initiation in a lodge must be proposed in writing by an Elk of the lodge; said proposition shall state the name, age, business, birthplace, residence and references of the person and also whether he has ever been proposed by any lodge of the Order and with what result, over the signature of the applicant."

This requirement was placed in the Revised Statutes in 1907 and became a statutory requirement of the Order. Since the chief purpose of the Order was social, and social equality between the races was taboo, this position even in a democracy was explained on this basis.

This requirement would have kept out of the Order all non-white persons after 1890. Whether prior to this date or not, rumor has it that there were Negro members of the Order who were not known as Negroes. For long years some Negroes, light in color, have moved back and forth across the color-lines without being recognized as persons of color. "Passing" has been a continuous process with the appearance of mulattoes in the United States. The assumption that all of the people who came first from Africa were black is false, for the mulatto is as typically African as the one with the darker color. Slaves were

Harry Vandermark, clerk, Mills Hotel, N. Y.

E. W. Platt, clerk, 610 East 138th street, N. Y.

Harry Bosworth, clothing business, Fourth avenu street, N. Y.; residence, Hallett's Point, Astoria, L.

John H. Blume, who was a clerk in Pettingil's Agency; residence, No. 411 North Twenty-seventh S

Frank Langhorn, photographer, Plainfield, N. J.

Wm. L. Bowron, leader of the Fourteenth Street chestra, N. Y.; a member of New York, No. 1.

Thomas G. Riggs, actor, now residing in Australi

The deceased members are:

Chas. A. S. Vivian, comic singer.

M. G. Ashe, photographer, who died in New Orlea fever in 1868.

Wm. Carleton, Irish comedian.

Wm. Sheppard, negro minstrel.

George F. McDonald, actor.

J. G. Wilton, wood-turner.

In Bro. Wilton's case there has never been any po gence of death, but he has not been heard from for fifteen years. It was he who made the original small which is now in the possession of the G. E. R. for th being handed over, at New Orleans, to the G. L. f preservation. Of the names given above, those who Mrs. Giesman's were Vivian, Steirly, Wilton, Kent, B worth and Blume.

The popularity of the new organization soon cause tax the capacity of the boarding house parlors. Acco quarters were secured in a portion of the building N

A page from Detweiler's *An Account of the Origin and Early History of the Benevolent and Protective Order of Elks of the U.S.A.* (1898).

taken from many parts of Africa and even from the West Coast there came the browns, the yellows, and the blacks. While mulattoes have increased through miscegenation, and intermarriage where it was permitted, it must not be overlooked that colors of Negro people have not changed from an exclusively black color to white or lighter color. These Negroes and the near-white have joined various community and fraternal organizations, especially in the larger cities where people are not so well known to one another, but the extent of this crossing is impossible to ascertain.

There were also Negro actors in most of the cities where the "Jolly Corks" and the Elks were organized. The census of 1900 reports that there were 2,043 actors and showmen who were Negroes. The rumor has been persistent and has been passed on from one generation to another that there were "light-skinned" Negroes who were members of local lodges of the Benevolent and Protective Order of Elks. Some members were said to have known these members but made no reference to this knowledge in their local circles. M. D. Detweiler states in his *An Account of the Origin and Early History of the B.P.O.E. of the U.S.A.* (1898) that among the original "Jolly Corks" was "William Sheppard, Negro Minstrel." There may be some question as to whether he was a Negro or whether this designation referred to the theatrical part played by him, especially, since there was above his name that of "Wm. Carleton, Irish Comedian." Whether true or false, it is known that such a membership was not beyond the realm of possibility, and it is well known that the signs, colors, symbols, paraphernalia and ritual made their appeals to Negroes as to others.

This period in Negro life witnessed many instances of restriction and exclusion on the basis of color, similar to the action of this fraternity. The word "white" as a qualification for membership had been written into the Constitution and was a part of the customs of labor unions and other national and local organizations. The American Federation of Labor, organized in 1881, declared its interest in the organization of workers without regard to race, creed or nationality. This declaration was interpreted at first by local unions to mean the organization of separate white and Negro unions which would agree to work together for the advancement of all workers. However the separate racial organization became the historical practice.

These results were reflections of the depths to which the second class citizenship of the Negro had descended. The Fourteenth Amendment of 1868 and the Fifteenth Amendment of 1870 were nullified during this period by state action and court decisions. The Civil Rights Act of 1875 prohibiting discrimination against

Negroes in public places was short-lived. Reactions against these defenses of citizenship and Civil Rights for Negroes were swift. Organizations to maintain white supremacy had been started. Among these were the Ku Klux Klan, the Knights of the White Camellia, the White Brotherhood and the Constitutional Union Guards. Negroes were terrorized and kept from the polls and the courts. The United States Supreme Court in 1883 declared the Civil Rights Act unconstitutional. This decision opened more widely and made legal the segregation and discrimination of Negroes. Greater emphasis was given to the second class status of Negroes in the Supreme Court decision in 1896 in *Plessy v. Ferguson.* This decision declared that a state law providing for separate but equal accommodations on railroads was constitutional. Separate but equal accommodations became the rule in Northern and Southern sections where the two racial groups met. With this background, it was not difficult for the Order of Elks to take action which excluded Negro members from its fellowship. While the emphasis was placed upon the type of membership, "white" to be accepted, the exclusion of Negroes was by direct action.

Efforts were made over a long period to prevent the use of the name, the ritual and the insignia of the Order of Elks by the organization of Negro-Americans under the title of the Improved Benevolent and Protective Order of Elks of the World. In each case Negroes ultimately gained the opportunities to continue their work, either by court action or the strategy of approach and contact. This was the result in the case in Tennessee in 1909.* While the New York Court of Appeals restrained Negroes from using a name similar to the Order of Whites, and from wearing its emblem, it did not enjoin the use of the fraternity colors and the name of officers.*

Case after case was tried in state after state as injunctions were sought against the Negro organizations and their use of Elk symbols and rites. Gradually as failure resulted from these efforts, Grand Exalted Ruler Fred Harper of the Benevolent and Protective Order of Elks stated the case for the Grand Lodge in 1918 when he reported:

> "In my opinion, the most dignified and effective course for our Order to pursue in the premises is to refrain from further litigation and to pay no further attention to the Negro Elks, except to show them such consideration as may be properly

---

*(Benevolent Order of Elks v. Improved Benevolent Order of Elks. 122 Tenn. 141, 118 S. W. 389.)

*(Benevolent and Protective Order of Elks v. Improved Benevolent and Protective Order of Elks. 205 N. Y. 459.98 N.E. 7 56.)

> due an organization which claimed to be engaged in benevolent and charitable work among a race which both needs and deserves such service."

After this period there was sporadic action of local origin against the Improved Benevolent and Protective Order of Elks of the World but there was no support given to these efforts by the Grand Lodge or its officers. The two Orders were to go their separate ways, each of them building separately and dispensing charity and brotherly love. There can be no doubt that from the point of view of American democratic principles, the tenets of the United Nations and the trends toward One-World, the Order known as the Improved Benevolent and Protective Order of Elks of the World could face the future with the confidence that its membership provisions would need no change as to race, color or national origin.

Chapter II
The Beginnings of Organization

Elkdom among Negro-Americans had its rise in the Queen City of Cincinnati, Ohio, during the closing years of the Nineteenth Century. In the latter part of the month of February, 1897, Arthur J. Riggs, who was a pullman porter and a man who was active in public affairs among Negro citizens in Cincinnati, began the conception of the plan which led to the organization of the Order of Elks among Negroes. Riggs had assisted L. H. Wilson in the organization of the Knights of Pythias Lodge in Ohio. He was also described by Editor Wendell P. Dabney of the *Cincinnati Union* as a "great Orator." Dabney wrote of the pullman porters in Cincinnati, "They have contributed greatly to the course of good citizenship since many of them have been prominent in every walk of church, business and fraternal life. They own a great deal of property and are noted for being listed among our most solid and law abiding people, since the sporty, spendthrift element is dead or eliminated from the source."

Riggs stated that while carrying the idea in mind of organizing an Elks lodge, he met B. F. Howard of Covington, Kentucky, on the street in Cincinnati. He found that Howard was thinking of the same project for the organization of a lodge of Elks among Negroes in Cincinnati, which might ultimately extend throughout the United States. Howard asked Riggs about how they could obtain a ritual and the necessary lodge materials. Riggs said that he thought that a copy of the ritual could be secured. Howard then urged him to go ahead, secure the ritual, and have it printed so that the organization could be effected. Riggs obtained a copy of the ritual and undertook to have it printed.

This action was typical of Arthur J. Riggs, who is rightly called one of the founders of Elkdom among Negroes. He was born in Shelbyville, Kentucky, March 7, 1855. He was the son of Lloyd and Rachael Tevis, who were the slaves and servants for life of Reverend John Tevis, a Camelite preacher. It seems strange to us of a later generation that a preacher, as a man of God, should hold slaves, but this was not unusual in a section of the nation in which forced labor was regarded as a necessity and had become a social custom sanctioned even by religion. When his mother died, Riggs was six years of age. After freedom was declared in Kentucky, the name of "Riggs" was selected by him, instead of "Tevis", as the former was the family name of his grandparents on his father's side.

Arthur J. Riggs
Founder
Honorary Past Grand Exalted Ruler

His formal education was limited for there were no schools for Negroes in Shelbyville and in the State of Kentucky prior to the emancipation of slaves. These schools were prohibited by statute. However, in 1869, E. Munford of Ohio opened a school in the basement of the A.M.E. Church. The tuition charge was two dollars a month. Although a good size boy who was quite capable of working, Riggs was sent to school by his father. The failure to pay the tuition in advance led to the termination of his schooling, for he was asked to leave the school having been there only one month and four days. Riggs stated, my "ABC book, as it was called in that day and time, was laid aside and I was soon introduced to Old Beck, a stubborn mule, and the 'plow'."

Riggs then worked for the Crenshaw family, receiving thirty five dollars a year with board and clothes. Crenshaw was a lawyer and had to make trips to Louisville. Riggs listened to his description of the city of Louisville and determined himself to go there. He arrived in Louisville in March, 1871, and made friends with a young man who took him to the home of the William Hornsbys who was a steward on the steamer "Mary Huston." Hornsby gave Riggs a job as dishwasher on the steamer's run from Shelbyville to New Orleans. He remained at work on this steamer until May, 1872, during which time he was promoted to pantryman and then to third cook. He was later employed at the Galt House in Louisville until February, 1876, when he decided to go to Cincinnati where he secured employment at the Grand Hotel as a waiter.

Riggs married Lucy Hendricks on December 13, 1876, but because of his limited schooling was compelled to sign the marriage record book with a cross mark, which was not unusual in those days. With improvement in his economic life and after two children were born to his family, the opportunity came to him to continue his education under the private instruction of a Professor Johnson, who was said to have been a Negro of English birth and training.

After the organization of the Knights of Pythias Lodge with L. H. Wilson in 1896 and after serving as the Pythian Grand Chancellor of the State, he conceived the idea of an Elk Lodge in Cincinnati. It was not strange that there should be an inclination to organize a lodge of Elks, since the Pythians were well organized and staffed with an apparently capable leadership. Ambitious and qualified men, such as Riggs and Howard, looked for openings for leadership in other fields of fraternal activity. The prospects for the organization of a lodge of Elks and of its development through other lodges into a Grand Lodge were challenges not too difficult of acceptance by ambitious men like Riggs and Howard. In the meantime, Riggs had entered the railroad pullman service and remained in it for seven years. His participation in the organization of an Elks Lodge among Negroes led to the termination of his pullman service, for as Riggs said, "The white Elks made it so warm for me that I left Cincinnati."

It was while he was in the pullman service that Riggs had contacts with Elks who had copies of the Elks ritual. His procural of this ritual was the first active step in the inception of an Elks lodge. Moreover, the Grand Lodge of the Benevolent and Protective Order of Elks had met in Cincinnati in 1896. The office of Grand Secretary was located in Cincinnati from 1890 to 1894 and the Grand Exalted Ruler, John Galvin, was a resident of this city from 1898 to 1899. It is not unlikely that observations and contacts such as these incidents made possible awakened still further the purpose of Riggs and Howard. Whether Riggs secured an Elk Ritual by gift or by one being left inadvertently on his train, or in an office, or elsewhere, cannot be ascertained as Riggs did not reveal his method of obtaining it. The traditions of the pullman service were of such high caliber and the integrity of Riggs was such that it seems that the stealing of it was beyond the realm of probability, although it was entirely possible.

William L. Anderson, Printer of the First Ritual, 1898; Acting Grand Secretary, 1907-

At any rate, Riggs later prepared an affidavit in the Virginia Case, which stated that he wrote the ritual. With the encouragement of B. F. Howard, Riggs took the manuscript of the ritual to a printer, William Anderson, whose shop was at the corner of Eighth and Plum Streets and asked his price for printing one hundred rituals. Riggs said that when he was informed of the price he "threw up his hands," for he saw no way to secure the funds. However, Howard agreed that since Riggs had furnished the manuscript, he would advance the money to pay for the printing and get his money back after the lodge was organized.

In order to obtain legal advice, Riggs approached an attorney, George H. Jackson, concerning the possible infringement on the rights to the ritual of the lodge of white Elks, which might result from the organization of the lodge of Negro Elks in Cincinnati. Attorney Jackson took up the matter with the Register of Copyrights of the Library of Congress in Washington, D. C., and the reply was received that no Elks' ritual had received a copyright. This ritual was forwarded by Riggs on September 28, 1898, and the copyright was granted to him. It should be noted that Riggs did not claim in his application to be the "author" of the ritual, but its "proprietor." This action gave protection to the use of the ritual, without reference to the attitude of white Elks.

This historic document in the history of the Improved Benevolent and Protective Order of Elks of the World is as follows:

1898, No. 56981

LIBRARY OF CONGRESS, to wit:

BE IT REMEMBERED,

That on the 28th day of September, 1898, Arthur J. Riggs, of Cincinnati, O., hath deposited in this Office the title of a book, the title or description of which is in the following words, to wit:

Ritual of the Benevolent and Protective Order of Elks of the World.

Cincinnati, O. The Rostrum Press, 1898.

the right whereof he claims as proprietor in conformity with the laws of the United States respecting Copyrights.

OFFICE OF THE REGISTER OF COPYRIGHTS,
WASHINGTON, D. C.

John Russell Young
Librarian of Congress.

By

Thorwald Solberg
Register of Copyrights.

Having worked for more than six months on the ritual, arranging the sections and reading the proof sheets, it was with satisfaction that Riggs and Howard began to look forward to the event of organization. They were assisted in this organization of the ritual by Frank Hunter, who later became Exalted Ruler of the Cincinnati Lodge. These men, Riggs, Howard, and Hunter, may be regarded as the "Three Musketeers of early Elkdom

B

1898 . No. 56981

Library of Congress, to wit:

Be it remembered,

That on the 28th *day of* September *, 189*8*,*
Arthur J. Riggs *, of*
Cincinnati, O. *, hath deposited in this Office the title of a* book *,*
the title or description of which is in the following words, to wit:

Ritual of the Benevolent and Protective Order of Elks of the World.

Cincinnati, O. The Rostrum Press, 1898.

the right whereof he *claim*s *as* ~~*author*~~ ~~*and*~~ *proprietor in conformity with the laws of the United States respecting Copyrights.*

Office of the Register of Copyrights,
Washington, D. C.

John Russell Young
Librarian of Congress.

By

Thorvald Solberg
Register of Copyrights.

I hereby certify that the foregoing is a true copy of the original record of copyright.
In witness whereof, the seal of this Office has been hereto affixed this thirteenth *day of* July *, 19*54*.*

Copyright Office of the United States of America,
Washington, D. C.

Arthur Fisher
Register of Copyrights.

Copyright of First Ritual,
September 28, 1898, by Arthur J. Riggs

among Negroes. A temporary body was selected from Negro citizens who were called to meet in October, 1898, after a preliminary meeting had been held during the previous month in the basement of the home of Riggs in the 300 block of Perry Street in Cincinnati where a Committee on By-Laws was also appointed. Riggs and Hunter worked together on the completion of the Constitution and By-Laws, in cooperation with B. F. Howard by whom, Hunter reports, "all of this work was overseen." A charter was proposed. Funds were collected and Howard was repaid for his advances. Frank Hunter, B. F. Howard, and Arthur J. Riggs then called the first Lodge of Elks among Negroes to assemble on Monday evening, November 17, 1898, at the Masonic Hall on George Street, near John Street.

FRANK H. HUNTER, First Exalted Ruler of the First Lodge of Elks of the World, Alpha Lodge, Cincinnati, Ohio.

The following officers were elected: Exalted Ruler, Frank Hunter; Esteemed Leading Knight, Dr. J. C. Erwin; Esteemed Lecturing Knight, Arthur J. Riggs; Esteemed Loyal Knight, B. F. Howard; Secretary, Dr. Frank Johnson; Treasurer, H. T. Jackson; Chaplain, William Fielding; Esquire, W. H. Thompson; Tiler, Vincent Dean; Out Side Guard, Benn Hall; Trustees; Peter Bates, Edward Smith, John Stowers, Edward Gastin, Edward Gaither and Sam Brown. The list of floor members included Detective Richard Read, Louis Clark, Sam Taylor, Randolph Kelly, Edward Cleveland, Harry Davis, George Butler, and John Fitzhugh.

Shortly after this meeting, a rumor was persistently circulated describing the fact that Arthur J. Riggs had stolen an Elk Ritual from a traveling man on a pullman car and had set up a Negro Elk Lodge in Cincinnati. In describing this event, Riggs states, "Whoopee! How the whites did howl, threats of all kinds were made against the members of the colored Elks Lodge. They assembled their artillery and attempted to march in, take our rituals and put the whole bunch in jail. We demanded to know what right they had to stop a Negro Elk Lodge from existing.

We also demanded that the Exalted white Ruler show us his copyright for his ritual. He said we were here first, and you Negroes have no right to use the B.P.O.E. Ritual. I said, look at this, and I produced my copyright signed by Uncle Sam and said, if I hear another word about a Negro Elk Lodge I will put the entire white Lodge in Jail for infringing on my copyright. After they found out that they could not put the lodge out of business, they turned their guns on Riggs and they shot from every angle.''

This picturesque description of this first encounter with a lodge of white Elks was indicative of the antagonism which accompanied the endeavors of these Negro pioneers in Elkdom. Riggs was taken from a train, on which he was serving as pullman porter between Cincinnati and New Orleans, when it reached Birmingham, Alabama, and threatened with lynching unless he told where he had secured the Elk Ritual. He agreed to bring the ritual back on his next trip south but instead, he changed places with another porter, and never went on this trip again.

It was said that subsequently the pullman porters going out of Cincinnati were suspected of being members of the Elk Lodge and were questioned about it by the railroad pullman service superintendent. As a result of this disturbing situation, Riggs who had a wife and six children left Cincinnati in 1899 for Springfield, Ohio. Riggs described the cause of his action in these words, ''By my action in getting the Order started the white Elks in Cincinnati boycotted me and I could not hold a job, my family suffering because I could not get work to sustain them, and when I left Cincinnati and came to Springfield I went under an assumed name. I went to work at a hotel where the proprietor was a Director and the head clerk, Exalted Ruler of the white Lodge and as a burnt child dreads the fire, you know the rest.'' At that time, Riggs gave all of the rituals, papers and printed matter to B. F. Howard who lived in Covington, Kentucky. This city was then made by him the headquarters of the lodge.

The next step was the procural of the first charter. The first charter for the incorporation of an Elk lodge among Negroes was issued by the State of Ohio on June 16, 1899, following the application for it on June 10, 1899, drawn up at the First Grand Lodge assembled on this date. It was the second legal document in Elk history among Negroes laying a foundation for the permanence of the organization, the first step being the copyrighting of the ritual. This Charter was as follows:

These Articles of Incorporation
of
The Improved Order of Elks of the World witnesseth that we, the undersigned, a majority of whom are citizens of the State of Ohio, desiring to form a corporation, not for profit, under the general corporation laws of said State, do hereby certify:

First, The name of said corporation shall be the Improved Order of Elks of the World.

Second, Said corporation shall be located, and its principal business transacted at the City of Cincinnati in Hamilton County, Ohio.

Third, The purpose for which said corporation is formed is benevolent and social intercourse among its members.

In witness whereof, we have hereunto set our hands, this tenth (10th) day of June A. D., 1899.

(Signed)
B. F. Howard
E. A. Williams
Jas. C. Erwin
W. L, Anderson
John S. Fielding

The last two named, W. L. Anderson and John S. Fielding were said by Frank Hunter to "have never been Elks." However, it is well known that W. L. Anderson was later made an Elk with Judge William Hueston presiding.

The official approval of this incorporation was as follows:

The State of Ohio, Hamilton County, SS.

On this 10th day of June A.D., 1899, personally appeared before me, the undersigned, a Notary Public within and for said County, the above named B. F. Howard, E. A. Williams, James C. Erwin, W. L. Anderson, and John S. Fielding, who each severally acknowledge the signing of the foregoing articles of incorporation to be his free act and deed, for the uses and purposes therein mentioned.

Witness my hand and official seal on the day and year last aforesaid.

(10¢ I. R. Stamp)

Jos. E. Church
Notary Public
(Seal)

State of Ohio
Hamilton County } ss.

I, Geo. B. Hart, Clerk of the Court of Common Pleas, within and for the County aforesaid, do hereby certify that Joseph E. Church, whose name is subscribed to the foregoing acknowledgment as a Notary Public was at the date thereof a Notary Public in and for said County, duly commissioned and qualified, and authorized as such to take said acknowledgment; and further that I am acquainted with his handwriting, and believe that the signature to said acknowledgment is genuine.

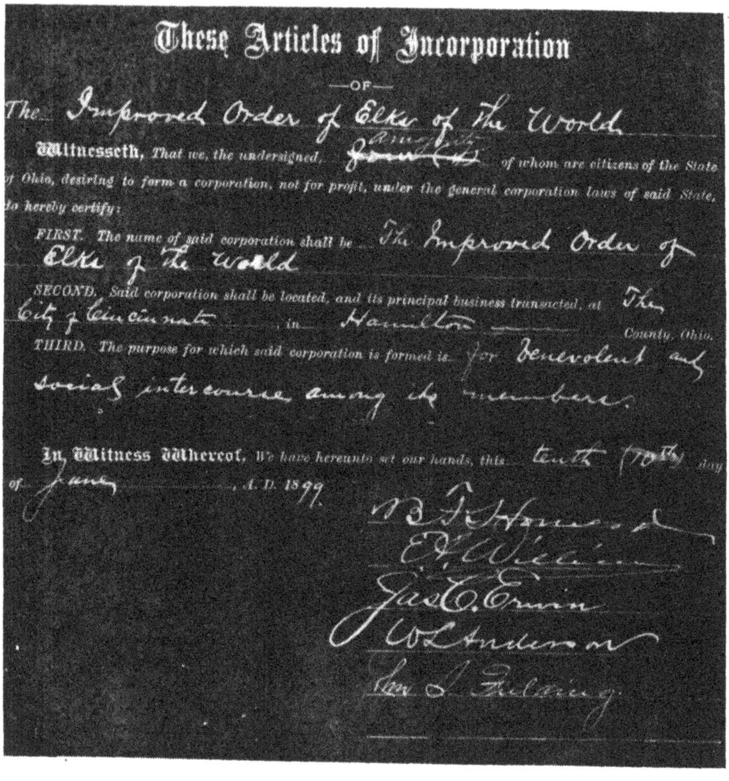

These Articles of Incorporation

—OF—

The Improved Order of Elks of the World

Witnesseth, *That we, the undersigned,* [illegible] *of whom are citizens of the State of Ohio, desiring to form a corporation, not for profit, under the general corporation laws of said State, do hereby certify:*

FIRST. The name of said corporation shall be The Improved Order of Elks of the World

SECOND. Said corporation shall be located, and its principal business transacted, at The City of Cincinnati *in* Hamilton *County, Ohio.*

THIRD. The purpose for which said corporation is formed is for benevolent and social intercourse among its members.

In Witness Whereof, *We have hereunto set our hands, this* tenth (10th) *day of* June *, A. D. 1899.*

B. F. Howard
[illegible]
Jas. C. Erwin
W. L. Anderson
[illegible]

The First Charter
Articles of Incorporation
of the Improved Order of Elks of the World, Approved June 10, 1899, and Filed at Columbus, Ohio, June 16, 1899

In witness whereof, I have hereunto set my hand and affixed the seal of said court, at Cincinnati, this 15th day of June, A.D., 1899.

(10¢ I. R. Stamp)

(Seal)

Geo. B. Harte, Clerk
By Louis N. Reaf, Deputy

United States of America, }
State of Ohio, Hamilton County } ss.

I, Charles Kinney, Secretary of State of the State of Ohio, do hereby certify that the foregoing is an exemplified copy, carefully compared by me with the original record now in my legal custody as Secretary of State and found to be true and correct, of the Articles of Incorporation of the Benevolent and Protective Order of Elks of the World, filed in this office on the 16th day of June, A.D., 1899, and recorded in Volume 76, Page 92, of the Records of Incorporation.

In testimony whereof, I have hereunto subscribed my name and affixed my official seal at Columbus, the 16th day of June, A. D., 1899.

Charles Kinney, Secretary of State

As a result of this incorporation, the Cincinnati Lodge was reorganized under the charter and title of "Improved Order of Elks of the World," with B. F. Howard as Exalted Ruler. It was reported by Riggs that after a short time Howard and Alpha Lodge "got into trouble," particularly when "he had styled himself Grand Exalted Ruler." Then, Riggs states "The members of Alpha Lodge No. 1, later named, would not stand for his ruling and dictation so the lodge disbanded."

After this division had occurred, Howard took Dr. E. A. Williams, head of the Knights of Pythias into his confidence, and with his cooperation kept Elkdom active among Negroes. They revised the ritual and inserted in the Elks' literature the one word "Improved" before "Order of Elks," and the words, "of the World" as official parts of the title. Howard with dynamic action kept his section of the Elk lodge active and maintained a leadership as organizer and founder which gave to the subsequent generations a significant heritage.

In order to carry out this objective in a legally authorized manner, Howard as "proprietor" and not as "author" obtained a copyright for the *Ritual of the Subordinate Lodges Under the Jurisdiction of the Grand Lodge of the Improved Benevolent and Protective Order of Elks of the World.* This Copyright is as follows:

Class A, XXc. No. 35177

LIBRARY OF CONGRESS, to wit:

BE IT REMEMBERED,

That on the twelfth day of June, 1902, Benjamin Franklin Howard, of Covington, Ky., hath deposited in this office the

E

CLASS A, XXc. No. 35177

Library of Congress, to wit:

Be it remembered,

That on the twelfth *day of* June, 19 02, Benjamin Franklin Howard, *of* Covington, Ky., hath *deposited in this Office the title of a* book

the title of which is in the following words, to wit:

Ritual of the subordinate lodges under the jurisdiction of the Grand Lodge of the Improved, Benevolent and Protective Order of Elks of the World.

The Grand Lodge, I.B.P.O.E. of W. 1898.

the right whereof he *claim* s *as* ~~*author*~~ ~~*and*~~ *proprietor in conformity with the laws of the United States respecting Copyrights.*

Office of the Register of Copyrights,
Washington, D. C.

Herbert Putnam
Librarian of Congress

By

Thorvald Solberg
Register of Copyrights.

I hereby certify that the foregoing is a true copy of the original record of copyright. In witness whereof, the seal of this Office has been hereto affixed this thirteenth *day of* July, 19 54.

Arthur Fisher
Register of Copyrights

Copyright Office of the United States of America,
Washington, D. C.

Copyright of Ritual of Subordinate Lodges under the Jurisdiction of the Grand Lodge, June 12, 1902 by Benjamin Franklin Howard.

title of a book, the title of which is in the following words, to wit:

> *Ritual of the subordinate lodges under the jurisdiction of the Grand Lodge of the Improved Benevolent and Protective Order of Elks of the World.*
>
> The Grand Lodge, I.B.P.O.E. of W. 1893

the right whereof he claims as proprietor in conformity with the laws of the United States respecting Copyrights.

COPYRIGHT OFFICE OF THE UNITED STATES OF AMERICA, WASHINGTON, D. C.

(Seal)

This copyright gave Howard the authority not only to proceed with the organization of subordinate lodges but also to furnish them with rituals. Howard's organization arose and developed not only through his ambition and leadership but also as a result of the need for organization and protests of Negro Elks against the exclusion of their numbers from membership in the previously organized Elk lodges of whites. Led by Howard, Negroes began to organize and fight with persistence for the right to develop lodges among themselves, but with the assurance that their lodges would be open to all the qualified. This assurance was given in the last words of the title, which described the lodge as "of the World." It was inevitable that this struggle would lead to a clash of ambitions as well as to bitter personal dissension among the group. These antagonisms could be motivated in open hostility by the common foe in the person of the white Elks who would be pleased to witness a division if not a breakup of Negro Elkdom. It was almost as if they had used the phrase, "divide and conquer."

This concept of division came into reality when B. F. Howard organized a lodge in Covington, Kentucky, and was declared its Exalted Ruler. It was the second attempt in Negro Elkdom to keep alive the traditions of the first lodge, Alpha Lodge, No. 1 of Cincinnati. With Arthur Riggs hastily leaving Cincinnati as a consequence of white Elk opposition and taking up his residence in Springfield, Ohio, and the determination of some authorities of the pullman authorities in Cincinnati to prevent the spread of the Elks organization by the porters in its service, the transfer of the activity of Elkdom among Negroes across the Ohio River to Covington in Kentucky, and the temporary decline of Elk activity among Negroes in Cincinnati were the accompaniments of these developments. Frank Hunter continued to be the Exalted Ruler of the first Elk Lodge of Negroes.

However, Howard remained the dominant and undoubted leader, who refused to yield his leadership. Lodges were organized under his leadership and direction in other parts of the United States, at Norfolk, Virginia; Pine Bluff, Arkansas; Shreveport, Louisiana; and Natchez, Mississippi. These organized units of Elkdom among Negroes were due largely to his dominant action. Riggs seemed almost to go into retirement so far as the continued organization of Elks was concerned and did not emerge from these shadows until nearly two decades had passed. Howard carried forward the organization of lodges, so that the basis was laid by him for the establishment of a Grand Lodge. Howard was the Founder and organizer of Negro Elkdom, and Riggs was its precursor and Founder.

Both of them are Founders of the Improved Benevolent and Protective Order of Elks of the World and have left their footprints in the paths of its history. Their souls go marching on in the thousands of the Antlered Herd who compose the Order in our time. Their contributions to the beginnings of Negro Elkdom should not be forgotten by those of this generation who wear proudly the purple and the white. The errors and weaknesses of their day can be paralleled by those of our day. Let us honor and revere them for their great accomplishment in the initiation of the Order, exemplifying their virtues and avoiding their faults. There are those who want our forebears to be angels and the most perfect of men. There are those who would debunk them and show that their feet were feet of clay. Howard and Riggs were heroes at the time when Elkdom needed them. We praise their deeds. We honor their lives. It is for us the living to be worthy of the great cause and goodly heritage which these founding fathers have bequeathed to us. This is our challenge from them.

Chapter III

First Steps in Expansion

With the organization of the first lodge of Elks among Negroes in Cincinnati, and the lodge in Covington, Kentucky, it happened, as A. J. Riggs states, "that lodges sprang up like mushrooms all over the country." It then seemed desirable and necessary to organize a Grand Lodge. With several local lodges in operation and a strong, ambitious leader like B. F. Howard who was the Founder of the Order, seeking to unite these locals, the scene was laid for larger group action and the first establishment of national foundations. However, the emphasis given by Howard to the Covington Lodge and the reactions in Cincinnati, to the lodge there, "caused Cincinnati Lodge No. 1 to go out of existence," as Frank Hunter stated. Before this happened the Grand Lodge had been organized in the Queen City.

The First Grand Lodge under the leadership of B. F. Howard assembled on June 10, 1899, in Cincinnati, where Howard acted and was elected as Grand Exalted Ruler. The session was held in Room 19 of Temple Court, and was opened in ritualistic form. From a temporary organization, the lodge moved into a permanent organization with the formulation of constitutions for the Grand Lodge and subordinate lodges. The following officers were present in person or by proxy: B. F. Howard of Covington, Kentucky, Grand Exalted Ruler, presiding; Charles F. Jackson of Norfolk, Virginia, Grand Esteemed Leading Knight, Proxy; John H. Young, Pine Bluff, Arkansas, Grand Esteemed Loyal Knight; Dr. E. A. Williams of True Light Lodge No. 2, Shreveport, Louisiana, Grand Organizer and Acting Grand Esteemed Lecturing Knight; G. F. Bowles of Natchez Lodge, Natchez, Mississippi, Grand Secretary; Dr. James C. Erwin of Cincinnati, Ohio, Grand Treasurer.

Grand Exalted Ruler Howard stated the object of the meeting and presented the charter which would be sent for approval to the Secretary of State at Columbus, Ohio. This approval was secured under date of June 16, 1899. A committee of three, on motion of E. A. Williams, was appointed to draw up the Constitution and By-laws. They were E. A. Williams, Chairman, G. F. Bowles and John H. Young. A one hour recess was granted to the committee to complete its work. After the recess, the committee reported the Constitution and laws, which were adopted

Proceedings of the First Session, Constitution and Laws of the I.B.P.O.E. of W. Grand Lodge, June 10, 1899.

unanimously and were ordered to be the foundations for government of the Grand Lodge and the subordinate lodges.

The Constitution was presented for "The Improved Benevolent and Protective Order of Elks of the World." This title was an extension of the title listed in the State of Ohio Incorporation which was "The Improved Order of Elks of the World," and of the title in the copyright by Riggs of "The Benevolent and Protective Order of Elks of the World." The Preamble of the Constitution declared:

> "Section 1—The members of the Improved Benevolent and Protective Order of Elks of the World, representing the subordinate lodges in the Grand Lodge, at its annual session, June 10, 1899, at Cincinnati, Ohio, do establish, ordain and consent to the following constitution.
>
> Section 2—The name of this organization shall be 'The Improved Benevolent and Protective Order of Elks of the World.'
>
> "Section 3—Its objects shall be and are benevolent, social and altruistic — to promote and encourage manly friendship and kindly intercourse, to aid, protect and assist its members and their families."

The Grand Lodge was declared to be the only legitimate source of power and authority. It was granted the power to organize and create subordinate lodges and to provide for their government and ceremonial usage. The fundamental tenets of the American Government were approved, "the greatest freedom of thought and liberty of speech, consistent with good order and manly deportment." The membership provision was that it was "limited to male citizens of legal age of the world, having such qualifications as may be provided by law." An additional statement was that the membership should be confined to male citizens of sound mind and body, good reputation, and of the age of twenty-one years and over. The membership application would have to state that the applicant was "a citizen of the World and of the State." What a contrast this membership qualification was to the one by the older lodge restricting its membership by the word "white"! There can be no doubt about which one was not only on the side of right but also on the wave of the future.

Provision was made to assist "any Elk who finds himself actually in need of the necessities of life, or sick and in distress." Social sessions of lodges were authorized after regular sessions but there was to be "true gentlemanly decorum, and no gambling was to be permitted in any lodge room, social or club quarters." The purpose of these additional laws was to maintain

The First Grand Lodge in Session, Cincinnati, Ohio, 1899.

high ideals and practices among Elk members and to maintain worthy and acceptable standards for the lodges.

It was also provided in the Constitution that "the present Grand Exalted Ruler, B. F. Howard, who by his unwearied zeal in securing the ritualistic ceremonies of this Order, shall hold the said office for a term of ten years, from the date of issuing of this Constitution, June 10, 1899." For his services, the Grand Exalted Ruler was to receive the sum of seven hundred and fifty dollars and an annual income of fifty per cent of the gross receipts from taxes, after the seven hundred and fifty dollars were paid and he was also to receive a bonus of twenty-five dollars for each lodge organized. A precedent was established by this action for the payment of a salary and income to the Grand Exalted Ruler. A salary to be determined by the Grand Lodge was also to be paid to the Grand Secretary. Grand Lodge laws and rules and order of business were adopted. After the adoption of the Constitution and laws, the Grand Lodge adjourned to meet at the call of the Grand Exalted Ruler, B. F. Howard, and this was not to be later than 1902.

PROCEEDINGS

—OF THE—

First, Second and Third

SESSIONS

—OF THE—

Improved, Benevolent

—AND—

Protective

ORDER OF ELKS

OF THE WORLD.

1903.

Proceedings of the First, Second, and Third Sessions of the Improved Benevolent and Protective Order of Elks of the World, 1903.

The Second Grand Lodge was not only larger in lodge representation and in Elk members but it was also colorful and more representative of Elk presentations. On September 5, 1901, the Grand Lodge met at Norfolk, Virginia and a Grand Full Dress Parade was held for the opening day. The line formed at Fishermen's Hall on Church Street and proceeded along the principal streets. In the first division the Grand Marshal was John Alexander, Berkeley Lodge, No. 12; the Grand Aids all mounted were Major George L. Pugh, Pandora Lodge, No. 2, Newport News, Virginia; Lieutenant R. M. S. Brown, Excelsior Lodge No. 4, Hampton, Virginia; M. J. Stephenson and William Brown of Eureka Lodge, No. 5, Norfolk, Virginia. The Hampton Brass Band was composed of 18 men; the Berkeley Lodge No. 12 of 30 men; Excelsior Lodge, No. 4, of 25 men; Pandora Lodge No. 2, 40 men. The second division of the parade had as Marshals, J. E. Mills, Louis Ashbey and Alexander Wright, Exalted Ruler of Eureka Lodge, No. 5. The Grand Exalted Ruler, B. F. Howard, was presented a large bouquet of roses and ferns by Eureka Lodge and carried this with him in the parade. It was said that "Too much praise cannot be given the brethren for their grand appearance on this occasion; their tailor-made pants, white vests and shining silk hats, and their beautiful badges, magnificent jewels, formed a picture inspiring and grand."

Another social spectacle, closing the Grand Lodge, was the Grand Banquet at Fishermen's Hall in the evening. The scene was described by Grand Secretary Bush in the following words: "Big (4) Four Orchestra opened up with a lively quick step. The beautiful new hall was filled with the elite of the city by the sea. Handsome ladies in their evening gowns, gallant Elks in their rich evening dress made a picture long to be remembered. 11:00 P.M., Floor Manager, William Brown ordered the Grand March, the signal to prepare for supper. Grand Deputy, William A. Noel, led the Grand March, followed by the Grand Exalted Ruler B. F. Howard with Mrs. Addie Brown, Norfolk, Virginia; Grand Secretary J. H. Bush with Mrs. Rosa A. Jackson, Richmond, Virginia; Grand Treasurer, Dr. E. A. Williams with Mrs. Hester Noel; Grand Inner Guard, William Freeman with Miss Inez M. Jackson of Richmond, Virginia; Master of Social Sessions, Col. M. D. Meekins with Miss Lewis; Dr. C. B. Jackson, Grand Organizer with Miss Beatrice E. Jackson of Richmond, Virginia; Grand Representative, J. P. Wright of Hampton, Virginia with Miss Esther E. White, Norfolk, Virginia; Grand Representatives, J. T. Brandy, Washington, Pennsylvania; William Lewis of Baltimore, Maryland; William H. Corprew of Berkley, Virginia; Visiting Elks, Dr. W. T. Jones of Newport News; W. E. Atkins of Hampton; J. E. Mills of Norfolk; Sir Robert Lowry and wife of Norfolk, and others kept time with the inspiring strains of the Grand Orchestra. We were ushered into the dining hall. Brother J. J. Corprew, Louis Ashbey and Thomas Burts had prepared a lovely table, handsomely decorated with ferns and potted plants; the choicest delicacies of the season were served bountifully. After supper the giddy waltz was continued until the beautiful pink of the morning warned us of approaching day and the great Second Annual Reunion of the Improved Benevolent and Protective Order of Elks of the World passed into history."

This first appearance of the ladies at a Grand Lodge was significant historically, for it presaged the activity and cooperation which was to lead ultimately to the organization of the Daughter Elks. Their participation in the social affairs of the Grand Lodge and the subordinate lodges gave them acquaintances and contacts which led to their decision for organization.

Between the parade and the banquet a considerable amount of business was undertaken. On September 7, with Grand Exalted Ruler B. F. Howard presiding, the Grand Lodge was opened in ritualistic form. The roll was called and the Minutes were read. The report of the Grand Secretary showed the following taxes had been received from lodges and paid to the Grand Treasurer:

Alpha, No. 1	$12.00
Pandora, No. 2	34.00
Monumental	49.00
Excelsior, No. 4	14.00
Eureka, No. 5	61.00
Keystone, No. 6	17.50
Phoenix, No. 7	25.00
Light House, No. 9	20.00
Capitol City, No. 11	13.50
Berkeley, No. 12	5.00
Total	$251.00

This report gives some idea of the continuing expansion and growth of the Order within the period of the first two years of its origin. The development represented in these lodges and members was a remarkable tribute to the pioneering and organizing abilities of the Grand Exalted Ruler and his associates in the Grand Lodge as well as the leaders of the subordinate lodges in their local communities. Motivation for expansion continued to be directed from the headquarters of the Grand Exalted Ruler and the leadership of B. F. Howard was demonstrated in these results.

The committee on obituary, consisting of M. J. Stephenson, Frank Jackson and J. Paul Wright made its report, closing with the words "thus may we ever act and may our actions be forever controlled by the Exalted Ruler above and when any of our number shall be called into the spirit world, may we write their faults upon the sand and their virtues upon the tablets of love and memory."

Resolutions were adopted extending gratitude to Eureka Lodge No. 5 of Norfolk, Virginia, for its hospitality and to the citizens and press of the city. The newspaper known as *The Cincinnati Brotherhood* was adopted as the official organ of the Order.

When the question arose of the next place of the meeting of the Grand Lodge, Lewis Hall nominated Richmond, Virginia; William Lewis nominated Baltimore, Maryland; J. H. Brandy nominated Washington, Pennsylvania. The vote resulted finally in an unanimous vote for Washington, Pennsylvania, the first Tuesday in September, 1902. The Committee on Finance made its report of its examination of the books and records of the Grand Secretary and the Grand Treasurer and stated that they were found correct. The payment of bills was then ordered by the committee.

The first payments of the Grand Lodge expenses of officers for attendance were made at this Second Grand Lodge, and the payments were authorized in the committee's report. This report showed that the first convention payments to officers were for living expenses during the Grand Lodge. There were no evidences that traveling expenses were included at this time.

The closing words of the session were by Grand Exalted Ruler Howard who said, "I feel proud of this session and the manner in which every brother has conducted himself during our stay in this beautiful city by the sea. I shall forever hold in my breast for the brethren of the tide water, that devotion and respect as expressed in the motto of our beloved Order. May you all go home more determined than before to build up and spread the Order in every city and town and may the Lord bless each one of you and spare us to meet again. I hope it will be the pleasure of some brother to sing, 'God Be With You Till We Meet Again.' " It was at this point that the Grand Exalted Ruler was overcome with the emotion of the occasion. It was reported by the Grand Secretary that "involuntarily tears trickled from his eyes." The brethren rose and sang. Short but spirited speeches were made by Sirs Wyatt Roane, Pandora Lodge No. 2; B. F. Jackson, Pandora Lodge No. 2; William A. Noel, Eureka Lodge No. 5; William Lewis, Monumental Lodge No. 3; Dr. C. B. Jackson, Eureka Lodge No. 5; William H. Corprew, Berkley Lodge No. 12; J. T. Brandy, Keystone Lodge No. 6. A motion was then made by William Lewis that a rising vote be given to "the Grand Exalted Ruler for his courage and devotion to our great Order."

In the period between the Grand Lodge sessions of 1901 and 1902, Grand Exalted Ruler Howard secured the second copyright of the Elk ritual containing the ceremonies for the subordinate lodges of the Order on June 12, 1902. This copyright gave Grand Exalted Ruler Howard the basis for the claim of the ownership of the ritual which was used by subordinate lodges of the Order during the ten years of his term of office.

The Third Grand Lodge assembled at Washington, Pennsylvania, on September 2, 3 and 4, 1902. The Grand Exalted Ruler presided. The other Grand Officers who were present were: Grand Secretary, J. H. Bush; Grand Exalted Knight, C. K. Lewis; Grand Exalted Lecturing Knight, William Lewis; Grand Organizer, Dr. J. E. Mills and Grand Esquire, Lincoln Clark. The Grand Officers who were absent were Dr. E. A. Williams and Wyatt Roane.

The Grand Exalted Ruler B. F. Howard appointed the following committees: *Committee on Credentials* — Harry Henry, Baltimore, Md.; Dr. W. T. Jones, Newport News, Va.; Dr. J. E. Mills, Norfolk, Va.; *Committee on Appeals and Grievances*— L. Clark, Hampton, Va.; J. J. Corprew, Norfolk, Va.; W. T. Jones, Newport News, Va.; *Committee on Obituary*—William Lewis, Baltimore, Md.; John A. Bailey, Norfolk, Va.; C. K. Lewis, Atlantic City, N. J.; *Committee on Law and Supervision* —J. T. Brandy, Washington, Pa.; Dr. J. E. Mills, Norfolk, Va.; R. M. S. Brown, Hampton, Va.; *Committee on Address*—C. C. Lewis, Lewis Hall, L. Clark; *Committee on State of Order*— R. M. S. Brown, Hampton, Va.; J. H. Bush, Cincinnati, Ohio; Dr. James E. Mills, Norfolk, Va.; *Committee on Mileage and Per Diem*—Dr. J. E. Mills, R. M. S. Brown, David S. Miller.

The delegates at this Grand Lodge represented the following lodges and their members:

> J. H. Bush, Alpha Lodge, No. 1, Cincinnati, Ohio—60 members. W. T. Jones, Pandora Lodge, No. 2, Newport News, Va.,—58 members. Harry Henry, Monumental Lodge, No. 3, Baltimore, Md.,—89 members. R. M. S. Brown, Excelsior Lodge, No. 4 Hampton, Va.,—81 members. J. E. Mills & J. J. Corprew, Eureka Lodge, No. 5, Norfolk, Va.,—204 members. C. A. Strawthers, Keystone Lodge, No. 6, Washington, Pa.,—55 members. D. S. Miller, Phoenix Lodge, No. 7, Paris, Ky.,—25 members. Proxy—Maceo Lodge, No. 8, Jacksonville, Fla.,—25 members. C. K. Lewis—Light House Lodge, No. 9, Atlantic City, N. J.,—30 members. Proxy, Capitol City Lodge, No. 11, Richmond, Va.,—35 members. Proxy, Berkley Lodge, No. 12, Berkley, Va.,—53 members. Proxy, Birmingham Lodge, No. 14, Birmingham, Ala.,—63 members. Proxy, Bell Sumter, No. 15, Birmingham, Ala.,—31 members. Proxy, H. F. Weaver Lodge, No. 16, Selma, Ala.,—35 members.

One of the first evidences of misunderstanding in the Order was evidenced in a resolution adopted during this session. It was sponsored by Pandora Lodge No. 2 of Newport News, Virginia. The declaration was made that some misunderstanding had arisen among brother Elks in Virginia and especially in Eureka Lodge No. 5 of Norfolk, Virginia, and that Pandora Lodge

No. 2 had been interfering in a matter which did not concern them. This lodge denied any charge of having taken part with any lodge not recognized by the Grand Exalted Ruler, B. F. Howard, or not in good standing with the Grand Lodge. Pandora Lodge further declared that its officers and members deplored the acts causing the difficulty with Eureka Lodge and stated that they had never wavered from their allegiance to the Grand Lodge under whose charter they were working and that they would stand by the present administration, and the improvement of the Order. This resolution brought into the open session a difficulty which was to cause further division among the lodges and members of the **Order.**

It was necessary to adopt resolutions for the enforcement of regulations as the Order grew in lodges and members. The Committee on Laws and Supervision reported the requirement, which was adopted that all delegates must report to the Grand Lodge all funds expended by their lodges before they would be seated. Since lodges had been chartered with small numbers and limited funds, it was provided that no lodge could be chartered with less than 20 members and the payment of $3.50 per member.

Dr. James E. Mills, First Grand Organizer; Third Grand Exalted Ruler, 1909-1910.

The provision was adopted also that if a member of a subordinate lodge would remain three months in arrears in the payment of dues, he would be suspended. The power of the Exalted Ruler of subordinate lodges was extended to include a demand for an explanation for the casting of black balls against candidates, and if the explanation was not satisfactory, a majority vote of the lodge would be sufficient for the candidate's election. It was also required that a tax of $1.50 would be levied to pay the bills of the Grand Exalted Ruler and the the Grand Secretary, and it was stated that the itemized bills would be paid within thirty days after communication from the Grand Exalted Ruler to the Committee on Laws and Supervision. The expenses of officers were authorized for payment. These expenses were for travel and living costs at the Grand Lodge. These were the first payments for mileage and per diem.

The exercise of power by Grand Exalted Ruler Howard in the expulsion of Dr. Charles B. Jackson, D. Milkens, J. Stevenson and A. Noel was endorsed by the special committee. These were the first expulsions approved by a Grand Lodge. Since there was an indebtedness of six hundred dollars due the Grand Exalted Ruler, the committee recommended that there would be a per capita tax of twenty-five cents per annum and that each subordinate lodge be required to pay twenty-five dollars annually until this debt was paid. The committee's report on these two matters was signed by Lincoln Clark, L. H. Hall and C. C. Lewis. A committee was then appointed to revise the constitution and report its findings to the next Grand Lodge session at Hampton, Virginia, in September, 1903.

The Grand Officers elected for the next year were: Grand Exalted Ruler, B. F. Howard; Grand Esteemed Leading Knight, Dr. W. T. Jones, Pandora Lodge, Newport News, Virginia; Grand Esteemed Loyal Knight, C. C. Lewis, Light House Lodge, Atlantic City, New Jersey; Grand Esteemed Lecturing Knight, William H. Hall, Monumental Lodge, Baltimore, Maryland; Grand Esquire, Lincoln Clark, Phoenix Lodge, Paris, Kentucky; Grand Master of Social Sessions, J. A. Bailey, Eureka Lodge, Norfolk, Virginia; Grand Organizer, Dr. J. E. Mills, Eureka Lodge, Norfolk, Virginia; Grand Inner Guard, Calvin Strawthers, Keystone Lodge, Washington, Pennsylvania; Grand Outer Guard, D. S. Miller, Phoenix Lodge, Paris, Kentucky; Grand Trustee, H. Henry, Monumental Lodge, Baltimore, Maryland; Grand Chaplain, J. J. Corprew, Eureka Lodge, Norfolk, Virginia; Grand Organist, D. S. Miller; Grand Tiler, Lewis Hall, Capitol City Lodge, Richmond, Virginia and Grand Treasurer, J. F. Brandy, Keystone Lodge, Washington, Pennsylvania.

Another aspect of expansion was the establishment of the Daughters of the Improved Benevolent and Protective Order of Elks. This movement had been in the making almost directly after the First Grand Lodge and had gained momentum with each Grand Lodge. The idea of an organization of women Elks had its beginning with Mrs. Emma V. Kelley, who is regarded as the Founder and the Supreme Mother of the Daughters of Improved Benevolent Protective Order of Elks of the World.

Mother Kelley was born at Barretts Neck, Nansemond County, Virginia, February 8, 1865. She was educated in the public schools and attended Hampton Institute. She became a teacher in the Virginia public schools, and in 1893 she was married to Robert Kelley, who died seven years later. She then came to

DAUGHTER EMMA V. KELLEY, Founder and Organizer of the Daughter Elks, First Grand Daughter Secretary.

Norfolk where she gave considerable time and thought to an Elks organization among women.

Mrs. Kelley, in describing this origin stated, "we well know that it was never intended for men to be alone, so the auxiliary to this Order was established." She then in these brief words described the organization in Norfolk, Virginia of the Daughter Elks: "It was on a bright summer evening on June 13th (1902), a small number of ladies had decided they wanted to be an auxiliary to the brother Elks, and in spite of some of the brothers not wanting such a department we were determined and thirteen of us were organized in the hall at that time at the corner of Smith and Queen Streets in a Temple of Daughters of Elks by Dr. James E. Mills, Grand Organizer then for Mr. B. F. Howard."

This first meeting stands almost alone, however, as the group soon disbanded, for as Mrs. Kelley describes it, after the hardships of three months, "the daughters were no more." Then she states that she began to realize that the Order had a wonderful mission not only for men but also for women. On October 25, 1902, she called another meeting, and with three members present, organized for the second time the first Temple, Norfolk Temple, No. 1, Dt. Mary P. Barnes, Daughter Ruler; Dt. E. V. Kelley, Secretary and Dt. Julia Fraction, Treasurer. However, when the third Sunday in July, 1903, came and their first anniversary sermon was preached at the St. John's A. M. E. Church in Norfolk, there were about forty members. Other Temples were also formed.

Following the meeting of the Grand Lodge of 1903 at Hampton, Virginia, Mrs. Kelley began the organization of a Grand Temple on September 9, 1903, with the approval of Grand Exalted Ruler Howard, at Bassett's Academy, Hampton, Virginia. Represented at the meeting were Norfolk Temple, No. 1; Birmingham Temple, (Alabama) No. 2; Western Star Temple, (Washington, Pa.) No. 3; and Beulah Temple, (Berkeley, Va.) No. 4.

The following Grand Officers were elected: Mary P. Barnes, Grand Daughter Ruler, Norfolk, Va.; Dora Fuller, Grand Vice Daughter Ruler, Berkeley Va.; Margaret Chatman, Grand Chaplain, Washington, Pa.; Eliza England, Grand Assistant Daughter Ruler, Birmingham, Ala.; Emma V. Kelley, Grand Secretary, Norfolk, Va.; Annie Spencer, Grand Treasurer, Norfolk, Va.; Malinda Roy, Grand Organist, Norfolk, Va.; Sarah Armstrong, Grand Daughter Knight, Norfolk, Va.; Mary Stevens, Grand Gatekeeper, Berkeley, Virginia; and Dts. E. F. Sneed, Fannie Hicks, Norfolk, Virginia, and Edith Brandy, Washington Penn-

DAUGHTER MARY P. BARNES, First Grand Daughter Ruler, 1903-1906.

sylvania, Grand Trustees.

Mrs. Kelley was appointed to draw up the first Constitution and the first degree rites. There were eighty-six members and ninety-one dollars had been received during the year and expenses were $88.75 leaving a balance of $2.25. This was the day of small beginnings and if numbers and amounts were the tests of success the Daughters could be easily judged as failures, but this was far from being the truth. Mrs. Kelley said, "We suffered hardships and abuses, almost ashamed to have our names enrolled on the book to call ourselves Elks." These women had within them a determined spirit which in value far outweighted material considerations. Men might smile in derision at their feeble efforts but they were confident that they were "building better than these men know." A report by a Committee on Education is of interest. The Committee stated, "Dear Sisters, as we can see the great necessity of education, especially for our boys, be it resolved that we send our children to school and not only send them to school, but let us give them a home training and teach their hands to work as much so as to teach their mental faculties to study."

The purpose of the Grand Temple Organization was described as for the "sole purpose to unite all women of sound bodily health and good moral character; to give moral and material support and elevate its members; and to put women in touch with one another, from the Atlantic to the Pacific and from the Great Lakes to the Gulf of Mexico; and extend our borders into the Isles of the Sea, and if possible join hands with our sisters on the shores of Africa."

This purpose seemed to be succeeding when the Grand Temple met at Atlantic City in 1904. There were six Temples represented. The Grand Temple Degree was constituted and awarded on the day the Grand Degree Chamber was called and the constitution was adopted. The foundation had been laid for the women in Elkdom. They had been attending the public functions of subordinate lodges and were present at some of the social sessions of the Grand Lodges. They had learned the value of the Order from their husbands and male relatives. They associated with the Elks and the organization which had developed from its emblem, for Charity, Justice, Brotherly Love and Fidelity were as dear to the hearts of women as they were of men—and some believed that they were even dearer to women. This expansion to include women was one of the most significant achievements in the history of Elkdom.

The work of these first Grand Lodges and the Daughter Elks and their Temples was registered not only in the records of their meetings but also in the inspiration which was given to the representatives and delegates of lodges who were present. Men and women returned to their communities determined to spread the influence and membership of the Order of Elks so far as they could. Stimulation was given to the host lodges and Temples where the sessions were held. A leadership in lodge, temple and community activities was created and experience was secured by men and women in the conduct of large meetings and participation in them. The fellowship and friendly relations of these contacts of Elks with Elks gave new hope to many of the discouraged and disillusioned in local lodge and temple circles. These organizations grew in number and in membership as Brother Elk and Elk Daughter leaders eagerly looked forward from Grand Session to Grand Session to make their reports of their growth and expansion.

Chapter IV
Division and Antagonism

The Improved Benevolent and Protective Order of Elks of the World continued its expansion and its first steps were implemented by many additional ones. The Grand Lodges of 1903, 1904 and 1905 showed unusual developments. These reports were presented with enthusiasm at the Grand Lodge of 1903 at Hampton, Virginia, the Grand Lodge of 1904 at Atlantic City, New Jersey, and the Grand Lodge of 1905 at Washington, D. C. As the year 1906 approached, the number of lodges in operation had increased to more than one hundred.

During this period active opposition also developed among white Elks against the manifestations of Elkdom among Negroes. This activity was centered at first in the State of New York. The legal basis for opposition was found in Section 674-A of the New York Penal Code, the Grattan Law, which prohibited the wearing of an emblem, button or insignia of any lodge or order of ten years' standing by any persons except their members. Additional legislation was introduced in the legislature to prevent further violation of this rule.

The New York Law concerning the wearing of emblems was as follows: "Any person who wilfully wears the badge or the button of the Grand Army of the Republic, the insignia, badge or rosette of the Military Order of the Loyal Legion of the United States, or the badge or button of the Spanish War Veterans, or the Order of Patrons of Husbandry or the Benevolent and Protective Order of Elks of the United States of America or of any society, order, or organization of ten years' standing in the State of New York, or uses the same to obtain aid or assistance within this State or wilfully uses the name of such society, order or organization, the titles of its officers or its insignia, ritual or ceremonies, unless entitled to use or wear the same under the constitution and by-laws, rules and regulations of such order or of such society, order or organization is guilty of a misdemeanor."

Agitation over incidents developing out of this law came just at the time of a division in the Grand Lodge, the period of the first expansion of Negro Elkdom and the organization of subordinate lodges. It was inevitable that these movements would clash and that incident after incident would occur in these tense situations.

In April, 1906, a Deputy Grand Exalted Ruler of the Benevolent and Protective Order of Elks, Hughes, of Yonkers, New York had George B. Miller, a Negro Elk who wore an Elk emblem arrested and hauled into court. Miller claimed that he was a member of an Elk lodge in Norfolk, Virginia, and had the right to wear the emblem as a member of the Improved Benevolent and Protective Order of Elks of the World. Judge Beal who heard the case declared that only bona fide members of an Order could wear its emblem under the section of the Penal Code and found Miller guilty. However, the judge suspended the sentence on Miller's promise not to wear the emblem again. Miller said that he was engaged in organizing a lodge in Yonkers but that he would not continue his operations, "pending a decision of the higher courts in the case."

This statement by Miller shows a determination which was characteristic of the founders of the Order. They would not be stopped in their endeavors to expand Elkdom. They refused to yield on their Elk mission, but they would be law abiding. They would not admit that negative decisions against them were the final words and they would appeal the case to higher authorities while abiding by the law as interpreted by the lower courts. This experience of Miller's was repeated in other places.

In Rochester, New York in May, 1906, H. D. Murray, a Negro Elk was arrested on a warrant by Dr. Richard Decker, Exalted Ruler of Rochester Lodge, No. 24, Benevolent Protective Order of Elks, charging him with unlawfully wearing an Elk emblem. This charge was also under the section of the Penal Code. Opposition had arisen in Rochester as a result of the organization of a Negro Lodge of Elks, of which Murray was a member. In reporting this incident, the *New York Tribune*, May 28, 1906, stated that "a petition for an injunction restraining members of the Improved Benevolent and Protective Order of Elks from wearing the Elk's head and antlers, the distinguishing emblem of the Benevolent Protective Order of Elks, will be made this week before a Supreme Court Justice in behalf of the Rochester Lodge of Elks. This will be the beginning of a fight that will undoubtedly be carried to the United States Supreme Court as the constitutionality of a state law is involved. The Improved Benevolent and Protective Order of Elks is a Negro organization. A member was discharged in police court last week when arraigned for violating the statute in question, which provides that one may not wear the badge of an organization of ten years' standing unless he is entitled to wear it under the constitution of that Order."

During the following month of June, a Negro Elk, O. R.

Johnson of 129 W. 134th Street, New York City, was charged with unlawfully wearing a button of the Elks. Justice McKeon, McAvoy and Dual of the Court of Special Session, on June 19, 1906, acquitted Johnson of the charge, declaring that it was not shown that he had violated the Elks' constitution. Evidence showed that the names of the two Orders were different, that the words "Improved" and "of the World" were added and the "I" and "W" were added to the antlers, which made it look like the older Elk emblem but as a matter of fact it was different. This decision gave additional courage to Negro Elks both to be active Elks and to continue their permanent organization.

An evidence of this permanence was given in the nearby state of New Jersey. This was the incorporation of the Grand Lodge of the Improved Benevolent and Protective Order of Elks of the World under the laws of the State of New Jersey on July 30, 1906. The incorporation stated:

> 1. The undersigned persons desiring to associate themselves into a corporation pursuant to the act of the legislature of the State of New Jersey entitled "An Act to incorporate associations not for pecuniary profit" approved April 21, 1898, and the amendments and supplements thereto, do hereby certify that the name by which such corporation is to be known is "GRAND LODGE OF IMPROVED BENEVOLENT AND PROTECTIVE ORDER OF ELKS OF THE WORLD."
>
> 2. The purpose for which it is formed is the social and recreative enjoyment of its members and to promote friendly and fraternal relations between them and to provide for the relief of destitute members or their families, and to maintain a fund for that purpose, and to contract with its members to pay death benefits according to the rules or by-laws adopted by it or by any subordinate lodge, and to agree to pay the same to the husband, wife, father, mother, son, daughter, brother, sister or legal representative of such member after his or her death.
>
> 3. The said corporation shall have the power to organize, conduct and supervise subordinate lodges throughout the United States and Canada, which lodges shall have the same powers as are herein conferred, but shall be subject to and under the control of the Grand Lodge herein incorporated.
>
> 4. The corporation is to be located and its principal business to be conducted in the City of Jersey City in the County of Hudson and State of New Jersey.
>
> 5. The number of trustees shall be .... and the names of the trustees selected for the first year are:

Name	Residence
George E. Bates	Newark, N. J.
Edward E. Brock	Brooklyn, N. Y.
J. Thomas Brown	Jersey City, N. J.

David W. Parker	New York City
George W. Griffin	Jersey City, N. J.
Sandy P. Jones	New York City
George E. Cannon	Jersey City, N. J.
Wiliam Preston Moore	Brooklyn, N. Y.
John W. Carter	Jersey City, N. J.

6. The corporation may have an office or offices outside of the State of New Jersey for the convenience of the Grand Officers and Trustees or the officers and trustees of subordinate lodges, where meetings may be held at such places as may be determined or authorized by the Grand Lodge herein incorporated.

7. The corporation shall maintain an office in the State of New Jersey in accordance with the requirements of the statute in such case made and provided, at No. 15 Exchange Place, in the City of Jersey City, in the County of Hudson and Frank J. Higgins shall be the resident agent in charge of said office upon whom process against said corporation may be served.

IN WITNESS WHEREOF we have hereunto set our hands and seals the thirtieth day of July, nineteen hundred and six.

Witness

J. Herbert Potts

Geo. E. Bates
Edward E. Brock
J. Thos. Brown
David W. Parker
George W. Griffin
Sandy P. Jones
Geo. E. Cannon, M.D.
William Preston Moore
John W. Carter

STATE OF NEW JERSEY }
COUNTY OF HUDSON } SS

BE IT REMEMBERED, that on this thirtieth day of July, nineteen hundred and six, before me, a Master in Chancery of New Jersey, personally appeared George E. Bates, Edward E. Brock, J. Thomas Brown, David W. Parker, George W. Griffin, Sandy P. Jones, George E. Cannon, William Preston Moore and John W. Carter, who, I am satisfied, are the persons named in and who executed the within certificate of incorporation, and I having first made known to them the contents thereof, they did each acknowledge that they signed, sealed and delivered the same as their voluntary act and deed for the uses and purposes therein expressed.

J. Herbert Potts
Master in Chancery of New Jersey."

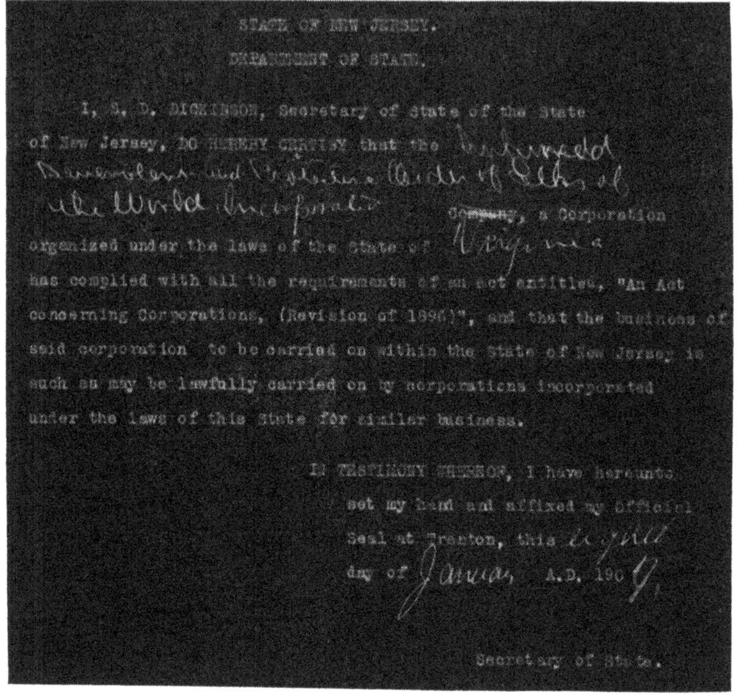

STATE OF NEW JERSEY.

DEPARTMENT OF STATE.

I, S. D. DICKINSON, Secretary of State of the State of New Jersey, DO HEREBY CERTIFY that the [illegible] the World Incorporated ~~Company~~, a Corporation organized under the laws of the State of Virginia has complied with all the requirements of an act entitled, "An Act concerning Corporations, (Revision of 1896)", and that the business of said corporation to be carried on within the State of New Jersey is such as may be lawfully carried on by corporations incorporated under the laws of this State for similar business.

IN TESTIMONY WHEREOF, I have hereunto set my hand and affixed my Official Seal at Trenton, this eighth day of January A.D. 1906.

Secretary of State.

Certification of the Incorporation in New Jersey, January 8, 1906.

Three of the incorporators were described by the *New York Tribune* as John W. Carter, a porter of Charles M. Schwab's private car, the Loretta; George E. Bates, an attendant in the office of Frank E. Sheppard, general superintendent of the Pennsylvania Railroad, Jersey City, and Dr. George H. Cannon, Jersey City physician. This incorporation was another contribution to the internal development of the Order, for while there were forces antagonistic to it and exerting pressure from the outside, there was solid building within its ranks in the midst of increasing division.

This division occurred in the same year, 1906, when the call went out from Grand Exalted Ruler Howard for the Seventh Annual Session of the Grand Lodge. This session convened in Odd Fellows Hall, Garfield and Long Streets, Columbus, Ohio, on August 28. It had been decided in the Grand Lodge of 1905 in Washington, D. C., that the next Grand Lodge would be held

[illegible] may be [illegible].

[illegible] we have hereunto set our hands and seals the thirtieth day of July, nineteen hundred and six.

STATE OF NEW JERSEY : S. S.
COUNTY OF HUDSON :

BE IT REMEMBERED, that on this thirtieth day of July, nineteen hundred and six, before me, a Master in Chancery of New Jersey, personally appeared [illegible] [illegible] Brown, [illegible] Parker, [illegible] [illegible] Jones, [illegible] William [illegible] and John [illegible],

who, I am satisfied, are the persons named in and who executed the within certificate of incorporation, and I having first made known to them the contents thereof, they did each acknowledge that they signed, sealed and delivered [illegible]

Signatures to the Incorporation of the Grand Lodge in New Jersey, July 30, 1906.

in 1906 in Brooklyn, New York. When the opposition of the New York officials and members of the Benevolent and Protective Order of Elks had reached its height in 1906 and members of the Improved Benevolent and Protective Order of Elks were being arrested, and the General Assembly was giving consideration to additional bills prohibiting the operation of the Order among Negroes, Grand Exalted Ruler Howard decided to change the place of meeting of the Grand Lodge from Brooklyn to Columbus.

This change was explained in the following words at the Grand Lodge by Grand Exalted Ruler Howard, "To my great regret I was compelled to change the Grand Lodge meeting from Brooklyn, N. Y., to this city of Columbus, Ohio, on account of the Grattan Bill, which was passed by the State Assembly of New York and which prohibits colored Elks from wearing badges or pins. However, a committee has waited on the Attorney General and he informed the members thereof that this bill would be set aside in the near future." He then added, "I advise this Grand Body to employ the very best counsel to take hold of the New York Case, as some of our members have been ordered to take off their badges and pins. We must put our full force on the case and make every effort to have it taken to the Supreme Court."

This change of the meeting place from Brooklyn, which had been selected for the 1906 meeting, to Columbus was not satisfactory to the lodges in the Eastern part of the country, nor were they pleased with the arbitrary manner in which it was done. They sent a committee to confer with the Grand Exalted Ruler to request that the decision of the previous Grand Lodge be observed. On his refusal they made plans to hold a meeting in Brooklyn in spite of the Grand Exalted Ruler's action, which they reported as "arbitrary action." The Grand Exalted Ruler would not withdraw his call for the Columbus meeting and the Eastern faction would not consent to the Columbus meeting. Howard wanted to avoid embarrassment to his members by meeting in New York State and the possible troubles which he thought would arise. Such a decision does not classify him as one who was unwilling to face the issue. He was always regarded as a brave man and as one who did not hesitate in a fight. His entire life is a testimony to his steadfastness in these respects. However, he felt that the Grand Lodge should not go to New York until this particular issue was settled, and in this matter he was obdurate.

The result was that there were two Grand Lodge sessions held in 1906. One at Columbus with Grand Exalted Ruler Howard

The Seventh Annual Session

—OF THE—

Grand Lodge of Improved Benevolent and Protective Order of Elks of the World

---

Convened in Odd Fellows' Hall, Corner of Garfield Ave. and Long Street, Columbus, O., on Tuesday, Aug. 28th, 1906, at 1 o'clock, P. M.

The officers and delegates of the Grand Lodge of the Improved Benevolent and Protective Order of Elks of the World met at the Elk's headquarters, corner of 3rd Street and Mt. Vernon Avenue, at 10 o'clock A. M., and headed by the Citizens Band, marched to the Trade Auditorium where a public session was held.

A letter from Governor A. L. Harris was read. In it the Governor stated his inability to be present; but welcomed the Grand Lodge to the City and extended to it the freedom of the same.

Honorable Graham Deuwell of Columbus, Ohio, delivered the following address of welcome:

BROTHER GRAND EXALTED RULER AND GRAND OFFICERS, brother members of the Improved Benevolent and Protective Order of Elks of the World. LADIES AND GENTLEMEN:

In behalf of Euterpe Lodge No. 52 of the Improved, Benevolent and Protective Order of the Elks of the world and of the capital city of the great Stat eof Ohio, we take profound pleasure in welcoming you as Grand Exalted Ruler and Officers, and delegates, visitors and guests of this assembling of the seventh annual session and meeting of the Grand Lodge of the Improved Benevolent and Protective Order of the Elks of the world. It is a sincere re-

First Page of the Minutes of the Seventh Annual Session of the Grand Lodge, August 28, 1906.

presiding and the other at Brooklyn with George E. Bates, Grand Esteemed Leading Knight presiding at the opening meeting, since he was the highest ranking Grand Lodge officer present. He was later succeeded by Dr. William E. Atkins as presiding officer and Grand Exalted Ruler. There were forty-two lodges represented at the Columbus Grand Lodge, and it was reported that there were seventeen represented at the opening of the Brooklyn session. This number was later increased to twenty-one. These meetings inaugurated a division in the ranks of the Improved Benevolent and Protective Order of Elks of the World which was to continue for the next four years, 1906-1910, under Brother B. F. Howard as Grand Exalted Ruler and Brother Dr. William E. Atkins of Hampton, Virginia, as Grand Exalted Ruler.

While some lodges and member Elks were criticizing Grand Exalted Ruler Howard, his Grand Lodge opened with a Welcome Address by Graham Denwell of Columbus, on behalf of Enterpe Lodge, No. 52. This address described the Grand Exalted Ruler as "the distinguished founder, organizer, exponent and father of Negro Elkdom." Another resolution endorsed the action of the Grand Exalted Ruler in changing the meeting of the Grand Lodge from Brooklyn to Columbus. This resolution was adopted unanimously. Further evidence of the warm regard held for Howard by the Grand Lodge was shown when he returned to the sessions, after an absence from the lodge sessions to answer an injunction against holding the Grand Lodge in Columbus. It was recorded in the Minutes that "The Grand Exalted Ruler's return was hailed with triumphant eclat."

A third resolution was adopted and was important because its main purpose was to correct an error in the incorporated title of the Order, while incidentally referring to the Grand Exalted ruler. It was, "Whereas, B. F. Howard, being the first colored man to give to our race the Colored Elks of the World, and further in consideration of the fact that error in name was unintentional, and knowing full well that there are some whose efforts are to destroy the Order under B. F. Howard, we hereby present to this honorable body resolution, to wit: That the Charter of Incorporation of the Improved Order of the Elks of the World be amended to read the 'Improved Benevolent and Protective Order of Elks of the World.'" This error had been made in the Ohio incorporation of 1899 in which the title was used. This title was now to be changed. Fifty dollars was appropriated to defray the expenses incurred in the correction of the Charter.

Regret was expressed by Dr. J. W. Ames of Detroit, Michigan, concerning the withdrawal of some members who were holding a

Dr. William E. Atkins, Second Grand Exalted Ruler, 1907-1910.

meeting at the same time in Brooklyn. He spoke of the disadvantage of such a meeting and expressed the hope that a committee on unification and arbitration would be appointed to meet a similar committee of Brooklyn Elks, with power to adjust all questions in controversy that the rupture could be remedied and the factions united. This note of unity was also sounded by Grand Exalted Ruler Howard when he said in his annual address, "My advice to the Order of Elks is to stand together as a united body." A committee was appointed by the Grand Exalted Ruler and a telegram was sent to the Grand Lodge in Brooklyn, New York, requesting the appointment of "a like committee to meet said committee at a time and place which may hereafter be designated." The Brooklyn Lodge agreed also to appoint a committee.

DR. JAMES W. AMES, Grand Secretary, 1907-1908.

A similar note was sounded by the Committee on the Good of the Order when it recommended that "any Committee chosen or appointed by the Grand Lodge for the purpose of affecting a reconciliation or arbitrating any misunderstanding between the lodges here assembled in this our 7th Grand Lodge Session; and the belligerent lodges at Brooklyn, N. Y., act in a spirit of firmness for what is right and just, for the best interest of the lodges; yet having in mind the spirit of conservation as their best judgment and intelligence shall demand. We would also suggest that every member of the Order bear in mind, that the I.B.P.O.E. of W. is an Order devoted to the fraternal welfare of the colored race all over the world and that no selfish or sectional demarcations of interest should enter into this rank, but rather a united effort be exerted in the future as in the past, to make it the Order of the Elks of the North, South, East and West."

Another report to the Columbus Grand Lodge concerned the publication of the *Elks Journal*. The first publication was in

March, 1906, when 500 copies were printed. During the period March to August there were 2,100 copies published and sent to the lodges and members. When the Grand Secretary, P. A. Nichols reported concerning the *Journal,* it was ordered that it would be adopted as the official organ, that a publication board of five be appointed, the refund to go to the Grand Secretary of funds previously expended and new assessments were approved for future publications.

Fred W. Ernst, Editor-Manager, *Elks Journal,* 1907-

The division of the Grand Lodge of the Improved Benevolent and Protective Order of Elks of the World was continued under the respective leaders B. F. Howard and William E. Atkins. Lodges and individuals made their choices and pledged their respective allegiances. Each claimed to be the successor of the First Grand Lodge of 1899. Each session was harmonious and without acrimony and each was searching for some method of unification and reunion.

Separate Grand Lodge sessions for each faction became the practice, while the committes endeavored to iron out the difficulties in periods of discussion. In 1907, the Grand Lodge under Grand Exalted Ruler Howard met at Reading, Pennslyvania, on August 27, 28, and 29, and the Grand Lodge under Grand Exalted Ruler Atkins met at the same time in Chicago, Illinois. Each group reported growth in its number of lodges and its membership, and orderly business procedures were maintained by each of them.

At the Reading Grand Lodge, Dr. J. E. Mills, the Grand Organizer declared, "We are not unmindful of the fact that our ranks have been rent asunder by some of our people whose efforts have been made in trying to set aside the founder of this

Order, and we would hope that in this city of equality and friendliness a solid front of all forces could have been presented. We hope that time will heal the breach and that upon one common platform every Negro Elk will be in accord, and render homage to one Grand Lodge. May God hasten the day when strife from within shall vanish and the angel of peace shall spread her wings over a united I.B.P.O.E. of the World." In the same vein, the Committee on the Good of the Order recommended that the Arbitration Committee be continued and instructed to use all proper efforts to heal the breach existing and to bring "the strayed and misguided brothers into the fold."

The officers of this Grand Lodge were: B. F. Howard, Grand Exalted Ruler; D. T. Coles, Grand Leading Knight; J. A. Blume, Grand Chaplain; W. H. Nicholson, Grand Esquire; Sandy Daugherty, Grand Tiler; R. B. Dandridge, Grand Inner Guard; Dr. Phillip Scott, Grand Medical Director; Dr. J. E. Mills, Grand Organizer; Dr. James W. Ames, Grand Secretary; Dr. W. T. Jones, Grand Treasurer; William Freeman, M. of Social Sessions; T. H. Williams, Grand Trustee; H. H. Griffin, Grand Trustee.

The membership report of the Grand Secretary showed that there were sixty-one lodges with a total membership of 3,740; thirty-nine lodges reported an increased membership of 1,249 members; 32 lodges reported property valued at $6,124.18; 49 lodges had $7,333.35 in the banks and twenty-eight lodges had spent for charity $3,079.75. Eighty lodges were on the rolls representing thirty states.

The Grand Lodge Session in Chicago, Illinois, convening at the Pekin Theater at this same time had the following officers: Dr. William E. Atkins, Grand Exalted Ruler; Raymond L. Phillips, Grand Esteemed Leading Knight; Sandy P. Jones, Grand Esteemed Loyal Knight; Cabel Calloway, Grand Es-

Grand Officers and Delegates of the Eighth Annual Session, Reading, Pennsylvania, B. F. Howard, Grand Exalted Ruler, 1907.

teemed Lecturing Knight; E. M. Shoecraft, Grand Inner Guard; I. W. Warden, Grand Tiler; J. Welford Holmes, Grand Secretary; J. T. Brandy, Grand Treasurer; William E. Lewis, Grand Organizer; Samuel E. Jones, Grand Esquire; J. H. Gray, Grand Chaplain.

Fifty-four lodges were represented in this Grand Lodge. There were enthusiastic delegates and visiting Elks at the sessions. One of the lodges, Anthracite Lodge No. 50, presented an ink stand and paper weight made of anthracite coal to the Grand Exalted Ruler. In making the presentation Brother Charles E. Battles said of Grand Exalted Ruler Atkins, "We are mindful of the fact that when he took the reins of government one year ago, it was amid confusion, and at a time when free men wanted to rebel against tyrannical rule and oppression, and when the leaders were looking about for a Moses to lead us in our battle against the wrong, the mantle fell on our present Grand Exalted Ruler, Dr. William E. Atkins, who has led us safely for one year, and under whose matchless leadership we are gaining the confidence of our friends and putting our opposers to flight."

The annual report of Grand Exalted Ruler Atkins was delivered in the midst of outbursts of applause which interrupted its presentation. He described the objections of white lodges to Negro Elks, the case in Georgia, the attitude of the Howard faction in setting up new lodges in cities where lodges were already established; and his regret at the division. Shortly thereafter, the rules were suspended and Grand Exalted Ruler Atkins was reelected by acclamation.

In the meantime, plans were being completed for the incorporation of the Grand Lodge in the states of Virginia and New York. Dr. Atkins and his group applied and received approval and the certificate for the incorporation of the Improved Benevolent and Protective Order of Elks of the World, in the State of Virginia. The application for the charter was filed on October 10, 1906, and was certified on November 3, 1906, by the Secretary of the Commonwealth of Virginia. Hampton, Virginia, was given as the principal office of business. The officers for the first year were reported as: Grand Exalted Ruler W. E. Atkins, Hampton, Virginia; C. H. Jones, Grand Esteemed Leading Knight, Elizabeth City, Virginia; S. T. Smith, Grand Esteemed Loyal Knight, Hampton, Virginia; J. J. Hooker, Grand Esteemed Lecturing Knight, Hampton, Virginia; R. M. S. Brown, Grand Secretary, Hampton, Virginia; Henry Stevenson, Grand Treasurer, Hampton, Virginia; the Grand Trustees were R. Watson, Hampton, Virginia; N. C. Barnes, Phoebus, Virginia. This group formed a definite Virginia organization, and at the same

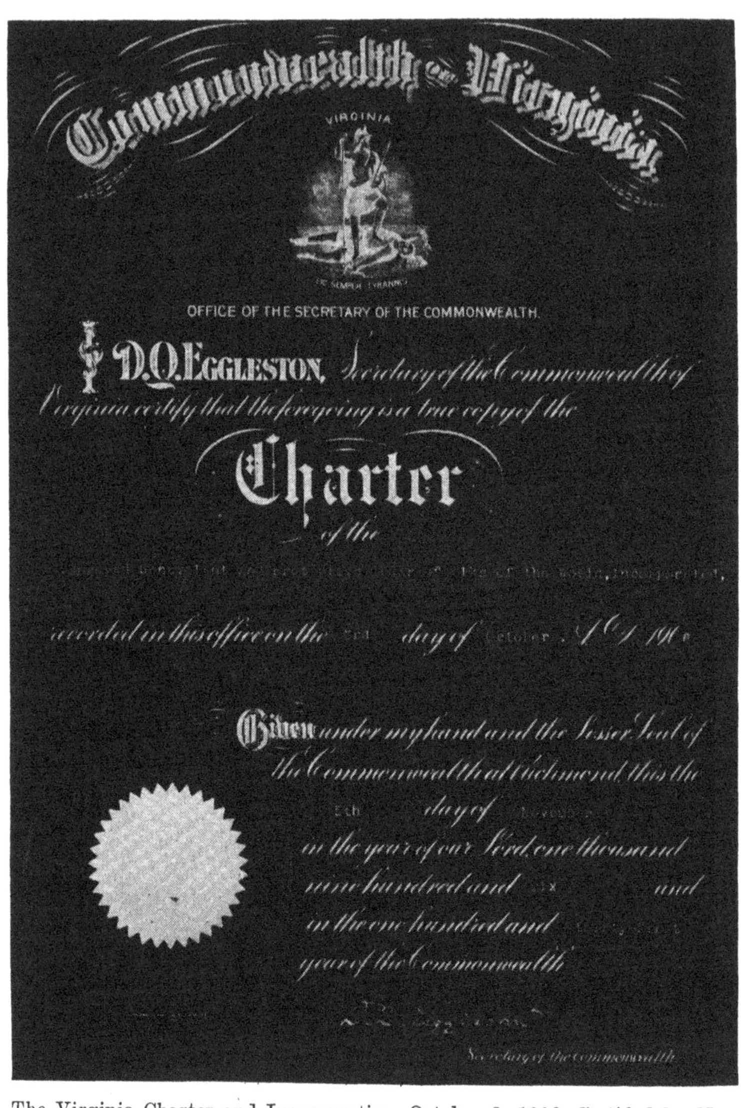

Commonwealth of Virginia

VIRGINIA

OFFICE OF THE SECRETARY OF THE COMMONWEALTH.

I, D.Q. EGGLESTON, Secretary of the Commonwealth of Virginia certify that the foregoing is a true copy of the

Charter

of the

recorded in this office on the 3rd day of October A.D. 1906.

Given under my hand and the Lesser Seal of the Commonwealth at Richmond this the 8th day of

in the year of our Lord one thousand nine hundred and six and in the one hundred and year of the Commonwealth

Secretary of the Commonwealth

The Virginia Charter and Incorporation, October 3, 1906, Certified by New Jersey, January 8, 1907.

time attempted to regard itself as a corporation for world purposes.

However, application was made on January 5, 1907, to carry on the business of the Improved Benevolent and Protective Order of Elks of the World, Incorporated, in the State of New Jersey. A copy of the Virginia Charter was submitted, the business office was given as No. 26, Exchange Place, Jersey City, New Jersey and George E. Bates was described as the agent of the corporation by William E. Atkins, President and W. T. Anderson, Acting Secretary. The officers were listed as W. E. Atkins, President; W. T. Anderson, Acting Secretary and Henry Stevenson, Treasurer. The Secretary of State of New Jersey certified on January 8, 1907, that compliance had been met with requirements of the Corporations Act and that business could be

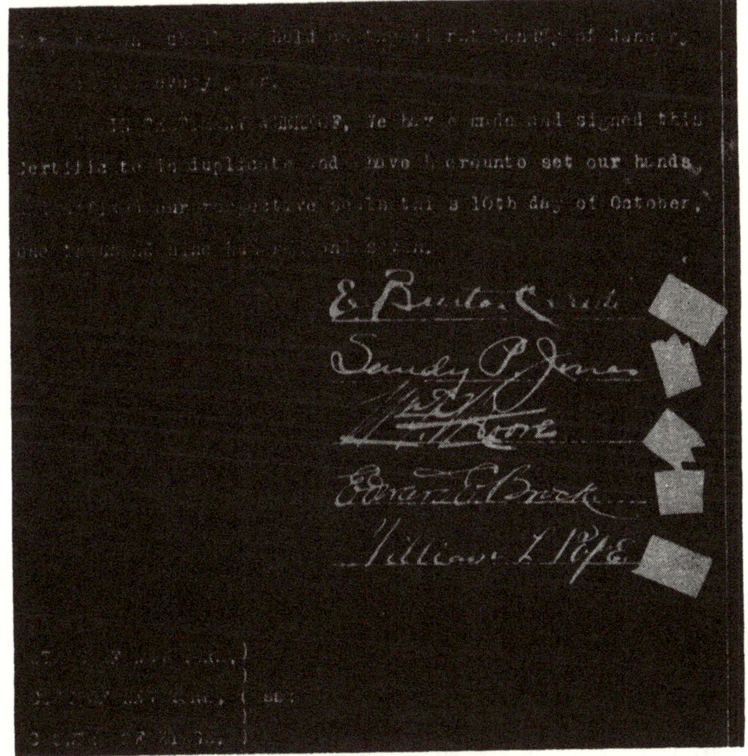

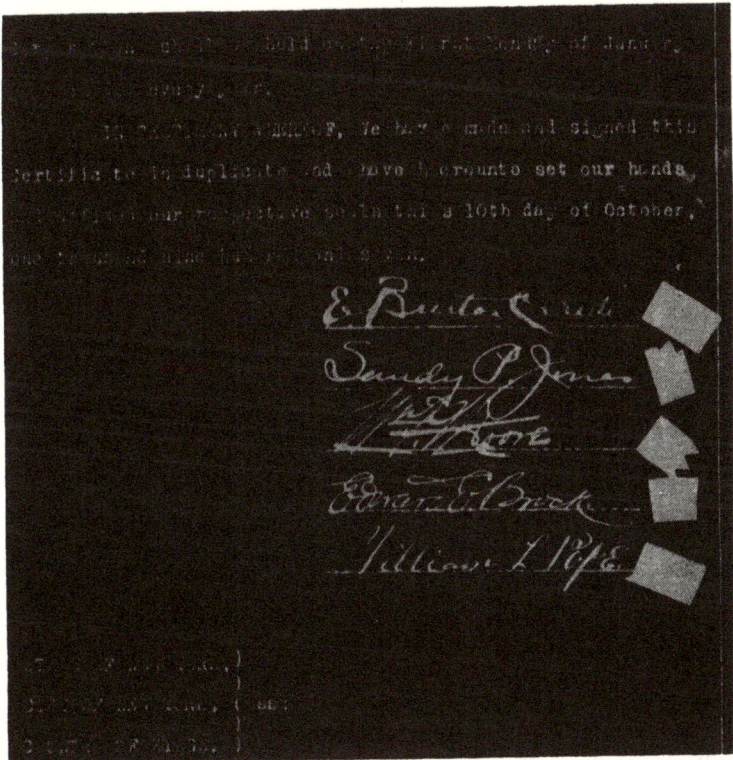

Signatures to the Incorporation in the State of New York, October 10, 1907.

carried on under the laws of the State. The Atkins group had thus fortified its position by charters in Virginia as well as in New Jersey.

The animosities and contentions which had developed between white Elks and Negro Elks and the division within the I.B.P.O.E. of W., influenced a New York group to undertake an incorporation of the Grand Lodge in that state. Application was made for a certificate of Incorporation of the Grand Lodge of the I.B.P.O.E. of W. It was stated that the undersigned, Edward B. Ceruti, Brooklyn; Sandy P. Jones, Manhattan; Edward E. Brock, Brooklyn, and William L. Pope, Brooklyn, "being desirous of associating ourselves together for the purpose of promoting the social, benevolent, charitable and protective interest of its members as hereinafter is more particularly described, pursuant to and in conformity with acts of the Legislature of the State of New York, relating to membership corporations, do hereby certify and declare that we are all of full age, two-thirds of us are citizens of the United States and all of us residents of the State of New York."

The additional proposals were to buy, hold, own, control, mortgage or sell real estate for the purpose of a home for the order; to provide for branches in different parts of the state, as the territory of operations were to be conducted in the State with the principal office in Brooklyn.

This charter was approved and filed with the Department of State of New York on October 17, 1907. The document served its purpose during the trying days of opposition, for the Grand Lodge was given legal status within the state through its certification. The corporation having served its purpose was dissolved by proclamation of the Secretary of State of New York published on October 15, 1952, after having been in legal operation from 1907.

During this period, the division in the Grand Lodge was continued. The next year, 1908, the Grand Lodge under Grand Exalted Ruler Howard assembled in St. Louis, Missouri, and the Grand Lodge under Grand Exalted Ruler Atkins met in St. Paul, Minnesota. This Grand Lodge group under Atkins had developed rapidly. Its numbers within two years had increased from 17 lodges to 90 lodges and 16 temples. They had taken 30 lodges from the Howard group and had lost not a single lodge to this group. Nevertheless, Grand Exalted Ruler Atkins had reported in 1908, "at times I have felt like giving up all in despair, but, being cheered by your words of encouragement, I have pressed on." He admitted that the hard times through which the nation was passing were affecting developments, together with "the litigations into which we have been dragged and the white man's stern opposition."

On May 9, 1907, a letter was addressed to Dr. W. E. Atkins, Grand Exalted Ruler by Dr. J. W. Ames, Grand Secretary of the Howard faction, which regarded itself as the legitimate Elk Lodge. Dr. Ames wrote that he was appointed Chairman of the Committee on Unification and Arbitration to see what could be done to harmonize the differences. He stated, "no people can grow strong and prosper divided. Our common enemy, the whites, are fighting us on the outside and on the other, internal strife is marring our growth and development." He added, "Personal aggrandizement should find no place in the hearts and minds of cultured men, when the race is panting for leaders of broad gauge, and their hope and future prosperity, materially, depends upon the earnest efforts of brave men who will not say, I do as others do, but whose self-abnegation is consecrated to their uplift. I would rather have it said that I was a true and faithful private in the ranks than a leader of discord and dissolution."

The reply of Dr. Atkins was under date of May 16. He wrote that he was as much opposed to the split in the Order as any living man. He stated that he would never treat with the group to which Dr. Ames belonged "upon the subject of uniting the two bodies as long as Mr. Howard comes in for consideration of any sort." He declared that he was personally opposed to Howard, and said he, "so long as I have any influence with our side I shall use it against him." His view was that the future of the Order was bright and that it would be unfortunate that "it should be killed by the stupidity of one man, whoever he may be." Howard had been called a tyrant and had been accused of high-handed selfish methods.

In defense of the Howard group Dr. Ames had stated that no tyrannical methods had marked the business dealings with his office and he believed that "a single personality never has, never can and never will dominate any Order and should not be the cause of a division now." Howard was the pioneer or buccaneer type of individual who seemed also to believe in rugged individualism. He was eager to fight those who opposed him. In 1906 he warned, "As Elks you will beware in the future of the assassin who stands with dirk in hand ready to get rid of such 'bad timber.'" He said that his hand was lifted and "ready to strike down oppression and to defend the order against all opposition that may arise against it." This attitude was well illustrated in the first year of the division when Howard entered suits against the three principal officers of the Atkins Grand Lodge, the Grand Exalted Ruler, the Grand Secretary and the Grand Treasurer.

It was again illustrated at the Grand Lodge Session in Detroit in 1909. Grand Exalted Ruler Howard entered the meeting and was escorted to the platform in the midst of an ovation. He started to pass Grand Exalted Ruler Atkins without any notice of him but the latter arose, advanced to Howard and clasped hands with him, as the house cheered to the echo. It was clear, however, that Howard was not his usual self and that the years were taking their toll of him, for he addressed the convention in such a lengthy disconnected talk that he "was finally asked to yield the floor by the Chairman."

In the meantime the opposition of white Elk lodges broke into the open in suits and injunctions in various states. This was not an unusual experience for Negro organizations, for this result in Elk relationships was paralleled in the life of other organizations with Negro membership. The white Odd Fellows of Mississippi sought to prevent Negro Odd Fellows from operating their organization. The white Knights of Pythias in Georgia and North Carolina fought the continuance of Negro Pythians. The white Masons opposed the Negro Masonic Lodges and questioned the legitimacy of their origin. In 1909 the Masonic Grand Lodge of Tennessee was restrained by a court injunction and its session was abruptly terminated. This period was characterized by a policy of whites for exclusion on the one hand and the determination to prevent the continuance of a similar separate organization. However, Negroes were prepared to fight in return. They too were proud. They would not fight at this time to be where they were not wanted as members, but they were resolute in their decisions to continue their organizations. The Elks were

DR. W. T. JONES, Grand Secretary, 1906-1907, Grand Treasurer, 1907.

among the most determined of these groups—the whites to run the Negro Elks out of existence and the Negroes to preserve their decade of development.

The protection of its emblem had been sought by the Grand Lodge of the Benevolent and Protective Order of Elks at its session in Philadelphia in 1907, when a commission of three was authorized "to secure legislation in the various states to protect our name and emblem from abuse by imitation and to prosecute any persons or organizations so imitating our name and emblem and to make such recommendations concerning an official emblem as may be deemed necessary." An attempt was made in 1908 to secure the passage of a bill in Congress to make it a misdemeanor for a person to wear fraudulently in the District of Columbia the badge, insignia or letters of the Benevolent and Protective Order of Elks of the United States of America. The bill passed the House of Representatives but failed to pass the Senate. Letters were sent to the Secretaries of State of all of the states protesting the issuance of charters to any persons using the name of the Order or any name bearing resemblance to it. Proceedings were started in several states. A permanent injunction was secured in Georgia against any society using a name bearing close resemblance to the older name. In Tennessee the white Elk lodges secured an injunction against the Negro lodge on October 19, 1907, and in Mississippi a Negro lodge was threatened with violence if it continued its meetings.

DR. P. A. SCOTT, Grand Medical Director, 1906.

This B.P.O.E. Commission reported in 1908 that legislation had been procured in several states and that the procedings in New York State should be prosecuted as may be necessary to the Court of Appeals. The Commission authorized the securing of a patent upon the design of the emblem. A patent was finally secured on "a combination of a dial showing the hour of eleven with a white face and red Roman numerals or circumscribed by a blue circle containing the initials B.P.O.E., on which dial and circle shall rest an elk's head and antlers which shall be surmounted by a red star.''

In the meantime this issue was joined in New York where there were smoldering fires. In spite of the incorporation in the State of New York under the membership Law in 1907 naming the order as the Grand Lodge of the Improved Benevolent and Protective Order of Elks of the World, the continuance of the activities of the Order was challenged by members of the B.P.O.E. Finally Deputy E. Burton Ceruti informed Grand Exalted Ruler Atkins that his lodge had been enjoined. The account of this case was given in the *New York Tribune,* June 8, 1908, ''Elks of the United States are interested in the final outcome of a temporary injunction which the Supreme Court Justice Morschauser at White Plains, has granted to the B.P.O.E. Elks of the Empire State against the I.B.P.O.E. Elks of he World, a colored organization, restraining it from using the name, title, emblem or membership card of the Order of Elks.

''The temporary injunction was obtained by John F. Brennan, a lawyer and member of Yonkers Lodge of Elks, and Lawyer Thomas F. Curran of Lodge No. 1 of Manhattan, who represented the Grand Exalted Ruler of the State of New York. Today Lawyer Brennan appeared before Justice Morschauser to argue a motion for a permanent injunction against the colored Order, and the matter was adjourned until Wednesday morning. The Elks seek a perpetual injunction against the colored lodge, which they say is in violation and repugnant to the corporate rights of the B.P.O.E. If the decision of Justice Morschauser is favorable, similar actions in other states of the union will be started by the Elks whose rules provide that only white members shall be admitted.''

WESLEY RANEY, Grand Treasurer, 1906-1907.

This decision was affirmed making the injunction permanent. Grand Exalted Ruler Atkins urged an appeal to the Court of Appeals and then on to the highest court in the land. Shortly afterward a bill was drafted by a legal committee of the B.P.O.E. for introduction in the legislatures of the several states.

In two instances, Massachusetts and New Jersey, the bill was defeated. It was introduced in the Illinois General Assembly with the following provisions: (1) No person, society, association or corporation was to adopt or use the name of any benevolent, humane, fraternal or charitable organization incorporated under the laws of the state or the United States or so resembling it as "to be a colorable imitation" of it, and where two or more such societies claim the same name the society which first became incorporated was entitled to the prior and exclusive use of the name; (2) No person was to wear or exhibit the badge, button, emblem, decoration, insignia or assume the name of such an organization incorporated under the laws of the state or any other state of the United States which may be calculated to deceive the people with respect to such prior incorporation unless he is authorized by the laws of the corporation to wear these emblems; (3) Upon application for an injunction to restrain these violations any and all hearings should be guilty of a misdemeanor and fined not exceeding fifty dollars or imprisoned in the county jail not exceeding thirty days or both."

There was an account of a conviction under a similar law in Arkansas in 1909. The Exalted Ruler and Secretary of the I.B.P.O. Elks of the World at Hot Springs, Arkansas, were arrested for wearing Elk emblems. The case was fought by the Grand Lodge and ultimately dismissed. Working quietly, Grand Exalted Ruler Atkins had succeeded in having the law so changed that it referred to the wearing and use illegally of any emblem by those not entitled to wear it under the provisions. This bill was general and gave protection to the members of all fraternal and non-fraternal organizations.

In order to secure funds for court costs, Grand Exalted Ruler Atkins called upon the lodges for contributions, urged the local lodges to spend their funds and repaid these lodges from receipts at the Grand Lodge sessions. He described himself as "the biggest beggar this year." He also insisted that the Order persevere in spite of the opposition which it was facing, for in his words, "The power to believe and the power to work make the genius and assure the destiny of men and that of the Order." Dr. Atkins' activity and interest extended even to the use of his own personal funds to fight these cases. Brother James E. Kelley, Grand Secretary, described this activity when he wrote his Eighth Annual Report that "the Atkins faction has taken a very

SULLY JAMES, Grand Legal Adviser, 1907.

definite stand against all cases in the courts, in the meantime sending out letters of encouragement to the various lodges assuring them that the Order would continue to live and grow in spite of all efforts to destroy it.''

When suggestions were made from different parts of the country that the name of the Order should be changed in order to prevent further opposition, Grand Exalted Ruler Atkins ridiculed the idea. When it was reported in a newspaper that Dr. J. W. Ames of Detroit had suggested that the name should be changed to the Fraternal Order of Meneliks, in honor of Emperor Menelik of Ethiopia, a committee was appointed to wait upon him so as to ascertain the truth. Dr. Ames later denied that he had made this statement. However, the attitude of the Grand Exalted Ruler was made evident. ''The idea of a strong and powerful organization like this showing fright and desiring to change its name simply because we have lost one lodge in Tennessee is more than strange.'' He stated that ''Luther persisted and the reformation arose. Washington persisted and America was set free,'' and then he asked, ''Might we not take fresh hope and try on?'' He said further, ''There is no occasion for weakness and less excuse for fear. If the foes of our Order, in ignorance of its purpose, have opposed its progress and sought its downfall, be yours the part to convince them of their error by furnishing in your lives and conduct a practical resistance to the grounds of their opposition, well knowing that the stability of any institution depends upon the faithfulness and fidelity of its members.''

This appeal had definite effect and the lodges all over the country remained firm and steadfast in these trying times. They permitted themselves to be taken to court. They met their enemies with legal talent. They were in complete agreement with the Grand Exalted Ruler who declared that he would not be content until the highest tribunal had passed on the matter. He recommended the creation of "a legal defense fund for the purpose of carrying the case to the court of highest resort." This is the direct origin of the legal defense committees and the Grand Legal Adviser who have continued to function effectively in the life and progress of the Order.

Chapter V
The Movement for Reunion

The unity of Negro Elkdom was the ideal of all of the leaders of the Order as the year 1909 approached. The Atkins faction continuously expressed this view, with Grand Exalted Ruler Atkins in the lead with the declaration, "with all my life and soul I have striven to bring peace and harmony in the ranks of Negro Elks, and from present indications I believe our hopes are about to be realized in the early consolidation of the two branches of the Order."

Similar expressions were made by Grand Exalted Ruler B. F. Howard. His Committee on Arbitration, headed by Dr. Ames made the following proposals: (1) that the Joint Committee representing the two factions hold a meeting in Dayton, Ohio on February 27, 1908; (2) that the meeting of the Atkins faction called for St. Louis, Missouri be declared off and that a reunion of the two bodies be held there; (3) that all charters be turned over to the parent body and all suits be dropped; (4) that all money held prior to the split be accounted for and returned to the parent body; (5) that all subordinate lodges of both jurisdictions be given legal standing, provided they are financial; (6) that all persons responsible directly or indirectly for the split be barred from holding office for a period of four years.

The reply to this proposal was made by Dr. Atkins who countered with (1) that in view of the fact that Mr. Howard's time expires in 1909 that the union Grand Lodge be held in that year and that the faction having the most lodges represented would select the presiding officer other than Grand Exalted Ruler Howard or Atkins; (2) that the place of the next Grand Lodge be selected by a special committee representing both Grand Lodges; (3) that after the meeting of the Committee on Arbitration neither Grand Exalted Ruler should issue charters to new lodges where lodges already exist; (4) that after the meeting of the Arbitration Committee neither side was to go to law against the other; (5) that in the event of reunion the two Grand Treasurers be required to turn over their funds to the reunited Grand Lodge for the debts of either; (6) that any reasonable plan be adopted of compensating Grand Exalted Ruler Howard for any debt of gratitude the Grand Lodge may feel and (7) that Grand Exalted Ruler Howard waive the right to any financial benefit from the Order except as agreed upon by it.

After consideration of the proposals and the counter proposal, the full Committee on Arbitration met in Chicago, Illinois at the Keystone Hotel, August 7, 1908. Representing the Howard side, there were Dr. J. W. Ames, Chairman, Detroit, Michigan; C. Clay Lewis, Atlantic City, New Jersey; E. A. Turpin, Camden, New Jersey; Harry Hammond Griffin, Philadelphia, Pennsylvania; and James T. Carter, Richmond, Virginia. Representatives of the Atkins side were J. E. Hawkins, Chairman, Seattle, Washington; W. L. Anderson, Cincinnati, Ohio; and James A. Ross, Buffalo, New York. J. E. Hawkins was selected as Chairman and J. T. Carter as Secretary.

The Committee was in session four days and parts of the nights to reach agreements for reunion of the 10,000 Negro Elks. The Committee prefaced its report with the statement that "no fears of punishment nor hopes of reward have influenced their performance of this task, but they have been governed entirely by a desire to do only what was just and equitable to all parties concerned." They declined to make a decision as to the right or wrong side, on the ground no good could accrue from this procedure, for it was now a fact that "if the Negroes of this country wish to continue in their enjoyment of the beneficent and morally elevating and social principles of Elkdom, they must come together for, in the language of the motto of Kentucky, 'united we stand, divided we fall' ". Therefore the decision had been reached unanimously that the two bodies should be one.

The following procedures were prescribed: (1) that the two Grand Lodges would meet at Detroit, Michigan, August 9, 1909, the two bodies winding up their separate business affairs and then going into a Union Grand Lodge, of which temporary body B. F. Howard would be Grand Exalted Ruler and W. E. Atkins Grand Esteemed Leading Knight; (2) the basis of representation would be one for each fifty members or fraction thereof; (3) the Grand Secretaries should submit the membership rolls ninety days prior to the Grand Lodge; (4) neither Grand Exalted Ruler was to issue a charter for a new lodge at any place where a lodge already existed; (5) all law suits were to be dropped and the two bodies were to bear the expenses of fighting suits by outside interests; and (6) the pass word after the adjournment of the two Grand Lodges was to be disseminated in alternate quarters of the year by each faction.

The seventh article of the agreement had occasioned most discussion as it concerned Grand Exalted Ruler Howard, who was the founder of the Order and had held office for ten years. Sensible of its appreciation, the committee declared, "Being deeply sensible of the debt of gratitude which the Negroes of

The Arbitration Committee, 1907. W. L. Anderson, Cincinnati, O.; J. E. Hawkins, Seattle, Wash.; James A. Ross, Buffalo, N. Y.

this country owe to Mr. B. F. Howard for turning over to them the great Order of Elks, and in order to demonstrate that sense of gratitude, we do ordain that the sum of $5,000 shall be paid to him in full settlement of all demands and claims of every kind, nature and description, present or prospective, up to and including August 15, 1909." The eighth, ninth, tenth and eleventh articles were procedural ones referring to the Union Grand Lodge of 1909.

This agreement was accepted and approved by the Grand Lodge of the Howard faction on August 13, 1908, at the Annual Session in St. Louis, Missouri, both the Grand Exalted Ruler and Grand Secretary J. E. Mills signing the resolution of approval as evidence of their acceptance. The Grand Lodge of the Atkins faction, meeting in St. Paul, Minnesota, August 27, 1908, after considerable debate savoring "only a good, sound, logic, gallant manhood and splendid examples of sincere fraternity never seen before," adopted the agreement in the midst of great cheering. All delegates were instructed by the committee's report to support any consistent measure toward unification without the sacrifice of any manly or honorable principle. The Grand Exalted Ruler and Grand Secretary were authorized to sign the resolution of approval, affix the seal of the Grand Lodge and forward copies of the same to Dr. J. W. Ames and Brother B. F. Howard.

At this same time Grand Lodge progress was made in 1908 at St. Paul Minnesota, when a Committee on an Elk's Home made its report through its Secretary, Brother C. H. Jones. The report stated that the Jonesboro Land and Improvement Company through its President, Dr. R. E. Jones, had donated certain land in Virgina for the erection of an Elk Home and that evidence of good faith, on the part of the Grand Lodge be shown by the construction of a building costing not less than $5,000. The committee recommended the acceptance of the land and that the deeds and title be placed in the hands of the Grand Trustees. This recommendation was approved by the Grand Lodge. A year later every member was taxed one dollar, to be collected prior to January, 1910, and the home not to exceed $12,000 in cost was to be known as the National Elks' Home and Summer Rest.

L. Melendez King, Grand Trustee, 1907.

Another matter of importance to the development of the Order had been referred to Brother L. Melendez King concern-

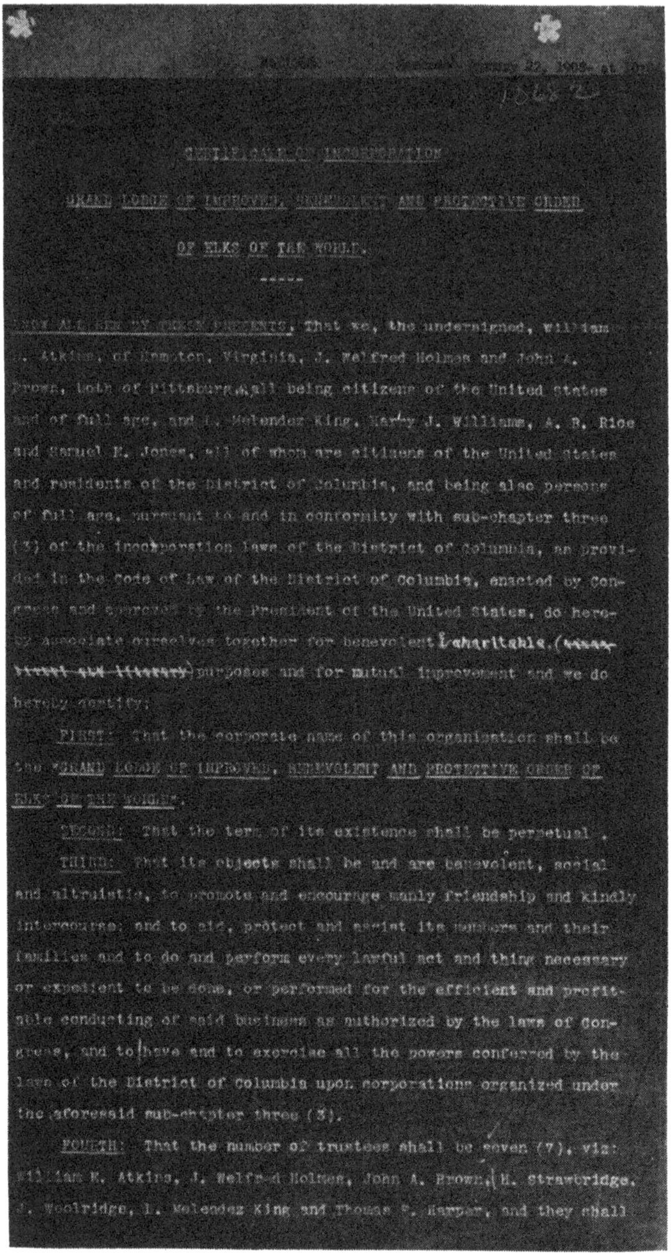

[illegible] Recorded January 22, 1908, at [illegible]

CERTIFICATE OF INCORPORATION

GRAND LODGE OF IMPROVED, BENEVOLENT AND PROTECTIVE ORDER

OF ELKS OF THE WORLD.

KNOW ALL MEN BY THESE PRESENTS, That we, the undersigned, William H. Atkins, of Hampton, Virginia, J. Welfred Holmes and John A. Brown, both of Pittsburg, all being citizens of the United States and of full age, and L. Melendez King, Harry J. Williams, A. R. Rice and Samuel E. Jones, all of whom are citizens of the United States and residents of the District of Columbia, and being also persons of full age, pursuant to and in conformity with sub-chapter three (3) of the incorporation laws of the District of Columbia, as provided in the Code of Law of the District of Columbia, enacted by Congress and approved by the President of the United States, do hereby associate ourselves together for benevolent, charitable, ~~(benevolent and literary)~~ purposes and for mutual improvement and we do hereby certify;

FIRST: That the corporate name of this organization shall be the "GRAND LODGE OF IMPROVED, BENEVOLENT AND PROTECTIVE ORDER OF ELKS OF THE WORLD".

SECOND: That the term of its existence shall be perpetual.

THIRD: That its objects shall be and are benevolent, social and altruistic, to promote and encourage manly friendship and kindly intercourse; and to aid, protect and assist its members and their families and to do and perform every lawful act and thing necessary or expedient to be done, or performed for the efficient and profitable conducting of said business as authorized by the laws of Congress, and to have and to exercise all the powers conferred by the laws of the District of Columbia upon corporations organized under the aforesaid sub-chapter three (3).

FOURTH: That the number of trustees shall be seven (7), viz: William H. Atkins, J. Welfred Holmes, John A. Brown, H. Strawbridge, J. Woolridge, L. Melendez King and Thomas S. Harper, and they shall

First page, Certificate of Incorporation, The District of Columbia, December 14, 1907, recorded January 22, 1908.

ing the incorporation of the Grand Lodge, I.B.P.O.E.W., and the information that the local lodge of white Elks was also incorporated under the title of Washington Lodge, B.P.O.E. Being aware of the opposition to Negro Elkdom in the capital of the nation as well as elsewhere, he studied the situation very carefully from the legal point of view. When he presented his certificate for recording, he was informed by the Deputy Recorder, who was a member of Washington Lodge, B.P.O.E., that it could not be filed since it was in derogation of the incorporate rights of the B.P.O.E. King then prepared a mandamus to compel the acceptance of the certificate and notified Grand Exalted Ruler Atkins. On the next day, he received a phone call stating that the matter had been referred to the United States District Attorney and that a date had been set for a hearing. King prepared a brief for his case while the white lodge also prepared a brief and submitted it through its attorney. The District Attorney finally decided in King's favor and the certificate was recorded. A vote of appreciation was extended to Brother King, who also admitted that credit was due Morning Star Lodge, No. 40 for cooperation with him. A motion was made to give to the Grand Deputy of New York the authority to publish in the newspapers of New York City, the *New York World, New York Sun, New York Press* and *New York Times,* a true copy of the national incorporation of the I.B.P.O.E. of W. This motion was not approved.

This incorporation under the laws of the District of Columbia gave a federal and national basis for the protection and operation of the Improved Benevolent Protective Order of Elks of the World. This legal document was another historical landmark in the legal establishment of the Grand Lodge. The report of this action was received with enthusiastic approval by the Grand Lodge Session. Provision was then made by the Grand Lodge for reference of all matters arising in courts of law involving the Grand Lodge to the Grand Legal Adviser, who was to confer with the Grand Trustees so as to protect the interest of the Grand Lodge. Since B.P.O.E., lodges were seeking injunction against subordinate lodges of the I.B.P.O.E. of W, for their use of the title "Elks," it was ordered that the Grand Lodge should defend these lodges in the courts in the use of the title "Improved Benevolent and Protective Order of Elks of the World," and that a fund be created by an assessment of ten cents per member from every subordinate lodge. Grand Exalted Ruler Atkins through correspondence endeavored to secure the cooperation of Grand Exalted Ruler Howard for aid in the defense of suits but the latter said that he could not respond to

HARRY H. PACE, Grand Master of Social Sessions, 1907-1908; Grand Secretary, 1908-1911; Fifth Grand Exalted Ruler, 1911-1913.

this request. The cost of the suit in New York alone was $3,879.82. The Atkins faction felt that it was carrying the defense of Negro Elkdom by itself since no aid was received from the Howard group.

The design of a pin on which letters patent had been secured was presented by Brother George E. Bates in behalf of Erle R. Sheppard, inventor. The committee recommended that the design and pin be adopted and that the necessary terms for the purchase and sale of the pins be agreed upon between the manufacturer and the Grand Exalted Ruler. The approval of the manufacture and sale of lodge supplies and paraphernalia for the Order by Captain S. T. Sneed was made, so as to establish legality for this activity. It had been also proposed that an Endowment Bureau be established by the Order and this was referred to a committee who reported that it was best for the subordinate lodges to attend to this matter for themselves and the delegates were urged to oppose "any measure for the establishment of any such bureau."

The Grand Lodge at St. Paul, Minnesota, of 1908 then elected and appointed its Grand Lodge Officers as follows:

Dr. W. E. Atkins, Excelsior, No. 4—Grand Exalted Ruler
Raymond L. Phillips, Pioneer, No. 10—Grand Esteemed Leading Knight
Dr. J. E. Dibble, Imperial, No. 101—Grand Esteemed Loyal Knight
Dr. A. A. Kellogg, Manhattan, No. 45—Grand Esteemed Lecturing Knight
Harry H. Pace, Bluff City, No. 96—Grand Secretary
J. T. Brandy, Keystone, No. 6—Grand Treasurer
Henry Jones, Great Lakes, No. 43—Grand Tiler
James H. Anderson, Manhattan. No. 45—Grand Inner Guard
E. M. Shoecraft, Great Lakes, No. 43—Grand Esquire
John H. Gray, Excelsior, No. 4—Grand Chaplain
C. A. Jamieson, Athens, No. 70—Grand Organist
E. E. Perkins, Charles Young, No. 103—Grand Master of Social Sessions
J. Welford Holmes, Iron City, No. 17—Grand Legal Advisor
Dr. R. E. Jones, Capitol City, No. 11—Grand Medical Advisor
William Jones, Monumental, No. 3—Grand Organizer
E. Burton Ceruti, Brooklyn, No. 32—National Receiver of Moneys

This Grand Lodge headed by Grand Exalted Ruler Atkins reported that there were ninety Lodges and over 10,000 members were claimed in its jurisdiction. By 1909 the number of lodges had increased to one hundred and three, and there were also nineteen temples. This Grand Lodge was an important part of

Elkdom and had become as valuable to Elkdom as the parent body. Its action looking toward unification was of great significance.

J. WELFORD HOLMES, Grand Secretary, 1907-1908; Grand Legal Adviser, 1908.

The Union Grand Lodge comprising the Grand Lodge led by Howard and Atkins, in accordance with the articles of agreement adopted by the Howard Grand Lodge in St. Louis, Missouri on August 12, 1908 and approved by the Atkins Grand Lodge in St. Paul, Minnesota, August 25, 1908, assembled in Arbeiter Hall, Detroit, Michigan on August 9, 1909. The meeting was called to order by the temporary chairman, James W. Thompson. The Mayor of Detroit extended greetings. The Grand Lodge was opened in ritualistic form by Grand Exalted Ruler Atkins. The roll call showed that there were 54 lodges represented by 105 delegates.

The Grand Exalted Ruler's address congratulated the delegates that they had been broad enough to lay down the fight and assemble to unite for a common destiny and cause. He said, "as regrettable as this affair is and has been it is gratifying that it is not peculiar to this organization alone. Governments have differed and seceded from each other. Even the Church of God is not exempt from this misfortune. We meet today with but one thought in view and that is to conserve our forces for the good this organization may be to future generations." Similar expressions were made by Grand Exalted Ruler Howard and the leaders of his group meeting in the hall below. A fraternal visit was made by a delegation consisting of Dr. J. E. Mills, G. Grant Williams, J. T. Taylor, Samuel Mitchell, J. E. Shepperson and H. T. Wycoff. Responses to addresses were made by J. Frank Wheaton and Grand Exalted Ruler Atkins.

One of the demands of the Committee on Arbitration was that the sum of $5,000 be paid to Grand Exalted Ruler Howard. This did not seem to be fair to the Atkins group when it was assessing its lodges and members for the costs of suits to save the Improved Benevolent and Protective Order of Elks of the World and planning for an Elks' Home, while the Howard group was demanding money to satisfy Grand Exalted Ruler Howard whose ten year term had almost expired. However, in an effort to carry out the articles of agreement, the Arbitration Committee addressed a letter to B. F. Howard during the Grand Lodge session proposing that after permanent union is completed, not later than August 12, 1909, one thousand dollars in cash would be paid and the balance of the $5,000 would be paid in quarterly installments equal to 10 per cent of the gross receipts of the Union Grand Lodge. On the other hand, Howard would agree to give up whatever right, title or interests which he had in the rituals, ceremonies and copyrights of the Order of Elks, and that he would cease to establish lodges or interfere with the establishment of lodges. To this proposal Howard sent the curt reply, "your proposition at hand. I cannot accept."

J. T. BRANDY, Grand Treasurer, 1902-1906.

Shortly afterward a committee from the Howard Grand Lodge consisting of John W. Patterson, J. A. Bloom and Martin Luther Davis read a resolution previously passed by their Grand Lodge and presented by T. G. Nutter of Kanawha Lodge No. 130 of Charleston, West Virginia:

Detroit, Michigan
August 12, 1909

> "Whereas, The two factions of the I.B.P.O.E. of W., known as the Howard and Atkins factions, have this day met in joint sessions for the purpose of consolidating and uniting said factions into one harmonious; and
> Whereas, we can have one harmonious body only by removing every possible cause which tended, in the least degree, to bring about the unfortunate division in our Order, and
> Whereas, we are constantly being hauled into the courts of justice by our white brethren and thereby put to great expense

and inconvenience in defending our rights, and, since we can meet said opposition only by presenting to the common enemy a solid phalanx, welded together by fidelity, love, charity and justice, and,

Whereas, we believe that it would be most unfortunate and inopportune to elect B. F. Howard or W. E. Atkins, Grand Exalted Ruler of the I.B.P.O.E. of the World, as neither of the two brothers mentioned, under the present chaotic conditions, and enmity existing between said factions could, under his leadership unite said factions into a harmonious body working to a common end; Be it

Resolved, that it is the sense of this Grand Lodge representing said factions that neither the name of B. F. Howard or W. E. Atkins be presented to this body as candidate for Grand Exalted Ruler of the I.B.P.O.E. of the World."

A discussion of this resolution led Dr. R. E. Jones to say that it was unjust and unkind to accept any proposition which would deprive any brother of his rights. However, Grand Exalted Ruler Atkins stated that he was willing to retire from the field with Mr. Howard if he was sincere in this matter. The Arbitration Committee then presented the following proposition:

"Whereas, the Howard faction has presented to the Atkins faction the proposition upon which unity shall be based, to-wit. That neither B. F. Howard or W. E. Atkins shall be a candiate for the office of Grand Exalted Ruler of this organization. Be it

Resolved, that this Grand Lodge commonly called the Atkins faction, do hereby agree to unite on said basis.

Provided, however, that this shall be the sole condition for the perfection of the organization of a United Grand Lodge, and that no other condition shall be imposed thereon.

(Signed) J. E. Hawkins, Chrmn. Arb. Com.
Jas. A. Ross
W. L. Anderson"

Brother Hawkins then stated that Howard had refused to consider the above proposition and that they could do nothing further in the matter and the committee asked to be dismissed. Brother Louis B. Anderson made the motion that prior to election of Grand Officers the Articles of Agreement concerning voting, charters and law suits be declared null and void by the Atkins Grand Lodge and his motion was unanimously adopted. The matter of union stood where it was before 1909. The two Grand Lodges proceeded to elect their Grand Officers and adjourned. However, the Howard faction elected Dr. J. E. Mills who had been Grand Organizer as Grand Exalted Ruler and the Atkins faction reelected Grand Exalted Ruler Atkins. A committee was appointed to prepare a statement for publication concerning the failure of arbitration. The leaders and delegates left the two conventions convinced that steps should be taken to unite the Grand Lodges. They looked forward to a later conference.

This conference, known as the "Peace Conference" was called by joint action of Grand Exalted Ruler Atkins and Grand Exalted Ruler James E. Mills. The delegates who assembled were designated the Peace Conference Commission. They were Dr. James E. Mills, Norfolk, Virgina; Dr. W. E. Atkins, Hampton, Virginia; Attorney J. Frank Wheaton, New York, N. Y.; Dr. W. T. Jones, Newport News, Virginia; Attorney J. W. Patterson, Washington, D. C.; Attorney L. Melendez King; James E. Dixon, Providence, Rhode Island; Rev. John H. Gray, Hampton, Virginia; Dr. P. A. Scott, Newport News, Virginia; Sandy Daugherty, Portsmouth, Virginia; and Archie Drew, Portsmouth, Virginia.

JOURNAL OF PROCEEDINGS

OF THE

Peace Conference Commission

OF THE

I. B. P. O. E. of W.

Wilmington, Delaware

Wednesday and Thursday, January 25-26

1910

———

GUIDE PUBLISHING COMPANY
NORFOLK, VA.

Journal of Proceedings of the Peace Conference Commission of the I.B.P.O.E. of W., 1910.

They assembled at the Paul Laurence Dunbar Lodge rooms on January 25 and 26, 1910. J. Frank Wheaton was elected temporary chairman and W. T. Jones secretary. Brother Wheaton opened the meeting with the following words, "we are here to decide the question of unification honestly, fairly, squarely and brotherly. We have met here on an important occasion. We have in our hands the destiny of thousands of our fellowmen. Whether we shall be faithful, realising the importance of our duty depends upon our actions. We must not only invoke our own personalities, but we must look for guidance to a power higher than we." He then requested Rev. J. H. Gray to lead in prayer. L. Melendez King spoke of the friendly relations between the two Grand Masters and predicted favorable action toward unification. The temporary organization was then made permanent. Grand Exalted Ruler Atkins suggested that Grand Exalted Ruler James E. Mills pre-

The Peace Conference Commission of the I.B.P.O.E. of W., Wilmington, Delaware, January 25-26, 1910.

side over the Union Grand Lodge meeting. This was approved by motion. Dr. Atkins said that the two Grand Lodges would have to meet in separate sessions at first in order to call off the respective Grand Lodge meetings scheduled for Brooklyn and Norfolk, after which they could go into the Union Grand Lodge over which Dr. Mills would preside. Dr. Atkins was made the Grand Esteemed Leading Knight of the Union Grand Lodge and the remaining officers now serving would continue jointly in their respective stations.

As to the place of meeting for the Union Grand Lodge, Brother L. Melendez King extended an invitation from Morning Star Lodge to meet in Washington, D. C., and Norfolk, Virginia was presented by Brother Dixon. After a brief adjournment, a motion was made by Brother Dixon that the Lodge meet in Washington, D. C. This motion was amended by Dr. Mills that the invitation be accepted from both lodges in Washington, D. C., and that the entertaining be placed in the hands of a local committee. The date was set as the last Tuesday in July for a period of four days. A resolution concerning the suits of the B.P.O., Elks against the I.B.P.O. Elks of the World was adopted, requesting Grand Exalted Ruler Mills to render whatever assistance possible in defense of the Lodge; the expense incident to these suits should be borne equally by both Grand Lodges and that both Grand Lodges levy an assessment of fifty cents per member. Dr. Mills later said that he believed that it was his duty to show that the side which he represented was "desirous of protecting the rights of the Afro-Americans," and that he would appoint an advisory committee relative to legal defense.

One of the visitors who was to play a leading role in the great future development of the Order was introduced and spoke briefly. This personage was J. Finley Wilson. This was the first of his public appearances before the leadership of the Order. He represented the press and was given the privilege of the floor. He expressed his high appreciation for the consolidation of the two factions and declared that the columns of the press were open to every Elk. He asked the conference to vote thanks to *The Norfolk Journal and Guide* for its kind expressions and its offer to publish Elk news. The vote to adopt this proposal was unanimous.

The Peace Conference adjourned with words of enthusiasm and hope for the Union Grand Lodge session. As the Chairman, J. Frank Wheaton, stated a sentiment shared by other members, "I know of no moment in my life which has brought more gratitude, joy and complete satisfaction to my life than the time covered by the deliberations of this conference." He said that the conference little realized the magnitude of its work and that while for five years they had been working apart "the work of the convention cements our Order" and "ties which were broken are now bound together."

The consummation of this dream of peace and union was reached in the meeting of the two Grand Lodges in Washington, D. C., on July 28, 1910, as the guests of Morning Star Lodge No. 40 and Columbia Lodge No. 85 in True Reformers Hall, Twelfth and U Streets. Proclamations concerning the meetings were issued by both Grand Exalted Rulers. The Chairman of the United Local Committee, Brother Benjamin L. Gaskins of Columbia Lodge No. 85, Washington, D. C., presided at the opening session. Prayer was offered by Brother C. H. Strothers of Columbia Lodge. Welcome addresses were made by the Secretary of the Commissioners of the District of Columbia, Dr. W. C. Tindall; Judge Robert L. Terrell, Ralph W. Tyler, Auditor of the Navy; Dr. W. Bruce Evans on behalf of the educational interests; Dr. M. W. Clair on behalf of the religious community; and Samuel E. Jones of Morning Star Lodge No. 40. Responses were delivered by Grand Exalted Ruler Mills and Grand Exalted Ruler Atkins, each of whom spoke enthusiastically about the union and when they clasped one another's hand, the applause and approval were tremendous. The response on behalf of the Peace Conference was given by Brother J. Frank Wheaton. Great applause followed his speech. The Elks Glee Club furnished the music.

BENJAMIN L. GASKINS, Chairman United Local Committees.

The parade was unusual and attracted considerable attention. A Washington daily newspaper reported, "Washington, as the Capital of the nation is accustomed to seeing processions, pageants and something of unusual interest in this line must be produced to attract the attention of the average Washingtonian. The parade of the colored Elks today was a parade that deserved all the attention that it attracted from the throngs that lined the streets during its entire length. It was orderly and showed skill in assembling and management, and in every respect reflected credit on the organization.''

On the second day the two Grand Lodges met in separate assemblies, as was planned, and brought their business to a close after receiving the reports of their respective officers. The question of the Union Grand Session was then raised. Resolutions were passed approving the actions of the Grand Exalted Rulers by the Atkins group to notify the Mills group in session on the lower floor of the same building ''that we have now completed our affairs and that we are ready to join them in Union Sessions at this time.'' A committee was appointed to convey this information. The committee reported that at 4:00 p.m. on the same day the Union Grand Lodge could go into session. This report was enthusiastically received.

The Union Session opened with Grand Exalted Ruler Mills presiding. The Joint Committee on Credentials retired to complete its report. Dr. Mills asked Acting Grand Esteemed Leading Knight, Dr. Atkins, to preside during his temporary absence. The Credentials Committe made its report the next day, July 28, showing that there were 108 lodges represented with 199 delegates. There was a large body of interested members who were present, the delegates occupying the lower floor and others in the gallery.

Grand Exalted Ruler Mills asked Grand Secretary Harry N. Pace to read the Minutes of the Peace Conference. After the reading, the motion to adopt and ratify the Minutes was unanimously approved. A rising vote of appreciation was given to the Peace Conference Committee for the statesmanlike manner in which they had worked. The members of the committee were called to the platform and three cheers were given to them. A motion was made by Dr. O. M. Waller to adopt the following resolution:

> "Whereas, the Grand Body is now duly and regularly composed of the Parent Body incorporated under the title I.B.P.O.E., and the Lodge of the I.B.P.O.E. of W.,
> Be it Resolved, that this Grand Body be and by virtue of this resolution now is the Grand Lodge I.B.P.O.E. of W."

This motion was referred to a committee of seven to consider the advisability of adopting it. A delegation of Daughter Elks requested permission to extend fraternal greetings and a committee was appointed to escort them into the session. Addresses were made by Daughter Emma V. Kelley and Daughter Scott. There were 26 temples at this time. The Daughters also asked for a closer relationship, submitting a resolution of their Grand Temple asking that a recognition sign and password between sisters and brothers be authorized and that Thanksgiving and Memorial Services be held jointly. The resolution was signed by Daughters Emma V. Kelley, Lottie Green, Mary Sneed, Grace Johnson, Alice Thornton and Julia Warner. It was referred for action to the Committee on Laws and Revisions.

The Grand Exalted Ruler, Dr. W. E. Atkins, delivered his address and among the pertinent statements was the one dealing with the union movement inaugurated by the two Grand Exalted Rulers and the Arbitration Committee: "Thus we come today not as a faction uniting with faction, for none but the most devoid in those manly and brotherly qualities that go to make up a worthy Brother Elk could inject such feelings here, but we come only to have you put the stamp of your approval upon the work already accomplished by Brother Mills and myself, aided by our faithful and determined Arbitation Committee." His address revealed the continued growth of the Order. It had extended beyond the United States with a lodge in Nassau, Bahama Islands and another lodge had been authorized for installation in El Calloa, Venezuela, and still another at Empire Zone, Panama.

Committees for the new Grand Lodge were appointed, the Past Grand Exalted Ruler's degree was formulated and the sign, grip and password were approved for use by the Brothers and the Daughters. Grand Exalted Ruler Atkins in making his report stated that the two lodges in Georgia had been compelled to change their name and title, since Georgia had passed an act prohibiting the operations of the I.B.P.O.E., of the World in that state and they had selected the name "Lions," and had assured him that they were still loyal to the Order and were paying their taxes.

The selection of a Grand Exalted Ruler for the United Grand Lodge occasioned considerable attention. A resolution had been offered but was not approved, ruling out of consideration both Grand Exalted Rulers, Dr. Mills and Dr. Atkins. Four Brother Elks were nominated—J. Frank Wheaton of Manhattan Lodge, No. 45; W. E. Atkins, present Grand Exalted Ruler; M. R. Bibb of Great Lakes Lodge No. 43; and Francis H. Warren of Wolverine Lodge No. 72. The first ballot showed, M. R. Bibb, 51; W. E. Atkins, 59; J. Frank Wheaton, 56; F. H. Warren, 15; Total, 181; necessary to elect 91. A second ballot failed to secure the number of votes necessary to elect from the three, Bibb, Atkins and Wheaton. Bibb was dropped from the list and the balloting resulted in Atkins receiving 57 and Wheaton 114, and he was declared elected.

J. Frank Wheaton, Fourth Grand Exalted Ruler of Reunited Elkdom 1910-1911.

The roster of officers was selected as follows: J. Frank Wheaton, Grand Exalted Ruler, New York, N. Y.; T. Gillis Nutter, Grand Esteemed Leading Knight, Charleston, W. Va.; Steward E. Hoyt, Grand Esteemed Loyal Knight, Boston, Mass.; Harry A. Jacobs, Grand Esteemed Lecturing Knight, Cincinnati, Ohio; Dr. William E. Gates, Grand Treasurer, Anacostia, D. C.; Harry H. Pace, Grand Secretary, Memphis, Tenn.; A. W. Russell, Grand Tiler, Atlanta, Ga. The appointed officers were J. J. Jones, Grand Esquire, Chicago, Ill.; P. H. Williams, Grand Chaplain, Pa.; D. T. Trezevant, Grand Inner Guard, N. Y.; Jesse W. Harris, Grand Organist, Pa.; F. H. Warren, Grand Organizer, Mich.; A. A. Seldon, Grand Master of Social Sessions, Mass.; J. W. Powell, Grand Medical Director, Ind.; William R. Morris, Grand Legal Adviser, Minn.; E. Burton Ceruti, Receiver of Monies for Legal Defense. After singing the closing ode and prayer by the Grand Chaplain, the Grand Lodge, now again united, adjourned to meet in Boston the next year, 1912.

There was similar reaction leading to a division by the Daughter Elks. When the divisions took place among the Elks, Norfolk Temple divided and the Grand Temple was also split into two divisions. This was a crisis which Mrs. Kelley said was one "that will be long remembered and shall never be forgotten." In 1906, the group siding with the Atkins faction met at Hampton, Virginia on November 10, and elected Mrs. M. E. Hodges as Grand Daughter Ruler. The group lining up with the Howard faction known as the "Parent Body of Daughters" organized at Smithfield, Virginia in the same year with Mrs. Kelley as secretary. This division continued, and when the two factions among the Elks sought peace, the same action was undertaken by the Daughters. An Arbitration Committee met in Detroit in 1909 but failed to accomplish its purpose. Three divisions developed after this meeting. Dr. J. E. Mills, who was Grand Exalted Ruler had a part of the Temple with him, B. F. Howard had a group with him and a third was with the Atkins faction. The temple was more than rent in twain.

In spite of these divisions the temples grew in number. Eight temples were instituted in 1907, and the income for the year was $266.83. Deputies were appointed and endowment policies were approved. In 1908 there were fourteen temples with 900 members. Eureka Temple No. 22 was the largest temple with 103 members. The Daughter Elks agreed at this Grand Temple to tax themselves twenty-five cents to help pay the legal expenses in the cases against Negro Elkdom. In 1909 the Grand Temple approved the organization of the Past Daughter Ruler Councils and the Executive Board and in 1910 Grand Daughter Secretary

DAUGHTER MAMIE E. HODGE, Second Grand Daughter Ruler, 1906-1923.

Emma V. Kelley was honored as the Mother of the organization as well as its Founder.

When the Peace Conference of the Grand Lodges met in Wilmington, Delaware in 1910, and the Union Grand Lodge assembled in Washington, D. C., in 1911, the Daughters were also prepared for union. The meeting of the Grand Temple in Boston, Massachusetts in 1911, was described as a "glorious" session, for it witnessed the union of the temples. The union of both men and women of Elkdom had been accomplished.

Chapter VI

Advancement in Spite of Handicaps

There were obstacles which faced the United Grand Lodge, as it began its first year of existence. Enthusiasm had marked the session of the Union Grand Lodge in Washington, D. C., and the delegates had returned to their home lodges with optimistic accounts and expectations for the future. However, there were delegates who were sympathetic and loyal to the Howard-Mills faction and were concerned that adequate consideration, in their opinion, had not been given at the Washington session to their views. One of the contentions grew out of the request of Past Exalted Ruler B. F. Howard for the sum of five thousand dollars as compensation for turning over the ritual to the Grand Lodge. This request was not given consideration and was ignored in the final settlement of differences.

In February, 1911, Past Grand Exalted Ruler James E. Mills brought suit against the Grand Lodge, on behalf of Past Grand Exalted Ruler B. F. Howard, basing the suit upon the ownership of the copyright of the ritual, which the Grand Lodge and subordinate lodges were using. This was one of the causes for discouragement and unrest among the lodges. When their members thought that the division and contentions were settled and that the brother Elks were united in common purposes, there arose this occasion for a new dividing of the brotherhood. Some lodges even refused to pay the regular taxation placed upon them by the Grand Lodge. In the midst of the exultation over the achievement of union, a new division over the ownership of the ritual made its appearance. It was not strange that many were asking, "would there ever be peace in Elkdom"?

In the meantime, another cause for this kind of questioning came with the service of papers for a temporary injunction against the Virginia lodges on Brother Carey Wheaton, Deputy of Grand Exalted Ruler J. Frank Wheaton who was named codefendant. The case was set for hearing on November 5, 1910, but was adjourned until December 3. Agreement was finally reached between Past Grand Exalted Ruler James E. Mills and Grand Exalted Ruler J. Frank Wheaton who had been named defendant in the suit to make permanent the temporary injunction issued by decree of Judge E. D. Waddel of the United States Circuit Court for the Eastern District of Virginia. It was agreed that the pending litigation should be superseded by

IN THE UNITED STATES CIRCUIT COURT

FOR THE EASTERN DISTRICT OF VIRGINIA

James E. Mills, Trustee and Grand Exalted Ruler of The Improved Benevolent and Protective Order of Elks of The World,

Complainant,

vs

J. Frank Wheaton,

Defendant.

TO THE JUSTICE HOLDING UNITED STATES CIRCUIT COURT FOR THE EASTERN DISTRICT OF VIRGINIA:

The complainant respectfully represents:

1. That he is a citizen of the United States and a resident of the City of Norfolk in the State of Virginia, and that he brings this suit on behalf of the Grand Lodge Improved, Benevolent and Protective Order of Elks of the World, a corporation, duly incorporated under the laws of the State of Ohio; and Benjamin Franklin Howard, a resident of Cincinnati in the State of Ohio. That by the constitution and laws of the said Order of Elks he is authorized and empowered to bring this suit as Grand Exalted Ruler.

2. That the defendant, J. Frank Wheaton, is a citizen of the United States and a resident of the City of New York in the State of New York.

3. That in 1889, the said Benjamin F. Howard organized a Grand Lodge that became known as the Improved, Benevolent and Protective Order of Elks of the World; and that the said organization was duly incorporated under the laws of the State of Ohio, as aforesaid; that the said Benjamin F. Howard presided over the said Grand Lodge as Grand Exalted Ruler, from the time of its beginning until the month of August 1909, continuously.

4. That in the said month of August, in the said year 1909, at the Grand Lodge meeting in the City of Detroit, in the State of Michigan, the said Benjamin F. Howard, upon the election, at the said meeting of his successor, James E. Mills, as Grand Exalted Ruler, agreed with the said Grand Lodge of the said Improved Benevolent and Protective Order of Elks of the World, over which he had up to this time presided, as aforesaid, to turn over to the said Grand Lodge the book or ritual aforesaid, for its exclusive use and benefit together with all the right title and interest that he, the said Howard could, or might have to the same by virtue of his copyright, for the agreed sum of Five Thousand ($5,000) dol-

The case of James E. Mills, Trustee and Grand Exalted Ruler I.B.P.O.E. of W., vs. J. Frank Wheaton, filed U. S. Circuit Court, October 12, 1910.

the arbitration by a commission consisting of the Attorneys for the contending parties, the plaintiff and the defendant, and an impartial Elk acceptable to the members of the commission. An amicable settlement was worked out to the satisfaction of all concerned, so that the Improved Benevolent and Protective Order of Elks of the World could continue its achievements in spite of obstacles.

In reporting this victory, Grand Exalted Ruler J. Frank Wheaton said, "What transpired during this night interval, apparently a curse, had developed into a lasting blessing upon the Improved Benevolent and Protective Order of Elks of the World. The many inevitable complications necessitated an investigation into the detailed construction, needs and shortcomings of our fraternal fabric, that on account of the happenings of this direful and discouraging period we emerged from the Slough of Despond into a smiling valley of promise and good cheer from which we behold the towering mountains of our fraternal victory."

The question of the ownership of the ritual through copyright was also tried in the Circuit Court of the United States for the Eastern District of Virginia at Richmond. The case was known as *James E. Mills, Trustee and Grand Exalted Ruler of the Improved Benevolent and Protective Order of the Elks, et al complainant, vs. J. Frank Wheaton, et al, Defendant* in Equity No. 614.

James E. Mills began this case as an individual Trustee and Grand Exalted Ruler of the Howard faction against Grand Exalted Ruler J. Frank Wheaton in his individual right. Brother Mills stated that he was bringing this suit on behalf of the Grand Lodge, Improved Benevolent and Protective Order of Elks of the World and Benjamin Franklin Howard, who had copyrighted the ritual, and that he was authorized under the constitution to bring this suit as Grand Exalted Ruler. He stated that when Grand Exalted Ruler Howard's term had expired in 1909, he had succeeded him as Grand Exalted Ruler. An agreement was reached, Mills said, for Brother Howard to turn over to the Grand Lodge the ritual for its exclusive use together with the right and title to it, and that five thousand dollars were to be paid for it. Brother Howard delivered the ritual to his successor Grand Exalted Ruler James E. Mills for the use of the Grand Lodge. Grand Exalted Ruler Mills said that he was responsible for the payment of the agreed sum.

It was then alleged that J. Frank Wheaton or his agents and followers caused the book to be printed, reprinted, and distributed, which amounted to an infringement of the copyright.

Because of these actions it had not been possible to pay the sum of five thousand dollars to Brother Howard. It was requested that the defendant, Brother J. Frank Wheaton, be restrained from publishing and vending this ritual, or as it was called in the suit, "said pirated ritual."

A supplemental complaint was filed by Brother Mills in the same court on December 10, 1910, stating that Charters had been secured in Virginia, New York, and the District of Columbia, which, it was stated, was in violation of the right of the copyright of the ritual as well as the rights under the original Charter granted by the State of Ohio. This had occasioned the use of two constitutions and by-laws, which had led to confusion and financial loss. Other irregularities had resulted, it was alleged. Since arbitration had been agreed to and a committee of Arbitration appointed consisting of Giles B. Jackson, John W. Patterson and Oscar D. Morries, it was requested that this would be ratified and confirmed by the court.

The decree having been temporarily entered in the record of February 7, 1911, the Special Master, Claude M. Dean, set June 23, 1911, as the time for executing the requirements of the decree. Notice was sent to the following attorneys of record: James M. Harrison, Norfolk, Virginia; John W. Patterson, Washington, D. C.; Benjamin L. Gaskins, Washington, D. C.; L. Melendez King, Washington, D. C.; and Giles B. Jackson, Richmond, Virginia. Testimony was taken on this date and counsel was allowed until July 29, 1911, to file briefs. The cause at issue was the enjoining of the Grand Lodge and the Subordinate Lodges from printing, reprinting, publishing, copying and distributing, and using any printed copy of the ritual. At the Advisory Committee meeting of Grand Officers in New York, March 30, 1911, it was proposed that $2,000 be paid to B. F. Howard payable in quarterly installments of $200 for the absolute transfer of the ritual to the Grand Lodge.

The decision in this case stated that a printed copy of the title of the ritual was deposited with the Librarian of Congress on June 12, 1902, by B. F. Howard, but there was a publication of the ritual prior to this date by Arthur J. Riggs under a copyright on September 28, 1898. It was said that "B. F. Howard is not entitled to a copyright of the same under the laws of the United States." The copy had also been used without the copyright notice required by law to be inserted on the title page or the page following. Accordingly, the complainant, B. F. Howard, whom Grand Exalted Ruler Mills represented, was declared not entitled to maintain an action for the infringement of the copyright, even though he was otherwise entitled to it.

It was alleged by his attorney that he was "the absolute owner of the said ritual" and that "for ten long years his sole support had been from the income being derived by the use of his ritual among the subordinate lodges of the Improved Benevolent and Protective Order of Elks of the World; that he could not have afforded to part with his ritual without just compensation in view of his old age and inability and his utter dependence upon the income from the said ritual for the support of himself and his family."

It was declared by the decision that B. F. Howard was not the author of the book or ritual, and the conclusion was that the alleged copyright of the book or ritual involved in this cause was an invalid one, and that "the copyright does not belong to anyone." Testimony showed that "Howard was mentally incapable of producing such a ritual as involved in this cause and that it was not Howard's work to copyright; Riggs' affidavit, which was admitted without objection, is to the effect that he, Riggs, wrote the ritual and entered the same for copyright and that Howard's entry was without his consent and a fraud upon him, and that the two books are identical." When it is realized that the Librarian of Congress is not required to inquire into the question of the right when granting a copyright and that the one who claims the title states it, the possibility of this kind of contention becomes more apparent.

The report on this case to the lodges and members of the Order recited the fact that, "It must be pleasing to all loyal members that our victory in this case has served to stop the long, tiresome and disrupting internal strife, and is an impetus for greater activities and efforts on their part toward making our beloved Order a potential power in the social, moral and intellectual uplift of its members and the race in general."

No decision had been rendered in the New York Case. It hung like a dark cloud on the horizon of the future for the lodges in the eastern part of the nation. This case and those in other states to prohibit the existence of lodges of Negro Elks caused the indifferent to grow negligent and affected generally the growth of the lodges. Fortunately, the leadership selected for this trying period was equal to the challenges placed before it. J. Frank Wheaton, an attorney of record, maintained peace and aroused interest and worked continuously during his year in office as Grand Exalted Ruler for the advancement of the Order. The Grand Secretary, Harry H. Pace, worked indefatigably in maintaining contacts with the lodges and their secretaries. He was capable and conscientious in his work, for he knew that the times called for this type of activity.

H. H. PACE, Grand Exalted Ruler,
392 Beale Avenue,
Memphis, Tenn.

GEO. E. BATES, Grand Secretary
36 Thomas Street,
Newark, N. J.

DR. W. E. GALES, Grand Treasurer,
Anacostia, Washington, D. C.

Newark, N. J., Nov. 1st, 1911.

To Members of the I. B. P. O. E. W.

Greeting:

The Report on the **"VIRGINIA CASE"** by Special Master Claude M. Dean, Esq., printed on the following pages, was made two months after adjournment of the Grand Lodge in Boston. The Grand Exalted Ruler has already issued a circular citing the salient points in said Report, but it is thought advisable to publish the same in full, that it may be filed in the archives of your Lodge for future reference.

It must be pleasing to all loyal members that our victory in this case has served to stop the long, tiresome and disrupting internal strife, and is an impetus for greater activities and efforts on their part toward making our beloved Order a potential power in the social, moral and intellectual uplift of its members and the race in general.

Yours in C. J. B. L. & F.,

Geo. E. Bates

Grand Secretary.

First Page of the Report on The Virginia Case, 1911.

The attitude of these Elk leaders of this day is best illustrated by a statement from the annual report of Grand Secretary Pace,

> "When the history of the Order of Elks is some day told by one with power to tell, it will be the story of one of the fairest creatures of the brain of man, the most beautiful allegory of the reality of human brotherhood, and the most sacred vows of an institution erected by humans for human beings, an order destined to grow and to flourish, full of hope and promise and capable of the highest development, but which from first to last was trampled on, abused and robbed by those who were among its creators and sworn defenders."

This report was made at the Grand Lodge session of 1911. This session met in Paine Memorial Hall, Boston, Massachusetts, on Appleton Street from August 9 to 11. The Public Session was held in Fanueil Hall, "the Cradle of Liberty," where a large and enthusiastic audience assembled. It was said that, "The fair sex being greatly in evidence made the scene one long to be remembered." The meeting was opened by Brother Raymond L. Phillips, Chairman of the United Committee for Entertainment of the Grand Lodge, who presented Brother Samuel B. Noble, Deputy for the State of Massachusetts, the presiding officer. Among the speakers was the Mayor of Boston who delivered an unusual address showing familiarity with Negro history. This address was applauded enthusiastically. Grand Exalted Ruler J. Frank Wheaton responded to the address of the Mayor. The Minutes report that he was at his best and left a lasting impression by his masterly eloquence. Other addresses were by Brothers Stewart E. Hoyt, later Grand Esteemed Leading Knight and George E. Bates, Grand Esteemed Loyal Knight. When the session closed the delegates and visitors were taken on a sight-seeing trip around Boston and to a picnic at Bass Point.

On the next day, the Twelfth Annual Convention assembled with Grand Exalted Ruler Wheaton presiding. The following committees were appointed:

Committee on Credentials—C. P. Lancaster, William R. Morris, Charles D. Freeman, Raymond L. Phillips, I. W. Warden.

Committee on Resolutions—S. B. Noble, I. H. Nutter, J. Finley Wilson, William H. Jones, C. R. Richardson, W. H. McFarland, D. W. Parker, J. E. Dixon, James T. Carter, Charles W. Gant.

Committee on Appeals and Grievances—Edward D. Thompson, William Shands, H. A. Howell, John E. Gills, Jackson Spencer, Carey Wheaton, J. Clay Smith, George W. Clarkson.

Committe on Law and Revision—D. Macon Webster, Francis H. Warren, A. W. Scott, E. Burton Ceruti, Dr. P. M. Edwards.

Committee on Obituary—Stewart E. Hoyt, Daniel Ware, E. M. Johnson, Rev. W. P. Gibbons, Robert Jackson, J. T. Brown, J. H. Chiles.

Committee on State of the Order—David McDaniel, E. C. Haller, Henry Brown, Dr. J. W. Stubbs, William McKenzie.

Committee on Audit—Dr. J. Leroy Baxter, J. R. Dunn, Robert P. Phea, A. T. Webster, A. J. Enty.

Committee on Grand Officers' Reports—James H. Anderson, Edward D. Thompson, J. T. Brandy, J. Finley Wilson, Edgar A. Still.

Committee on Fraternal Visit—Dr. W. E. Atkins, D. Macon Webster, O. M. Waller, Henry E. Jones, John W. Harris.

Committee on Mileage and Per Diem—Dr. R. E. Jones, James H. Anderson, R. M. Hyde, Edgar A. Still, Jacob Williams.

Press Committee—James H. Anderson, Oliver E. Robinson, Perry G. Leonard, George W. Chavis.

When the Committee on Credentials reported it was noted that there were seventy-two lodges represented with one hundred and fifty-eight accredited delegates. This number was less than those at the previous meeting of the Grand Lodge in 1910, the Union Grand Lodge, where there were ninety-eight lodges represented and two hundred and two delegates. There was no doubt that the pressure of lawsuits, the consciousness of being on the defensive and the assessments for court expenses played their part in reducing the attendance and affecting the loyalty of some lodges and members. However, those who were present were loyal and determined to carry on the work of the Order. They repeated this determination throughout the session of 1911.

One wing of those who were discouraged was represented by Dr. O. M. Waller who introduced a resolution to organize a new Order. He prefaced the resolution with references to the fight being made against the Order in the states of New York and Virginia, the three thousand dollars which had to be assessed in order to prosecute the New York Case, the Howard-Mills Case over the ritual and the eighty-three lodges not heard from in this Grand Lodge. He proposed that consideration be given to the appointment of a committee of fifteen to consult concerning "the question of the voluntary formation and construction of an original order, with original ritual, with and upon which we can, without disrespect, face the whole world and go forward." After debate the motion to adopt was "overwhelmingly lost."

The Grand Exalted Ruler's report and the report of the Grand Secretary mentioned the annoying court cases but each stressed the determination to go forward on the bases of the Elk principles of Charity, Justice, Brotherly Love and Fidelity. Grand

Secretary Pace reported that "the past year, which is ended when this meeting goes into history, has been perhaps the most crucial one that this Order of Elks has ever had, and but for the fact, which is paramount in my belief, that it is destined to stand in the forefront of organized bodies and has a mission to perform that all of its enemies cannot thwart, it could not have withstood the trials and vicissitudes of this year through which it has come." He said that his report was a story of mingled sorrow and joys—"sorrow at our weaknesses, our struggles and our failures; and joy in the ultimate triumph of our cause, the culmination of a year of discouragement and despair in this meeting so full of hope and promise for those principles we love." He concluded his report with the request that he should be relieved as Grand Secretary.

It was reported that collections of income had fallen off during the months of the Howard-Mills Case and that it was necessary for the officers to advance their personal funds to carry on the work of the Grand Lodge or else this work would have stopped. Of 201 lodges existing, there were 121 which had reported during the year, and there were 7,728 members, an increase of 2,709 members over the last report. Grand Secretary Pace added, "This increase is due to the combination effected at Washington last year, and if this union is further cemented this year, so that these men really and truly believe it is permanent, this number will double within the ensuing year." Columbia Lodge, No. 85 led the membership with 620 members. Great Lakes Lodge No. 43 came second with 409 members. O. V. Catto Lodge No. 20 had 272, Manhattan Lodge No. 45 had 267 and Lawrence Lodge No. 18 had the smallest lodge with 18 members. Among the states, Pennsylvania led with 20 lodges, Virginia had 17, Ohio and New York had 11 each.

One of the first efforts to assemble the historical records of the Order was advanced by Grand Secretary Pace and was approved by the Committee on Grand Officers' Reports. This committee urged action at this session and recommended that some lodge with a home of its own should become the custodian of these records. Commendation was given by this committee to Brother E. B. Ceruti who had served as National Receiver of Funds for the legal defense of the Order.

The visit of the delegation from the Grand Temple was another important event of the Grand Lodge sessions. Grand Secretary Emma V. Kelley was the speaker and it was recorded that she delivered a soul-stirring address. She reported that thirteen temples had been organized since the Washington meeting in 1910. Grand Legal Adviser William R. Morris responded and "elo-

E. BURTON CERUTI, National Receiver of Monies for Legal Defense, 1908. Grand Legal Adviser.

quently portrayed the beauties of Elkdom and the great assistance rendered by the Ladies' Temple."

Proposals were made by committees for an Endowment Fund with death benefits, the beneficiary to receive two hundred dollars. A Mortuary Fund was to be created by a tax of twenty cents a month from each member. These proposals were indefinitely postponed by motion, but this was not the end of these proposals.

The roster of Grand Lodge Officers included the following: H. H. Pace, Grand Exalted Ruler, Memphis, Tenn.; T. G. Nutter, Grand Esteemed Leading Knight, Charleston, West Va.; Stewart E. Hoyt, Grand Esteemed Loyal Knight, Boston, Mass.; W. H. Leonard, Grand Esteemed Lecturing Knight, Philadelphia, Pa.; George E. Bates, Grand Secretary, Newark, N. J.; Dr. William E. Gales, Grand Treasurer, Anacostia, D. C.; A. W. Russell, Grand Tiler, Atlanta, Ga.; Daniel Trezevant, Grand Inner Guard, New York, N. Y.; F. H. Warren, Grand Organizer, Detroit, Mich.; J. J. Jones, Grand Esquire, Chicago, Ill.; J. Clay Smith, Washington, D. C.; E. M. Johnson, New York, N. Y.; R. M. Hyde, Des Moines, Iowa, Grand Trustees; Rev. W. P. Gibbons, Grand Chaplain, Washington, D. C.; Dr. R. E. Jones, Grand Medical Director, Richmond, Va.; E. Burton Ceruti, Grand Legal Adviser, New York, N. Y.

Opposition continued during the following year and New York was the center of the contest in the courts. The Order was prepared, as Grand Exalted Ruler Pace said, to get a proper and complete hearing before the Supreme Court of the United States and the Attorney, Brother D. Macon Webster, was authorized to prepare the appeal to the higher court. The court modified its original injunction by directing it to apply to the name "Elk." The original one applied not only to the name but to Elk Colors, purple and white, and the use of similar names for offcers. This was the case of Benevolent and Protective Order of

Elks, vs. Improved Benevolent and Protective Order of Elks.* While this was a concession, the Grand Officers were not satisfied. They were heartened by the decision of the U. S. Supreme Court rendered by Chief Justice White in the Pythian Case. This court reversed the decision of the state court because the white fraternal order had been guilty of "laches" or negligence in not objecting more immediately to the Negro organization. It had waited for years before objecting, and the state court was therefore declared in error. Since the Negro lodge of Pythians was incorporated in the District of Columbia, it was decided that a federal right was involved. This case was Creswell vs. Grand Lodge, Knights of Pythias.** It seemed to point out the way for the appeal of the Improved Benevolent and Protective Order of Elks of the World in its New York Case.

The 1912 Grand Lodge, the Thirteenth, assembled in Dayton, Ohio, according to the action of the Grand Lodge and the call of the Grand Exalted Ruler, August 27-29, at the Lodge Room of Waldorf Lodge in Memorial Hall. Grand Exalted Ruler Pace declared that the year had been one "of continual struggle because we have had to battle with various forces and contend against various elements antagonistic to us." Nevertheless, he added that there had been a settlement and hopefulness that at some time the lawsuits would end and the Grand Lodge would meet without various kinds of litigations. The settlement referred to the Howard claim that the ritual was his personal property. This assertion, according to the Grand Exalted Ruler, "was knocked completely in the head, and his individual ownership of this Order and all its finances was given its death blow." He said that whatever debt of gratitude may have been owed to Howard for

DR. WILLIAM E. GALES, Grand Treasurer, 1910-1913.

---

*(205 N.T. 459, 1912.)
**(225 U.S. 246, 32 Sep. Ct. 822, 1912.)

his part in the foundation of the Order had been wiped out in dollars and cents. The loss of cases and the indefinite outcome of others caused some dissatisfaction among the lodges, and the Grand Exalted Ruler said that he "hesitated to call upon over-burdened and over-taxed lodges to contribute to a cause which seemed so hopeless." He doubted the willingness of the lodges to respond again, since they had been taxed for the same purpose over a long period. But he added, "my doubts were only for an instant and hardly had my letters reached their destination, when I was showered with messages from every section of the country and from every lodge in response to my letter of appeal, coinciding in my decision to continue to fight for every one of our rights, and to go down together like men or stand in a solid phalanx victorious."

The Grand Exalted Ruler's report described the homes purchased by the local lodges, particularly the O. V. Catto Lodge No. 20 in Philadelphia and Cuyahoga Lodge No. 95 in Cleveland. On the question of Endowment and the provision for after death payments, he did not believe in it, for he said there should be a scientific arrangement of rates and benefits based upon the experiences of life insurance companies. He regarded any other method as worse than folly, and yet he recommended the appointment of a commission to devise plans and methods concerning the legal phase of the establishment of an Endowment Department of the Grand Lodge. This proposal was referred to the consideration of the Trustees. He advised every Elk to become a qualified voter and to become active in politics, recommended the candidacy of Brother James H. Anderson for the New York General Assembly, and Brother R. R. Jackson to the State Senate of Illinois. He also recommended the incorporation of the Grand Lodge and of all subordinate lodges. This was approved by the Grand Lodge in a resolution.

The question of the relation of the Daughters of Elks to the organization was raised and he suggested that a closer relationship should be developed.

A resolution on this matter was adopted as follows:

> "Whereas, The association of women of our race known as Daughters of Elks, operating through a Grand Temple and Subordinate Temples, are using the name, colors and other distinguishing colors of our Order, and
>
> Whereas, The relations existing between the two grand bodies are, at present, not clearly defined and regulated, therefore,
>
> Be it Resolved, That a committee of three be appointed to investigate the subject and report some plan for the adjust-

ment of this chaotic condition and report at the next Grand Lodge Session."

The committee reported later that the Grand Exalted Ruler of the I.B.P.O.E. of W., be and is hereby recognized as the Grand Exalted Ruler of the Temple, that he shall issue all charters, and have supervision over the Temple, that all Elks may become honorary members of the Grand Temple and local Temples and that the two bodies may hold joint sessions.

The Grand Secretary and the Grand Treasurer gave reports which indicated continued progress in spite of opposition, and the Committee on the State of the Order commenting on these reports reported that the Order was "in a prosperous condition, financially and numerically."

When the election of Grand Officers occurred, considerable discussion arose on the matter of the election of the Grand Exalted Ruler. The Washington Grand Lodge of 1910 had adopted a resolution to the effect that "the incumbent of the office of the Grand Exalted Ruler in the future be ineligible to succeed himself." Brother T. G. Nutter, Esteemed Leading Knight, who was presiding quoted the constitution that the officers were to be elected annually and that according to Art. 4, Sec. 1, "all other Laws in conflict with this are repealed by this fundamental law." He ruled that Brother Pace was eligible for re-election. Brother J. Finley Wilson of Norfolk, Virginia who, later at this convention, was elected "Grand Organizer," remarked that the Washington action was only "a war measure necessary at the Washington Convention." A motion was made to table the resolution opposing the re-election of Grand Exalted Ruler Pace. Brother Armond W. Scott defended the motion to table. On the roll call the motion to table was adopted.

Dr. G. W. Owens, Grand Medical Director, 1912-

The Grand Officers elected for 1912-1913 were: H. H. Pace, Grand Exalted Ruler, Memphis, Tenn.; George E. Bates, Grand Secretary, Newark, N J.; T. G. Nutter, Grand Esteemed Loyal Knight, Boston, Mass.; James

GEORGE E. BATES, Newark, N. J., Grand Secretary, 1911-1928.

T. Carter, Grand Tiler, Richmond, Va.; William H. McFarland, Grand Inner Guard, Brooklyn, N. Y.; J. Finley Wilson, Grand Organizer, Norfolk, Va.; Dr. G. W. Owens, Grand Medical Director, Atlanta, Ga.; William Freeman, Grand Esquire, Paris, Ky.; and J. J. Jones, Grand Trustee, Chicago, Illinois. The next Grand Lodge session was voted to meet at Atlantic City, New Jersey.

Advancement had been made in spite of handicaps as represented in lawsuits and decreased lodge support. The report of the Grand Treasurer showed a balance of only $22.86 in 1911 but in 1912 the balance was $742.66. Similar developments were noted in all lines of fraternal activity.

One of these aspects of great development was seen in the work of the Daughter Elks of the Grand Temple. They were so proud of their temples and their relationships to the Order that a history of their eleven years was presented to their Atlantic City session in 1913 by Daughter Emma V. Kelley, who was the Founder. She had organized the juvenile department in 1907, incorporated this department and by 1912-1913, it was one of the strongest of Elkdom. These years were filled with individual deeds of women who sacrificed and worked for the expansion of the Order through temples and state associations. In spite of handicaps, they too were advancing with continuous success.

Chapter VII

Peace, Progress and Opposition

Under the continuing leadership of Grand Exalted Ruler Pace and the assistance of the Grand Secretary, George E. Bates, peace was coming to the organization in its internal operations and progress was being made far beyond previous years. The Grand Secretary had made many improvements in the keeping of records of the Grand Lodge and had recommended similar and additional improvements for the maintenance of good records by the subordinate lodges. Lodges and members were increasing and good fraternal work was being done in individual communities. Real estate was being purchased and lodges were acquiring homes for themselves. However, the lawsuits continued and the opposition of the "White Elks" was also expressed in court action.

These contests in the courts were costly and there were periods when disagreements arose among the attorneys even about the amount of fees. L. Melendez King in the Virginia Case demanded a fee, in addition to the one paid to the attorney of record, B. L. Gaskins. Early in May, 1912, suit was reported to have been filed by Brother King against the Grand Lodge for $600.00 as his fee for services at Richmond. A compromise was accepted by Brother King in the amount of $85.00, with his agreement also to pay the costs of the court. A similar suit was filed by Attorney Giles B. Jackson for $3,000.00 for his services in the same case. It seems that he was not officially employed but, as the Grand Exalted Ruler reported, "continued to meddle until the very end, and had the unmitigated nerve to file claim for his services in the sum which I have named." This case was settled also for a cash payment of $250.00, through the assistance of Grand Secretary Bates, Grand Legal Advisor Scott and Brother James T. Carter. These men rendered good professional service in their respective capacities, and they expected to receive fees commensurate with their efforts, but the Grand Officers wanted them to realize that they too were brother Elks and that this fact should weigh heavily in their submission of bills for services.

An instance showing the need for further coordination with the Daughters of the Elks arose when a complaint was received from Ultra Lodge No. 130 at Orange, New Jersey, that a Temple had been organized in that city without the consent and over the lodge's protest. The Temple was instituted in spite of the action of the lodge and the opposition of the Body Deputy. This brought the matter up for discussion at the next Grand Lodge, which ruled that no Temple could be made without the consent of the subordinate lodge in that city. The Grand Trustees reported in 1913 on this subject, resolving that the Daughters of Elks were an adjunct body of the Grand Lodge, that the Grand Exalted Ruler should be Grand Patriarch and the Grand Chaplain should be Grand Orator with other officers females, and that the Grand Temple should meet in its sessions at such time and place as the Grand Lodge. When the Grand Temple voted against coming under the protection of the Grand Lodge, this action was tabled by the Grand Lodge.

This Grand Lodge of 1913, the Fourteenth Annual Meeting, convened in Fitzgerald's Auditorium, Atlantic City, New Jersey, August 26-29, with eighty-six lodges represented with one hundred and seventy-six delegates. The Grand Exalted Ruler's report stated that a part of the year had been one of peace and that while all that he desired had not been accomplished, he had tried in his five years of service as Grand Secretary and Grand Exalted Ruler to lay "a foundation that would in some way make the future of this Order secure." Grand Exalted Ruler Pace said that the year had been the best in history, that more money had been collected and the expenses of the administration had been less. The report was so complete and satisfactory that the Grand Exalted Ruler was not only commended by motion but a committee was authorized to present him with a loving cup as a token of appreciation. A similar gift was later made to the Grand Secretary.

The report by the Grand Secretary, George E. Bates, stated that a setback had come to the Order in the decision of Justice Hughes of the U. S. Supreme Court denying the requested writ of error, whereby the New York Case could be reviewed by the highest court. Grand Exalted Ruler Pace declared on this case, "If this is the final attitude of the court in this matter, then indeed are our misfortunes greater than we have ever contemplated they should be." This pessimistic note was not shared by the Grand Lodge. The New York delegation reported that they had decided to continue the fight with the object of having the state law known as the Grattan Law enacted in 1905 repealed. This effort was endorsed by the Grand Lodge.

A resolution was also adopted that in view of the friction developed between the B.P.O.E., and the I.B.P.O.E. of W., that a more thorough understanding between the two groups was necessary, and that a committee of five members of the Grand Lodge should be appointed by the Grand Exalted Ruler and directed to seek a conference with the Grand Exalted Ruler of the Benevolent and Protective Order of Elks or such other officials as may be desirable, looking toward a better understanding and the adoption of steps to eliminate the dangers of misunderstanding and friction in the future. This action was the adoption of a new procedure and method. Having met the opposition on its own ground in the courts, an attempt at conference and compromise was to be attempted. When a suggestion was made that incorporation in an English country be sought, Brother T. G. Nutter said that incorporation in one country is not recognized in another unless there is a treaty to this effect and that there was no such treaty between this country and England.

In the meantime the Grand Legal Adviser, Armond W. Scott, gave his report and stated that he had been interested in the Dayton Case since the last Grand Lodge and had asked Brother Thomas Norris to represent the Grand Lodge for a fee of fifty dollars, that the case had gone against the Lodge and that sufficient legal questions had been raised to carry the case through the courts of Ohio and to the U. S. Supreme Court. One of his finest suggestions was that this session of the Grand Lodge should formulate some plan, "whereby we can put an end to so much litigation, and use the money which is coming into our coffers in a way and manner that will accomplish tangible results for this organization which is composed of the noblest and most loyal set of men who constitute any colored organization ever established among Negroes of this country." And yet, he proposed a continued fight to get a proper case before the Supreme Court for a final decision as to whether the Order could or could not continue to exist and operate as the Improved Benevolent and Protective Order of Elks of the World. This report was received "with enthusiasm and noisy demonstration lasting for several minutes."

The Grand Organizer, J. Finley Wilson, made a report describing his travels and activities, and among these was a statement that Past Deputy Settle had given him a letter from the first Grand Exalted Ruler B. F. Howard, who had conspired with the white Elks to bring about an injunction in Dayton against the lodges. This letter was forwarded by Brother Wilson to the Grand Exalted Ruler. Brother Wilson recounted his visits to lodges and then requested that his office as Grand Organizer be more clearly defined. The Committee on Ways and Means, however, recommended that the offices of Grand Organizer, Grand Medical Director and Grand Organist be abolished. This recommendation was approved by the Grand Lodge.

T. GILLIS NUTTER, Grand Esteemed Leading Knight, 1910-1913; Sixtl Grand Exalted Ruler, 1913-1916.

The Grand Lodge Officers were T. G. Nutter, Grand Exalted Ruler, Charleston, W. Va.; Stewart E. Hoyt, Grand Esteemed Leading Knight, Boston, Massachusetts; J. H. Starkey, Grand Esteemed Loyal Knight, Cleveland, Ohio; J. R. Dunn, Grand Esteemed Lecturing Knight, Chicago, Ill.; George E. Bates, Grand Secretary, Newark, New Jersey; James T. Carter, Grand Treasurer, Richmond, Va.; W. H. McFarland, Grand Esquire, Brooklyn, N. Y.; W. H. Johnson, Grand Inner Guard, St. Paul, Minn.; R. V. Ridley, Grand Tiler, Terre Haute, Ind.; Rev. W. R. Gullins, Grand Chaplain, Providence, R. I.; A. W. Scott, Grand Legal Adviser, Washington, D. C.

The Grand Exalted Ruler chosen at this 1913 Grand Lodge, T. G. Nutter, showed himself to be a capable leader who guided the Order into a period of peace and progress. For these goals, there had to be a cessation of external opposition and the increase of internal cooperation. After reading the decisions of the Court of Common Pleas of Montgomery County, Ohio, and of the Court of Appeals, he concluded that if it applied to any organization, it was the Howard Grand Lodge, which had operated under the Ohio incorporation, and not to the united Grand Lodge operating under incorporation in New Jersey and the District of Columbia. He sent a letter to the lodges of Ohio under date of January 10, 1914, presenting the facts in the case and his interpretation of the ruling of the court and said that he saw "no reason why the work should not go right on as though nothing had happened, and should any attempt be made to prevent the members of Ohio from using the name, etc., the Grand Lodge will come to their defense, and see to it that all necessary questions are raised which will fully protect the members in exercising their rights in this respect." This letter was well received by the lodges in Ohio and the work in Ohio was continued. He had had an agree-

JAMES T. CARTER, Grand Treasurer, 1913-1928.

ment with the white Elks that they would not interfere with the lodges while the case was pending.

It was also reported by Grand Exalted Ruler Nutter that pursuant to the Peace Resolution, as it was called, of the Fourteenth Annual Session presented by Brothers W. H. Randolph and R. D. Burton of Old Dominion Lodge, No. 181, a committee was appointed to carry out the resolution. This committee, composed of W. H. Randolph, Lynchburg, Va.; J. Frank Wheaton, New York; Armond W. Scott, Washington, D. C.; W. George Avant, Newbern, N. C.; and T. Gillis Nutter, Grand Exalted Ruler representing the Grand Lodge, and Brothers D. Macon Webster, H. Adolph Howell of New York representing the New York lodges, held a conference with Grand Exalted Ruler, Edward Leach, of the Benevolent Protective Order of Elks of the United States of America on November 24. 1913, at the white Elks Home in New York City. Grand Exalted Ruler Leach told the committee that he was sympathetic with their resolution, requested that it should be placed in writing and that he would make it a part of his report to his annual session at Denver, Colorado, July 13-19, 1914. This written statement was drawn up from individual statements of committee members by the Grand Exalted Ruler.

STEWART E. HOYT, Grand Esteemed Leading Knight, 1913.

Among the statements in the draft, signed by the committee, was the reference that they had no desire for the continuance of the friction of the past, that they had not sought any fraternal recognition by the white Elks by signs, grips and passwords, and they had not imposed themselves on the members of their Order. Their desire was to exemplify the great principles of Elkdom, Charity, Justice, Brotherly Love and Fidelity. The question was asked and answered, "Why should there be any objection to our Order practicing the great principles of Elkdom? Surely no confusion can grow out of our doing so, for the line of demarcation between the races in this country is so distinctly drawn that there cannot be the least confusion as to the identity of the two Orders, or as to their membership any more than there can be question as to the identity of the white churches and the colored churches of this country or their membership." In addition, attention was called to the white and colored Masons, the white and colored Odd Fellows and the white and colored Pythians, and the fact that it was to be to the best interests of the two Orders that peace, harmony and good-will should prevail and that misunderstandings be removed. The request was made that the session at Denver would consider the passing of a resolution prohibiting all lawsuits either by the Grand Body or the Subordinate Lodges. The resolution was forwarded to Grand Exalted Ruler Leach of the B.P.O.E., but he failed to acknowledge it, and neither a letter nor personal approaches brought explanations or replies. It was also found that the petition was not presented to the Denver convention.

Nevertheless, Grand Exalted Ruler Nutter was determined to motivate the program of peace between the two Orders. He sent proclamations and letters to the Subordinate Lodges urging them to take up this matter with local white Elks. At St. Paul, Minnesota, a harmony banquet was held by Amos Lodge No. 106 and members of the white lodge attended. Promises were secured from prominent Elks that they would do everything possible to have the petition acted upon at Denver.

No explanation was received concerning the failure of Grand Exalted Ruler Leach to present the petition, but a prominent white Elk informed Grand Exalted Ruler Nutter that "it was agreed that there should be no further legal action against the colored Elks, and the delegates were instructed to that effect, without putting the convention on record." Subsequently, he noted changes of attitudes, and he called upon all to cultivate the friendship and esteem of white Elks and citizens in their respective communities.

This year, 1913-1914, despite the Dayton lawsuit was called "the Banner Year of Negro Elkdom" by the Grand Exalted Ruler. He said, "the plaintive notes of the dying swan have been succeeded, as it were, by the chirps of the mocking bird"—and "today Negro Elkdom stands on the threshold of the greatest awakening in the history of secret orders." He reported that nine new lodges had been made and seven old lodges reinstated. He added that Brother Finley Wilson whom he appointed Grand Traveling Deputy had the credit of making the first lodge at Canonsburg, Pa. The report was made that the Grand Secretary and the Grand Treasurer were now bonded and the recommendation was made that an endowment department based upon scientific insurance be established. Additional recommendations were for State Elks' Grand Reunions, the revision of the Grand Lodge Constitution, a uniform system of bookkeeping for the subordinate lodges. This report was received with enthusiasm, and with the Chautauqua salute a great demonstration followed.

There were ninety lodges with seven thousand members and they had contributed three thousand dollars to charity, according to the report of Grand Secretary Bates, who also alleged that this year had been a peaceful one. He said that the lodges were still active in New York State in spite of the legislation there, and that apparently the white Elks had resolved that they would not annoy them again. He proposed that a list of thirty-nine lodges, for which every possible way to revive them had been made, would be dropped from the list of lodges, in order not to keep carrying "a lot of dead wood on your books." He believed that the wheat was being separated from the chaff and the foundation laid for a better day for young Negro manhood. The receipts and disbursements revealed a balance of $2,296.57, which was an increase over the last year.

A list of lodges with a membership of 100 or more gives an idea of the numerical strength of the Order:

O. V. Catto No. 20, Philadelphia	316
Morning Star No. 20, Washington, D. C.	265
Eureka Lodge No. 5, Norfolk, Va.	252
Capitol City No. 11, Richmond, Va.	252
Lighthouse No. 9, Atlantic City, N. J.	205
Columbia No. 85, Washington, D. C.	202
Great Lakes No. 43, Chicago, Ill.	201
Smithfield No. 65, Smithfield, Va.	199
Manhattan No. 45, New York, N. Y.	193
Williams No. 11, Richmond, Va.	175
Old Dominion No. 181, Lynchburg, Va.	172
Beacon Light No. 34, Portsmouth, Va.	170
Cuyahoga No. 9, Cleveland, O.	165
Monumental No. 3, Baltimore, Md.	153
Progressive No. 35, Jersey City, N. J.	136
Bay State No. 19, Boston, Mass.	132
Jones Valley No. 14, Birmingham, Ala.	125
Lexington No. 27, Lexington, Ky.	123
Pride of Newark No. 193, Newark, N. J.	118
Royal No. 77, Petersburg, Va.	118
Pioneer No. 19, Boston, Mass.	112

Keystone No. 6, Washington, Pa.	112
Imperial No. 12, New York City	110
Iron City No. 17, Pittsburgh, Pa.	104
Gate City No. 54, Atlantic City, N. J.	102
Excelsior No. 4, Hampton, Va.	100
Wolverine No. 72, Detroit, Mich.	100

Some of the funds were deposited in the two Negro banks, the Mechanics Savings Bank, Richmond, Va., of which John G. Mitchell, Editor of the *Richmond Planet,* was the President and in the St. Luke Penny Savings Bank of the same city, of which Maggie L. Walker was the President. The opinion of Brother James L. Carter was that this recognition should be given to these Negro enterprises.

Not a single suit had been filed against the Order since the Atlantic City Grand Lodge a year ago, according to the report of Grand Legal Adviser, Armond W. Scott. He discussed the Dayton Case and again proposed the final determination of the issue of the two Orders in the U. S. Supreme Court, if it should be forced upon the Grand Lodge. There was a demonstration following the presentation of this report, as it was unanimously adopted.

A charter for the Grand Lodge was introduced and recommended for adoption by a committee appointed at the last Grand Lodge. This charter in design was drawn by Brother W. H. Johnson, Grand Inner Guard, of St. Paul, Minnesota. The committee reported that "it adequately and artistically symbolizes the fundamental principles of our Order." The recommendation was adopted including the tender of a gift of fifty dollars.

The Grand Officers for 1914-1915 were: T. G. Nutter, Grand Exalted Ruler, Charleston, West Va.; S. E. Hoyt, Grand Esteemed Leading Knight, Boston, Mass.; J. H. Starkey, Grand Esteemed Loyal Knight, Cleveland, Ohio; W. H. Leonard, Grand Esteemed Lecturing Knight, Philadelphia, Pa.; George E. Bates, Grand Secretary, Newark, N. J.; James T. Carter, Grand Treasurer, Richmond, Va.; William H. McFarland, Grand Esquire, Brooklyn, N. Y.; William Hopkins Johnson, Grand Inner Guard, St. Paul, Minnesota; H. Clay Stevens, Grand Tiler, Wilmington, Del.; J. Clay Smith, Chairman Trustee Board, Washington, D. C.; J. J. Jones, Grand Trustee, Chicago, Ill.; William H. Jones, Grand Trustee, Philadelphia, Pa.; William H. Stanton, Grand Legal Adviser, Pittsburgh, Pa.; James E. Churchman, Grand Chaplain, Orange, N. J.; Samuel B. Noble, Grand Master of Social Sessions, Danville, Va.

The year 1915-1916 was a significant one in the change from

litigation to peace. In state after state, the opposition grew less and less and gradually faded from the respective scenes of former antagonism. This trend was accompanied by marked progress for the Order. However, the antagonism was continued in several states. In New York an Elk brother was arrested for wearing an Elk pin and a fine of $100 was imposed on him. The brothers in New York were urged to live within the law in respect to the wearing of insignia bearing the elkhead. This situation in New York was different from the situation in Florida and North Carolina, for there had been no tests of the law in these states, as there had been in New York.

The Florida Legislature passed a law in 1913 prohibiting the unauthorized wearing or using of badges, insignia or uniforms of certain orders and societies and prescribing penalties. Warrants were sworn out by H. M. Bethel of Tallahassee, Florida, on February 8, 1915, for Brothers James Washington, Exalted Ruler and J. A. Bryant, Chairman of the House Committee of Maceo Lodge, No. 8, Jacksonville, Florida, for wearing a badge of the Benevolent and Protective Order of Elks of the United States of America in violation of the law. Again on April 11, 1915, warrants were issued against Brothers Arthur Reddick, T. L. Reddick, Exalted Ruler; Henry R. Speed, Secretary and Sam Farris of White Hall Lodge No. 179 of Palm Beach, Florida, for the same. These Elk brothers were held for the Grand Jury. As a matter of fact, these brothers were wearing the insignia of the Improved Benevolent and Protective Order of Elks of the World and not the insignia of the Benevolent Protective Order of Elks of the United States of America.

When it became known that the Grand Lodge was going to fight the case, and the attiude of white Elks as a Grand Lodge was known to its members, through the denial to endorse the action for arrest, there was a change in their determination to carry on the case. Grand Exalted Ruler Nutter was advised that the white Elks did not want the case brought up and they had refused to furnish money for it. The case was postponed when it should have been heard in the June term of the court. and then again in the July term. This was declared by the Grand Exalted Ruler as "The First Victory in the courts." The Grand Legal Adviser. William H. Stanton, received a letter from a counsel in Florida stating that after investigation he had come to the conclusion that the Florida statute upon which the case was based was unconstitutional. The case was later nolle-prossed by the county attorney.

A second case, the Dayton Case, was carried through the same procedures. The attorneys for the white Elks said that they had

WILLIAM H. STANTON, Grand Legal Adviser, 1914-

no desire to pursue the lawsuit. This attitude was further evidence that there might be no further pressure in the case. Neither of these cases was prosecuted by the sanction of the Order of Elks but by individuals acting upon their own initiative. The New York Case was authorized for reopening by the Grand Lodge in 1915, but Grand Exalted Ruler Nutter regarded such an action as unsound and that no good could come out of it. Having spent more than five thousand dollars on the case, he had decided not to go further in the case. There, he let the matter rest. In 1916, another case arose on warrant in Washington, North Carolina, for a similar violation by Elk members, and the result was the gradual termination of the case.

The Sixteenth Annual meeting of the Grand Lodge assembled in Chicago, Illinois, August 31, September 1-3, 1915. The main speakers at the Public Session were Mayor William Hale Thompson, Honorable Oscar DePriest, Grand Exalted Ruler Nutter and State Representative S. B. Turner. With the opening of the Business Session, the Grand Exalted Ruler reported that the Order was in splendid condition—the best in its entire history. The year, he declared, "was a great year in Elkdom and the progress of our noble Order has been remarkable during the depression of the present year." The Grand Exalted Ruler and the Grand Legal Adviser, W. H. Stanton, had prepared careful legal defenses, describing the Order's history, its incorporation and its legal status.

The Grand Secretary, George E. Bates, gave a report which showed progress in lodges, members, real estate and bank balances, together with the death and sick benefits paid and the charitable work accomplished. No law had been adopted for the legal affiliation of the Grand Temple with the Grand Lodge. During the official visit of the committee representing the Grand Temple at the Grand Lodge, Mrs. Emma V. Kelley made a strong appeal to the Grand Lodge to annex the Temples so that they could come under the protection of the Grand Lodge, and they requested an answer at once. The Grand Trustees recommended that the same plan which had been formerly adopted by the Grand Lodge be adopted so that the lodges and temples should be more closely affiliated. The Grand Temple thus became a recognized auxiliary of the Grand Lodge, but the conclusion of the matter was referred to the next Grand Lodge when the Committee on Law and Revision would report. The real estate purchased or being purchased by the lodges was reported to have the estimated value of $81,450.00, listed as follows:

Lodge	*Value*
Monumental No. 3, Baltimore	$ 8,000.00
Phoenix No. 7, Paris, Ky.	200.00
Jones Valley No. 14, Birmingham, Ala.	5,000.00
Brooklyn No. 32, Brooklyn, N. Y.	7,500.00
Progressive No. 35, Jersey City, N. J.	4,500.00
Great Lakes No. 43, Chicago, Ill.	4,000.00
Alexandria No. 48, Alexandria, Va.	3,000.00
Shackelford No. 48, Winchester, Ky.	500.00
Unity No. 71, Harrisburg, Pa.	3,000.00
Pride of Camden No. 83, N. J.	1,500.00
Cuyahoga No. 95, Cleveland, O.	15,000.00
Mountain State No. 117, Clarksburg, W. Va.	50.00
Conestoga No. 140, Lancaster, Pa.	200.00
Mt. Vernon No. 151, Coatesville, Pa.	1,000.00
O. V. Catto No. 20, Philadelphia, Pa.	20,000.00
P. L. Dunbar No. 106, Wilmington, Del.	3,500.00
Lincoln No. 145, Gettysburg, Pa.	1,500.00
Eureka No. 114, Nassau, Bahama Islands	3,000.00
Total	$81,450.00

The Grand Officers elected for 1915-1916 were: T. G. Nutter, Grand Exalted Ruler, Charleston, West Va.; George McMechen, Grand Esteemed Leading Knight, Baltimore, Md.; George W. Holbert, Grand Esteemed Loyal Knight, Minneapolis, Minn.; H. Adolph Howell, Grand Esteemed Lecturing Knight, New York, N. Y.; George E. Bates, Grand Secretary, Newark, N. J.; James T. Carter, Grand Treasurer, Richmond, Va.; Henry Chisman, Grand Esquire, Hampton, Va.; William H. Johnson, Grand Inner Guard, St. Paul, Minn.; H. C. Stevens, Grand Tiler, Wilmington, Del.; J. J. Jones, Grand Trustee, Chicago, Ill.

When the Grand Lodge met in its Seventeenth Annual Session in Philadelpha, Pa., August 21-25, 1916, at St. Peter Claver's Hall, it was with the realization that peace and progress were present at this session and these were evidenced with the appointment of the Committee on Credentials, which reported that there were 114 lodges represented with 271 delegates.

At the first session, the parade was formed. It was described as "unquestionably the largest and most imposing street demonstration made by the Order, composed as it was of sixteen bands and four thousand of the Antlered Herd, and requiring over one hour to pass a given point. The uniforms and general deportment of the marchers caused much favorable comment of the spectators along the line of march and the opinion was freely expressed by both white and colored spectators that it was the finest parade of a colored organization ever held in Philadelphia."

A large part of Grand Exalted Ruler Nutter's report dealt with the litigation. He closed this section of the report by urging the Grand Lodge to act on the wearing of the emblem, since much trouble had developed over the question of some members wearing what was claimed to be the official badge of the white Elks. He said that the body should direct that no brother should wear a pin with simply the letters, "B.P.O.E." He did not regard such advice as yielding in any respect and he did not wish to have it so interpreted. He was ready to continue the fight for all of the rights of Elkdom. His action in this latter respect was given impetus by the Committee on the State of the Order, who declared that having noted that the smouldering fires of prejudice on the part of the B.P.O.E., had burst into flames, they stated that "the stalwart personnel of this Order intend to fight to the death, till the scales of justice be evenly balanced and the Improved Benevolent Protective Order of Elks of the World come rightfully into their own."

The Grand Exalted Ruler reported twenty-eight new lodges and nineteen old ones reinstated and said that substantial progress had been made all along the line. He also referred to the passing of Booker T. Washington, "a great leader of the people—a man with 'a vision that was to raise him above his fellows and place him upon the dizzy heights of philosophy, from which eminence he was to pour down a benediction, not only upon his own race, but upon mankind in general.'"

The membership had increased to 144 active lodges with a membership of 10,317. This was an increase in members of 3,390 and was the largest membership ever reported. Eight new lodges were instituted, which equalled the number instituted last year and six were reinstated. These figures show that there had been progress, but it should be recalled that in 1910, the year of consolidation, there were 140 active lodges, and by 1916 there was only an increase of four new lodges. This small increase was due to the fact that many lodges under pressure of legal opposition had disbanded or had become inactive. The balance in the Treasury in 1916, according to the report of the Grand Secretary and Grand Treasurer was $5,746.56, as against a balance of $3,032.21 in the previous year, 1915.

A pertinent section of the report of Grand Secretary Bates is of interest in relation to the history of the Order. He wrote, "Some day some literateur will write the story of Elkdom and were he to do it tomorrow, he would tell how seventeen years ago a little band of men determined to become Elks, and did become Elks, how through all of those seventeen years they encountered opposition without and dissensions within, how they fought the opposition, aye, oppression it might be termed, how finally their perseverance and dogged determination to succeed—to surmount all obstacles, was rewarded by the blossoming forth of a mighty fraternity whose geographical limitation is bounded only by help to humanity. That, brother would be the nucleus of the story, and finally he might say, 'Man is unjust, but God is just and finally justice triumphs.'"

Historic action was taken in connection with the Daughter Elks, a matter which had been considered from time to time without finality. The Committee on Law and Revision reported in accordance with the resolution of the Grand Lodge of 1915 and its report was adopted by the Grand Lodge of 1916. This action was as follows:

> "*Therefore,* be it enacted that this Grand Lodge, now in session in Philadelphia, Pa., adopt the Daughter Elks as an auxiliary body in the I.B.P.O.E. of W.; that the Grand Exalted Ruler of the Grand Lodge I.B.P.O.E. of W. shall be the Grand Patriarch of the Daughter Elks; the Grand Esteemed Leading Knight of the Grand Lodge I.B.P.O.E. of W., shall be the Grand Supervisor of the Daughter Elks and the Grand Chaplain of the Grand Lodge I.B.P.O.E. of W., shall be the Grand Orator of the Daughter Elks; that membership in the Daughter Elks shall consist of the present regularly initiated members of Daughter Elks in good financial standing in their several Temples and none other than the mothers, wives, widows, Daughters and Sisters of members of the Improved Benevolent and Protective Order of Elks of the World.
>
> *Be it Further Enacted,* That no Daughter Elks' Temple shall be instituted in any city or town, where there is no local Lodge I.B.P.O.E. of the World; nor shall they be instituted without the approval of said local lodge; that the Grand Temple of Daughter Elks shall meet and hold its sessions at such time and place as the Grand Lodge, I.B.P.O.E. of the World.
>
> *That,* nothing in the Constitution and By-Laws of the Daughter

Elks of Grand Temple of Daughter Elks shall conflict with the Constitution or General Laws of the Improved Benevolent Protective Order of Elks of the World, and that the present constitution of the Grand Temple of Daughter Elks shall be submitted to the Grand Exalted Ruler and Grand Legal Adviser of the I.B.P.O.E. of W., for revision, in keeping with the above resolution.

That, the signature of the Grand Exalted Ruler and Grand Secretary of the Improved Benevolent and Protective Order of Elks of the World be attached to every charter granted to the subordinate lodges of the Daughter Elks."

The Grand Officers for 1916-1917 were: Armond W. Scott, Grand Exalted Ruler, Washington, D. C.; George E. Bates, Grand Secretary, Newark, N. J., James T. Carter, Grand Treasurer, Richmond, Va.; George McMechen, Grand Esteemed Leading Knight, Baltimore, Md.; W. M. Hoyt, Grand Esteemed Loyal Knight, Atlantic City, N. J.; Paul H. Bray, Grand Esteemed Lecturing Knight, Yonkers, N. Y.; P. H. Southhall, Grand Esquire, Minneapolis, Minn.; T. C. Strickland, Grand Inner Guard, Atlanta, Ga.; A. A. Selden, Grand Tiler, Boston, Massachusetts; W. H. Stanton, Grand Legal Adviser, Pittsburgh, Pa.; Riley Woodard, Grand Chaplain, Richmond, Va.; J. Clay Smith, Chairman, Trustee Board; J. J. Jones, Grand Trustee, Chicago, Ill.; H. Clay Stevens, Grand Trustee, Wilmington, Del.

Chapter VIII
War and Victory

At the Eighteenth Annual Session of the Grand Lodge at Cleveland Ohio, August 28-30, 1917, composed of 118 lodges and 243 delegates, Grand Exalted Ruler Armond W. Scott in his report spoke of war and victory. The war was World War I and the victory was the beginning of the end of the litigation which had dogged the advancing steps of the lodges for long years. "You will appreciate the fact that during this entire year," said the Grand Exalted Ruler, "we have labored under the most unusual disadvantages, in that we have been in the midst of a world war and our own country, because of the arrogance, brutality, inhumanity and utter disregard for international laws by the Imperial German Government, has been compelled, in defense of its own national honor, to accept the German challenge to battle and, notwithstanding the fact that this race of ours has been continually the victim of caste prejudice and injustice, yet every member of this Order has been and is willing now to do his bit and make any sacrifice necessary to maintain the honor and integrity of our country's flag."

While this situation had arisen in 1917, it had been developing for three years. Since 1914 the United States had lived in the shadows of war, although President Woodrow Wilson had appealed to the American people urging neutrality in the words, "Every man who really loves America will act and speak in the true spirit of neutrality." The attempt at neutrality continued during the next three years with protests and state papers supporting it, but within two months in 1917, six American ships were torpedoed. The President then asked Congress to declare the course of Germany nothing less than war, stating that the world must be made safe for democracy. On April 6, the war resolution was passed by Congress. Acting quickly to win the war, Congress passed a draft act of able-bodied males, in age from twenty-one to thirty-one years and at a later period from eighteen to forty-five years. Taxes were increased and restrictions were placed upon all living conditions. President Wilson, a master phrase-maker, called for sacrifices by the people characterizing the war as "a war to end war" and "a war for democracy." By June, 1917, an advance guard of the American Expeditionary Force had reached France. Over two million Americans, Negroes and whites, went to France as parts of this

ARMOND W. SCOTT, Grand Legal Adviser, 1913-1914, Seventh Grand Exalted Ruler, 1916-1919.

force, and another two million were in the training camps of the United States before the war had ended.

One of these training camps was Fort Des Moines, Iowa, where Negro Officers were being trained. This camp started on June 15 was the result of a long period of agitation by Negroes to secure the opportunity to train and to serve as officers in the United States Army. There were members of the Improved Benevolent and Protective Order of Elks of the World who were at Fort Des Moines, and some were commissioned as officers. Others served as privates, who were not fortunate enough to undergo officer training. Many subordinate lodges began the purchase of liberty bonds, which was kept up through the years. The Eighteenth Grand Lodge recommended to the subordinate lodges that the members in good standing who were drafted for the Army should be given some consideration of honor by them, and the lodges responded. The record made by the lodges and Brothers later occasioned the statement from the Grand Exalted Ruler that the Negro people had demonstrated early in the war that they were "patriotic and loyal American citizens," who could be depended upon for services to their country as needed, and his conclusion was that they were therefore entitled to all of the rights and privileges enjoyed by other peoples.

In addition to these war experiences, the lodges were facing a type of domestic war. They were being pressed by arrests of individual members and court trials occasioned by actions of white Elks. In Pennsylvania, it was contended in the United States Circuit Court for the Eastern District, that since the cases in Tennessee, New York and Ohio had been decided against the I.B.P.O.E. of W., the U. S. Court should also decide against the case on the full faith clause of the Constitution which each state gave to the other. While the I.B.P.O.E. of W., had retained attorneys, again they left the next move up to the white Elks. The North Carolina Case remained undecided. Another case had started in Chicago in December, 1916, involving an injunction. In the same year two brothers were arrested in New York for wearing B.P.O.E. pins. The first was acquitted and the second was convicted but was given a suspended sentence. An attempt was made to carry the New York Case to the U. S. Supreme Court but that court decided that no Federal question was involved and jurisdiction was denied.

In June, 1917, a member of Mizpah Lodge, Phoebus, Virginia, was arrested in New York City and charged with wearing an Elk emblem. The brothers of Manhattan Lodge No. 45 engaged Brother Philip Thorne to defend him. It was proved at the trial that the defendant wore a copyrighted B.P.O.E. pin. Two judges concurred in his guilt, with one dissenting. Attorney Thorne urged that the brother did not know that the pin he wore was a copyrighted pin of the B.P.O.E.

Another case of unusual consequences arose in New York, and only the wise actions of the members of Manhattan Lodge prevented further legal trouble. Brother Robert H. Holmes, a member of Manhattan Lodge No. 45 and a policeman, was killed in performance of his duties. A white man named Fitzgerald claiming to represent a local lodge of white Elks threatened to get an injunction to prevent the Negro Elks from using anything emblematic of the Elks at his funeral, since the courts had ruled against such use. When Manhattan Lodge learned of this proposed action, it was decided that their members would not wear any emblems or use any display at the funeral ceremonies. This action prevented any additional court trouble over the emblem.

It is of interest to observe that these incidents grew out of the wearing of B.P.O.E. pins. The members of the I.B.P.O.E. of W. had been warned by the Grand Exalted Rulers and the Exalted Rulers to discontinue this practice which continued to cause trouble for the Grand Lodge and for themselves. Grand Exalted Ruler Scott gave this warning at the 1917 Grand Lodge Session, and he was supported by Grand Legal Adviser Stanton, who added that these pins were bought in stores, at public sales, and that such action should be condemned and prohibited officially. Brother George Bates, Grand Secretary, recommended that the Order make it a punishable offense for a brother of the I.B.P.O.E. of W. to wear a B.P.O.E. emblem. He said that, "while they have been warned from time to time, many of them do not heed the warning and as a consequence cause much trouble." He also advised that a pin should be adopted for use of the members, and as one had been approved in St. Paul in 1907, this one could be placed in general use. The court incidents arose, he said, through the purchase of pins by members in stores where B.P.O.E. pins were on sale and the arrests or overt actions would follow from such actions.

A resolution was adopted providing for a ten dollar fine for the first offense of wearing an unauthorized pin and suspension for the second offense. Another resolution presented by Monarch Lodge No. 145 of New York City, was heartily adopted as follows:

> "As the I.B.P.O.E. of W. has never had an official button, and there being in consequence a great number of conflicts and vexatious problems arising from the fact that the Lodges of the I.B.P.O.E. of W. have no definite emblem which leads many in our Lodge to wear emblems of the B.P.O.E., therefore,

> *Be it Resolved,* The Grand Exalted Ruler, Grand Secretary and Grand Treasurer act as committee of this Grand Lodge, to model a button, same to be adopted by this Grand Body and to be used universally by all the Lodges in the jurisdiction of the I.B.P.O.E. of W."

Since these difficulties were continuing between the two organizations but were centering more upon the simple issue of the badge or pin and not upon their existence, it seemed to Grand Exalted Ruler Scott that this was a propitious moment to approach the leadership of the B.P.O.E., as it was manifested that official sanctions were lacking in most of these cases. He knew also that victory could be won not only by direct attack but by diplomatic negotiation of issues. He began this activity with a letter to the Grand Exalted Ruler of the B.P.O.E., Fred Harper of Lynchburg, Virginia, extending congratulations to him on his election to his Order's most exalted office and "the good wishes of the colored Elks of the world to you, because we have been advised that you have always manifested a peculiar interest in our welfare." He called attention to the information given to the convention in Atlantic City in 1913 by Brother W. H. Randolph of this city, that he was one who was opposed to the closing of the door against colored Elks. He also had observed that there was a large majority of the members of the B.P.O.E. who were more disposed to encourage rather than hinder them. He concluded that the I.B.P.O.E. of W. was trying to help improve conditions for Negroes as well as humanity and they were aiding the country in its hour of peril with loyal and patriotic service to their motherland. This letter was graciously answered by Grand Exalted Ruler Harper of the B.P.O.E., with assurance of his sincere appreciation.

This correspondence was the first breach in the solid wall of opposition and antagonism between white and Negro Elks. Similar expressions concerning friendly contacts between members of local lodges were made from time to time, showing the development of favorable attitudes. Others would have chosen the single method of direct assault on the citadel from which the opposition forces came, but Grand Exalted Ruler Scott saw that in addition to this program there was the advantage of beginning the creation of good will, while not retreating one step from his original position of carrying a good case to the highest court in the land. He saw money spent by subordinate lodges and the Grand Lodge in defense endeavors in the courts and the effects which these incidents had upon the developments within the Order. Progress was being made but more could be made in periods of peace.

Grand Secretary Bates paid a deserved tribute to Grand Exalted Ruler Scott when he said, "His administration has been able and intelligent, and I believe that I can say without fear of successful contradiction that his energetic and forceful personality has been the cause of much of the great success we have achieved this year, and when the history of the Order is written his name and record as Grand Exalted Ruler will shine as a bright and radiant star among the galaxy of able men who have been or shall be called to fill that office."

The realization of an approaching period of better relations was seen also by Grand Secretary Bates in his 1917 report. He said, "Looking back through the dark pages of our history, when to be an Elk was considered by many to be a badge of dishonor, when even among our own people the object of our organization was misunderstood and the personnel of our membership severely criticized, when our legal entanglements and the seemingly irrepressible trend of adverse circumstances enveloped us in doubt as to the permanency of our existence, we should indeed be happy that the Eighteenth Annual Session of our Grand Lodge finds our organization in a robust condition, with all doubt as to the permanency of its structure dispelled, with a better feeling existing for us by those who were once prone to criticize, with a largely increased membership and a flourishing Treasury, with less antagonism for us on the part of the antlered herd of the other race, with a higher conception on the part of many of our members of the essentials in living upright lives, thus placing our Order in the sphere of a moral as well as fraternal force among our people."

In order to work out a solution for the problem of the relationship of the Daughter Elks to the Grand Lodge, Grand Exalted Ruler Scott held a conference with Grand Daughter Ruler, Dt. Mamie E. Hodges and Dt. Emma V. Kelley, Grand Daughter Secretary, in Washington, D. C., on December 1, 1916. The Constitution of the Grand Temple was reviewed, section by section, and suggested changes were made. A Proclamation was sent out to the temples giving details of the new relationship and suggesting the cooperation of the temples with the lodges. The result was an immediate working agreement which was developed with the Daughters, and the expectation was that the Order would thus become, in the words of Grand Exalted Ruler Scott, "the greatest and most powerful secret organization among our people in this country." This association of the Daughter Elks with the I.B.P.O.E. of W., approved by the Grand Lodge of 1916, had led to issuance of the following charters: Liberty of the Valley Temple, Phoenixville, Pa.; Evening Star Temple,

Uniontown, Pa.; Washington Light Temple, Crisfield, Md.; Polar Wave Temple, St. Louis, Mo.; Harriet Tubman Temple, Los Angeles, Calif.; Keystone Temple, Donora, Pa.; Manhattan Temple, New York City.

The report on expansion and growth of the 1917 Grand Lodge was that the membership had risen to 13,181, which was an increase of 2,291, over the previous year, and there were forty-one lodges with numbers ranging from 604 to 100. Twenty-three lodges had purchased real estate during the year, bringing the total valuation of real estate held by the lodges to $146,150.00 as compared with $91,425.00 the last year. There were $15,375.20 paid out in sick benefits and twenty-six lodges had paid out death benefits ranging from $630.00 to $200.00 per lodge. The grand total of receipts for the year was $12,151.33.

The Grand Officers for 1917-1918 were: Armond W. Scott, Grand Exalted Ruler, Washington, D. C.; George E. Bates, Grand Secretary, Newark, N. J.; James T. Carter, Grand Treasurer, Richmond, Virginia; A. J. Brown, Grand Esteemed Leading Knight, Richmond, Va.; C. Henri Lewis, Grand Esteemed Loyal Knight, Detroit, Mich.; Samuel E. Bailey, Grand Esteemed Lecturing Knight, Philadelphia, Pa.; George E. Wibecan, Grand Trustee, Brooklyn, N. Y.; P. A. Southall, Grand Esquire, Minneapolis, Minn.; H. P. Kennedy, Grand Inner Guard, New Bern, N. C.; George W. F. McMechen, Grand Legal Adviser, Baltimore, Md.

The Nineteenth Annual Meeting of the Grand Lodge was called to order at St. Peter Claver Hall, Baltimore, Maryland, on August 27, 1918, by Grand Exalted Ruler Armond W. Scott. The Committee on Credentials made its report showing that there were 133 lodges with 327 delegates. There were four Past Grand Exalted Rulers, Dr. William E. Atkins, Hampton, Virginia; J. Frank Wheaton, New York City; Harry H. Pace, Atlanta, Georgia; T. Gillis Nutter, Charleston, West Virginia.

One of the first actions of the lodge was the adoption of a motion for the appointment of a committee to draft resolutions of fealty and loyalty of the Grand Lodge, I.B.P.O.E. of W., to the President of the United States in the present crisis. The committee was appointed consisting of Brothers George W. Holbert, H. Adolph Howell and Harry H. Pace. The parade was then begun. It was declared to be, by the *Baltimore-American*, "one of the finest demonstrations in the City of Baltimore by either a white or colored organization." There were twenty-five bands, over 5,000 marchers, one hundred automobiles and representatives of the Army, Navy and Red Cross.

The order of the day was then the Report of Grand Exalted

Ruler Scott. The first section of his report was described, "True Patriots." Said he, "Neither injustice, caste prejudice, nor proscription have dampened our ardor, nor deadened our spirit of patriotism and devotion to this our mother country. This is our country for which, in every one of its conflicts, our forefathers have fought, bled and died on a thousand battlefields, that this nation might live. Since we last met, hundreds, yea thousands, of our members have joined the colors, and we can safely predict that they will maintain that same splendid record of our forefathers on Boston Commons and Bunker Hill, on Lake Erie with Commodore Perry, at Fort Wagner and Milliken's Bend, at San Juan Hill and Carrazal, Mexico, and with Roberts and Johnson in the trenches of France."

He said that subordinate lodges and individual members had contributed to the Red Cross and purchased many thousands of dollars of Liberty Bonds and Thrift Stamps. Later a committee recommended the purchase of $10,000 worth of Liberty Bonds by the Grand Lodge, and this recommendation was adopted. A letter was read by the Grand Exalted Ruler from Newton D. Baker, U. S. Secretary of War, who had been invited to be present. He expressed his regret at not being able to be present, and wrote of the splendid work of the Order for the betterment of humanity and the stimulation among all elements of the colored people of the nation a keener realization of their duty to their Government in this hour of peril when the civilization of the world practically hung in the balance. He said that more than $50,000 in Liberty Bonds had been purchased, for which the Order deserved highest commendation.

The condition of the Order was reported as good both according to the report of the Committee on the State of the Order and as shown by membership increases, receipts and the payment of mortgages on five lodge homes. Other lodges had undertaken the purchase of homes. There were also eight Temples of Daughter Elks instituted during the past year.

The death of B. F. Howard, First Past Grand Exalted Ruler, was announced by the Grand Exalted Ruler, the debt of gratitude owed to him for the organization of the Order was described, and he concluded that "as the years come and go, let us think only of his virtues, and remember that he, like all the rest of us, was only a human being." Later, a monument was authorized for erection at the expense of the Grand Lodge over his grave, as a continuing testimony of the gratitude referred to by the Grand Exalted Ruler.

Correspondence had been conducted by the Grand Exalted

Ruler with Grand Exalted Ruler Fred Harper of B.P.O.E. of the U.S.A. Among other things, direct mention was made in December, 1917, by Grand Exalted Ruler Scott of the instruction to proceed in the Philadelphia Case, that the members of the I.B.P.O.E. of W. had been ordered to wear only its new pin, somewhat in the form of a star with raised letters on each point, I.B.P.O.E.W., with an Elk head in the center; and that through his good offices the members of his Order might be persuaded so that his liberal views might permeate the rest of his membership. Grand Exalted Ruler Harper wrote his New York City Lodge requesting that all friction be avoided pending the final settlement of the policy of his lodge. On May 30, 1918, Grand Exalted Ruler Scott wrote that it was his confidential belief that the men of the B.P.O.E. would ultimately realize that no harm would come to them through the existence of the I.B.P.O.E. of W. Again on July 16, 1918, Grand Exalted Ruler Scott wrote commending the friendly attitude of the Grand Exalted Ruler Harper that in years to come he would realize how much he had helped and encouraged a group of men who were loyal to their country and to the Order whose chief mission was to dispense charity among the unfortunate.

Finally at the B.P.O.E. Convention at Atlantic City, New Jersey, on July 8, 1918, Grand Exalted Ruler Harper made the following recommendation: "I have never been in accord with the attitude which the Grand Lodge has assumed for a number of years toward the Negro organization which has adopted the name of Improved Benevolent and Protective Order of Elks of the World. I have thought that our Order was so permanently established, so distinctive in character and membership, that we could well afford to ignore any attempt at imitation on the part of those who for obvious reasons could never impose upon the public or our own members even if they so desired. So far as I am advised no evidence of any such desire or intention has ever been displayed by the organization in question.

"In my opinion the most dignified and effective course for our Order to pursue in the premises is to refrain from further litigation, and to pay no further attention to the Negro Elks, except to show them such consideration as may properly be due an organization which claims to be engaged in benevolent and charitable work among a race which both needs and deserves such service. At my request the Committee on Good of the Order has made a careful study of this whole question and have embodied their views in a report which will be made at this session of the Grand Lodge. I commend that report to your careful consideration.'' This recommendation was adopted by his Grand Lodge.

The Order was urged by Grand Exalted Ruler Scott to do nothing to renew the unpleasantness, to wear the pin of the I.B.P.O.E. of W., and no other Elk lodge pin, and if this should be done, he was confident that the troubles would end and the future would hold peace, prosperity and happiness. This result was a victory. The report was described in the Minutes of this session as marking ''the greatest epoch in the history of the I.B.P.O.E. of W., for it told of the consummation of peace between the white and colored Elks.'' There was great demonstration of approval, and the Grand Exalted Ruler received an ovation as men vied with one another to grasp his hand. Many were overcome with emotion and wept with joy ''at the dawn of fraternal freedom for the Order after years of strife.'' Many wanted to reelect Grand Exalted Ruler Scott for another term at once, but he unselfishly declared that he preferred to wait until the proper time for elections.

The sense of victory was continued in the report of Grand Secretary Bates, who described the result as ''a signal victory for the tact, intelligence and diplomacy displayed by our Grand Exalted Ruler.'' The report on membership showed 15,224 in 151 active lodges, an increase of over two thousand members since the Grand Lodge in 1917. The Order had lodges in twenty-nine states and one each in the Bahama Islands and the Republic of Panama. It was reported that 923 members of subordinate lodges had gone into the service of the Army and Navy, and that nearly every lodge had contributed a quota to these services of the nation. The Grand Treasurer's report showed a balance of $12,216.71.

The election resulted in the choice of the following Grand Officers: Armond W. Scott, Grand Exalted Ruler, Washington, D. C.; George E. Bates, Grand Secretary, Newark, N. J.; James T. Carter, Grand Treasurer, Richmond, Va.; Andrew J. Brown, Grand Esteemed Leading Knight, Richmond, Va.; Henri Lewis, Grand Esteemed Loyal Knight, Detroit, Mich.; William H. Shands, Grand Esteemed Lecturing Knight, Philadelphia, Pa.; Jesse S. Jones, Grand Trustee, Portsmouth, Va.; H. P. Kennedy, Grand Inner Guard, New Bern, N. C.; P. A. Southall, Grand Esquire, Minneapolis, Minn.; Richard B. Kane, Grand Tiler, Hartford, Conn.

The committee appointed to draft a resolution on the fealty of the Order reported the following in the form of a telegram:

To His Excellency,
Woodrow Wilson, President of the United States, Washington, D. C.

We have the honor to transmit to you the following resolution which has been unanimously adopted:

Whereas, our beloved country is engaged in a worldwide struggle for Democracy, and

Whereas, the man-power of this nation has been called upon to make the most extreme sacrifice known in history,

Be it Resolved, That the Improved Benevolent and Protective Order of Elks of the World in its Nineteenth Annual Session assembled hereby pledges the country and the President of the United States the loyal and unconditional support in this, the great crisis in the world's history to the full extent of its man-power and resources, and

Be it further Resolved, That Ten Thousand Dollars be and the same is hereby set aside for investment in the Fourth Liberty Loan.

Harry H. Pace
H. Adolph Howell
Geo. W. Holbert

This resolution had additional emphasis in the report of the Committee on the State of the Order, which urged that "each Brother enlarge upon his efforts to do his part as an American citizen in aiding the Government in whatever way that is possible to bring the war to a successful conclusion." The Committee went a step further in not only pledging allegiance and expressing approval and gratitude to the President of the United States, the Secretary of War and his assistant Emmett J. Scott, but also to encourage the efforts to minimize unreasonable racial prejudices and barbaric practices and "to secure an honest deal for the Negro soldier whose acts of bravery, at home and abroad, have already won the admiration of the world."

Another resolution called for the organization of a Juvenile Department of the Order to be then known as cadets of the I.B.P.O.E. of W., which was approved by the Grand Lodge. A request from the Grand Temple that the provision that its members had to be wives, widows, daughters and sisters of members of the I.B.P.O.E. of W., should be changed to read any female member of good moral character being vouched for by five members of their respective Temples is eligible for membership. This request was tabled. The Committee on Appeals and Grievances found in its report that an edition of Daughter Emma V. Kelley's ***Brief History of I.B.P.O.E. of W.,*** contained some references in the Ritual which should not be made public and declared that its sale and distribution should be discontinued. Brown's *Brief Manual and History of the I.B.P.O.E. of W.*, was proposed for ownership by the Grand Lodge but because it described some of the ritualistic work, this proposal was tabled. The Grand Lodge closed to meet at Atlantic City, New Jersey.

R. M. S. BROWN, Author of Brown's *Brief History*; Grand Secretary, 1907-

This Twentieth Annual Session of the Grand Lodge at the Light House Lodge on Arctic Avenue, August 26-28, 1919, marked an epoch in the history of the I.B.P.O.E. of W., not only because it closed twenty years of its history but also because it marked the termination of the war and demonstrated the permanence of victory for the independence of the Order. There was the combination of war and victory.

This Grand Lodge was the largest in history, with one hundred and forty-seven lodges, an increase of eighty-three over last year, representing 465 delegates. The parade had twenty-six bands, magnificent floats and displays, costumed brothers and sisters, and it took two hours for it to pass a given point. An enthusiastic reception was given to it by white and Negro onlookers and by the daily press.

Grand Exalted Ruler Scott in his Report congratulated the Order on its magnificent progress and the removal of its many obstacles both without and within. He said that every year for many years, lawsuits had been reported but that since the last Grand Lodge, the Philadelphia Case, the last of the series had been discontinued. He stated that there had "not been a legal ripple upon the bosom of our fraternal sea," and that internally it had been a year of absolute peace and harmony. He called it also "The Dawn of a New Day." He reported that the lodges as well as the Grand Lodge were in flourishing conditions with good amounts in their treasuries and with the ownership of properties; and he proposed the appointment of a committee of three who would consider the question of the ways and means to invest their funds. The Grand Lodge had established a National Home for Indigent Elks, he said, and it had proven to be a complete success.

The membership report by Grand Secretary Bates showed 21,107, an increase of 4,237 over last year. There were sixty-seven lodges with membership of over one hundred, and eleven new lodges were instituted. Pennsylvania again had the largest number of lodges, thirty-two; with Virginia holding second place with twenty-five, New Jersey was third with eighteen and New York fourth with twelve. This report also showed that 1,587 lodge members were in the Army and Navy during the war. He reported that the $10,000 in Liberty Bonds had been purchased principally through colored banks. The total cash and bonds were $19,652.10, and the total receipts were $23,486.51, according to the report of Grand Treasurer Carter. He paid a tribute to Grand Exalted Ruler Scott in the words, "His magnetic personality, his rugged honesty of purpose, his executive ability of a high order—all have been an asset to the Order, the result of which shows very plainly through the reports that shall be rendered here today." A watch was later presented to Brother Scott as a token of appreciation for his great service to the Order.

The Committee on the State of the Order stated that "the Order has made the greatest progress in the history of its existence" and the Grand Trustees styled the session as the "victory meeting," when "our beloved country has been victorious over the cruel Huns and we are glad to say that victory has crowned our efforts."

The comment of the Grand Exalted Ruler on the death of Past Grand Exalted Ruler B. F. Howard was implemented by the following resolutions:

> "*Whereas,* The man who founded this grand organization is dead, and being of the opinion that his memory should be preserved, always having in mind, the ground work and foundation of our Order, and,
>
> *Whereas,* Today our organization stands second to none among our people, having attained the apex of efficiency through the untiring efforts of those who have followed him, and, to show to the world we practise what we preach,
>
> *Be it Further Resolved,* That this grand organization do allow Mrs. B. F. Howard $20 a month, for the rest of her natural life, and that the monument be erected at a cost of $500.00.
>
> Fraternally submitted,
> D. M. McDaniel
> W. McKenzie
> Monarch Lodge, No. 45

This last clause concerning the payment to Mrs. Howard was changed to pay her $20.00 a month for five years.

The Past Exalted Rulers' Council previously organized was given additional status by designating the council of New York State as Council No. 1. An effort to have the *Elks Bulletin,* published by Pocahontas Lodge No. 129, Cambridge, Massachusetts, accepted as the official organ failed to secure adoption. A committee to make a survey for a National Elks' Home was appointed consisting of George E. Bates, Grand Secretary; H. H. Pace, Past Grand Exalted Ruler and William H. Shands.

The Daughter Elks were also interested in a national home, which was to be called their "Shrine." At their session in 1919 in Lighthouse Lodge auditorium, Atlantic City, N. J., a resolution was introduced by Daughher Emma V. Kelley taxing each member ten cents annually toward the purchase of this home.

The following Grand Officers of the Grand Lodge for 1919-1920 were elected: George W. F. McMechen, Grand Exalted Ruler, Baltimore, Md.; George E. Bates, Grand Secretary, Newark, N. J.; James T. Carter, Grand Treasurer, Richmond, Va.; W. Cary Trueheart, Grand Esteemed Leading Knight, Atlantic City, N. J.; W. W. Green, Grand Esteemed Loyal Knight, Birmingham, Ala.; H. A. Watkins, Grand Esteemed Lecturing Knight, Chicago, Ill.; H. P. Kennedy, Grand Trustee, New Bern, N. C.; La Rue Paxton, Grand Esquire, Pittsburgh, Pa.; Richard B. Kane, Grand Inner Guard, Hartford, Conn.; Joseph V. Greene, Grand Tiler, Toledo, Ohio; C. Henri Lewis, Grand Legal Adviser, Detroit, Mich.; C. G. Cummings, Grand Chaplain, Charleston, West Va.

The installation of these officers was conducted by Past Grand Exalted Ruler Atkins who, with Past Grand Exalted Rulers Wheaton, Pace and Nutter, was present at this session. As the meeting closed, it was said that this was "the most successful meeting ever held by the Order."

Chapter IX
Expansion and Growth

The period following the close of World War I witnessed a period of expansion particularly into the West and internal growth of the Improved Benevolent and Protective Order of Elks of the World. The numerical membership and financial strength of the Order increased. Its growth in these areas was remarkable. The confidence of the leadership in the potentialities of the Order was confirmed and the loyalty of the members was assured by the outcome of these later years and the record of fraternal achievement. For the past decade there had been a continuous increase in membership in spite of the war and the stringent times through which the lodges were passing. Obstacles were met and surmounted. The Order had declined to terminate when it seemed that an organized effort was at work in all the states to destroy its work. Facing this opposition, Elk brothers were manly and courageous. Their decision was that they were going to stick by their guns and they would fight it out along legal and organizational lines.

The new expansion was felt in the growth of lodges particularly in the Mid-west and Western section, where there had not been much development and in some cases none. Thirty-two lodges were instituted between the last convention in 1919 and the session of 1920. This was the greatest number of new lodges in the Order's history. This westward development made the Order's membership realize that they constituted a brotherhood in which there were no sectional lines. The State of Oklahoma had no lodges in 1919 but there were six in 1920. There were five new lodges in Kansas, where there had been only one. However, North Carolina had the largest number, nine, of newly organized lodges. Reference was made to the status of the Order in Georgia where it had been enjoined years before from instituting any lodge. This injunction had not been dissolved, and a prominent member of the white Elks was willing to assist, but the Grand Exalted Ruler stated that he felt that the Grand Lodge should consider the matter. The Grand Lodge later approved a resolution that the Grand Exalted Ruler and Grand Legal Adviser were authorized to exercise their discretion in bringing the Georgia Case to a successful conclusion so that a lodge may be instituted in the state. While Grand Exalted Ruler George W. F. McMechen was mainly responsible, there were also to share in this accomplishment the deputies whom he had appointed and special requests sent to brothers to assist in the accessions.

An important action in the cementing of unity was the carrying out of the resolution of the Grand Lodge concerning the B. F. Howard Monument. On Sunday afternoon, July 4, 1920, this monument was unveiled at Linden Grove Cemetery, Covington, Kentucky. The monument was of hammered Bedford stone. It was three feet ten inches by two feet six inches at the base, with a ten foot shaft carrying emblems and lettering. The plans for the monument were submitted by Brother William H. Johnson of Indianapolis who gave assistance in the delivery and installation of the monument.

Grand Exalted Ruler McMechen had issued proclamations and had given publicity to the event. The cooperation of the lodges in Cincinnati, Negro police, a marching band, Alpha Lodge No. 1 of Cincinnati, Etta Wah Temple of Cincinnati and Ira Lodge of Covington participated in the parade which passed through the principal streets of the two cities to the cemetery. Ira Lodge had been inactive for more than three years as a result of their sympathy and respect for Past Grand Exalted Ruler Howard. The lodge was reinstated on the evening of July 3 by Grand Exalted Ruler McMechen. Alpha Lodge through a committee headed by Brother Toran helped with the program and secured the consent of the cemetery officials to conduct the dedication. The Grand Exalted Ruler delivered the address of dedication, and addresses were made by Brothers William Lewis, Baltimore, Md.; R. E. Pharrow, Atlanta, Ga.; John T. Brandy, Washington, Pa.; Frank Hunter, St. Louis, Mo.; and James T. Howard, Great Lakes Lodge No. 43, Chicago, Ill., and Buckeye Lodge No. 73, Youngstown, O., and Summer Lodge of Providence, Rhode Island, placed a floral wreath at the base of the monument.

The widow of B. F. Howard was present at the services. Her reaction to the occasion was expressed in a letter to the Grand Exalted Ruler dated July 10, 1920, from Indianapolis, Indiana. She had remarried and her name was Mrs. M. L. Howard-Person. Her letter stated to Grand Exalted Ruler McMechen:

> Dear Sir:
>
> As I was present at the dedication of the monument to the memory of my hubsand, the late B. F. Howard, Founder and Organizer of the Elks, I wish to congratulate them and also extend to them my deepest apreciation for such lasting tribute of respect.
>
> May the Elks live long and become a power for good in this and succeeding generations. "Cast thy bread upon the waters, for thou shalt find it after many days."

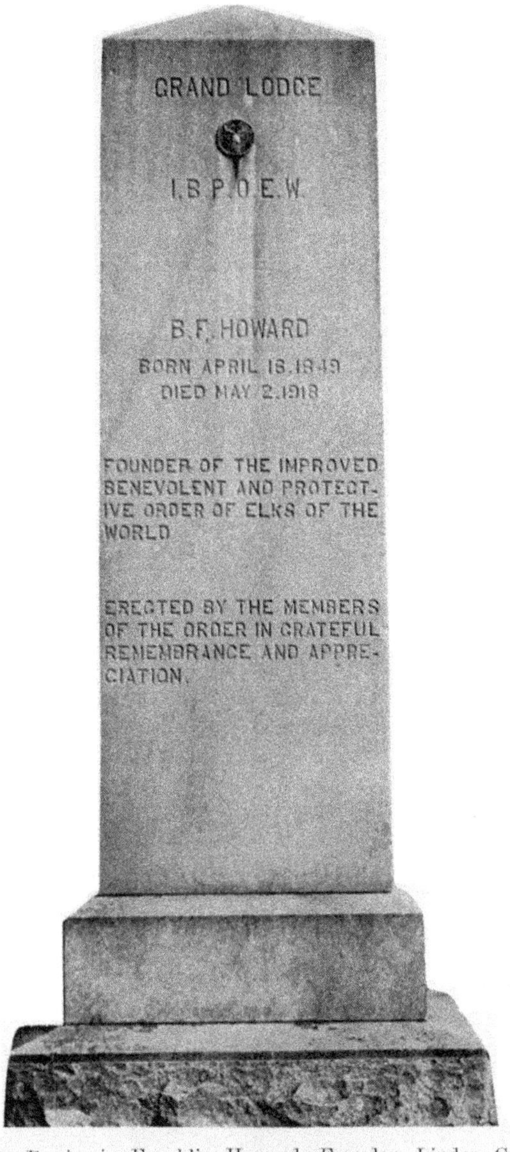

GRAND LODGE
I.B.P.O.E.W.
B.F. HOWARD
BORN APRIL 16.1849
DIED MAY 2.1918
FOUNDER OF THE IMPROVED BENEVOLENT AND PROTECT-IVE ORDER OF ELKS OF THE WORLD
ERECTED BY THE MEMBERS OF THE ORDER IN GRATEFUL REMEMBRANCE AND APPRE-CIATION.

Monument to Benjamin Franklin Howard, Founder, Linden Grove Cemetery, Covington, Ky.

I am sure it will, if such prominent men as those who directed the building and dedication of the monument continue to lead this great fraternal Order. Many thanks and best regards.

Sincerely,
M. L. Howard-Person

With the erection of the monument, the second part of the action of the Grand Lodge of 1919 was the next consideration. This second provision authorized the payment of $20.00 a month to the widow of B. F. Howard for five years. The impression was that she was in need, and this was the basis for this action. It was learned shortly after the 1919 session that Mrs. Howard had remarried. A member of the lodge, Brother John W. Johnson, Secretary of Indiana Lodge No. 104 of Indianapolis visited her and his report to Grand Secretary Bates indicated that she was not in need. The Grand Exalted Ruler was informed that she owned two pieces of real estate in Covington, Kentucky and had recently disposed of one house, while another had a value of $1,500. She was desirous of having the monthly allowance but it was withheld by the Grand Exalted Ruler and the Grand Secretary until the Grand Lodge Session in August, 1920.

This Twenty-first Annual Meeting of the Grand Lodge met in the Auditorium of the Lincoln Theater, Kansas City, Missouri, August 24-26, 1920. Grand Exalted Ruler McMechen called the session to order. After the ritualistic services, the Grand Exalted Ruler appointed the committees. The Committee on Credentials later reported that there were 140 lodges represented with 488 delegates. Last year's session was represented by 465 delegates, so that this 1920 convention was larger than the 1919 convention, which was the largest prior to its assembly.

The opportunity for expansion was emphasized in the words of the Grand Exalted Ruler, "There are splendid fields which await an opportunity to come within our fold." This was said also because the Grand Lodge was meeting in a section where it had not met previously, and because the Grand Exalted Ruler believed that "westward the course of empire takes its sway." He said that Indiana, Ohio, Illinois, Kentucky, Missouri and other states with large Negro populations offered opportunities for the spread of Elk principles, but he added that new legislation would be necessary to accomplish these objectives. He told of the new lodges and the increases in membership and in finances. At the close of his address, Brother William R. Morris of Amos Lodge No. 106, after commending the Grand Exalted Ruler, moved that the rules be suspended and that he be given the unanimous vote

George W. F. McMechen, Grand Legal Adviser, 1917-1919; Eighth Grand Exalted Ruler, 1919-1921.

of the Grand Lodge to succeed himself as Grand Exalted Ruler, and the motion was adopted.

The expansion in members was detailed by the report of Grand Secretary Bates, who stated that there were 29,143 members, an increase of 8,036 over last year's membership. There were 166 active lodges in 1919 but there were 209 active ones in 1920. The total evaluation of real estate owned by the lodges was $454,626 and there were fifty-six lodges which either owned or were purchasing real estate. In addition to the thirty-two lodges instituted, there were twenty-seven Temples organized. He had issued a small journal under the title of *Elks' Official News,* in April, 1920, although there was no amount in his budget for its publication. The balance in the Treasury, according to the Grand Treasurer was $17,933.09, with the total receipts, $24,394.15.

The election resulted in the following officers: George W. F. McMechen, Grand Exalted Ruler, Baltimore, Md.; George E. Bates, Grand Secretary, Newark, N. J.; James T. Carter, Grand Treasurer, Richmond, Va.; W. C. Trueheart, Grand Esteemed Leading Knight, Atlantic City, N. J.; Walter T. Dixon, Grand Esteemed Loyal Knight, Washington, D. C.; John P. White, Grand Esteemed Lecturing Knight, Richmond, Va.; Quincy J. Gilmore, Grand Trustee, Kansas City, Mo.; Edgar A. Still, Grand Esquire, Reading, Pa.; Leslie T. Ash, Inner Guard, Chicago, Ill.; Roy R. Morgan, Grand Tiler, Atlanta, Ga.

C. Henri Lewis, Grand Legal Adviser, 1919-1921; Grand Esteemed Loyal Knight.

The report of the Grand Trustees called attention to the unprecedented growth and development of the Order, its expansion and the hope and optimism held by the members of the Order. A change in the election procedure was approved. After the nominations, the secretaries were to prepare a sheet with names listed in proper columns, the roll of lodges would then be called in numerical order, the delegation from each lodge would elect a Chairman who would poll the delegation of those members actually present, and announce the vote and the secretaries would record the votes and the sheet would be handed to the presiding officer. This method had been proposed at the session of 1919 but failed to secure approval. The resolution was adopted limiting the term of the Grand Exalted Ruler, the Grand Esteemed Leading Knight, the Grand Esteemed Loyal Knight, and the Grand Esteemed Lecturing Knight to one year, and neither should be able to succeed himself. The committee recommending this resolution included Brothers C. W. Holbert, Robert R. Jackson, T. W. Fleming, C. Henri Lewis, W. H. Randolph, W. H. Johnson and J. Finley Wilson. Another resolution was adopted stating that since the duties of the Grand Officers had increased materially and had become more exacting, salaries should be paid to them; the Grand Exalted Ruler, $1,200 a year; the Grand Secretary, $2,400 a year; the Grand Treasurer, $600 a year and the Grand Legal Adviser, $200 a year. This resolution was adopted with only two dissenting votes.

The first action looking toward the educational program of the Order was approved at this Grand Lodge of 1920. It was declared:

> "*Whereas,* The Improved Benevolent and Protective Order of Elks of the World is an organization of progressive thought and action and recognized as one of the leading Orders of the race, and,
>
> *Whereas,* the members of the fraternity believe in giving our boys and girls every educational advantage, be it hereby
>
> *Resolved,* That the Grand Exalted Ruler be empowered to appoint a committee of five to consider the advisability of setting aside a certain amount of money each year to be used as a scholarship fund to provide education for some boy or girl in one of our institutions of learning."

This resolution was submitted by Daniel Ware of Pochahontas Lodge No. 129, Cambridge, Massachusetts. The Committee on Resolutions concurred in the resolution but recommended that no mileage or per diem be allowed the committee, and the Grand Lodge also concurred. The Grand Lodge brought its business to a close with the resolution, "Long live Kansas City and its lovable and hospitable citizens."

The movement into the Mid-West was not without its incidental opposition. In April, 1920, application was made to the Grand Secretary for a charter for a lodge at Bloomington, Indiana. About a month later, the white Elks obtained an injunction against the institution of the lodge. The Grand Legal Adviser, Brother C. Henri Lewis, went to Bloomington and the matter was tried in the Monroe County Circuit Court. It was shown that the suit was started without the approval of the Grand Exalted

Ruler of the B.P.O.E., or the Grand Lodge officials. The Court took the briefs filed in the case under advisement. It was the opinion of the Grand Officers of the I.B.P.O.E. of W., that this would be the end of the litigation in this case, for there was no reason to believe that the new Grand Exalted Ruler of the B.P.O.E., had or would change the expressed opinion of Past Grand Master Harper in 1918, and the adopted resolution of the Grand Lodge.

Attention was directed to the origin of the Improved Benevolent and Protective Order of Elks of the World by the receipt by Grand Exalted Ruler McMechen of a letter on June 18, 1921, from J. Arthur Riggs of Springfield, Ohio, who was associated with B. F. Howard in the founding of the Order. He sent with his letter "the original manuscript of the Order." The Grand Exalted Ruler acknowledged this gift and suggested that the Grand Lodge express its thanks to Brother Riggs for this historical document.

Shortly after the rise of the Bloomington case, the Twenty-second Annual Meeting of the Grand Lodge, I.B.P.O.E. of W., met in Ruggles Hall, Boston, Massachusetts, August 23-25, 1921, with Grand Exalted Ruler George W. F. McMechen presiding. The parade was one of the largest and most magnificent of its kind. The *Boston Post* described it as follows: "Boston's pavements re-echoed yesterday to the tread of the feet of the largest procession of colored people in the history of the race in America. With a rainbow show of colors, a snapping galaxy of drum majors and many bands, 10,000 members of the Improved Benevolent and Protective Order of Elks of the World paraded from Arlington and Beacon Streets, down town through the South End, to Frederick Douglass Square, Cabot and Tremont Streets.—Governor Fuller when interviewed said, 'I have seldom enjoyed a parade as much as that one,' as he left the reviewing stand, 'It was a splendid turn-out and they have my most cordial congratulations on the fine showing'."

On the following day, after the opening ceremonies, the committees were appointed. The Committee on Credentials reported that there were 169 lodges represented, with 651 delegates, an increase of 163 delegates over the number in 1920. There were six Past Grand Exalted Rulers present—Past Grand Exalted Rulers Atkins, Mills, Wheaton, Pace, Nutter and Scott.

The Grand Exalted Ruler's address described the bad conditions through which the country had come with business slowed down and work scare, but the Order had reflected these conditions only in part. Thirty new lodges had been instituted in different sections with one in New Orleans, Louisiana, and another in Cheyenne, Wyoming. This made a total of sixty-two lodges instituted under the two-year administration of Grand Exalted Ruler McMechen, the largest number organized in any similar period. He wanted the Order expanded beyond continental United States. He appointed James S. Walker of Buffalo, N. Y., Grand Traveling Deputy of the Dominion of Canada; John S. Melbourne of Brooklyn, N. Y., Grand Traveling Deputy of Cuba. When the 1922 Grand Lodge met there were lodges in the making at Hamilton, Toronto, Montreal and Cuba. In making these assignments, the Grand Exalted Ruler said that the Order was "a world-wide organization and can be organized in any country, under any flag and any language." There was a lodge in Nassau, the Bahama Island "under the British flag," and another in the Republic of Panama.

The reports of the Grand Exalted Ruler and the Grand Secretary described the Tulsa, Oklahoma, riot of 1920 and the outbreak of race antipathy on the part of groups of white persons. Hundreds of Negroes were killed or wounded and their homes and businesses destroyed. The lodge there, Cosmopolitan Lodge No. 247, lost its lodge home, with one member killed and several wounded. A proclamation was sent out by the Grand Exalted Ruler requesting donations for the distressed, and as a result $1,346.75 was received by the Grand Treasurer. The two delegates from Oklahoma were each given $150.00 to assist them in their need. This situation was repeated in other sections of the country. Henry Lincoln Johnson, according to the *New York Times,* told a Senate Committee in 1920 investigating presidential campaign expenditures, "that Negroes had been lynched for voting the Republican ticket." Intimidation of Negro voters was described as a general practice at this time in hundreds of areas of the South.

First Elks' Home built from the ground, by a lodge, Jones Valley Lodge, No. 14, Birmingham, Alabama, 1921.

The membership was reported to have reached 42,236

in 1921, an increase of 13,093 over the report of 1920. The Grand Secretary declared, however, that it was his "honest opinion that our membership is actually over 50,000," and that there were lodges which did not report their full membership. There were some lodges with remarkable increases, such as Monumental Lodge, No. 3, Baltimore, Md., with an increase of 429; Great Lakes No. 43, Chicago, Ill., with an increase of 425; and Eureka No. 5, Norfolk, Va., with an increase of 409. There were 231 active lodges representing thirty-two states and the District of Columbia. The real estate owned by these lodges was valued at $534,675.00 and the total cash of the subordinate lodges in the banks was reported to be $220,916.00. The total amount of death benefits was $34,162.00 and sick benefits were $36,119.55. Twenty-five new Temples were instituted during the year and one reinstated. The Grand Secretary reported that "the temples are growing almost as fast as the lodges." State associations of lodges and Past Exalted Rulers' Councils were approved by the Grand Lodge. In the latter case the sum of $300.00 was appropriated for the reimbursement of Past Exalted Rulers' Council No. 1 of New York for the expenses entailed in constructing the charter design, editing rituals and the advanced thought and knowledge of creating them. A commission of seven members to be known as a National Temple Commission was appointed. Resolutions were passed commending the President of the United States and Governors of states who had taken stands against lynching and mob violence. The Ku Klux Klan and similar organizations were condemned. The treatment of the Twenty-fourth Infantry was declared unjust and colored Americans were urged to join in achieving their civil rights.

The cash balance was $30,072.14 and the Liberty Bonds were $10,000.00 making a total of $40,072.14. The lodge in 1920 adjourned with a surplus of $27,773.74 and met in 1921 with a surplus of $40,072.14. When compared with the situation which the Grand Lodge faced in Boston in 1911, there was then only $22.88 in the Treasury and an indebtedness of $565.00. It was clear from these reports that there had been both great expansion and unusual growth. Grand Secretary Bates paid a deserved tribute to Grand Exalted Ruler McMechen when he said, "He who lays down the sceptre of authority placed in his hands two years ago is truly one of God's noblemen—a man and Brother whom I learned to admire because of his genial personality and gentlemanly qualities.—The record of sixty-two lodges made under his administration of two years has never before been equalled and will be difficult to surpass, and he retires with our good wishes for his success in whatever may be his future undertakings." The gift of a watch and chain was later presented to Grand Exalted Ruler McMechen as a token of appreciation.

The Grand Officers for 1921-1922 were: George E. Wibecan, Grand Exalted Ruler, Brooklyn, N. Y.; Zachariah Alexander, Grand Esteemed Leading Knight, Charlotte, N. C.; John P. White, Grand Esteemed Loyal Knight, Richmond, Va.; William J. Wheaton, Grand Esteemed Lecturing Knight, San Francisco, Calif.; George E. Bates, Grand Secretary, Newark, N. J.; James T. Carter, Grand Treasurer, Richmond, Va.; Victor Walker, Grand Esquire, Denver, Colo.; William Henry Johnson, Grand Inner Guard, Philadelphia, Pa.; Samuel E. Robinson, Grand Tiler, New London, Conn.; Thomas W. Fleming, Grand Legal Adviser, Cleveland, O.; W. C. Brown, Grand Chaplain, Brooklyn, N. Y.; H. P. Kennedy, New Bern, N. C.; Quincy J. Gilmore, Kansas City, Mo.; George F. Hatton, Washington, D. C., Grand Trustees. These officers were installed by Past Exalted Ruler J. Frank Wheaton who had been appointed Assistant District Attorney of New York, and the Grand Lodge adjourned to meet at Newark, N. J. in 1922.

The efforts of Grand Exalted Ruler Wibecan were directed during the following year to expansion of the Order. He planned to travel about the country in order to visit the lodges and stimulate their development and expansion. He said afterwards that he was the first Grand Exalted Ruler elected for one term and that he tried to crowd all the energy he possessed into one year and to inspire confidence in the Order's membership. He had traveled 10,000 miles visiting sections not previously visited by Grand Exalted Rulers. In Oklahoma City on June 26, he slipped upon a muddy sidewalk as he descended from an automobile. He was taken to the hospital for X-ray examinations. It was found that there were no broken bones but he had to continue his journey on crutches across the continent.

In spite of the economic depression, the work of organizing lodges and increasing members continued through the year. The Grand Exalted Ruler granted seventy-six dispensations to various lodges to make new members, and he was able to report at the close of the year that twenty-five new lodges were instituted during the year. He was ably assisted by deputies who were as devoted to the cause of expansion and growth.

The Twenty-Third Annual Meeting of the Grand Lodge convened in Roosevelt Memorial Temple, Newark, New Jersey, August 22-24, 1922. The Public Session on August 21 was called to order by Brother John T. Cheshire, Chairman at the Convention Committee. Grand Secretary George E. Bates served as

George E. Wibecan, Grand Trustee; Ninth Grand Exalted Ruler, 1921-1922.

Master of Ceremonies. Addresses were delivered by Honorable Frederick Breidenback, Mayor of Newark, with a response by Brother W. R. Morris; Rev. W. P. Coon with a response by Past Grand Exalted Ruler Armond W. Scott; Counsellor George A. Douglass, Exalted Ruler of Newark Lodge No. 93, Alexander Braithwaite; Mrs. A. E. O. Cooke, Daughter Mamie E. Hodges, Grand Daughter, Emma V. Kelley, Grand Secretary and Grand Exalted Ruler Wibecan.

On the next day, August 22, the Grand Lodge was opened and afterward the Convention Committees were appointed. The report of the Committee on Credentials showed that there were 186 lodges represented with 442 delegates. There was an increase of fifteen lodges over last year's attendance and a decrease of 211 in the number of delegates. Progress was shown in the number of lodges but the effort of the lodges and members to save money in this postwar period of economic stress was demonstrated in the sending of fewer delegates.

The report of Grand Exalted Ruler Wibecan, because of his incapacity was read by Past Grand Exalted Ruler H. H. Pace. The report revealed the progress made in new lodges and showed that the finances increased nearly 50 per cent, from $38,000 to $54,000. He gave the facts about the Bloomington, Indiana Case and stated that there was no litigation pending between the Grand Lodge of the B.P.O.E., and the Grand Lodge. He had corresponded with Grand Exalted Ruler William M. Mountain, B.P.O.E., of Flint, Michigan. Among other things, he wrote that since there was no conflict between the lodges and their principles, they should have an interest in continuing the friendly relationships which would permit I.B.P.O.E. of W., to organize in any part of the Republic. He asked, "is there not some common ground upon which we may meet to adjust the matters," and avoid litigation. The reply was that there was no need of controversy about the matter. His lodge, Grand Exalted Ruler Mountain of the B.P.O.E., stated was for men "white in color" and that there was no chance of taking in members other than these. Like other legal matters of this type, this one died slowly.

A reference was made in the report to the admission of a white man into the Order. Trinity Lodge No. 183, Newport, Rhode Island, had requested through its secretary to reply to his inquiry if there would be any objection to a white man's admission to the Order, and the additional fact was that he had married a colored woman. The reply of Grand Exalted Ruler Wibecan was:

> "The I.B.P.O.E. of W., says nothing about color, and there is nothing in our Constitution or By-Laws that could prevent a white man being admitted as a member. I doubt the wisdom

> of having a white man as a member in any local lodge, even though he might be the husband of a colored woman. We have so many colored men in the Order who look like white men, and there are so many white people in the country who look like colored, that maybe some white man could get into an Order unnoticed, but where the fact is actually known that the applicant is white, I am afraid it might disturb the relationship of some of the brothers, and for that reason I doubt whether it would be expedient. At the same time, I would not want to be put on record as saying that a white man could not become a member of the I.B.P.O.E. of W., because we try to be broader than the white organization, which closes the door to the colored man."

This was the expression of a tradition which had been existent in the Order from its inception, that its doors were open to all qualified applicants. In commenting upon the history of the Order in this respect, the Grand Exalted Ruler had said that no color or racial lines were drawn in the organization. This was the basic reason for the addition of the words, "of the World," to its name and title. While this was the policy and fact, the Grand Exalted Ruler took the position that the Order was primarily for Negroes. He advocated therefore the cultivation of "a stronger race consciousness by urging the setting aside of days by the lodges to commemorate with proper ceremonies Emancipation Day, the commemoration of the birthday anniversary of Frederick Douglass, that great American of his race; Paul Laurence Dunbar, the greatest poet that America has yet produced, white or black, considering his origin and his struggle; of Crispus Attucks, the Negro, the first to shed his blood in behalf of American independence, and other immortals of the race who have risen to leadership or distinguished themselves in time of war or peace. We should urge the appropriation of a sum of money large enough to sustain a chair for Negro history at some leading college of the race, in order to encourage our youth to know more about the history of the race."

It is of interest to observe that there were lodges of both racial groups who were friendly and helpful to each other. One such incident is referred to by Grand Legal Adviser Thomas W. Flemin East Liverpool, Ohio. The white and Negro lodges there mingled with one another as "true Elks," and the white lodge assisted the Negro lodge in securing its home.

A group insurance plan had received consideration by Grand Exalted Ruler Wibecan because he thought it would be a moral force for the good of the order and a constructive effort. He called a meeting of his Advisory Committee consisting of three Grand Trustees, the Grand Treasurer, the Grand Legal Adviser, the Grand Secretary and his secretary at the lodge home of Columbia Lodge No. 85, Washington, D. C., on November 26, 1921. The President, the Attorney and representatives of the North Eastern Life Insurance Company of Concord, New Hampshire were present. The contract was submitted, discussed and the committee by a standing vote approved the plan. There was proposed a small outlay by the membership and a million dollars would be returned to the Order in three years; there was no physical examination and no age limit and there would be a working force of Negro men and women. The decision was that the Grand Exalted Ruler would send out the "Proclamation Extraordinary" informing the lodges of the action of the Advisory Committee. Some of the replies showed that there were brothers who questioned the proposition and protested its adoption. It was reported that about sixty lodges adopted the proposal.

THOMAS W. FLEMING, Grand Legal Adviser, 1921-1922.

At the Grand Lodge of 1922, the Grand Exalted Ruler requested the appointment of a committee of seven to take up the question of Group Insurance for consideration. He suggested that the heads of Negro life insurance companies be advised and encouraged to submit proposals. Several lodges submitted insurance plans to the Grand Lodge session. The proposal adopted by the Advisory Committee was reported to the Grand Lodge and laid on the table indefinitely. Another proposal for a committee of three to investigate all forms and propositions on insurance were also presented to the Grand Lodge.

Some of these proposals were being made with the objective of interesting additional members in the Order, for while there had been expansion and growth there was a decrease in active members in 1921-1922. In July of 1921, the Grand Secretary reported that the membership was 42,236, but that the membership in 1922 was 35,000, although several lodges had not reported. He regarded this as "a loss of about 7,000 members." This loss in membership was not paralleled by a reduction in finances. On the contrary the receipts were greater in 1922 than in 1921. The total receipts and balance from 1921 was $51,254.61, with a cash balance on hand of $41,718.84, whereas the balance in 1921 was $37,726.73. While there had been a loss as a whole, there were substantial increases in six lodges in Brooklyn No. 32, Monarch No. 45, Manhattan No. 45, Wolverine No. 72, Pride of Newark No. 93 and Imperial No. 127. In 1921, there were six lodges with memberships above one thousand but in 1922 there were only three. The twenty-five new lodges instituted during the year also helped to increase the total membership figures. There were thirty-two new Temples instituted, seven more than the number of lodges. Eighteen charters were issued for Past Exalted Rulers' Councils, and two states reported their activity, one in North Carolina and the other in Kansas. The failure of the Negro banks, the Mechanics Bank of Richmond, Va., and Mutual Savings Bank of Portsmuoth, Va., along with hundreds of others during this period, in which the Order had $1,684.75, was an occasion for discussion at the Grand Lodge. The Grand Treasurer, who regarded himself as personally responsible for opening these accounts in these banks, advanced his own funds to reimburse the Grand Lodge for these losses. The Grand Lodge repaid this amount to Grand Treasurer Carter for this evidence of his loyalty and service to the Order.

When all of these factors were taken into consideration, Grand Secretary Bates concluded, "The success achieved this year under such adverse conditions should certainly cause us to look to the future with much encouragement."

The Grand Officers chosen for the following year were: J. Finley Wilson, Grand Exalted Ruler, Washington, D. C.; R. Adolph Howell, Grand Esteemed Leading Knight, New York, N. Y.; George W. Shafer, Grand Esteemed Loyal Knight, Louisville, Ky.; Alexander Braithwaite, Grand Esteemed Lecturing Knight, Newark, N. J.; George E. Bates, Grand Secretary, Newark, N. J.; James T. Carter, Grand Treasurer, Richmond, Va.; E. M. C. Richards, Grand Esquire, Newport, R. I.; Edward Green, Grand Inner Guard, Alexandria, Va.; James R. Wilson, Grand Tiler, Harrisburg, Pa.; Henry Lincoln Johnson, Grand Legal Adviser, Atlanta, Ga.; W. George Avant, Grand Chaplain, Franklinton, N. C.; Quincy J. Gilmore, Chairman, Grand Trustees, Kansas City, Mo.; George F. Hatton, Washington, D. C.; William H. Shands, Philadelphia, Pa., Grand Trustees; Grand Auditors, Dr. O. C. Clayborne, Savannah, Ga.; Thomas H. Browne, Connellsville, Pa.; William S. Moore, Boston, Mass.

Grants of aid were given to several organizations by this Grand Lodge. The National Association for the Advancement of Colored People was given $200.00, the National Urban League and the local Newark League were given $25.00 each. The proposal for a National Elks' Home was again referred to a committee. A resolution approving the Dyer Anti-Lynching Bill and urging its passage was approved. A resolution was proposed endorsing the plan to erect a monument in Washington, D. C., to the memory of Pietro Alonzo, "An eminent explorer of the Negro race" and pilot of the Nina on the Columbus voyage to the West. Nothing ever came of this proposal as it was not conclusively proved that Pietro Alonzo was a Negro. The *Fraternal Record* of Chicago, with Brother Gerald Jamison of Dearborn Lodge as editor, was made the official journal of the Grand Lodge, which was later described by the Grand Secretary as a real, live, healthy, up-to-date organ, regularly and promptly issued. The adoption of the new Constitution was regarded by the Grand Trustees as a remedy for friction and for the promotion of greater peace and harmony.

The Grand Officers were installed in an impressive manner by the Past Grand Exalted Ruler J. E. Mills. Then the Minutes concluded significantly, "Grand Exalted Ruler Wilson then assumed the chair." This was the first time that the record showed this conclusive statement. This was good description in this case, for a new era opened for the Improved Benevolent and Protective Order of Elks of the World after J. Finley Wilson assumed the chair.

Chapter X
The First Steps of the Master Builder

The Master Builder of Elkdom elected at the Grand Lodge of 1922 was J. Finley Wilson. Under his administration and direction continuing over a period of years the greatest number of lodges and members and the most remarkable development of Elk services were to take place. It is true that he had a good foundation upon which to build, but many poor buildings are erected on good foundations. However, a good building was erected by Grand Exalted Ruler Wilson upon the good foundation laid by his predecessors in the Grand Exalted Ruler's chair, B. F. Howard, William E. Atkins, J. E. Mills, J. Frank Wheaton, Harry H. Pace, T. Gillis Nutter, Armond W. Scott, George W. F. McMechen and George F. Wibecan.

Because of Grand Exalted Ruler Wilson's great contributions to the history of his Order, it is desirable that we should know something of his background. He was a native of Tennessee, born near Nashville, August 28, 1881. He was elected Grand Exalted Ruler on his forty-first birthday, August 28, 1922. He was the son of Rev. James L. and Nancy Wiley Wilson. He was educated in the public schools of Nashville, and was awarded the Doctor of Laws degree by Allen University. He had many experiences in reaching the zenith of his career as Grand Exalted Ruler, all of which seemed to make some contribution to his colorful leadership in Negro-life. He was, according to his own statement, "bell-boy, newsboy, boot-black, porter, hotel waiter, head waiter, cow-boy, miner, newspaper reporter, newspaper editor and publisher, and President of the Negro Press Association."

After leaving Nashville, he journeyed westward, working at periods in Kansas City, Missouri; Denver, Colorado; and in cities in Arizona, Wyoming, Utah and in Klondike, Alaska. Some of his Western adventures in ranching and mining were thrilling experiences for him, and gave him sympathy and understanding with all kinds of people. It is said that he once conducted a dance hall with Tex Richard in Nevada. In Salt Lake City, he edited the *Plaindealer*. Returning to the East, he worked as a reporter on the *Baltimore Times*, edited *The Washington Eagle*, and contributed to *The Norfolk Journal and Guide* and *The New York Age*.

His interest in Elkdom began at Norfolk, Virginia, where he acknowledged, according to his statement, "the supervision of

J. Finley Wilson, Tenth Grand Exalted Ruler, 1922-1952.

the late G.E.R., B. F. Howard and P.G.E.R., Dr. James E. Mills, at the first convention.'' He did not become active until 1903 in Mountain Lodge No. 39, Denver, Colorado; and Parker Lodge No. 24, Pueblo, Colorado. He was a delegate to the annual Grand Lodge session in 1904. He served either as Deputy or Grand Organizer under every Grand Exalted Ruler. It was his claim that as a Deputy, he ''made more lodges than any other Deputy.'' He was a member of the Peace Conference at Wilmington, Delaware, in 1910, and of the Union Conference at Washington, D. C. There can be no doubt that his calling was to Elkdom where his yearning for the common touch could reach more of the people and his desire for leadership could be satisfied with an organization which needed his forceful abilities. As a dynamic, courageous leader with an unusual personality and an intriguing friendliness, who could use picturesque, flowery language effectively, he became an attractive leader for the people who heard and willingly followed him.

The favorite word of J. Finley Wilson was ''forward,'' and when he was elected Grand Exalted Ruler in 1922, the command ''forward'' was heard by every lodge in the Order. The Grand Officers, the deputies and the rank and file of members put their shoulders to the wheel and the lodges began to move forward. Men of every station in life moved forward with him. Grand Secretary Bates said that ''college presidents, grand officers of kindred organizations, business men, and last, but not least, the horny-handed sons of toil have vied with each other in their eagerness to taste of the munificent benefits to be derived from membership in the Order.''

Grand Exalted Ruler J. Finley Wilson wanted the Order to expand to all available territories and to increase all lodge memberships. When he learned that an Oriental, Chu John, known as a millionaire hotel keeper and cafe owner had applied for membership in Imperial Lodge No. 127, he advised the District Deputy to admit Chu John, who after his initiation gave the lodge a certified check for $500 to make the first payment on its home.. In defending this position, Grand Exalted Ruler Wilson said that he had made this decision, ''remembering always that the Chinese represent a century-old civilization, number more than four hundred million people, control billions of wealth, were the discoverers of gunpowder, and further, that in these days of war and pestilence, it behooved the black man to make friends with all the sons of men—and still further, that in view of the fact that our organization is based upon the Christian religion, it should be our slogan, 'whosoever will, let him come' ''. At Cheyenne, Wyoming, another inquiry was raised concerning the initiation of a Japanese in a lodge to be instituted at Casper. The initiate was a Japanese merchant. Grand Exalted Ruler Wilson advised also to proceed with this initiation and "Brother Togo became one of the enthusiastic Elks of the nation."

When the question arose of the establishment of a lodge in the State of Tennessee, the Grand Exalted Ruler opened correspondence with the Governor of the State and the Secretary of the State. He made an engagement with the Governor and went to Nashville. He reported that the situation was discussed and in response to the Governor's question where the trouble began at first for the Order, Grand Exalted Ruler Wilson said that it was in New York although the work in Virginia and Kentucky had not been disturbed. Whereupon he reported Governor Austin Peay as saying, "Wilson, we are both Tennesseeans—and we are all Tennesseeans, whether black or white. You are quite right, when you say that if you died tomorrow you could not be buried in Tennessee with the rites of your Order. It shall be so no longer. While I am the Governor of Tennessee, no Yankees in New York, or in any other state, shall interfere with you here. I shall grant you a charter for this state, and you may be permitted to establish a lodge in any city or town you may desire, and can secure your quota of men—and I defy anybody to disturb you." The Grand Exalted Ruler was assisted in this work in Tennessee by Brother John T. Rhines, also a native of the state, who exercised similar diplomacy in the re-establishment of Elkdom in Tennessee, for there had been a lodge previously at Memphis.

This work of expansion was reported at the Twenty-Fourth Annual Meeting of the Grand Lodge at the Auditorium of the Avenue Theatre, Chicago, Ill., August 28-30, 1923, with Grand Exalted Ruler Wilson presiding. After the regular opening the Committee on Credentials reported and the committees were appointed. The parade was reported to be up to standard and the press stated that it was the longest and best of the parades held by any Negro organization in the city's history. The number of lodges represented in the convention was reported by the Committee on Credentials to be 257, an increase of 73 over 1922, with 622 delegates, an increase of 182 over the last year.

Grand Exalted Ruler Wilson stated in his annual report that while there had been a decrease of 7,000 members reported in 1922, he had issued proclamations and had traveled himself 50,000 miles in the interest of Elkdom within twelve months, without taking a single penny from the Grand Lodge. He said "as we traveled, Elk lodges sprang up everywhere." He traveled into the deep South and to the extremes of the Far West.

The record of lodges and members was very unusual, as a result of his work in cooperation with the deputies. The membership at the close of the Newark meeting in 1922 was 36,306, but at this 1923 meeting, the membership roll had reached 51,491, an increase of 15,185 or 40 per cent. There were eighty-five new lodges instituted during the year 1922-1923, and there had never been such a number created in one year in the history of the Order or any other among Negroes. Thirty-three Temples were also made during the year, which showed that the female branch of the organization was also growing rapidly. Protests were being made, however, that the law was not being observed in admission by some Temples, which had not restricted their membership as the law required to wives, mother, sisters, daughters and widows of Elks. Many of the lodges had large increases. These extended in number from Fort Dearborn Lodge in Chicago with 950 increase to Brooklyn Lodge, N. Y., with 200. There were nine Lodges with more than one thousand members and one lodge with over two thousand, Imperial Lodge of New York City.

There was no Negro fraternal organization which could boast of a larger membership than the Improved Benevolent and Protective Order of Elks of the World. As Grand Secretary Bates alleged, "the country is literally ablaze with Elkdom." In South Carolina, Arkansas, as well as Tennessee, the planting of the banner of Elkdom was in process. There were 340 lodges in the following states: Ohio 16, Virginia 37, Maryland 13, Pennsylvania 45, Missouri 5, Kentucky 8, Florida 5, New Jersey 27, Alabama 3, Massachusetts 9, North Carolina 38, Georgia 2, New York 21, West Virginia 20, Iowa 3, Colorado 6, California 5, Michigan 6, Nebraska 1, Indiana 6, Minnesota 3, Washington 3, Oregon 1, Tennessee 3, Louisiana 3, South Carolina 8, Arizona 2, Arkansas 1, Oklahoma 7, Wyoming 2, Nassau Bahamas 1, and Dominion of Canada 1. Pennsylvania had the largest number, 45, followed by North Carolina, Virginia and New Jersey. The Grand Exalted Ruler stated that there was another lodge started at Windsor, Canada, the first in Canada being Prince of Wales Lodge at Niagara, South Ontario and he said that there was one also in Monrovia, Liberia, West Africa.

The finances showed similar increases. The total balance with $10,000 in Liberty Bonds was $59,658.72, an increase of $10,-412.27, despite the fact that the per capita tax was reduced from fifty cents to twenty-five cents a year. The Grand Lodge adjourned at Newark the year before with a balance of $49,186.58. The Grand Lodge auditors reported that the total receipts for the year were $64,826.06. The Grand Lodge had gone forward in both numerical and financial ways. The increasing finances again led to the discussion of projects for a National Elks' Home.

It was inevitable that with this progress, there would be difficulty and criticism. Grand Exalted Ruler Wilson traveling by automobile was in an accident which dislocated his patella and confined him to bed for five weeks. The acts of kindness of the brethren during this period touched him deeply. In the midst of this illness, there was criticism and vilification, he said, which was published and would have done harm to the Order if there had not been supreme confidence in him. One criticism was that a Grand Exalted Ruler was wanted with "more dignity." Slander and gossip were said by the Grand Exalted Ruler to characterize the entire matter. His answer as to dignity was contained in his annual report when he referred to the growth of public esteem for the Order and the men of high quality who had become members.

He called attention to a few of these: "Perry W. Howard, Assistant Attorney-General of the United States; John D. Gainey, the biggest political appointee the railway mail service ever had; Prof. Silas Harris, President of the Negro Educational Congress; Bishop W. E. Chappelle of the A.M.E. Church; Fred. Ramer, Principal of the high school at Martinsburg, West Virginia; Dr. J. R. Wilson of Florence, South Carolina; Dr. Clark, President of Southern University, established by Governor P. B. S. Pinchback; Dr. Baranco of Baton Rouge; Hon. John L. Webb of Hot Springs, Arkansas; Dr. James E. Shepard, President of the National Training School at Durham, N. C.; C. C. Spaulding, President of the North Carolina Mutual Insurance Company; Dr. Rakes of Dover, Delaware; Major Milton T. Dean of Cheyenne, Wyoming, the ranking United States Officer of Colored forces on the Western front in the World War; Dr. Wiseman, Pastor of Avery Chapel, Columbia, South Carolina, the most noted preacher in that section; Dr. Ratcliffe, wholesale druggist of the same city; Dr. Eaves, surgeon of Hot Springs; Dr. Wade of the Pythian Bathhouse fame; Dr. J. C. Hill, who pastors the largest colored church in Hot Springs during the winter, and the second largest for white people in Toronto, Canada during the summer — now Chaplain of Vapor City Lodge. Nothing could be plainer than that the dignity of the Order is rapidly being elevated."

Resolutions were adopted by this Grand Lodge expressing the views of the Order on questions affecting its members. The first of these resolutions urged the suppression of mob violence, and this was not requested for Negroes alone but for all people in the United States. It was resolved that the Grand Lodge mem-

Daughter Nora Taylor, Third Grand Daughter Ruler, 1923

bers were ready to defend the Constitution, their citizenship and homes with every dollar and every drop of blood. An address to the country affirmed allegiance to the flag, requested Congress to continue wise regulations on immigration and to encourage the employment of American labor, condemned all organizations practicing overthrow of law such as the Ku Klux Klan and urged the suppression of them, condemned the crime of lynching, demanded the enforcement of the Fourteenth and Fifteenth Amendments and declared that if segregation would be established through a Government Hospital for colored soldiers at Tuskegee, Alabama they were confident that there were colored men capable and qualified to manage this institution. A National Home for the aged, needy and sick members of the Order was again proposed, a committee was appointed, an appropriation of twenty thousand dollars was authorized as a first payment on the property and approval was made by the Grand Lodge. The property was in the State of Pennsylvania and was described by Brother Edward W. Henry of O. V. Catto Lodge No. 20, Philadelphia, Pa.

The results of the election were the following officers for 1923-1924: J. Finley Wilson, Grand Exalted Ruler, Washington, D. C.; John R. Marshall, Grand Esteemed Leading Knight, Chicago, Ill.; H. H. Hucle, Grand Esteemed Loyal Knight, Gary, Ind.; Emmett R. Chainey, Grand Esteemed Lecturing Knight, Seattle, Wash.; George E. Bates, Grand Secretary, Newark, N. J.; James T. Carter, Grand Treasurer, Richmond, Va.; George Rideout, Grand Inner Guard, Baltimore, Md.; John W. Johnson, Grand Tiler, Indianapolis, Ind.; Henry Lincoln Johnson, Grand Legal Adviser, Atlanta, Ga.; W. George Avant, Grand Chaplain, Franklinton, N. C.; Edward Green, Grand Master of Social Sessions, Alexandria, Va.; J. M. Avery, Grand Organist, Durham, N. C.; George F. Hatton, Washington, D. C.; William H. Shands, Philadelphia, Pa.; C. Tiffany Tolliver, Roanoke, Va., Grand Trustees; O. C. Clayborne, Savannah, Ga.; Thomas H. Browne, Connellsville, Pa.; William S. Moore, Boston, Mass., Grand Auditors. The installation of these officers was performed by Past Grand Exalted Ruler Mills in ritualistic form.

The Grand Temple in session at this time elected Daughter Nora Taylor Grand Daughter Ruler, but she died twelve days afterwards. Grand Vice Daughter Ruler Laura E. Williams took her place. She served until 1926 when Daughter Ella G. Berry was elected. The year 1926 was a banner year for the Temples for the Child Welfare Department was created with Daughter Ethel Frazer as chairman and eighty-eight temples were made.

Daughter Laura E. Williams, Fourth Grand Daughter Ruler, 1923-1926

During the next year after the 1923 Grand Lodge, considerable opposition developed to the purchase of the Pennsylvania property for a National Elks' Home. The Grand Legal Adviser, Henry Lincoln Johnson, was so disturbed over the matter that he suggested that it should be held in abeyance until a referendum could be had and the results reported to the next Grand Lodge session. The referendum was participated in by 218 lodges, a minority number, with 149 voting for the purchase and 69 against. Nothing was done toward the consummation of the purchase as a result of this report. The price of $70,000 had been set for the property, but before these negotiations had been completed, the property had been sold for $100,000, which ended the discussion of its purchase by the Elks.

HENRY LINCOLN JOHNSON, Grand Legal Adviser, 1922-1925.

Immediately following the Grand Lodge of 1923, the Grand Exalted Ruler was called to Wisconsin as there was a developing obstacle in Milwaukee to the establishment of a lodge there. The B.P.O.E., Grand Exalted Ruler did not want the lodge of I.B.P.O.E. of W., instituted in this state. Grand Exalted Ruler Wilson held a conference with him, and finally agreement was reached after questions were raised about the word "Improved," to which Brother Wilson replied that this referred to "territorial expansion" while their lodge confined itself to "white Americans between the Oceans." Almost the same interpretation was given to the question, "of the World," and its meaning. Grand Exalted Ruler Wilson replied, "when the gavel sounded in New York to open the lodge, the boys were saying the 11 o'clock toast in Bermuda, and the relatives of Brother Chu John and Harry Joe in the Celestial Empire and in the Kingdom of the Mikado were arising in the morning from their slumbers. That while the toast was being said in New York, President King was sounding the gavel for his cabinet meeting in Monrovia in the Republic of Liberia. And therefore I believed we were of the world."

These replies, and the good humor back of them, seemed to satisfy his questioners. The lodge was set up at Milwaukee with 350 paid members, and 297 present. This was the largest lodge set up in the history of the Order.

During the first part of August, Grand Exalted Ruler Wilson made the journey to Cuba, where he met the Mayor of Havana and the first Exalted Ruler of El Moro Castle Lodge No. 525. There were thirty men who were initiated including former President Menocal, the Chief of Police, Senator Gomez and other dignitaries. This lodge in Cuba was a significant step in the history of the Order.

These steps in expansion were continued in various places in the United States. This country seemed to be taken by a storm of Elkdom. The Grand Exalted Ruler was inspired and the Deputies were enthusiastic. When the Grand Lodge assembled in 1924, it was reported that there was an addition of one hundred and twelve lodges, an unprecedented number of new lodges. It was also a matter of record that the first Drill Patrol was organized in Lighthouse Lodge No. 9 on March 23, 1923. The patrols were features of subsequent parades.

The Twenty-Fifth Annual Meeting, the Silver Anniversary session, of the Grand Lodge convened in Central Baptist Church, August 26-29, 1924, at Pittsburgh, Pa. Grand Exalted Ruler J. Finley Wilson called the session to order and appointed assistants to the regular officers. The convention was organized and the Committee on Credentials was appointed with Committees on Grand Lodge Degrees, Fraternal Greetings, Press, Law and Revision, Appeals and Grievances, State of the Country, Resolutions, Charity, Obituary, Mileage and Per Diem. The parade formed shortly afterwards. It was praised by onlookers. The color scheme of purple and white made it a beautiful presentation, as newspapers stated. The public session was held with Brother Robert Vann of the *Pittsburgh Courier* presiding.

After the ritualistic service, the Grand Lodge opened for business on its second day. There were so many delegates and visitors present that it was necessary to use a rope for a dividing line between them. The Grand Legal Adviser, Henry Lincoln Johnson, was the first to report. His report included no major problems. In closing the report he congratulated the Grand Exalted Ruler referring to him as "our Mighty Chieftain—our Little Captain," "our Little Phil Sheridan," and to his ceaseless journeys to every part of the country and abroad, in his dissemination of Elkdom. He described a threat to the Grand Exalted Ruler when he was returning northward in a drawing-room on a pullman car. A group of Southerners attempted to break into his Drawing Room but he displayed such courage with his "blue-steel trusty forty-five, that he and his bride were not disturbed." Grand Legal Adviser Johnson then added, "God grant that the day will come when leaders generally will follow the example of J. Finley Wilson and give to the oppressed Negroes of this country the beautiful lesson of self-defense, although numbers prevail against them."

A delegation from the Grand Temple was admitted for their annual visit. Brother Ceruti presented Madam Daisy Henderson of Forest Temple No. 9 of Washington, D. C., who then presented Daughter Georgia Tucker of Ocean City Temple No. 23 of Atlantic City, N. J. After appropriate remarks she presented a beautiful shaving set to Grand Exalted Ruler Wilson. His interest was constantly manifested in the Temples. He always reminded the lodges that it was important for them to form auxiliaries of the women. Past Grand Exalted Ruler Armond W. Scott was also presented with a token for his services to Elkdom. Past Grand Exalted Ruler Nutter responded fittingly. The Temples had experienced great success this year, for they had instituted sixty new Temples.

The next reports were made by the Grand Secretary Bates and Grand Treasurer Carter. These reports showed increases in membership and finances. The total increase in members was 15,117, and the total membership had reached 66,608, with 112 new lodges. There were only seven states in which there were no lodges, North Dakota, South Dakota, Montana, New Mexico, Maine, New Hampshire and Vermont. Lodges were reported in forty states. The real estate owned by the lodges had increased to over a million dollars. Imperial Lodge No. 127, New York City, had dedicated a $200,000 home, which was described as the finest and most commodious of any owned by the Order. Other lodges also had fine homes. The total cash surplus with Liberty Bonds was $73,928.42, an increase of $17,859.96 over 1923. According to the report of the Committee on Credentials, there were 322 lodges represented in the convention, an increase of 55 over last year, with 760 delegates, and an increase of 138 over the previous year.

The Grand Exalted Ruler's report dealt with the Wisconsin situation and the pledge that he had kept that he would have 100 new lodges but instead there were 125 and he said that there would be forty new Temples but instead there were sixty. He described El Moro Lodge, the Fidelity Fund of a million dollars which he was undertaking to raise, Expansion, Dispensations Granted, Work of the Deputies, Growth in Public Estimation, The Virgin Islands, Necrology, Filling the Breach, Cabinet and

Deputies. An effort to elect him by acclamation just after his report was ruled out of order.

After other reports, Brother W. C. Hueston was recognized, and, as the Minutes state, "in rich oratorical language nominated J. Finley Wilson to succeed himself as Grand Exalted Ruler." This was seconded by Brother Arthur J. Riggs of Prince Humby Lodge No. 469 of Springfield, Ohio, who was one of the founders. Past Grand Exalted Ruler George E. Wibecan was placed in nomination. On the balloting the vote was Wilson 698 and Wibecan 52, whereupon the latter moved that the election of Brother Wilson be made unanimous.

The Grand Officers elected at this time were: J. Finley Wilson, Grand Exalted Ruler, Washington, D. C.; John R. Marshall, Grand Esteemed Leading Knight, Washington, D. C.; F. H. Watkins, Grand Esteemed Loyal Knight, Washington, D. C.; George E. Bates, Grand Secretary, Newark, N. J.; James T. Carter, Grand Treasurer, Richmond, Va.; Joseph Brown, Grand Esquire, New York City; George W. A. Scarville, Grand Inner Guard, Paterson, N. J.; J. Walter Stafford, Grand Tiler, Wilmington, Del.; Carlos C. Valle, Grand Organizer, New York, N. Y., and Durham, N. C.; Henry Lincoln Johnson, Grand Legal Adviser, Washington, D. C.; W. George Avant, Grand Chaplain, Durham, N. C.; William H. Shands, Philadelphia, Pa.; C. Tiffany Tolliver, Roanoke, Va.; Edward F. Berry, Chicago, Ill., Grand Trustee; O. C. Clayborne, Gary, Ind.; Edward W. Henry, Philadelphia, Pa.; Littleton McDuff, Los Angeles, Calif. Grand Auditors. Seven Past Grand Exalted Rulers were present, William E. Atkins, Hampton, Va.; James E. Mills, Norfolk, Va.; Harry H. Pace, New York City; T. Gillis Nutter, Charleston, West Va.; Armond W. Scott, Washington, D. C.; George W. F. McMechen, Baltimore, Md.; and George E. Wibecan, Brooklyn, N. Y.

It was resolved that the *Fraternal Record*, having served the lodges as their "mouth-piece" for over two years, each lodge should pay two dollars a year as subscription, and in return the *Record* was to publish in each issue the official roster and send two issues to each lodge. Major N. Clark Smith who had conducted the annual band contest for the past three years was appointed official Bandmaster and supervisor of music for the next Grand Lodge meeting. The gavel used by Past Grand Exalted Ruler J. Frank Wheaton was accepted by Grand Exalted Ruler Wilson.

An address to the country was issued by the Grand Lodge urging loyalty to the nation, good relations between the races, enactment of the Dyer Antilynching Bill, the condemnation of all religious and racial intolerance, commendation of the

N.A.A.C.P., alignment of Negro workers with organized labor, commendation of President Coolidge and the emulation of the cardinal principles of the Order.

The historical question of the copyright of the manual and ritual of the I.B.P.O.E. of W., was again presented to the Grand Lodge of 1925 by the report of the Special Committee on Revision of Ritualistic Work. On November 29, 1924, the Committee, Brothers J. E. Mills, Armond W. Scott, Harry H. Pace, James M. Harrison and J. P. Quander, Jr., met in New York City to hear the claim of John Patterson for compensation for copyright of the Elks' manual. Mr. Patterson claimed that he was rightfully entitled to the control of the copyright, as he had rendered service in consideration of its assignment to him. He asserted that the contractual relations between the Howard faction and himself had been subsequently ratified by the I.B.P.O.E. of W., through the consolidation of the Howard and Wheaton factions. He suggested that the Grand Lodge take over this copyright and make payment to him for his claim and fee of fifteen thousand dollars, which had been fixed by Past Grand Exalted Ruler Howard and the controllers of the Howard faction.

When asked for the specific basis of his claim he asked his Counsel to state it. His Counsel said that the copyright and assignment were matters of record and that he was authorized to present the claims. He directed attention to the case in the Federal Court of the Eastern District of Virginia in 1910 by James E. Mills against J. Frank Wheaton and the Master's decision that the copyright was the common property of the public. The Counsel contended that subsequent amendments had changed this situation so that a judical decision could not impair proprietary rights in a copyright. This was by Acts of Congress in 1909, 1912, and 1914.

After hearing the case the committee concluded:

1. That Judge Waddell of the United States Court for the Eastern District of Virginia, in or about the year 1910 decided that the said claimants had no exclusive right to use the said ritual or to share the fruits from the sale of the same, and no proprietary interest therein, that the I.B.P.O.E. of W. had a common right in and to the said ritual and could not and should not be disturbed in the quiet and useful enjoyment of the same. The decision of Mr. Justice Waddell will more fully appear by reference to the Minutes of the Grand Lodge of 1911.

2. That even if the claimants had any rights under the said ritual, they had failed within reasonable time to assert the

same in a court of competent jurisdiction and continuously acquiesced in the use of it by the I.B.P.O.E. of W.

This report was made to the Twenty-Sixth Annual Meeting of the Grand Lodge in Rayo Theater, Richmond, Va., August 25-29, 1925. This session was the farthest South of any Grand Lodge sessions, Baltimore, Maryland, Washington, D. C., and Wilmington, Delaware having previously served as host cities. The Committee on Credentials' report showed that the Richmond Convention was the largest of all Grand Lodge sessions with 401 lodges represented and 839 delegates. All seven of the past living Grand Exalted Rulers were present, Atkins, Mills, Pace, Nutter, Scott, McMechen and Wibecan. There were also present Arthur J. Riggs of Springfield, Ohio and Frank H. Hunter of St. Louis, Missouri, who were made Honorary Past Grand Exalted Rulers because of the work which they had done in the founding of the Order. The parade of the Elks and Daughter Elks was regarded as "the most picturesque and beautiful in the annals of the Order." The uniformed marching clubs and leading bands received the continuous applause of the spectators all along the way of the parade. This demonstration in the Capital of the Confederacy was so impressive that the far-off *New York Times* carried the following boxed column on its front page:

> *60 bands head 20,000 Negroes in Elk Parade in Richmond,* August 25, 1925—Sixty brass bands blared the marching time for upward of twenty thousand uniformed Negro Elks today as the largest parade of Negroes in the history of Richmond winded down Monument Avenue.
>
> Eighty thousand Negroes watched the parade from places of vantage along the line. Every state and several foreign countries were represented among the marchers.

The prominent visitors included the Governor of the State, Dr. R. R. Moten, President of Tuskegee Institute, the Mayor of Richmond, Mayor Allen Washington of Hampton Institute. Judge W. C. Hueston introduced Dr. Moten to the Grand Lodge who said that this Order of Elks was the most progressive of all fraternities and that he was proud to have been a member for seven years. He also stated that the wonderful parade the previous day would do more to cement the good relationship between the two races than anything transpiring lately.

Difficulties which Grand Exalted Ruler Wilson had had with several lodges over the recognition of the authority of the Grand Exalted Ruler occupied a considerable part of the report of the Grand Legal Adviser. He found evidences of lack of loyalty to Elkdom during the past year and that some were forgetful of their vows. But what could be expected of an organization which had grown so rapidly and had taken in so many who were not acquainted with the history and tradition of the Order. There were many who did not know its laws and others took advantage of its weaknesses. He said, "our Order is not composed of the Negro lowest down, nor is it composed of the Negro highest up, but thank God, it is composed of the average men and women of the race which makes it truly representative of the Negro racial group in this country."

The Grand Secretary showed that there had been an increase in members from 66,608 in 1924 to 72,171 in 1925, but there were many lodges which had not yet reported when he closed his books. There were seventy-four new lodges and sixty-five new Temples. In 1924, he said that there was the sum of $69,290.70 in cash and bonds and the next year this had increased to $83,695.31. State associations had been holding sessions, and he quoted the law for these meetings. The law for juveniles was read by the Grand Secretary, that "The Juvenile Class of the I.B.P.O.E. of W., as now constituted shall be entirely under the supervision of the Grand Temple and the Grand Temple shall have full authority to make laws, not in conflict with this constitution, to govern said Juvenile Class."

The conclusion of the Grand Secretary's report was an appeal for the Elks to get closer together, to construct a program of value to the race, establish a National Legislative Bureau in Washington to fight racial legislation in conjunction with the N.A.A.C.P., create scholarships for worthy youth of the race, aid to hospitals, and in various ways to make Elkdom the synonym for racial service.

The Grand Exalted Ruler's report gave a wide coverage of his relationships with subordinate lodges and the growth of the Order. He claimed no special credit but with the work of the deputies the Order had more than doubled in size in three years. He said that the Order was only a skeleton in the South three years ago and there were injunctions in Georgia, Arkansas, South Carolina, Texas, Tennessee and Louisiana. Said he, "now, after we have interceded with the governing powers in those states, by common consent not only may we operate in them all, but we have made it possible for other colored organizations to operate." This growth was represented also by the dedication of fifty-two homes and the burning of fifty mortgages. He listed again the growth of the Order in public esteem as evidenced by types of members enrolled and good will generated by local lodges. He concluded that "we must go on and on, around the world, and those who stand today in the path of progress must be swept aside, so that we may go onward and upward to the supreme heights of glory."

The Daughter Elks at the session of their Grand Temple in Bethel A.M.E. Church had adopted the program for the organization of the Purple Cross Nurses Units. This was one of the historic moments, for these units have developed their services in various communities. With the background of this work behind them, the Daughter Elks sent a delegation to extend fraternal greetings to the Grand Lodge, and again through Daughter Ella G. Berry, Vice Grand Daughter Ruler, they requested that the law be changed confining their membership to relatives of Elks. The delegation presented the Grand Exalted Ruler with a traveling bag. Brother Thomas H. Browne and the Grand Exalted Ruler responded.

When the time for election arrived, Brother William C. Hueston, it was said, "in a burst of real eloquence placed the name of Brother Finley Wilson in nomination to succeed himself." J. Dalmus Steele and T. B. Watkins were nominated. The ballots resulted in Wilson 423, Steele 134 and Watkins 60. The re-election of Grand Exalted Ruler Wilson was then conceded, and he was declared elected. The Grand Secretary's election showed in the balloting, Bates 387 and Harry H. Pace 100, and the former was declared elected. The Grand Treasurer, James T. Carter was re-elected by acclamation. Others elected were: Dr. S. H. George, Grand Esteemed Leading Knight, Paducah, Ky.; Dr. Roland R. Johnson, Grand Esteemed Lecturing Knight, Brooklyn, N. Y.; Joseph Brown, Grand Esquire, New York City; Sidney B. Thompson, Grand Inner Guard, Cleveland, Ohio; A. B. Grasty, Grand Tiler, Welch, West Va.; Carlos C. Valle, Grand Organizer, Newark, N. J.; Perry W. Howard, Grand Legal Adviser, Washington, D. C.; W. George Avant, Grand Chaplain, Durham, N. C.; Grand Trustees: C. Tiffany Tolliver, Roanoke, Va.; Edward F. Berry, Chicago, Ill.; and R. E. Pharrow, Atlanta, Ga.; Grand Auditors: Littleton McDuff, Los Angeles, Calif.; H. A. M. Johns, Lynchburg, Va.; E. H. Copeland, Winston-Salem, N. C.

Several important actions established historical precedents and milestones for the Order in 1925. One of these was the adoption of the Report of the Committee on Law and Revision making the *Washington Eagle* the official organ of the Grand Lodge. Each lodge was to pay two dollars, annual subscription, and in return the paper would publish such official publications and documents as would be needed in the judgment of the Grand Exalted Ruler and Grand Secretary. This resolution was reported from Gibralter Lodge No. 461, Kingstree, South Carolina, to the Grand Lodge and was adopted.

This Convention of the Grand Lodge terminating the first year of the administration of J. Finley Wilson as Grand Exalted Ruler, revealed the first steps in a program of ideas and visions which would give definite advancement to the Grand Lodge and the subordinate lodges. The watchword, "Forward," was passed from one to another of the Antlered Herd, and the march toward great heights for the organization had begun. The travels of the Grand Exalted Ruler were far and wide. Wherever he went new life appeared among the lodges. Their attendance and activities were increased by his appearances. The fellowship of each lodge was expanded. Its purpose of charity was given stimulus and its patriotism was enlivened. Grand Exalted Ruler Wilson brought together men of widely different views and of varied political opinions under the tent of Elkdom. His great showmanship helped to dramatize his ultimate purposes for the Order, as he undertook his first steps not only as a builder but as a master-builder.

Chapter XI

Builders of Education, Health and Civil Liberties

Important historical actions which were of great significance to the future of the Improved Benevolent and Protective Order of Elks were the adoptions of resolutions establishing a permanent interest of the Order in education through its own Department of Education, a survey of Negro Health and a Department of Civil Liberties. There were incidental references to the cause of education in the Grand Lodge sessions of earlier years but the great step in this direction was taken in the Grand Lodge of 1925, when a resolution was adopted, a department of education established and Judge William C. Hueston elected as Commissioner of Education.

The man who was more responsible than any other one person for the launching of this educational program was William C. Hueston. He was born in Lexington, Kentucky, was educated in its public schools, the University of Chicago, received the Bachelor of Laws degree from the University of Kansas, and was awarded the honorary degree of Doctor of Laws by Wilberforce University. He began the practice of law immediately after graduation and also the manifestation of interest in Elkdom. He served in public office as magistrate in Gary, Indiana; Assistant Solicitor of the U. S. Post Office Department, Washington, D. C., and as President of the National Negro Baseball League. Despite the busy activities of his legal practice and the public offices which he held, his abiding interests were in the Improved Benevolent and Protective Order of Elks of the World and in an educational program through which it might serve youth. His friendship and association with J. Finley Wilson were factors which contributed to the greater building of the services of the Order to the people whom it served.

At the 1925 Grand Lodge session, the resolution establishing the Department of Education was introduced. This resolution was submitted by Brother W. C. Hueston, who was the founder and later efficient and capable Commissioner of Education for many years. This resolution was as follows:

> Be it enacted by I.B.P.O.E. of W. represented in the Grand Lodge:

JUDGE WILLIAM C. HUESTON, Commissioner of Education in 1925

That WHEREAS, the most needful thing for the advancement of the American Negro is Education,

And WHEREAS, our Order stands primarily for the improvement of the human race, and more particularly for those of the Negro Race,

And WHEREAS, it is apparent that a passion for Education must be instilled in the youth of our Race,

And WHEREAS, it is well known to us that there are many capable young men and women, who are denied Educational Opportunity because of insufficient means,

And WHEREAS, it is absolutely necessary that it must be plain that the American Negro appreciate the wonderful generosity of those who are not of our group, but who notwithstanding this fact are contributing in some instances by the millions to Negro Education,

And WHEREAS, owing to our individual lack of large means, we are unable as individuals to give large sums of money for Education,

THEREFORE BE IT RESOLVED:

That the I.B.P.O.E. of W., in this Grand Lodge assembled, create and establish a department of Education under the following terms and circumstances:

(1) There shall be and is hereby established the department of Education of the I.B.P.O.E. of W.

(2) Said department shall be operated and controlled by a Board of Education composed of the Grand Exalted Ruler, Grand Secretary, the three Grand Lodge Trustees and a Commissioner of Education who shall be Secretary of the Board and who shall be elected by the Grand Lodge annually.

(3) That it shall be the duty of the Board of Education to provide Scholarships for deserving Negro youth in the various Schools of Higher and Secondary Education, giving preference as far as possible to those who are children of parents who are members of this Order, it being fully understood, however, that scholarships may be granted to deserving students who are not members of our Order,

(4) That said Board of Education shall at the first meeting provide Rules and Regulations for the government thereof. Said rules when published shall stand as the governing Law of the said Board. The Grand Lodge, however, when in session shall have the right to revise, or abrogate said rules, and provide others in their stead or place.

(5) It shall be the general duty of the Commissioner of Education subject to the approval of the Board of Education to arrange scholarships in the various Schools of the Country and to recommend after careful investigation persons for said Scholarships distributing them as far possible in the various Sections where our lodges are located, and to do such other things as the rules of the Department may require of him.

(6) In order to provide funds necessary to the granting of

Scholarships in this Article herein provided, be it enacted that every Subordinate Lodge shall pay annually into the Education Fund Sixty ($.60) Cents for every member carried on its rolls. This amount shall be paid in Quarterly installments of Fifteen ($.15) Cents on or before the 15th day of the months of October, January, April and July of each year. The failure of any lodge to make such payments when due shall deprive said lodge of its rights to receive the quarterly password and of representation in the Grand Lodge.

(7) The Education Fund when collected shall be immediately turned over by the Grand Secretary to the Grand Treasurer and shall be deposited separately from other funds of the Grand Lodge to be paid out on the order of the Board of Education, said Checks to be countersigned by the Grand Exalted Ruler and the Commissioner of Education.

(8) The Board of Education through its proper officers shall present a printed report of all of its undertakings annually to the Grand Lodge.

Submitted by W. C. Hueston. Approved and adopted by Lake City Lodge No. 182, Gary, Indiana.

H. H. Hucle, Exalted Ruler
C. C. Norris, Secretary

This resolution marked the rise of an interest in education under the leadership of Judge William C. Hueston which was to be maintained in constantly increasing proportions. Scholarships were to be awarded. Contests were to develop friendly rivalries and unmeasurable good was to be accomplished as the people heard the oratorical contests of their youth. This was one of the great steps approved by Grand Exalted Ruler Wilson, the Master-Builder, and initiated by his long-time friend and co-worker, Brother William C. Hueston, who was himself a master-builder in the field of the educational interests of the Improved Benevolent and Protective Order of Elks of the World. He was appointed by the Grand Exalted Ruler to head this department after the Grand Lodge of 1925 had closed and began his work with enthusiasm directly after the close of the convention. The election of Grand Officers had taken place prior to the enactment of the legislation for the department. The death of Brother Henry Lincoln Johnson, Grand Legal Adviser, made it necessary for Judge Hueston to serve temporarily in this capacity. In October, 1926, he began to carry on the duties of Commissioner of Education. The Grand Exalted Ruler constituted the Board of Education to include the Grand Trustees, the Grand Secretary, the Grand Treasurer, the Commissioner and the Grand Exalted Ruler.

Emphasis was given to his endeavors by the Proclamation of

Grand Exalted Ruler Wilson, January 1, 1926. He said, "The Commissioner of Education, W. C. Hueston, has rung the school bell, and invaded the realms of ignorance. He fired the first volley of his attack just before Christmas and promises to keep up the drive from now until next August. He has dedicated himself to the proposition and will be a relentless foe of the Monster that is holding our people in darkness and slavery."

The establishment of this Department of Education was praised by such newspapers as *The Afro-American, The Chicago Defender, The Pittsburgh Courier, The Afro-American, The Kansas City Call* and others. Letters poured into the Grand offices congratulating the Order on taking this advanced step in assisting the educational movement among Negroes. This activity was at once one of the most popular movements undertaken by any fraternal organization.

The First Bulletin, No. 1, was issued by Commissioner of Education Hueston on December 12, 1925, and was sent to the secretary of each lodge. It contained a full statement of the objectives of the Department of Education. The lodges were requested to acquaint the temples with these purposes since scholarships would be granted to females as well as males. Four communications were sent by mail to each lodge with correspondence to individuals. The Commissioner stated that "the response in many instances was wonderful." The educational program was endorsed at the Council of Bishops of the African Methodist Episcopal Church at New Orleans on February 18, 1926.

In order to arouse interest and organize the lodges and temples for an effective program, the week of April 11, 1926, was set apart and designated as "Elks First Educational Week." A suggested program was sent out to the lodges. On Sunday, April 11, they were requested to send speakers representing the Elks to the churches. On Monday, committees were requested to visit the public and private schools to encourage pupils to remain in school through high school and if possible to enter college. Visits were to be made on Tuesday to public school authorities to discuss the improvement of unsatisfactory conditions in school systems and to commend the good conditions. Wednesday and Thursday were survey days and contact days with parents concerning out of school children and the problems of parents in relation to their children. On Friday, the lodges with the cooperation of the temples were to give public entertainments, the net proceeds of which were to go into the Scholarship Fund. In spite of handicaps, this period of activity during Educational Week was regarded as "a great success."

The Twenty-Seventh Annual Meeting of the Grand Lodge assembled in the Auditorium of the Mt. Zion Congregational Church, Cleveland, Ohio, August 24, 1926. Following the usual opening ceremonies, the committees were appointed. The Grand Lodge adjourned for the parade, which was carried out, it was said, with precision and grace. The report of the Committee on Credentials showed that there were 527 lodges with 965 delegates in attendance. These figures revealed that there was an increase of 118 lodges and 120 delegates over the attendance and representation at the Richmond Grand Lodge in 1925.

The membership report by the Grand Secretary had reached 82,069. He admitted that it was becoming a difficult matter to give an exact account of the membership because all of the lodges did not report in time to be included in the Grand Secretary's annual report. The real estate holdings of the lodges approximated $1,500,000, the death benefits paid by the lodges totalled $89,101.67, the sick benefits were $76,466.54 and the charity distributed amounted to $27,811.11. The total receipts of the Grand Lodge for the year 1925-1926 were:

Grand Lodge Tax	$29,584.35
Educational Tax	14,818.18
New Lodges	12,550.00
Supplies	4,778.76
Total	$61,731.29

The Grand Treasurer, J. T. Carter, reported that there was a cash balance in the General Fund of $85,474.32, and a total balance of $101,969.91. These reports were evidences of the expansion and advancement of the Order. Grand Exalted Ruler Wilson said that the Order of Elkdom had experienced "the most glorious year in all its hstory." New lodges were instituted in Puerto Rico, Panama, Kingston, Jamaica, Costa Rica and cities in Canada. The Grand Lodge was so pleased with these reports that the Grand Officers were congratulated. Grand Exalted Ruler Wilson was "the Napoleon of Fraternal Organizations." Grand Sec-

C. C. VALLE, Grand Organizer

PERRY W. HOWARD, Grand Legal Adviser, 1925.

retary Bates was "the hero of the old and new Elks of our beloved Order" and Grand Treasurer Carter was "our trusty Treasurer and Financier."

The complete story of this expansion was presented by the Grand Exalted Ruler and the Grand Organizer Brother C. C. Valle. Brother Wilson had traveled widely — more than 80,000 miles, he said, and he had many experiences in transportation. Accidents occurred and he was in the hospital for periods due to automobile injuries. He had been presented with a Buick car by the Grand Lodge and traveled extensively in it, and at other times he had traveled in cars owned by members of the Order, as well as on trains. The Committee on Grand Officers' Reports commended the Grand Exalted Ruler for his visits to foreign territories and expressed pleasure at seeing the number of delegates from Puerto Rico, Panama, Cuba, Canada and other Latin-American countries.

His report stressed the importance of the Fidelity Fund, which he had presented to the Richmond convention. Through this idea he had planned to raise a million dollars and the fund would be used for a home for the aged, a national shrine and an endowment for the benefit of widows and orphans. Consideration should be given, he said, also to the Education Fund to provide for scholarships. This fund was raised through a 15 cents per capita tax on the quarterly basis.

After this report the election was held with the results that the following were selected: J. Finley Wilson, Grand Exalted Ruler, Washington, D. C.; Dr. S. H. George, Grand Esteemed Leading Knight, Paducah, Ky.; Leonard Foreman, Grand Esteemed Loyal Knight, Akron, Ohio; Dr. Roland R. Johnson, Grand Esteemed Lecturing Knight, Brooklyn, N. Y.; George E. Bates, Grand Secretary, Newark, N. J.; James T. Carter, Grand Treasurer, Richmond, Va.; William A. Turner, Grand Esquire, Wheeling, West Va.; C. E. A. Starr, Grand Inner Guard, Denver, Colo.; French

Dr. Roland R. Johnson, Grand Esteemed Lecturing Knight

Gillison, Grand Tiler, Hartford, Conn.; William C. Hueston, Commissioner of Education, Gary, Ind.; Carlos C. Valle, Grand Organizer, Newark, N. J.; Perry W. Howard, Grand Legal Adviser, Washington, D. .; W. George Avant, Grand Trustees, David Cardwell, John R. Marshall, Wayman Wilkerson; Grand Auditors, Floyd C. Payne, A. C. Cannal, Jr., H. A. M. Johns.

Several propositions were adopted by the Grand Lodge. One provided that in cities having 50,000 or more Negroes, there could be only two lodges, except where there are now more than two. It was also provided that in cities with two or more lodges, it would be lawful to institute one Temple of Daughter Elks for each lodge so organized. Five Grand Trustees instead of three were approved. Authorization was given to the celebration of the "birthday anniversaries" of Crispus Attucks, Frederick Douglass and Paul Laurence Dunbar. Discrimination in the government departments was attacked by resolution and President Calvin Coolidge was called upon to terminate it. A committee of six physicians and a statistician were authorized for appointment by the Grand Exalted Ruler to make a study of the infant death rate among Negroes. This resolution indicated a trend toward the reappearance of the work of the Grand Medical Director who had served the Order in earlier years.

HISTORY
OF THE
ELKS OF THE WORLD
BY
ARTHUR J. RIGGS
Past Grand Exalted Ruler
First Edition
May, 1926
Title Page of Pamphlet-History of the Elks of the World by Arthur J. Riggs, May, 1926.

Another resolution commended Commissioner of Education Hueston for the showing of his department and for "the wise step taken in adding this feature to our splendid Order, as it means so much for the organization." Brown's *Brief History* was noted and a proper cipher was authorized. The organization of Pullman Porters as the Brotherhood of Sleeping Car Porters was unqualifiedly endorsed and the members of the Order were requested to give every possible aid to this organization. The place of the meeting of the next Grand Lodge was New York City.

Two publications were of significance during this period. One of these, a forty-two page pamphlet edition was announced of Arthur J. Riggs' *History of the Elks of the World*, publication endorsed by the Grand Lodge held at Richmond, Va., August, 1925. The second was by Daughter Emma V. Kelley, the Grand Secretary of the Daughters, who wrote and published a small pamphlet of seventy-two pages with the title, *Kelley's History of the Daughters of I.B.P.O.E. of W.* These publications were hailed by the Elk brothers and sisters.

The selection of New York City for the next Grand Lodge session was the cause of much controversy throughout the remainder of 1926 and the first part of 1927. It was rumored directly after the Cleveland Grand Lodge that efforts would be made to change the meeting to another city. The movement grew so widespread that Grand Exalted Ruler Wilson appointed a committee of lawyers to go to Albany, New York. A resolution was adopted by the Grand Trustees directing the Grand Exalted Ruler to notify the lodges in New York that the court injunction against the Order would have to be vacated on or before June 15 or he would call the Grand Lodge to assemble elsewhere.

Title Page of Emma V. Kelley's History of the Daughters of I.B.P.O.E. of W., 1926

This discussion then mounted and the newspapers took up the presentation of the matter. The New York Elks served the Grand Exalted Ruler, the Grand Secretary and the Grand Treasurer with papers enjoining them from transferring the meeting to any other place. The counsel for the New York lodges were Pope B. Billups and Francis E. Rivers. They began work to get the injunction and the Grattan Law vacated. They went to Cincinnati where the Grand Lodge of the B.P.O.E. was meeting and had conferences which resulted in a letter stating that so far as the B.P.O.E. was concerned the injunction against Negro Elks was a dead letter and there was no objection

Daughter Ella G. Berry, Fifth Grand Daughter Ruler, 1926-1929.

on their part to it being vacated. Affidavits were then made by the Grand Exalted Ruler and Grand Secretary, and with the able assistance of Grand Legal Adviser Perry W. Howard and the associated counsel, Judge Taylor of White Plains, New York, the injunction was vacated temporarily at first and later it was made permanent. However the Grattan Law was still a state statute.

The New York Times, July 24, 1927, noted the lifting of the ban against Negro Elkdom in the following account:

> *Ban on Negro Elks Lifted*
>
> 19-YEAR-OLD INJUNCTION OFF TEMPORARILY SO THEY CAN CONVENE
>
> White Plains, N. Y., July 23 ....
>
> An injunction of nineteen years standing against the I.B. & P. Or. of Elks of the World, a Negro Organization, was suspended temporarily today by Supreme Court Justice Taylor to enable the Negro Elks to hold a national convention in N. Y. next month.
>
> Justice Taylor reserved decision on the motion of attorneys for the Order to vacate the injunction granted on July 20, 1908 by Supreme Court Justice Morshauser. He will confer with the latter, but the injunction is lifted pending decision, and there is every indication that it will be vacated.
>
> Soon after the Negro order was formed the Grand Lodge of the B.P.O.E., obtained the order restraining the I.B.P.O.E. of W., from using the name "Elks," or wearing regalia similar to that used by the white Elks. Perry W. Howard of Washington, special assistant to the Attorney-General, told Justice Taylor that the white organization had believed that colored Elks might intrude upon them. Howard said the Elks now held no such feeling.

Victory celebrations were held by Elks in New York State and in other places. Injunctions were rapidly dissolved elsewhere as an aftermath of the New York action. As the year advanced, scholarships were granted by the Board of Education consisting of Grand Exalted Ruler Wilson, Grand Daughter Ruler Ella G. Berry, Grand Secretary Emma V. Kelley, the Grand Trustees Pharrow, Berry, and Toliver, Grand Secretary Bates and the Commissioner of Education. Individual students of merit and promise were selected. Applications were received from sixty-six students and grants were made to twenty-three and the amount of these scholarships was $4,686.35. A complete record was kept of each student, his scholastic work, his personal needs as to books, food and in rare instances clothing. Three of the twenty-three graduated in 1927; Edgar A. Hawley, Bradley Polytechnic Institute; J. Welford Holmes, University of Pittsburgh, and Peter D. Johnson, Dartmouth College.

A second significant part of the educational program was the Elks National Oratorical Contest. The country was divided into six sections and rules were drawn up for contests in each section. By recommendation of the Commissioner of Education, the subjects to be used by the contestants concerned the Constitution of the United States with special emphasis upon the Thirteenth, Fourteenth and Fifteenth Amendments. So many entrants were offered from lodges and temples that it was necessary to divide the nation into eight sections rather than six. More than five hundred young men and women entered these contests, studied and spoke about the Constitution. The final contest was held in Washington, D. C., on June 10.

The Lincoln Theater was the scene of this event with the Grand Exalted Ruler and the Grand Daughter Ruler presiding. Commissioner Hueston described the scene as follows: "Eight contestants beautifully and properly attired; the audience made up of men and women, brothers and daughters of this Great Order of Ours and many who were not, but all who had the spirit of the evening. The contestants were not only profound but letter perfect in the preparation and delivery of their orations. Not a one hesitated. None forgot a word. It was a battle, the best in our country were contesting." The prizes ranged from $500 to $50, and in addition each contestant was granted a scholarship. The report of the full work of the Department of Education was presented at the Grand Lodge session of 1927.

This grand Lodge, the Twenty-Eighth Annual Meeting, was called to order in New York City at Mother Zion A.M.E.Z. Church, August 23-27, 1927. There were 565 lodges represented with 1,034 delegates. There had been 527 lodges and 965 delegates at the Cleveland Grand Lodge in 1926. Fraternal Greetings were brought on behalf of the Grand Lodge of Masons of the State of Maryland, the National Medical Association, the National Negro Bankers Association and the National Negro Bar Association. When Acting Mayor McKee welcomed the 2000 delegates and visiting members in session, amid loud applause following the response, Grand Exalted Ruler Wilson said, "Governor Smith (Al) will receive Republican as well as Democratic Negro votes, sufficient to put him in the White House if he will obtain the repeal of the Grattan Law."

For the first time in history Grand Secretary Bates reported a loss in membership, for which he made excuses. The lodge year was closed on July 31, and reports had come in showing that the membership was about 73,000, whereas in 1926 it was given as 82,069. He admitted that a larger number of lodges had not reported. Eighty-three new lodges were instituted during the year and he added, "everywhere the word Elkdom is the Synonym of enthusiasm and progressiveness until the institution of new lodges is an easy task being only contingent upon the financial ability of those who would join, as the desire to do so burns practically in the breast and desire of every young or old man in the country." He felt that the summit of their achievement had not been reached. His report dealt further with real estate owned, sick and death benefits, charity, the educational department, the Mississippi Relief Fund, deputies and organizers, auditing, grievances, past exalted rulers for meritorious service

Souvenir Program
SIXTH ANNUAL CONVENTION
OF THE
OHIO STATE ASSOCIATION
OF THE IMPROVED, BENEVOLENT, PROTECTIVE ORDER OF
ELKS of the World
SPRINGFIELD, OHIO . . . . JUNE 5, 6, 7, 1927
Prince Hunley Lodge, No. 469
Sonora Temple, No. 396
GEORGE WHITE, Chairman
WESLEY WHITE, Gen. Sec.
VALERIA WHITE, Cor. Sec.
Hello Bill!

Sixth Annual Convention of the Ohio State Association, 1927

and bonds for Grand Officers. The report of Grand Treasurer Carter showed a grand total of book balances of $110,176.93, with the total amount in the Educational Fund during the year of $32,124.97, which agreed with the report of the Grand Auditors.

The extent of the expansion of the Order was demonstrated in Grand Organizer Valle's report, which contained a map of the United States with location of lodges. The state association had become increasingly valuable in the building of the Elk spirit. He reported the following foreign lodges, which gave emphasis to the title "of the World": Canada 5 lodges; Puerto Rico 6; Panama 4; Cuba 2; Jamaica 2; Honolulu 1; Mexico 1; Liberia 1. He presented the first copies of the Spanish ritual. He said that the lodges could do better work and that expansion in the Spanish areas would be facilitated.

Health was another important subject of presentation in the Report of the Commission of Health and Infant Mortality, of which Dr. William J. Thompkins was Chairman and Dr. Charles B. Fisher was Executive Secretary. Other members of the Commission were Dr. Algernon B. Jackson, Washington, D. C.; Dr. Phillip A. Scott, Newport News, Va.; Dr. John B. Hall, Boston, Mass.; Dr. T. T. Wendell, Lexington, Ky.; and Mr. Charles E. Hall, statistician. The report stated that for twenty years statements had been made about the health of Negroes but they were made without research and that the truth was not known. The Grand Exalted Ruler in observing these conditions appointed the Commission to begin the first of the health surveys of Negro health. The Commission was called together by the Grand Exalted Ruler on January 17, 1927, in New York City. A questionnaire was planned for circulation in every city with a population of 5,000 in which Negroes constituted at least 10 per cent. Since no appropriation was made for this work the questionnaire was limited but it was prepared and sent to 699 Elk lodges and 451 cities. The preliminary report was presented in five sections: (1) General health conditions as pertains to Negro communities from the standpoint of environment and sanitation; (2) Population, mortality, rural and urban; (3) Infant death rates, associations of colored physicians, representation on boards of health, hospital facilities, housing facilities, sewerage; (4) Tuberculosis as pertains to Negroes in this country and (5) Recent changes in Negro mortality. The report cited as basic to these bad health conditions, poor housing, lack of sanitary inspections and the ignorance of public officials. Recom-

DR. WILLIAM J. THOMPKINS, Chairman of Health Commission

mendations urged the specific interest of lodges and members in health situations.

This was the first comprehensive survey on Negro health made by any organization. It was a notable addition to the fraternity's service to the nation, and was described as the most comprehensive report on Negro health ever made. The *New York Times* devoted an entire column to it and said that it showed that the Negro's health was "the worst in the country's history." The report was authorized for publication and distribution in pamphlet form and the sum of $5,000 was set aside for the use of the Commission and for free pamphlets to be issued quarterly to the public. The *New York Herald Tribune* carried a favorable article on the work of this Commission.

Education was dealt with in the comprehensive report of Brother W. G. Hueston, Commissioner of Education. He told of the establishment of the Department of Education in 1925 and that the first year was spent in organization. In the latter part of this year the work was launched and in the second year it had expanded and developed. He said in this report that "education and more education is the one essential element in race advancement that our group needs." Scholarships received a large part of the report, for he declared that the Board of Education was seeking "earnest, industrious, God-fearing, race-loving, upstanding young men and women of average ability who would appreciate the opportunity and then give every ounce that they possessed in order to justify their appointment." The Oratorial Contests were described. The cooperation of the Grand Officers and lodges, he said, had made possible his report of educational interest and advancement.

One of the proposals of the Grand Legal Adviser was that the Grand Lodge should be incorporated in the District of Columbia because of Federal protection. He believed that then some of the local charters could be vacated. However, the Grand Lodge did not act upon this matter at this session.

The Grand Exalted Ruler stated in his report which was described as "a three-hour report," that there was "a new emancipation" through a vacation of injunctions in the State of New York and that at this Grand Lodge they had won recognition of their manly stature. He called attention to state associations, bi-state and tri-state meetings, membership drives, the Mississippi and Florida contributions for the flood and hurricane victims, the Fidelity Fund and Health and Civil Liberties. He compared the Order with conditions in 1922 when he assumed office. Against 600 lodges in 1927, there were 186 then, with a treasury of $30,000 as compared with the present treasury of

$200,000. In 1922 there was a membership of 29,000 and today it was 250,000, said the Grand Exalted Ruler.

He stressed the educational program with special mention of the work of Commissioner Hueston. Among other things he said, "In carrying out this educational program, there is and has been a master mind behind the wheels. Who is he that has labored in season and out of season for the practical success of this educational program? None other than Commissioner Judge W. C. Hueston, who occupies the high position as Municipal Judge of the city of Gary, Indiana—a true, loyal and trusted friend of the late lamented Honorable E. H. Gary, President of the United States Steel Corporation. Accomplished as a lawyer and as a jurist, Judge Hueston has not forgotten the members of his race farther down; having made good use of his own opportunities, he is seeking to make others make good use of theirs. This Brother Elk, Judge Hueston, is a genius at work. He dreams of the Board of Education in the day as well as the night; it is his 'pillar of cloud by day and his pillar of fire by night,' he has sacrificed his time, his energy and his influence to consummate this program." He regarded the Oratorical Contests in which there were discussions of the Constitution and the laws of the nation as of great value to American youth because he said that they were learning of their rights and privileges under the Constitution and were accordingly obtaining a new conception of their American citizenship.

The Civil Liberties Department was another of the projects which the Builders of Elkdom have established. The *New York Times* stated that "the creation of a Civil Liberties Commission for the advancement of Negroes by improving the relations between Negroes and whites was advocated yesterday at the third day's session."

One of the recommendations of Grand Exalted Ruler Wilson at the 1927 Grand Lodge called for the institution of a permanent Commission on Civil Liberties. This Commission was to work unceasingly until there were complete rights under the law accorded to Negro-Americans as citizens. Brother Wilson declared, "what we need is unity and solidarity of citizenship without regard to race, creed, color or previous condition of servitude! Then will America be safe against the world! I was so impressed by the zeal, intelligence and eloquence of these young colored boys and girls who took part in the recent Oratorical Contest, that I firmly believe that if we support them and back them up, our race will produce another Robert Brown Elliott—another John M. Langston—and another Frederick Douglass of this century." He urged that every effort be made to end the discrimination, Jim-Crow laws, and lynching so that law and order will be established; the opening of opportunities for employment; that respect and honor would be given to the women of the race; that the churches and educational institutions would be supported; that business enterprises would prosper and that the second class citizenship of Negro-Americans would end.

In accordance with this recommendation the following resolution was adopted by the Grand Lodge:

> "Resolved, that pursuant to the recommendation of the Grand Exalted Ruler, the Grand Legal Adviser and a committee of three to be appointed by the Grand Exalted Ruler, be and hereby constituted a Civil Liberties Commission and are charged with the duty of utilizing the full strength of our Order to remedy the fallen condition of law enforcement and Civil Liberties in our country, especially as the same affects our racial group."

Fraternal greetings were brought to the Grand Lodge by the Daughter Elks who were in session at Mt. Olivet Baptist Church. The reports from this Grand Temple were that they too had increased in number and finance during the past year and had made increases in this respect over the previous year. Grand Daughter Secretary Emma V. Kelley addressed the Grand Lodge, bringing greetings on the occasion of the Twenty-Fifth Silver Anniversary of their Temple. The Grand Lodge adopted fitting resolutions concerning the work of the Grand Temple of the Daughter Elks and also paid tribute to the work of Grand Daughter Ruler Ella G. Berry. The Grand Lodge again appointed a Committee on Fraternal Greetings to the Grand Temple which was headed by Brother G. Froe, Recorder of Deeds of the District of Columbia.

It was provided that the Grand Exalted Ruler should call a co-fraternal Congress, comprising the fraternities of the nation who were interested in the advance of the Negro population so that there would be produced a united movement toward this objective. The resolution declared that a committee, of which the Grand Exalted Ruler would be Chairman, to consist of not less than five members of the Order should be appointed to secure the cooperation of the heads of all national bodies of the race, that is the religious, business, civic, fraternities and national organizations of any kind to form mutual committees to work for the purpose of advancing the interest of the Negro people in the United States. A convenient place was to be chosen and time also for the meeting.

A Henry Lincoln Johnson Memorial was approved and a contribution was made toward the objective of assisting in erecting a Henry Lincoln Johnson monument as authorized by the Henry Lincoln Johnson Memorial Association of the State of Georgia. At a later period, the National Headquarters in New York carried the name of the Henry Lincoln Johnson Building and lodges were named after him, and notably Henry Lincoln Johnson Lodge No. 630 in New York City. Of its building, Mrs. Georgia Douglas Johnson, widow of Henry Lincoln Johnson, wrote:

> This is our Sanctuary bright
> Its mellow gleam of kindly light
> Says whosoever will may come
> And find in it a welcome Home.

The Fidelity Fund Committee made its report, recommending the establishment of the Fidelity Bureau to relieve the afflicted and the distressed. It was to be known as the Fidelity Bureau of the Improved Benevolent and Protective Order of Elks of the World and was to be under the direction of the Grand Lodge. There was to be a Board of Directors, a Secretary-Treasurer and a Grand Medical Examiner. Every member of the Order was to be eligible for membership on the payment of an application fee of $1.00 and a monthly premium. Each subordinate lodge was to become the agent of the Fidelity Bureau for the collection of these monthly dues. Certificates of insurance in the sum of $300, $500 and $1,000 were to be issued. The Grand Lodge approved a referendum on the Fidelity Bureau stating that within thirty days, lodges were to pass upon it and to report to the Grand Exalted Ruler and Grand Secretary.

An observation of the *Crisis* for October, 1927, on this Grand Lodge is of interest and historical value. "The meeting of the Colored Elks in Harlem during August was one of the most astonishing and hopeful occurrences that has ever taken place among Negroes of America. Never before has a great city been so elaborately and beautifully decorated for a visiting convention. There must have been at least six miles of flag bunting and electric lights which turned High Harlem into a fairyland.

"Then there poured into this Colored City, between 125th and 145th Streets, and from the crags of Washington Heights to Harlem River, a crowd of visitors estimated as high as fifty thousand. Streets were crowded day and night with automobiles, buses, men, women, and children. Theatres, dance halls, churches and cabarets were wide open. Private homes were filled with gay parties and entertainments, and yet the police force was not perceptibly increased in number; there was almost no disorder of any sort; there was very little drunkenness; very little quarreling. It was a happy, beautiful party.

"The conference despite strong rivalry for office and many matters of difference and dispute went off apparently without a hitch, and the parade, even in the rain, was a moving spectacle; while the great ball in the Armory of the Negro regiment was a little less than magnificent. The white city humming below was literally struck dumb. The *New York World* had regular accounts as usual. Some of the papers had a note now and then; but for the most part there was no news, no comment, no pictures; the white city sat and stared."

This last observation was only partly true for there were published accounts in the daily papers. Even the parade drew comment and was given space by a *New York Times* reporter who saw veiled humor in it, and yet some of his observations were valid:

30,000 PARADE IN RAIN

Harlem Throngs Cheer as Gaily Dressed Marchers Charleston to Tunes of 25 Bands

Under lowering skies and through intermittent showers 30,000 drenched but smiling and gaily clad Negro Elks marched, Charlestoned and cakewalked their way up Fifth Avenue from Sixty-First Street to Harlem yesterday afternoon in the four hour parade of the Grand Lodge of the I.B.P.O.E. of W.

Assembling at 1 o'clock under the command of Grand Marshal Joseph Brown, members of 900 lodges from every state and many foreign countries fell into line with their twenty-five bands and passed 100,000 cheering onlookers, who lined the streets and crowded the windows of Harlem buildings, gay with bunting and banners of every description. Leaving Fifth Avenue at 110th Street, the marchers went West to Lenox Ave., up to 125th Street, and again West to Seventh Avenue, finally disbanding at 149th Street and Lenox Oval.

For an hour the procession passed in review before Grand Exalted Ruler J. Finley Wilson and his staff in the grandstand at Seventh Avenue and 145th Street. Feminine members, known as Does, were almost as numerous as marchers of the other sex, while the leaders of the women's band set the toes of the Marchers and by-standers tickling with the notes of "Charleston," "Ain't She Cute," and "Me and My Shadow." A delegation of thirty Negro policemen from the West 135th Street Station among the marchers received loud cheers and applause.

White uniforms with purple trouser-stripes and collars were the fashion for the men, although tuxedo coats and white flannels were also seen and a heavy sprinkling of gold braid and brass buttons. One dignified group with top-hats and cutaways followed a score of mounted policemen who were in the van. The women ran strongly to white and gold, with an occasional group in brown, cerise, purple and other colors.

Rules against singing, talking, chewing gum and dancing while in marching order were issued by the Committee in charge of the parade, but the spirit of good-will which prevailed found many dancing to the music of the bands and shouting to friends at the sides. A motion picture concern made use of the parade as a background for a film, while 300 policemen under Inspector Thomas W. Ryan found that they had little to do.*

The Grand Lodge through its Grand Exalted Ruler J. Finley Wilson and the Commissioner of Education Judge William C. Hueston had undertaken the building of the Grand Lodge and the entire Order into a serviceable organization for the people as well as an organization for the individual members. Its Department of Education was the result of the foresight, the broad-mindedness and energy of both of these outstanding persons. The Health Department had been organized under its Health Director Dr. William J. Thompkins, who was subsequently appointed Recorder of Deeds of the District of Columbia and its work was to have a significant development in the future. The Civil Liberties Department under Robert J. Nelson, Executive Director, was to make notable contributions toward the advancement of the Negro, and legal battles were to be fought for individuals and for the racial group. These builders of the future of Elkdom have gone down in history as heroes of the Order.

ROBERT J. NELSON, Director of Civil Liberties; Chairman, Civil Liberties' Commission

New York Times, August 24, 1927.

Chapter XII
Advancing the Adopted Program

Having adopted a program which included emphasis upon education, health, civil liberties and services to the Negroes of the United States and other parts of the world, the Improved Benevolent and Protective Order of Elks of the World continued the advancement of this program as the year 1927 opened. The Grand Lodge Officers elected at this Grand Lodge of 1927 were: J. Finley Wilson, Grand Exalted Ruler, Washington, D. C.; Dr. S. H. George, Grand Esteemed Leading Knight, Paducah, Ky.; Joseph H. James, Grand Esteemed Loyal Knight, Brooklyn, N. Y.; George E. Bates, Grand Semretary, Newark, N. J.; James T. Carter, Grand Treasurer, Richmond, Va.; William L. Jackson, Grand Esquire, Philadelphia, Pa.; C. E. A. Starr, Grand Inner Guard, Denver, Colo.; William Emerson, Grand Tiler, Lexington, Ky.; William C. Hueston, Commissioner of Education, Gary, Ind.; Carlos C. Valle, Grand Organizer, Newark, N. J.; Perry W. Howard, Grand Legal Adviser, Washington, D. C.; W. George Avant, Grand Chaplain, Durham, N. C.; Grand Trustees, Colonel John R. Marshall, Chicago, Ill.; R. E. Pharrow, Atlanta, Ga.; Dr. D. T. Cardwell, Gary, Ind.; Wayman Wilkerson, Memphis, Tenn.; John W. Duncan, New York, N. Y.; Grand Auditors, Floyd C. Payne, Washington, D. C.; Dr. Thomas L. Love, Raleigh, N. C.; C. M. Hanson, New York, N. Y.

These Grand Officers undertook immediately at the close of the Grand Lodge sessions in New York to operate and advance the program which had been approved by the Grand Lodge. It was with enthusiasm that the work was undertaken by these Grand Officers. State associations began to operate in larger numbers. In 1922 there was only one state association but during 1927-1928 there had been five associations of state lodges organized. The Grand Exalted Ruler visited all of the meetings of these state associations which meant a considerable amount of travel.

Immediately after the adjournment of the Grand Lodge convention, Grand Exalted Ruler Wilson appointed the Commissioners on Civil Liberties. They were: Casper Holstein of New York; Robert R. Church of Memphis, Tennessee, and Robert J. Nelson of Wilmington, Delaware, the latter serving as Executive Director. The Grand Exalted Ruler stated that he appointed Brother Nelson as Executive Director because of the work which he had carried on in the State of Delaware for the civil rights of

Negroes. At a later period Robert R. Church was released as a member of the Commission and Brother George Lee of Memphis, Tennessee, was appointed in his place. The Commission had its first meeting on October 21, 1927, at the John Wesley A.M.E. Zion Church, Washington, D. C. Brother Nelson representing the Civil Liberties Commission joined the National Equal Rights League and the N.A.A.C.P., in a petition to the United States Congress urging the enforcement of the Fourteenth Amendment to the Constitution.

Again at Gary, Indiana, the Civil Liberties Commission through its representatives joined in the fight against segregation in the Gary High School. There were about 800 white pupils in this high school who refused to attend their classes until twenty Negro students were moved from the school. The Civil Liberties Commission sent its representatives who interviewed the mayor and individuals in this city. It was agreed ultimately to construct an additional high school which would be opened to both racial groups. In this way the school congestion and the problem of segregation were solved. Written protests were also filed by the Commission with representatives of the N.A.A.C.P., and the National Equal Rights League concerning segregation in the Federal service in Washington, D. C. In two departments responses came to the appeals, and segregation was abolished. Police brutality was also protested in the capital of the nation.

Further indication of the purpose to conduct a program of public service was demonstrated in the call by Grand Exalted Ruler Wilson, issued to 75 Negro fraternities throughout the nation to assemble in Washington, D. C. This call had been authorized by the Grand Lodge session of 1927. This meeting of the fraternity assembled in the lodge rooms of Morning Star Lodge No. 40 in the District of Columbia and also at the Columbia Lodge No. 85. There was a two day session of this group with the Grand Exalted Ruler presiding. William Pickens was made Vice-Chairman; Caesar R. Blake permanent Secretary and Nannie H. Burroughs, President of the Auxiliary of the National Baptist Convention was made Treasurer. These fraternities agreed to send a memorial to Congress concerning the wrongs inflicted upon the Negro people and the resolution was published in *Congressional Record,* having been presented by Senator Arthur Kapper of Kansas in the Senate and Representative William Hueston of Delaware in the House of Representatives. These fraternities dedicated themselves to continue their cooperation so that their influences might be felt in the circles of the National Government and that the status of Negroes would be advanced.

The publication of the first health bulletin brought out by a fraternal organization was reported to have been issued by the Commission on Infant Mortality and Health. There was also published a booklet containing the last report of this Commission at the convention of 1927. Lectures and publications in newspapers embraced other work conducted by the Commission. Interviews were held with parents, with school children and with family physicians. Public clinics were also organized so that there would be services given to the needy in several important areas where the needs were especially great. The survey ordered by the last Grand Lodge was conducted in fourteen cities in which the Negro population constituted 10 per cent or more of the total population of the city.

These subjects were presented and discussed again at the Twenty-Ninth Annual Meeting of the Grand Lodge which convened in Wendell Phillips High School, Chicago, Illinois, August 28-September 1, 1928. The session was called to order by Grand Exalted Ruler J. Finley Wilson. In the absence of Grand Secretary George E. Bates, Brother C. C. Valle, Grand Organizer, was appointed to serve as temporary secretary. Prayer was offered by Grand Chaplain W. George Avant and the Grand Lodge sang the opening ode. After organization the Committee on Credentials reported that there were 465 lodges represented by 1,013 delegates.

The first report was given by the Grand Legal Adviser Perry W. Howard who reported that for twelve months no suit had been pending against the Grand Lodge and that his policy had been to keep the Grand Lodge out of court. With Dr. J. E. Mills, Past Grand Exalted Ruler presiding, Grand Exalted Ruler Wilson delivered his annual report. He reported that the Order had reached this meeting in 1928 with 850 lodges, 600 temples of Daughter Elks, 350 juvenile organizations, 100 Past Grand Exalted Rulers' Councils, 35 state, bi-state and tri-state associations with an educational program, a health program and a Fidelity Fund endorsed by a majority of the lodges. He stated that a bill had been passed by the Legislature of Pennsylvania similar to the New York Grattan Law but that a similar bill had been defeated in New Jersey. He recommended the appointment of a Committee of Attorneys to study the situations in Tennessee, Ohio and Pennsylvania.

The Grand Exalted Ruler then paid tribute to the able leadership of Judge Hueston as Commissioner of Education, assisted

DAUGHTER LETHIA FLEMING, Grand Directress of Public Relations

by the Daughter Elks and particularly Daughter Lethia C. Fleming. Dr. William J. Thompkins, Chairman of the Commission on Health and Dr. Charles B. Fisher, the Executive Secretary of the Commission had achieved good results, he said, in their work. He noted that a Commission on the National Shrine had been at work, consisting of John J. Webb of Arkansas, Fred McCracken of Minnesota, Guy U. Blaine of Indiana and J. P. H. Westbrook of Colorado, and would report to the Grand Lodge. He recommended that the delegates at the first convention of 1901, 1902 and 1905 be made permanent delegates to the Grand Lodge with voice and vote; that an Order of Junior Elks be instituted instead of the Juvenile Organization and that the Civil Liberties Commission be placed on a permanent basis with appropriate support. The report was received, according to the Minutes, "amid vociferous applause," and an effort was made to reelect the Grand Exalted Ruler by acclamation.

The Grand Secretary, George E. Bates, stated in his report that he was glad to meet in Chicago, where there were two of the oldest and strongest lodges. The membership was reported up to 66,852, and there were sixty new lodges made since August 1, 1927. There were seventy-six lodges on the roll from which no report was received. Grand Organizer Valle had traveled extensively in the field work of organizing and reviewing lodges. He had visited 125 cities in fourteen states. He had reported in 1927 that the ritual had been translated into Spanish and printed and would be useful in the foreign world. The Grand Secretary said that copies had been sent to all lodges in Spanish speaking countries. The report was that the real estate owned by the lodges had increased in estimated value to $2,913,000.00 and that 132 lodges owned or were purchasing real estate; death benefits totaled $76,454.78 and sick benefits were $81,491.55, while charity amounted to $29,536.67. The Grand Treasurer reported that the total on hand in the General Fund was $98,735.99, and the Grand Auditors reported the actual worth of the Grand Lodge was $74,089.67.

One of the visiting groups to the Grand Lodge was a committee of ladies composed of Mrs. Alice Dunbar Nelson, Executive Secretary of the American Interracial Peace Committee and Mrs. F. E. Williams, Field Supervisor of Arkansas Negro Tuberculosis Association. The Daughter Elks had grown with phenomenal progress, their income had reached a total of $34,000, and a balance in 1927 of $11,450.65. Representing this strong organization, these ladies were escorted to the stage and Mrs. Nelson made an address which was described as "masterly and appealing." Mrs. Williams made an appeal for assistance to the Arkansas Tuberculosis Association. The appeal was referred to the Committee on Charity and a vote of thanks was extended to the ladies for their presence and address. The Shrine Commission of which Brother John L. Webb was Chairman and Brother J. H. P. Westbrook, Secretary, made its report recommending the purchase of a National Home to be bought or built in Washington, D. C., which would in the words of the Committee, "be truly a Shrine of Faith and Hope in the possibilities of the future, and the development of all that is dear to the I.B.P.O.E. of W." The motion was made to adopt and was approved by the Grand Lodge.

The report of the Commissioner of Education, Brother W. C. Hueston, was heard with great interest by the organization. He paid tribute to the cooperation which had been given him by Grand Exalted Ruler Wilson and the Grand Daughter Ruler, Ella G. Berry. His opening paragraphs explained his philosophy of education. He wanted the lodge to understand that he believed in creating the power of thinking on the part of the lodge members as well as youth. He said, "The purpose of the Department of Education in our Order is to train thinkers who can match themselves against the great minds of the world. If this race of ours is to still be known among the races of the world, then we must achieve more abundantly; we must build greater buildings; improve transportation; discover great cures; evolve financial systems and make our debtors the human race. And in order to do this, our minds must be trained to the highest possible standard. Individually we are unable to compete. Standing together, as exampled by the Improved Benevolent and Protective Order of Elks of the World, we shall."

He stated that in this second year of the exiestence of the department, there were four graduates from the University of

Pittsburgh, Bradley Polytechnic Institute, Dartmouth College, Walden University at Nashville, Tennessee, and that all of these students had graduated with honors. He said that there had been thirty-seven students in college who had been granted scholarships by the organizations and all had done well. The Oratorical Contests were again spoken of as great successes and the final contest was held at the Grand Lodge. He recommended that the final Oratorical Contest became a permanent part of the Grand Lodge sessions. He said, "keep up these contests, keep instilling into the minds of our young people their rights guaranteed by the Constitution, and one bright day you will awaken to know that you are indeed free."

He proposed that there should be organized in the Department of Education a Department of Athletics to be presided over by a Director of Athletics who would be nominated by the Commissioner of Education annually and appointed by the Grand Exalted Ruler. His duties would be to supervise athletic teams, arrange tournaments in the several branches of athletics and to have a national tournament. Through this department, it was planned that youth would be encouraged to develop physically and to be good sportsmen, thereby becoming assets in their communities. He referred to and described the Gary School Contest in which he and the Grand Exalted Ruler had participated. The report was received with considerable praise.

JAMES C. MARTIN, Grand Treasurer, 1928-1929.

The Grand Officers selected were: J. Finley Wilson, Grand Exalted Ruler, Washington, D. C.; Dr. S. H. George, Grand Esteemed Leading Knight, Paducah, Ky.; Joseph H. James, Grand Esteemed Loyal Knight, Jacksonville, Fla.; Andrew T. Mitchell, Grand Esteemed Lecturing Knight, New York City; James E. Kelley, Grand Secretary, Birmingham, Ala.; James C. Martin, Grand Treasurer, Maywood, Ill.; Sidney B. Thompson, Grand Esquire, Cleveland, Ohio; R. L. Derrick, Grand Inner Guard,

Spokane, Washington; Joseph B. Levy, Grand Tiler, Minneapolis, Minn.; William C. Hueston, Commissioner of Education, Gary, Ind.; Carlos C. Valle, Grand Organizer, Newark, N. J.; Perry W. Howard, Grand Legal Adviser, Washington, D. C.; W. George Avant, Grand Chaplain, Durham, N. C.; Dr. Roland R. Johnson, Grand Medical Director, Brooklyn, N. Y.; Dr. William J. Thompkins, Chairman of Health Commission, Kansas City, Mo.; John L. Webb, Chairman of the National Shrine Committee, Hot Springs, Arkansas; Robert J. Nelson, Chairman of Civil Liberties Bureau, Washington, D. C. The Grand Trustees were: Colonel John R. Marshall, Chicago, Ill.; R. E. Pharrow, Atlanta, Ga.; Dr. D. T. Cardwell, Gary, Ind.; Robert R. Church, Memphis, Tenn.; John W. Duncan, New York City. The Grand Auditors were: Dr. Charles A. Marshall, Washington, D. C.; Dr. Thomas L. Love, Raleigh, N. C.; and James B. Allen, New York City. Atlantic City was selected as the place of the 1929 Grand Lodge session.

An interesting proposal was made for the Office of Historian for the Order. After considerable discussion the Grand Exalted Ruler was authorized to appoint a special committee to attend to the collection of all matters connected with the origin and history of the Order and to guarantee the proper conservation of the same. A monument was authorized to be erected as a token of respect for the services rendered to the Grand Lodge by Brother Henry Lincoln Johnson.

In connection with the history of the Order, it is interesting to observe that a resolution was passed concerning the work of Brothers Arthur J. Riggs and Frank H. Hunter who were among the organizers of the Order in 1898. This resolution was as follows:

> "Whereas, it has been conclusively established by official records, printed documents and by the historians of the Order, that Brother Arthur J. Riggs and Frank H. Hunter were the actual pioneers and founders of this Order and,
>
> Whereas, in recognition of this work Brother Arthur J. Riggs and Brothers Frank H. Hunter were made honorary Past Grand Exalted Rulers, and.
>
> Whereas, in addition thereto Brother Arthur J. Riggs was granted a pension,
>
> Whereas, through inaction, over-sight or the pressure of voluminous business, Brother Frank H. Hunter was not given this recognition,
>
> Therefore, since it is a fact that Brother Frank H. Hunter was the first Exalted Ruler of Cincinanti Lodge No. 1; which lodge functioned three years as the Grand Lodge, and,
>
> Whereas, during the troublesome days, the privation which

he was forced to experience and the holding together the nucleus of the remaining 27 members of the original 327 of the first lodge, and,

Whereas, through his untiring efforts and foresights, the copyright of our work was established and though burdened with long years of service and mellowed by advancing years, he is present at every Grand Lodge session. Actively working for its uplift and advancement and has been since 1898, when in company with some of the old boys, all of whom have passed to the great beyond save two, this Order was conceived and born in the darkness of a cellar in Cincinnati, his home town,

Therefore, Be It Resolved, by the Grand Lodge of I.B.P.O.E. of W., that a life pension of fifty dollars per month be given to each of these Brothers.

This motion was approved by the Grand Lodge. After the presentations of gifts and addresses by the Grand Officers of the Grand Daughter Elks and the reports of committees, the officers were installed and the Grand Lodge adjourned.

The advancement of the adopted program could not succeed without opposition, which sprang up here and there in a number of lodges concerning not only the expenditure of funds, but the handling of the funds, in spite of the fact that in Grand Lodge after Grand Lodge, the Grand Auditors continued to find that the funds of the Order had been handled with honesty and efficiency. Some of the criticisms were regarded as malicious as they were directed against both the Grand Exalted Ruler and the Commissioner of Education. Defenses of the positions taken by these Grand Officers were given again at the Grand Lodge sessions as well as some replies were sent through the newspapers which at periods carried headlines.

Some criticisms were rather silly. One was that in the Oratorical Contest the audience was of the opinion, so it was reported, that the prize was taken from the real winner because she was dark and was given instead to a fair girl of no real ability. Judge Hueston made a reply to this accusation when he asserted that, "The first prize was won by an unbleached American boy of Alexandria, Virginia," which was a direct answer and denial of the criticism. Another such criticism was that there was a shortage in the Elks' funds and that the Grand Exalted Ruler was responsible for it. Again, the replies were the reports which were given at the Grand Lodge conventions, and those who came to the conventions soon discovered the falsity of these criticisms. It was reported that the Educational Fund suffered during 1928 and 1929 as a result of these criticisms and that there was a breakdown of morale during the Educational Week campaign. These types of criticisms could be expected by men who were building the Order and seeking to advance the adopted program of the Grand Lodge. Progress seemed to invite criticisms. Misunderstandings were easy to be created by those who were seeking to accomplish great deeds.

Upon this background the Thirtieth Annual Meeting of this Grand Lodge assembled in Atlantic City at the Senior High School, August 25-31, 1929. The Committee on Credentials reported 642 lodges present through 1,094 delegates and there were 36 Grand Lodge Officers in attendance. This was one of the largest of the conventions according to this report as compared with the previous year. The first of the reports of the Grand Officers presented at this session was the report of the Grand Secretary, Brother James E. Kelley, who stated that he was presenting a report to the Grand Lodge in its thirtieth year and that he was reporting that the Grand Lodge was in a healthy condition, spiritually, physically and materially, and that the promises of the future were beckoning to them. The success of the organization, he said, could be judged in part by its increase in membership and its financial standing. While the economic depression of the country had caused many members to cease their membership, the records showed that there were 631 financial lodges with membership of 73,362. This was an increase of more than 5,000 over 1928. At the same time there were some lodges which had not sent in their reports and accordingly the membership would probably be larger. He said that there were 57 lodges which had been organized during the year. He reported that real estate values had increased to $3,342,734.93 and that over $181,100.68 had been spent for charity, sick and death benefits. He closed his report of continued progress with the statement, "The world needs the program of our Order and we must unselfishly see to it that we carry on."

The Commissioner of Education, Brother W. C. Hueston, made his report showing the continued operation of the educational program on a successful basis. This was his third annual report. He said that in the first year of his administration of the department, $5,000 had been spent on scholarships; the second year, $7,452.23 and the third year, $9,425.36. There had been a gradual increase in the scholarship aid given to the students within the passing three years. He stated that the Board of Education had granted fifty-one scholarships, and that forty-six of these had been accepted. So far as the Oratorical Contests were concerned, six districts had been selected with a director over each of them and they seemed to be enthusiastic for the continuance of these contests because of the interest of the young people as well as the Elk Brothers in them. His report showed

James E. Kelley, Grand Secretary in 1928.

that the total receipts which had come to his department had been $45,631.49 and the expenses were $15,965.20, leaving a total balance in the Educational Fund of $29,666.29.

The Grand Exalted Ruler announced that "we have come to Atlantic City to fight if need be, with our last drop of blood and with every ounce of strength for the purposes and programs that have been inaugurated in the past seven years, and which have resulted in placing us before the world on the level which we now maintain." He said that there would be no retrenchment and no turning back, for his call was always forward. He described the progress briefly which had been made by the fraternity and the background of achievement which as he said, "has brought bishops and clerics into our midst on terms of equality, which has gathered professional men and women of highest standing. Leaders in politics and finance and social welfare may well be contrasted with the background of permutations and combinations and numerology—the science of numbers —and hitting on the backup—which is before me now as I render to you an account of the stewardship of the past twelve months."

The Grand Exalted Ruler referred to the work which had been done by Brothers Robert R. Church and John R. Hawkins in contributing to the success of the Republican Party in the recent elections and he stated that he had done what he could to bring the party back to its moorings. He was glad to see the Honorable Oscar De Priest, a member of the lodge, take his seat in the House of Representatives. Some of these statements by the Grand Exalted Ruler were criticized by other members of the convention because it seemed as though he was endeavoring to line up the Order with the Republican Party when there were members of the Democratic Party in the Grand Lodge sessions. This, however, seems to have been far from the point of view of the Grand Exalted Ruler who was expressing his personal opinion, and it was well known that he was a stalwart Republican. He referred again to the Fidelity Fund which was very close to his desires and hoped that the Grand Lodge would take some definitive action upon it. He described the hurricanes and devastation. The growth of the Order was summarized at home and abroad. The new lodges which were organized through the work of the Deputies and the Grand Organizer were also described.

The Health Commission, he said, had made great progress during the past year and that the first week in April had been designated as Health Week. A drive had been organized against disease by Dr. William J. Thompkins, Chairman of the Health Bureau. He called the work done by the Commissioner of Education a fine piece of work, and the Civil Liberties Commission had exercised, he said, vigilance in defending members of the racial group against sinister evils of proscription, segregation and discrimination.

A mid-winter conference had been called by the Grand Exalted Ruler in December of 1929, because the new Grand Secretary, James E. Kelley, had received only a part of his books from the former Grand Secretary, Brother George E. Bates, and it seemed necessary to plan for some action in order to secure the books to conduct the work of the Grand Lodge. He referred to criticisms which had been made by several of the members of the New York lodges and the proposal that there might be an effort made even to split the Order again. A number of cases had developed for adjudication by him, and dispensations had been granted.

In closing his annual report he gave this brief summary of the major part of the program which was now being operated. Said he, ''We have grown from one Grand Lodge to many Lodges, or state associations of which this body is the head supreme. Our Health Commission has demonstrated more than anything else to the Anglo-Saxon—the wisdom of the colored man of this generation who has organized a drive against disease and uncleanliness that he may be truly free. Likewise our Education Commission had demonstrated that we appreciate the need for eradication of ignorance in our group and the driving to the gutter of disorderly and criminal minds bent on our destruction. So too, our Civil Liberties Commission has made the Uncle Toms and Jim Crows hang their heads and sneak away before its fights for manhood rights and a square deal in America.'' He then added, ''We have girded for battle to fight those who would destroy our program.'' Paraphrasing a familar song, the final words of the report were:

> "We have sounded forth a trumpet that shall never call retreat;
> We are sifting out the hearts of Elks before this judgment seat;
> Be swift, your souls, to answer, be jubilant, your feet—
> For God is marching on.
> In the beauty of the lilies Christ was born across the sea,
> With a glory in his bosom that transfigures you and me;
> As He died to make men holy, let us live to make Elks free,
> While God is marching on."

Immediately following the address Brother John Marquess of Quaker City Lodge No. 720, Philadlephia, Pennsylvania, obtained the floor and made an eloquent speech moving that the rules be suspended and that J. Finley Wilson be re-elected Grand

Exalted Ruler by acclamation. The motion was seconded by Brother John R. Hawkins of Washington, D. C., but a point of order was raised by Brother Louis B. Anderson of Chicago and the point was sustained.

Grand Organizer Valle carried his work into New Mexico and into Texas where he had originally been ordered by the Klan to get out of the city of Fort Worth. However, he added that a strong organization was in the state and that there was a good state association. He moved into the Middle Western States, organizing lodges in a number of these states, especially Oklahoma, Missouri, Kansas, Illinois, Alabama, Mississippi, Tennessee, Arkansas and across the border into Mexico.

The Commission on Civil Liberties, reported through Brother Robert J. Nelson, calling attention to numerous endeavors and activities in Washington, D. C., in connection with cases of discrimination and the introduction of bills inimical to the interest of the Negro population in Congress. He made recommendations for a survey of Negro labor and business in cooperation with Brother J. A. Jackson of the United States Department of Commerce. Agriculture and the status of Negro farmers would receive some consideration, he said, by the Committee. The Commission on Health and Infant Mortality made an extensive report through Dr. Charles Fisher. The results of a questionnaire which had been sent throughout the Order, the importance of health work, periodic health examinations, the health units to be organized in the lodges, statistics concerning the births and deaths and the work of physicians in their distribution through the United States were all noted in the report. Recommendations also referred to the continuance of the work of the committee through additional surveys.

The report of Grand Treasurer Martin, showed that there had been total receipts of $105,276.88 and that there was a total balance as of August 15, 1939, of $46,484.43. So far as the finances were concerned the Grand Lodge continued its advancement and its use of funds to carry on its program. However, the Treasurer carried this note of warning, "Let economy be the watchword in order that the Improved Benevolent and Protective Order of Elks of the World shall not perish from the earth."

Several important actions were taken by the Grand Lodge. Among these was a prohibition of the publication of defamatory, malicious or scurrilous articles concerning any member or officer of the Grand Lodge or subordinate lodges. Any member engaging in these activities would be fined not less than $100 nor more than $250. A tax was placed upon the subordinate lodges and members of $.25 a quarter, or $1.00 for the year in order to maintain the program of the organization in education, health and civil rights.

The History Committee, which had been appointed at the 1927 Grand Lodge, reported that they had been searching for materials and had found one of the first charters issued Elks by the founders of the Order and had secured statements from the oldest members of the Order. The Committee requested the Grand Exalted Ruler to ask in his next proclamation that his office be supplied with any information of historical value to the organization, together with photographs, newspaper clippings or any matter that would pertain to the early growth of the Order. Very little material, however, was secured in this manner.

Another action of the Elks was the decision to elect a Commissioner of Junior Elks. This was an important movement for the youth work of the Order. Brother Robert H. Johnson, then Esquire of O. V. Catto Lodge, No. 20, of Philadelphia presented a resolution for the creation of a Legion of Honor composed of those who were ex-service men and members of the Order. This was one of the first efforts to interest the Grand Lodge in veterans and their affairs.

The Grand Lodge officers for 1929-1930 were: J. Finley Wilson, Grand Exalted Ruler, Washington, D. C.; Dr. S. H. George, Grand Esteemed Leading Knight, Paducah, Ky.; Joseph H. James, Grand Esteemed Loyal Knight, Jacksonville, Fla.; Andrew T. Mitchell, Grand Esteemed Lecturing Knight, New York, N. Y.; James E. Kelley, Grand Secretary, Birmingham, Ala.; Henry S. Warner, Grand Treasurer, New York, N. Y.; Sidney B. Thompson, Grand Esquire, Cleveland, Ohio; R. L. Derrick, Grand Inner Guard, Spokane, Washington; Joseph B. Levy, Grand Tiler, Minneapolis, Minn.; William C. Hueston, Commissioner of Education, Washington, D. C.; Perry W. Howard, Grand Legal Adviser, Washington, D. C.; W. George Avant, Grand Chaplain, Durham, N. C.; Carlos C. Valle, Grand Organizer, St. Louis, Mo.; Jessie Harris, Grand Organist, Pittsburgh, Pa; C. E. A. Starr, Grand Master of Social Sessions, Denver, Colo.; Dr. John Marquess, Commissioner of Athletics, Philadelphia, Pa.; Dr. Charles A. Marshall, Commissioner of Junior Elks, Washington, D. C.

Chapter XIII

"Forward"–In Spite of Depression

One of the favorite words of Grand Exalted Ruler, J. Finley Wilson was the word "Forward." His admonition was "Cross the Plains and scale the Rockies." He believed in the theory and concept of progress. He saw that Man had been a builder of his own destiny under God, as he studied history. His confident opinion was that he could build a greater future out of his past. He transferred this general belief to the work of the Improved Benevolent and Protective Order of Elks of the World. His optimism extended to the simple belief that next year would always be better than this one. There can be no wonder that, under the leadership of this man of vision, his Grand Officers caught parts of this optimistic view and carried on jointly with him in a forward movement towards the victories of which he spoke. These beliefs were the basis for the distinctive place occupied by this Order among the fraternities of the United States.

The real test of the value of these views came with the disastrous economic results of 1929 and 1930. Production had surpassed the purchasing power of the people and speculation had caused the boom of prosperity and plenty to burst. Late in 1929, panic developed in the stock market. This was the beginning of the spread of economic depression. Despite the measures of the Hoover administration, the depression continued its harmful effects. Unemployment developed and its effects were felt in all areas of the nation. There were bank failures, bankruptcies and mortgage foreclosures. The government turned rapidly to adopt measures of relief for these situations.

It was not unusual, therefore, to find the Grand Exalted Ruler paraphrasing the story of Hiawatha and referring to the approaching winter as "the winter of Nokomis." while the Grand Secretary was found stating that "the financial depression of the past year has seriously affected the economic status of our group." Nevertheless, the Order faced the depression with the watchword of the Grand Exalted Ruler before it, and continued its steady march forward.

Depression was not the only foe which the Order had to face. There was attempted division from defeated officers and their sympathizers which called for attention. Early in 1930, Grand Exalted Ruler Wilson was informed that Brother James T.

Carter, former Grand Treasurer, and others had secured a charter in 1929 from the State of Virginia and had incorporated under the same name as the I.B.P.O.E. of W., and had a similar corps of officers. Grand Legal Adviser, Perry W. Howard, was directed by the Grand Exalted Ruler to interest himself in the matter. He obtained a temporary injunction from the United States Circuit Court of Appeals restraining the other lodge from operating under their charter. The case was known as Grand Lodge of Improved Benevolent and Protective Order of Elks of the World, a Corporation versus The Grand Lodge, Improved Benevolent and Protective Order of Elks of the World, Incorporated and James T. Carter, Leon A. Reid, Joseph R. Pollard and John B. Neblett. The appeal was from the District Court of the United States for the Eastern District of Virginia. When the case came up for hearing, the Grand Exalted Ruler, the Senior Past Grand Exalted Ruler, the Grand Legal Adviser, the Commissioner of Education, District Deputy John P. White, the Grand Secretary, the Grand Treasurer and the President of the Virginia State Association were in attendance.

The most astounding occurrence was reported at the hearing. Brother James T. Carter was said to have told the court, "Your Honor, please, much contention is made by these men as to how we came into possession of this ritual and name. I want to tell you and be frank with the court, that we purloined them." This allegation of the theft of the ritual and name threw consternation into the ranks of those who were followers of Grand Exalted Ruler Wilson. They knew that the allegation was untrue, and as he said, "we hasten to assure you that there was no theft nor purloining." The worst aspect of this event was that this assertion was made by an Elk who had served by the suffrage of his brothers in one of the Grand Offices for fifteen years. The Grand Exalted Ruler gave a severe castigation in this instance.

The lower court held that the white Elks were the original users of the name Benevolent and Protective Order of Elks and that there was no exclusive right to the use of the name, Improved Benevolent and Protective Order of Elks of the World, although the prefix "Improved" and the suffix "of the World" were added. Judge Northcupp of the court also said that a similar suit had been brought in the court in 1910 by Grand Exalted Ruler B. F. Howard who claimed an incorporation under the laws of the State of Ohio; and there was another claim of an incorporation in New Jersey in 1906. An appeal was requested and granted, and the injunction remained in operation against Carter and his group.

United States Circuit Court of Appeals

FOURTH CIRCUIT

No. 3105.

Grand Lodge of Improved, Benevolent and Protective Order of Elks of the World, a corporation,
Appellant,

versus

The Grand Lodge, Improved, Benevolent and Protective Order of Elks of the World, Incorporated, and James T. Carter, Leon A. Reid, Joseph R. Pollard and John B. Neblett,
Appellees.

Appeal from the District Court of the United States for the Eastern District of Virginia, at Richmond.

(Argued February 11, 1931. Decided June 19, 1931.)

Before Parker, Circuit Judge, and Webb and Glenn, District Judges.

T. G. Nutter and Perry W. Howard (George E. C. Hayes and W. C. Hueston on brief) for Appellant, and James T. Carter (J. R. Pollard and W. W. Foreman on brief) for Appellees.

The Case of *The Grand Lodge, I.B.P.O.E. of W., vs. The Grand Lodge I.B.P.O.E. of W., a Virginia Corporation*, 1931.

This case was argued on February 11, 1931, before Judge Parker, Circuit Judge and District Judges Webb and Glenn. The Grand Lodge was represented by Attorneys T. G. Nutter and Perry W. Howard with George E. C. Hayes and W. C. Hueston on the brief. The suit was brought under the name of I.B.P.O.E. of W., a New Jersey Corporation against the I.B.P.O.E. of W., a Virginia Corporation.

Subsequently, on June 19, 1931, the U. S. Circuit Court of Appeals of the Fourth District through Judge John J. Parker rendered the decision granting not only the right to restrain others from the use of the name I.B.P.O.E. of W., but also giving the Order this exclusive right. It is of interest to note that this decision was delivered by Judge John J. Parker, who was nominated by President Hoover for a vacancy on the Supreme Court. Judge Parker was accused of being unfair to the Negro and to organized labor. The opposition developed from these sources became so strong that the nomination of Judge Parker was rejected. Of one thing Elks of the original Order were appreciative, Judge Parker had done them a good turn in the delivery of this decision in their favor, but seeing the larger good, they continued their opposition to his confirmation.

The decision declared that the older body was incorporated in Ohio, New York, New Jersey and the District of Columbia, but that these incorporations did not impair its rights as a New Jersey corporation. Unfair competition, the law of trademarks and the protection of names were discussed in detail in the decision.

The court declared, "In the case at bar the complainant for more than a quarter of a century had enjoyed the use of its name and had built up thereunder a large fraternal Order among the colored people of the United States. Its fraternal, charitable and educational activities had commended it to the public and had given membership therein a value to the people from whom it recruited its membership. It was entitled to enjoy the fruits of the organization which it had built up, unhampered by the efforts of others to appropriate to themselves its corporate name with the advantages thereto attaching. If the Virginia members were dissatisfied, they, of course, had a right to withdraw and organize a new Order; but they had no right, if they did so, to adopt the name of the original Order or to hold themselves out as a branch of the Order. To do so, constitutes a fraud upon the original Order and upon the public; and if allowed, would result in enabling the rival organization to appropriate to itself the advantages which the original Order had built up through years of effort. A more glaring example of unfair competition could not well be imagined.*

"Finally it is said that complainant is not entitled to the protection of its name because it has itself appropriated the name of the White Benevolent and Protective Order of Elks. In this connection it should be said that complainant claims not to have been a party to the Tennessee Case and an injunction granted in the New York Case has been dissolved by consent, but passing upon the rights of the White Order, which are not before us, we do not think that the rights of the complainant are to be ignored because it has adopted a name very similar to that of the White Order. Neither complainant nor defendant are seeking membership among white people and the similarity of their name to that of the White Order has no bearing upon the injury and wrong which the use of the name by the defendant will inflict upon the complainant. The White Order recruits its membership from among white persons only, and does not seek to enter into competition with either complainant or defendant. Defendants, however, are in direct competition with complainant and the use of its name gives defendants an unfair and unconscionable advantage.

"The case before us comes to this: complainant under a name very similar to that of the White Fraternal Order has built up a Fraternal Order among colored people, which has acquired a large membership and a splendid reputation among the people from whom it solicits members. The individual defendants have withdrawn from the Order and by the use of its name seek to secure for the new Order which they have incorporated the benefit of its reputation and standing. This, we think is a fraud upon the original Order and upon the public, which a Court of Equity should enjoin. The decree of the court below, denying the injunction and dismising the bill will accordingly be reversed and the case will be remanded for further proceedings not inconsistent herewith."

An appeal was taken to the U. S. Supreme Court and the Grand Legal Adviser, Perry W. Howard, again represented the Order and the appeal was denied. This decision, according to Grand Legal Adviser Howard "marked a new dav for Negro fraternalism in that it forever set at rest the abortive effort of some white fraternities to shut out the Negro." It also marked the beginning of the end of numerous court battles over the legal corporate existence of the Order.

**Benevolent and Protective Order of Elks* v. *Improved Benevolent and Protective Order of Elks of the World* 205 N.Y. 459, 98 N.E. 756, L.R.A. 1915B 1074; *Same* v. *Same,* 122 Tenn. 141, 118 S.W. 389.

The Thirty-first Annual Meeting of the Grand Lodge of the Improved Benevolent and Protective Order of the World was called to order by the Grand Exalted Ruler J. Finley Wilson in Detroit Armory, Detroit, Michigan, on August 26, 1930. After the appointment of officials and the opening exercises, the reading of the Minutes of the previous session was undertaken and the Chairmen of Committees began their work. Past Grand Exalted Ruler James E. Mills presided, while the Grand Exalted Ruler, J. Finley Wilson, gave his annual report. One of the keynote statements of the Grand Exalted Ruler was "there is but one way through," and according to Dr. Wilson this way was the right way.

Most of his presentations were centered around this point of view. He gave a statement of the expense account of his office and paid tribute to his co-workers. He called attention to the depression which was surrounding them and the fierce economic battle, as he termed it, which seemed to be aproaching during the next winter. He described the several cases which had come from the subordinate lodges to him for adjudication. He outlined again the Tennessee Case which had been against the Grand Lodge and was held up in Tennessee until the preliminary injunction in the Virginia Case was sustained or dissolved. Taxation was regarded by him as necessary for the maintenance of the Grand Lodge although he referred to the criticisms of it, but he said that he was able to report more financial lodges this year than ever before in the history of the Order and that only one temple had sent in a protest concerning taxes.

The Grand Exalted Ruler reported the foresight exercised in the midst of the financial depression which had struck America with the failure of bank after bank when he referred to the Commercial Bank at Wilson, North Carolina, in which the Grand Lodge had deposited $5,000. He said that the Grand Lodge had been able to cover this loss by an Indemnity Bond and so was able to collect the money just as though the bank was still in operation. He expected that they would be able to collect on the same bases from the Binga State Bank of Chicago. These collections were to come from the Bonding Company which stood for the losses. He referred to previous losses in the Tidewater Bank in Norfolk, Virginia, and the Wage Earners Bank in Savannah, Georgia, where there were no such bonds but he said as long as he was in office and had any influence, he would continue to urge that this method be used for the protection of funds and the rights of the members. He extended congratulations to several Brothers who had received appointments, notably Brother David E. Henderson of Kansas City, Kansas, who had been appointed Special Assistant to the Attorney General of the United States and Brother William C. Hueston who had been made Assistant Solicitor under the Post-Master General in the Post Office Department of the United States. This was the highest position ever given to a Negro in this Department. Congratulations were extended to Brother Oscar DePriest on securing the nomination for election to a second term as a member of the House of Representatives. The growth of state associations was described as well as the growth of the Order in spite of the various evidences of depression which were taking place all around the nation. He said that during the past year in the interest of expansion he had traveled more than fifty thousand miles, that he had planted the first lodge in Barbados, a lodge in the Phillipines at Manila Bay, a lodge at Portland, Maine, and he expected to learn shortly of the establishment of a lodge in London.

Thirty-three new lodges had been organized during the year. The Grand Exalted Ruler admitted that this was a smaller number than usual, but he alleged that it was due to the severe period through which they were going of storms, hurricanes, bank failures, drought and general depression. He paid tribute to the continuing good work of the Board of Education and the Commissioner of Education, the Health Commission, the Civil Liberties Commission and announced that a Junior Elk Group had been organized, of which he was proud, and that within another year he hoped to see 50,000 of these Junior Elks who would ultimately fill the ranks of the old heroes who were falling. Again at the close of the reading of this annual report an effort was made to reelect the Grand Exalted Ruler by acclamation, and this was finally accomplished after several points of order.

Grand Secretary, James E. Kelley, opened his report with the words, "The morning of another day has dawned." He described the twelve months previous as having been months of hard work and of suffering, but they had come to report to the Grand Lodge with the statement that the lodge was in good condition and was the strongest as well as the greatest of all fraternal organizations in the country. He felt that there was a worthy record of achievement through the various Grand Officers and departments of the organization. While the financial depresssion had been seriously affecting the economic status of the Negro, at the close of the books on July 31 there were 585 financial lodges with a membership of 52,685 with other lodges paying up but were not included in the report. From 302 lodges he had received reports which indicated that there were real estate, furniture, cash on hand totalling over $2,000,000 and that charity, including death benefits and sick benefits had been expended to the total of $105,904.35.

Grand Secretary Kelley also urged that consideration be given to the furnishing of regalia for the beautiful parades which were taking place. He spoke on the beauty and splendor of the parades and the costly uniforms which made a wonderful showing for the Order but he said that they were being manufactured by white regalia houses which give employment to white boys and girls. He suggested that the Grand Lodge itself should own and operate a regalia house and all lodges be required to buy their supplies from this house, and he urged the appointment of a committe to consider this project. He envisioned a glorious future for the Order, "increasing in membership, in financial ability, in power to serve and do good until its influence is exerted in a beneficial way in every matter that pertains to our welfare as a race." At the conclusion of this report a motion was made that a unanimous ballot be cast for Brother James E. Kelley to succeed himself as Grand Secretary and this motion was adopted.

Shortly afterward the Credentials Committee made its report showing that there were 579 lodges represented and that there were 986 delegates in the Grand Lodge. Considering the difficult financial stress which was upon many members of the lodges and the unemployment which had taken place, it was a little short of remarkable that so large a group of representatives of the subordinate lodges would be present at this Grand Lodge session. This too was a testimony to the fidelity and loyalty of the members of the Improved Benevolent and Protective Order of Elks of the World. It was also a tribute to the leadership of the Grand Exalted Ruler, the Grand Secretary, the Gand Treasurer and the Commissioner of Education, the Grand Legal Adviser and other Grand Officers who were cooperating in the development of a significant movement among Negroes.

The report of Grand Legal Adviser, Perry W. Howard, referred to the lawsuits, the bank failures and other notable cases which had been handled by his office. He concluded by recommending that the Grand Lodge reassert the domicile of the corporation as being in the State of New Jersey and as having been there since its incorporation in 1906. The Grand Lodge received and referred the report to the Committee on Grand Officers' Reports. The Executive Director of the Commission on Civil Liberties, Brother Robert J. Nelson, made a report concerning the work and activities of his committee. He referred to the cooperation which had been had with the National Association for the Advancement of Colored People and the successful opposition to the confirmation of Judge John J. Parker to the United

States Supreme Court. Strong representations were made to the Senate Judiciary Committee against a favorable report on Judge Parker's nomination. Protest was made against the segregation of Colored Gold Star Mothers by the War Department when they were sent to the battle fields of France to view the graves of their sons who had fallen in the First World War. Lynchings, unjust treatment, personal surveys of civic conditions in Maryland, Delaware, and Pennsylvania were also protested at this Grand Lodge Session. He recommended a study of the allotment of funds for educational purposes to the land grant colleges, a study of restrictive covenants and the problems of agriculture as they related to Negro workers as well as workers in industry.

The work of education was reported by Commissioner W. C. Hueston. He said that since 1925 they had granted 118 separate and distinct scholarships. He described individual young men who were making good in various parts of the nation. He said that there were three graduates in 1927 who had held scholarships, two in 1928, six in 1929 and six again in 1930.

The Commissioner of Education continued "We go forward in a comprehensive effort to bring into the race a spirit for full and complete education for every boy and girl," and that he wanted to keep up their enthusiasm so that they will ever keep up the effort of race advancement. He concluded his report with the words, "We go forward to greater things." On motion, the rules were suspended and Commissioner Hueston was reelected by acclamation.

The financial condition of the Order was shown in the report of Grand Treasurer Henry S. Warner. The balance on hand was $40,717.66. The Grand Auditors verified this report and complimented the Grand Officers on the manner in which the books of the Order were kept. The Grand Trustees reported that the economic conditions in the country were the worst in twenty years, with thousands being thrown out of work to make places for white men. These conditions had caused a tremendous loss of revenue for the Order and the loss of members in the subordinate lodges.

The report of the Health Commission was made by Dr. William J. Thompkins of Kansas City, Missouri. He reported on the results of the health questionnaire, noting community health machinery, birth registrations, communicable diseases, vital statistics, health of mothers, infants, school children, food control, general sanitation and education of the public. The report concluded with the determination to keep up this health work "until every health unit and organization of America heeds the call and gives to us our newer abolition—*a better bill of health.*"

One of the new reports to this Grand Lodge session was the re-

Daughter Abbie M. Johnson, Sixth Grand Daughter Ruler, 1929-1940.

port of Dr. Charles A. Marshall, Commissioner of Junior Elks. He reported that Philadelphia and Baltimore had taken the lead in organizing units of Junior Elks. The boys were to be organized in herds of thirty. They would be taught the Elk principles of charity, justice, brotherly love and fidelity and they would learn the Negro's history in Africa and America, he said. They would have their own ritual and constitution.

Numerous persons of prominence addressed the Grand Lodge and the Committee on Fraternal Greetings from the Grand Temple was admitted. Daughter Nannie Burroughs made a stirring address assuring the Grand Lodge of the cooperation and support of the Grand Temple. The death of Grand Daughter Ruler Ella G. Beery of Chicago, Illinois, caused a deep sense of sorrow through the area of the Grand Temple and the Subordinate Temples as well as in the Grand Lodge. She had wrought a great work during the three years of her active administration, 1926-1929. She was regarded by the temples as "The Teacher." The succession of Daughter Abbie M. Johnson, Sixth Grand Daughter Ruler in 1929, brought into leadership one whose efforts seemed to parallel the deeds of Grand Exalted Ruler J. Finley Wilson. She was known subsequently as "The Crusader."

The Committee on the State of the Country reported through Dr. John R. Hawkins asserting the loyalty of Negro-Americans and stating that they were ready and willing and anxious to uphold and defend the principles upon which the government was founded and at the same time they opposed crime, mob violence, Jim-Crow laws, unfair discrimination and enforced segregation against any people because of race, creed, color or previous condition.

The *Washington Eagle* was approved as the official publication of the Order and a commission was authorized to negotiate its purchase. The Board was to discharge and employ editors and managers and every member of the lodge was required to become a subscriber at the subscription of one dollar. The health work of the temples was authorized for coordination with the work of the Commission on Health of the Grand Lodge. A special Commission of three lawyers was approved to assist the Grand Legal Adviser due to the present magnitude of litigation.

The History Committee reported that the failure of the Grand Lodge to provide funds for more exhaustive research to secure the records of the first lodges and the personal papers of older Elks had prevented the work on a large scale. The original lectures of the Order had been printed at a cost of $125.00. When funds would be made available, the Committee stated that the

DR. S. H. GEORGE, Grand Esteemed Leading Knight

EDWARD W. SIMMONS, Grand Esteemed Lecturing Knight

SIDNEY B. THOMPSON, Grand Esquire

JOHN T. RHINES, Grand Director of Athletics

compilation of material would be completed, through the cooperation of the lodges and that the manuscript would be submitted to printing establishments to ascertain the cost of publication and the same would be submitted to the Grand Lodge.

An action connected with the history of the Order was adopted by this Grand Lodge when the widow of the Founder, B. F. Howard, was introduced and made remarks concerning the birth of the Order. When it was learned that she was in need, it was recalled by Past Grand Exalted Ruler Nutter that Founder B. F. Howard had requested compensation to the extent of $5,000.00 in 1909. A motion was made and adopted that Mrs. Howard be granted a pension of one hundred dollars a month, beginning October 1, during the balance of her life. A proposal for the creation of a Department of Veterans Affairs was presented but was not approved by the Grand Lodge.

The Grand Lodge Officers for 1930-1931 were: J. Finley Wilson, Grand Exalted Ruler, Washington, D. C.; Dr. S. H. George, Grand Esteemed Leading Knight, Paducah, Ky.; G. Lee Ratcliff, Grand Esteemed Loyal Knight, Columbia S. C.; Edward W. Simmons, Grand Esteemed Lecturing Knight, New York, N. Y.; James E. Kelley, Grand Secretary, Birmingham, Ala.; Henry S. Warner, Grand Treasurer, New York, N. Y.; Sidney B. Thompson, Grand Esquire, Cleveland, Ohio; R. L. Derrick, Grand Inner Guard, Spokane, Wash.; Joseph B. Levy, Grand Tiler, Minneapolis, Minn.; William C. Hueston, Commissioner of Education, Washington, D. C.; Perry W. Howard, Grand Legal Adviser, Washington, D. C.; W. George Avant, Grand Chaplain, Durham, N. C.; C. C. Valle, Grand Organizer, Memphis, Tenn.; Dr. J. L. Leach, Grand Organist, Flint, Mich.; C. E. A. Starr, Grand Master of Social Sessions, Denver, Colo.; John T. Rhines, Director of Athletics, Washington, D. C.; Dr. Adolphus W. Anderson, Special Grand Organizer, Philadelphia, Pa.

A definite case for the Order as a world order was made with the installation of a lodge in London, England in October, 1930, by Brother Beresford Gale of Philadelphia. An account of this installation by the *New York Times* is as follows:

"BRITISH NEGRO ELKS ENTERTAIN AT NEWLY ESTABLISHED CHAPTER

London, Oct. 10—The Improved Benevolent and Protective Order of Elks of the World, a Negro society, held its first guest night at its newly established British Chapter this week. The Order, which has 500,000 members in the U. S. and the West Indies besides a scattering of members in Africa, sent Beresford Gale, a Negro businessman of Philadelphia, to organize branches in Europe.

> At the first big ceremony, after the inaugural service at St. Giles in the Fields a fortnight ago, a Zulu Choir which came to London to make phonograph records, was entertained. The Order already has found jobs for some of its unemployed."
>
> N. Y. T., Oct. 12, 1930.

With the opening of the year 1931, the interest and desires of Elks were turned toward the convention which was to assemble in Philadelphia. This was the Thirty-Second Annual Meeting of the Grand Lodge of the Improved Benevolent and Protective Order of Elks of the World. The meeting was called to order by the Grand Exalted Ruler J. Finley Wilson. The continuous note that was heard throughout this meeting was the effect of the depression upon the development of the Grand Lodge and the subordinate lodges, but this was always met with the optimistic note of going forward in spite of the depression. The serious developments which had been affecting banks in the United States had not registered themselves in the treasury of the Grand Lodge because of the Surety Bonds which had been taken out with bonding companies. The Grand Exalted Ruler admitted in his report that the growth in the past year had been more largely spiritual than otherwise, and nevertheless, there had been organized 22 new lodges during what he called, "the hardest and toughest year in our economic history." He declared that the Grand Lodge and its officers and members constituted a fighting organization and that they were ready to lock horns with those members of the Order who had endeavored to bring opprobrium and division on its officers and its rank and file of membership.

Similar references were made by the Grand Secretary in his report to the effects of the depression. He said that there were few organizations which could boast of great achievements during the past year because times have been hard and employment has not maintained its previous standards. Nevertheless he reported progress that had taken place in the lodges, in the temples, in the payment of taxes and while some lodges had suffered in activities and in membership, others had gone forward at an increasingly satisfactory pace. He reported that the Department of Junior Elks had developed and that there were 9 Junior Elk herds. The first of which was organized with a membership of 500 under the auspices of Quaker City Lodge No. 720. As he looked in the future, he stated with emphasis that we have made, are making and will continue to make progress.

The Commissioner of Education reported for his fifth year in the operation of the department and announced that there were ten graduates for the year 1931, who had been helped with scholarships by the organization and all of them were honor students in their respective institutions. He said that the year had been a hard one for the Department to face because of the depression and the economic plight in which many of the parents found themselves in not being able to raise the necessary funds, even with scholarship assistance, to send some of the students who were selected to college. He said that there was a close connection between economics and education and that this was being considered and it seemed desirable that there should be in the Department a sort of research bureau in race, economics and education. In the case of each of these, three individuals motions were made directly after their reports to elect them with the unanimous vote of the convention as addresses were made commending these individuals, and the motions were adopted for their election immediately. In the case of the Grand Treasurer there was a division following his report, on his immediate election and it was necessary to have a ballot.

The election led to the following Grand Lodge Officers for the year 1931-1932, with other appointees by the Grand Exalted Ruler: J. Finley Wilson, Grand Exalted Ruler, Washington, D. C.; Dr. S. H. George, Grand Esteemed Leading Knight, Paducah, Ky.; Roy S. Bond, Grand Esteemed Loyal Knight, Baltimore, Md.; Edward W. Simmons, Grand Esteemed Lecturing Knight, New York, N. Y.; James E. Kelley, Grand Secretary, Birmingham, Ala.; Edward W. Henry, Grand Treasurer, Philadelphia, Pa.; Sidney B. Thompson, Grand Esquire, Cleveland, Ohio.; John F. Ross, Grand Inner Guard, Washington, D. C.; Joseph B. Levy, Grand Tiler, Minneapolis, Minn.; William C. Hueston, Commissioner of Education, Washington, D. C.; Perry W. Howard, Grand Legal Adviser, Washington, D. C.; W. George Avant, Grand Chaplain, Durham, N. C.; C. C. Valle, Grand Organizer, Memphis, Tenn.; Dr. J. L. Leach, Grand Organist, Flint, Mich.; C. E. A. Starr, Grand Master of Social Sessions, Denver, Colo.; John T. Rhines, Director of Athletics, Washington, D. C.; Dr. Charles B. Fisher, Grand Medical Director, Washington, D. C.; George A. Holland, Director Junior Elks, Phoebus, Virginia.; W. W. Barnum, Chairman Committee on Official Organ, Hagerstown, Md.; William H. Vodery, Grand Band Master, New York, N. Y. The Grand Trustees were: John R. Marshall, Robert R. Church, R. E. Pharrow, W. Carey Trueheart, B. J. Bryant. The Grand Auditors were: Dr. Thomas L. Love, James B. Allen, James T. Cooper. The Health Commission consisted of Dr. William J. Thompkins, Chairman, Dr. Charles B. Fisher, Executive Secretary, Dr. Phillip A. Scott, Dr. T. T. Wendell; Dr. A. R. Biggs; Dr. E. T. Belsaw; Dr. Charles A. Hall, Statistician. The Shrine Commission consisted of John

Henry S. Warner, Grand Treasurer, 1929-1931

B. J. Bryant, Grand Trustee

James E. Allen, Grand Auditor

Charles H. Hall, Statistician

L. Webb, Dr. J. H. P. Westbrook, Guy U. Blaine, Charles Joel; the Fidelity Fund Bureau—Thomas H. Browne, Stewart E. Hoyt, Dr. W. D. Thomas, A. Morris Williams and Charles Gent. The Civil Liberties Commission consisted of Robert J. Nelson, Walter H. Land and George W. Lee.

The Grand Lodge of 1931 authorized the meeting of the next Grand Lodge in Los Angeles, California but the situation of transportation into which the country was thrown as a result of the depression made it necessary to call the Grand Lodge to meet in the East. The meeting was called at Atlantic City, New Jersey, in the Fitzgerald's Auditorium, August 23-27, 1932. The Grand Exalted Ruler declared, "There can be no real wonder, with chaos everywhere that Elkdom was in a chaos of indecision as to the convention and its place of meeting." In his annual address to the convention, the Grand Exalted Ruler said, "We are here to celebrate the end of the depression, in equal scale weighing delight and dole. The poorest way to face life is to face it depressed. Our only defense against depression is obscurity and oblivion, but we make no defense, we have chosen the offensive. We have discovered that depression is but another name for bootleg Elkdom and there is no charity, justice, brotherly love nor fidelity in observing it and bowing down before it. We cannot grow in public estimation and public depression at the same time."

He added that the lodge was solvent and sound, substantial and solid and that they were both reliable and responsible in finances and in brotherly love. He praised the work of his associates and of the deputies in the development of the Order. He had appointed Robert J. Nelson as Editor of the *Washington Eagle*. Brother Nelson had served as Editor and Publisher of the *Wilmington Advocate*, 1920-1925, and as Executive Director of the Committee on Civil Liberties since 1929. He was the author of *Masterpieces of Negro Eloquence*.

Shortly after his appointment as editor of the official organ, the *Washington Eagle*, he was appointed by Governor Gifford Pinchot of Pennsylvania as a member of the Pennsylvania Athletic Committee. The Grand Exalted Ruler then requested Judge William C. Hueston, Commissioner of Education, to edit the official organ. The work of Brother Nelson on the Civil Liberties Commission was assumed, by appointment of the Grand Exalted Ruler, by Grand Legal Adviser, Perry W. Howard and the Grand Esteemed Loyal Knight, Roy S. Bond.

The Grand Exalted Ruler described successful state association meetings in many states, the dedication of lodge homes and special consideration was given to the burning of the mortgage on the excellent property of Columbia Lodge No. 85 in Washington, D. C., and at other places. He reported that the monument approved by the Grand Lodge for the grave of Borther Henry Lincoln Johnson in Lincoln Cemetery, Washington, D. C., had been erected and dedicated with fitting ceremony on June 26, 1932. His visit with a committee to the War Department to consult Secretary of War Hurley and General MacArthur, Chief of Staff, concerning the dissolution of the Tenth Cavalry and the Twenty-fourth Infantry was described by him. He was informed that these units were not to be destroyed immediately for there were retirements and the cavalry was becoming obsolete. These regiments would be distributed in various parts of the country instead of dissolving them entirely.

The criticisms of some of his policies and adverse publicity in some newspapers were discussed by the Grand Exalted Ruler. The newspaper references to expense accounts caused him to state that these accounts had been put into print and revealed to the world of Elkdom. He said, "we have held the ship of state together and no matter what figures may be printed by newspapers, whether they represent truth or cavilling, they do represent a vast retrenchment over previous years under the expert handling of the Grand Secretary, James E. Kelley." He recommended that certified public accountants be employed to audit the books of the financial officers annually, "so that everybody will be advised where the money's all gone." A Regalia Department was recommended. He said that there was change and decay all about due to the depression and that now is the time for Elks to get together for concerted action, for "we may survive if we close ranks and offer a solid front and united program to the common enemy." A unanimous ballot was cast for his reelection.

There was truth in his statement about the seriousness of the economic situation and the difficulty of holding "the Order intact in the years after the 1929 crash, industry was operating at less than one-half of its 1929 figure, wages were 60 per cent less in 1932 and dividends were 57 per cent less than in 1929. Over twelve million people were unemployed, cotton was selling at five cents a pound, wheat at less than fifty cents and corn at thirty-one cents a bushel."

It was the opinion of the Grand Secretary, James E. Kelley, that in spite of the continued depression, the Order had much for which to be grateful. They were meeting in annual session when other organizations had called off their meetings, and he said, "the old ship has been able to shun the rocks and reach the port because of the self-reliance and sacrifice of faithful members." It was recommended later by the Grand Trustees that as a measure of economy the salaries of all Grand Officers be reduced twenty per cent and the expenses accordingly. This recommendation was adopted, but the Grand Lodge did not use the proportion for reduction. The salaries of the Grand Exalted Ruler and Grand Secretary, who spend all of their time on their official duties were reduced only ten per cent. The Grand Secretary reported that there was a loss in membership. In 1931 there were 52,179 members reported and in 1932 this number was reduced to 39,416, but nine new lodges had been added and fifteen lodges had been reinstated. He saw progress in the Past Exalted Rulers Councils now represented in the Grand Lodge, the state associations, the temples which showed increases in membership and taxes paid, the Junior Elks who had fifteen herds and the Civil Liberties Department with six local civil liberties leagues.

He emphasized the need for a program of operation within the limits of the Order's income. He gave figures to show that the Grand Lodge had been endeavoring to accomplish this purpose for four years. In 1929 the cost of the Grand Lodge meeting was $19,648.24; in 1929 it was reduced to $13,492.86; in 1930 it was further reduced to $12,386.28 and in 1931 it was $9,986.65, which represented a considerable reduction in the four-year period. There had been a general falling off of taxes paid due mainly to the fact that so many members were out of work and unable to pay. He recommended that a committee be appointed to consider the matter and work out a program of operations. The receipts for the year for the general fund was $32,916.97 or $11,916.97 less than in 1930-1931, according to the report of the Grand Treasurer, Judge Edward W. Henry. The rules were suspended and the Grand Secretary and Grand Teasurer were elected by acclamation.

The program of education was described by Commissioner William C. Hueston who reported that by 1932, there were 103 students who had been granted scholarshops by the Order. In addition to the splendid record made by these students there were two students who did four years of college work in three years, Dorothy I. Height who graduated from New York University and Ruth Hood who graduated from Indiana State Teachers College. Judge Hueston had served also as editor of the *Washington Eagle* after Brother Nelson gave up the editorship. He proposed that the paper become a weekly instead of a monthly. He also suggested that an investigation should be made of the losses occasioned by the collapse of the Standard Life Insurance Company and the National Benefit Life Insurance Company. There were hundreds of applications, he said, in the Office of the Department but that they could not receive assistance because of the lack of sufficient funds. Judge Hueston was also reelected by acclamation.

The first formal report from a Grand Esteemed Loyal Knight was made by Brother Roy S. Bond, who gave some of his experiences in association with the endeavors of the Grand Exalted Ruler in continuing the advancement of the work of the Order. He too was reelected by acclamation. The Grand Legal Adviser, Perry W. Howard, reported that he was happy to announce to the Grand Lodge that the appeal in the Virginia Case to the U. S. Supreme Court had failed, and he said, "The Grand Exalted Ruler has been vindicated and the Grand Lodge, Improved Benevolent and Protective Order of Elks of the World, has now this name against the world, all the gates of hell cannot prevail against it. For it is yours to enjoy—untrammeled and unharmed—and a priceless legacy to pass on to the unborn generations." A standing vote of thanks was given to the Grand Legal Adviser.

The activities of the Executive Director of the Civil Liberties Commission, Robert J. Nelson, concerned discrimination in the nation's capital, protests against lynching, the expansion of segregated schools and the contrast furnished by the actions of Commissioner Hueston in making awards of scholarships in all types of colleges, the economic situation and the army's action on the Tenth Cavalry and the Twenty-fourth Infantry. He directed attention to the efforts of Communists among Negroes who realized that there was unrest among Negroes and he said, "although today the pride of our Race, our soldiery, has been reduced and suffered the ignominy of being almost a servant contingent, yet we cannot join any party that is recreant to virtue, liberty and independence. And, above all, we cannot join with any party that would alienate us from the God of our Fathers and the religion of Jesus Christ." He reported that the Grand Exalted Ruler had held a conference of a group of both races and as a result under Judge Henry a movement against Communist organization was undertaken. Brother Nelson urged that the power of the fraternity should be used in this struggle against Communism. It was at this period that Negro Elks decided to continue their program of protest within the framework of the Constitution and adopt the Bill of Rights as the platform upon which they would take their stand as they fought racism which was debasing the democratic philosophy of American life.

After only one year of activity the Junior Elks were reported by Dr. Charles A. Marshall to have fifty-two clubs and fifteen herds in twenty-nine states and in Montreal, Toronto and Vancouver, Canada. The work of the Health Commission had centered around the influencing of the appointment of Negro physicians as city and county health officers and Negro nurses as health nurses. Health units had been established in many temples. Dental clinics and the appointment of dentists to school systems had been secured. The report was submitted by Drs. William J. Thompkins, Charles B. Fisher, T. T. Wendell and E. T. Belsaw. The Shrine Commission and the Fidelity Bureau made progress reports.

The Grand Officers for 1932-1933 were J. Finley Wilson, Grand Exalted Ruler, Washington, D. C.; Dr. S. H. George, Grand Esteemed Leading Knight, Paducah, Ky.; Edward W. Simmons, Grand Esteemed Lecturing Knight, New Work N. Y.; James E. Kelley, Grand Secretary, Birmingham, Ala.; Edward W. Henry, Grand Treasurer, Philadelphia, Pa.; John Freeman, Grand Esquire, Philadelphia, Pa.; John F. Ross, Grand Inner Guard, Washington, D. C.; Joseph B. Levy, Grand Tiler, Minneapolis, Minn.; William C. Hueston, Commissioner of Education, Washington, D. C.; W. George Avant, Grand Chaplain, Durham, N. C.; Dr. J. L. Leach, Grand Organist, Flint, Michigan; David McDaniels, Grand Master of Social Sessions, New York, N. Y.; John T. Rhines, Director of Athletics, Washington, D. C.; Charles B. Fisher, Grand Medical Director, Washington, D. C.; George A. Holland, Director Junior Elks, Tuskegee, Ala.; W. W. Barnum, Chairman Committee on Official Organ, Hagerstown, Md.; William H. Vodery, Grand Bandmaster, New York, N . Y.

These Officers were installed by Past Grand Master James E. Mills. The advancement of the Order had been directed through the leadership of the Grand Exalted Ruler and the corps of Grand Officers given him by the Grand Lodge. Despite the difficult economic conditions, the delegates left the Grand Lodge sessions with hopes and plans for a greater future for Elkdom as it served the people of color.

Chapter XIV
Internal Developments in the Crisis

With the depression placing its impact firmly upon the Negro population and the reality of the loss of jobs under the accepted doctrine of this day of the last to be hired and the first to be fired among America's peoples, the Negroes faced a crisis more severe upon them than upon others. Not only their wages, but their living standards were forced lower than those of the white population. In 1935 their median income in selected Northern cities averaged a little less than half the income of white families. The facts showed that about one-half of all Negro families were on relief in the North. The economic situation in the South was worse. For example, in Mobile, Alabama, a Negro family had an income of $481 a year, while a white family had an income of $1,419. This disparaging picture was repeated in most of the areas of the United States.

While Negroes constituted one-tenth of the total population of the United States, they comprised an average of approximately one-sixth of the relief population. According to the Relief Census of October, 1933, Negroes on relief comprised 17.8 per cent of the total Negro population whereas only 9.5 per cent of all white persons and other races were on relief. This situation had increased by January, 1935, for it was found that 25.5 per cent of all Negroes were on relief as compared with 15.5 per cent of all white and other races on relief. This disproportion was more pronounced in the case of Negroes who lived in cities. According to the Relief Census of October, 1933, the percentage of the Negroes in cities receiving relief was almost three times that of the white population living in the cities.

Despite these disturbing factors, economic planning began in Congress in the spring of 1933 leading to the adoption of measures which President Franklin D. Roosevelt regarded as necessary for the New Deal Program and Negroes shared in the benefits of unemployment relief and in the rehabilitation measures. Along with other citizens they received relief benefits in the form of money, food, rent, orders, surplus commodities and in many places medical and dental aid. Their needs were great, however, because they constituted so large a proportion of the relief population. In round numbers the Negro families on relief in 1935 were 2.500 whereas the white families totaled 5,400, which indicated that the proportion of Negroes in the relief population was far in excess of their proportion in the general population. Discriminations in the government and the disproportionate plight of the Negro created unrest and dissatisfaction among Negroes themselves concerning the Recovery Program. The attitudes of Negroes were shown very clearly in the classic definition of the NRA, National Recovery Act, which was repeatedly used under the caption "Negroes Ruined Again."

While this situation affecting the Negro population was continuing, the Improved Benevolent and Protective Order of Elks of the World endeavored to carry on its program and was having success with its operation. It was holding its Grand Lodge and subordinate lodge sessions as usual, although the distressing information of situations throughout the nation affecting all types of business and industry as well as the families, city dwellers and farm population were being brought into their meetings.

When the Grand Exalted Ruler opened the Thirty-Fourth Annual Meeting of the Grand Lodge at the Walker Building in Indianapolis, Indiana, on August 21-25, 1933, he came as he said to make a report of his stewardship, "Without emphasizing the magnificent part played by Elkdom in the great economic crisis, at the same time outlining a fraternal policy for the antlered herd which will connect it with the main trunk line of the Roosevelt National Recovery Administration."

He called for a fighting program for Negro voters of America so that the Negro would be not only restored to his economic balance, but might be properly aligned for future economic progress with other constituent groups that make up the citizenship of this country. He called attention to the National Benefit Life Insurance Company which had become insolvent back in 1927 and was trying to make a come-back in the economic sphere, although it had been in receivership since that period. The receivers in 1933 petitioned the court for permission to sell or transfer the modified insurance. The Grand Exalted Ruler reported that he made answer as he thought that a successful program could be worked out for mutualization. He proposed a committee to endeavor to work out such a plan. He was very much concerned about this case, as well as other cases in which Negro financial institutions were involved.

He had served also as President of the Colored Voters League of America which had been constituted in 1928. He declared that there should be a larger number of Negroes who were voting in the United States and the League should undertake to suggest programs of activity for them. Among the questions which he suggested that should be asked was: (1) "Do you believe that NRA should signify Negro Recovery Also?" He was interested

MINUTES

OF THE

Thirty-Fourth Annual Meeting

GRAND LODGE

IMPROVED BENEVOLENT AND PROTECTIVE ORDER OF ELKS OF THE WORLD

B. F. HOWARD, Founder
I. B. P. O. E. of W.

CONVENED IN

Walker Building

Indianapolis, Indiana

August 21-25, 1933

Cover-Page of Minutes of the Thirty-Fourth Annual Meeting, Grand Lodge, I.B.P.O.E. of W., Indianapolis, Indiana, August 21-25, 1933

in Civil Liberties Leagues and stated that through his supervision there had been organized twelve units during the past year and these units were active in a number of ways assisting the people in their bad situations. He had taken an active part in the Scottsboro Case. In addition to raising money he had brought Judge Leibowitz to the nation's capitol where he spoke before an overflow audience with the Grand Legal Adviser Perry W. Howard presiding at the meeting. He was made President of the Ethiopian Federation, Inc., which became a national organization with *The Voice of Ethiopia* as its weekly organ.

The adopted program of the Order went forward as usual. The educational work under Judge William C. Hueston was continuing to maintain a good record for itself. The Grand Exalted Ruler stated that he had traveled more in this year, 1932-1933, than at any time since the beginning of the depression in 1929. Most of this traveling had been done at his own personal expense and for the purpose of encouraging and building up the subordinate lodges. A membership drive had been inaugurated and he had been able to make new candidates and reinstate old members in excess of some 40,000, so he reported. It was his belief also that as he traveled around at the end of 1934, the country would be on the road toward recovery and that the membership would exceed 50,000. Some lodges had become unfinancial but this was due mainly to the difficulties of the crisis which was before them and their individual members. He also stated that the support of the lodges had been responsible for putting over the program of the administration dealing with national recovery. He believed, however, that there must be "a comprehensive policy of financial rehabilitation of the colored race in America which is a part of the trunk-line program of the National Recovery Administration of Franklin D. Roosevelt." He was determined that there should be a program which would move in the direction of the defeat of Jim-Crowism and segregation everywhere in the United States, and he said that the fraternity must identify itself with the measures in order that it might deserve the high regard which the public had for it. Toward this end, the fraternity, he said. should be non-partisan politically with an interest in men and measures rather than in Republicanism or in Democratic Party politics.

The Grand Secretary was of the opinion that the New Deal was going to afford increased employment and that there would be a return of the members to their lodges with the resultant activity. He reported that nineteen of the old lodges had been reinstated, that seven new lodges had been added to the rolls during the past year and that this could be regarded as a most encouraging indication of the fact that Elkdom was making progress in the period of the crisis. The State Associations, the Temples, the Junior Elks with ten new herds and the Civil Liberties League with four new leagues were making progress in their activities to serve the sections of the membership allotted to them. He added that the lodge was still operating beyond its income and that in 1931-32 reductions had been made in the operating expenses but that the reductions were not sufficient to offset the decrease in receipts. He therefore appealed to the Grand Lodge to make the financial foundations of the lodge safer and that they might be able to balance the budget in spite of the decrease of income. This should mean the development of a budget, through a committee to be appointed by the Grand Exalted Ruler.

It is of interest to observe that following the reports of both of these general officers, Grand Exalted Ruler Wilson and Grand Secretary Kelley, the rules were suspended and the Grand Esquire was called upon to cast the unanimous ballot of the convention for their reelection for the ensuing term. It was evident also from a report of the Grand Treasurer that not only the country had been passing through, as he called it, "one of the most critical periods in its financial history," but that the Grand Lodge had also had similar experiences. He stated that it had been decided to make the Citizen's and Southern Bank and Trust Company the depository of all the lodge funds and that the bank had immediately agreed to deliver into the custody of the Grand Treasurer United States Bonds of sufficient value to cover doubly whatever amount the Grand Lodge might carry in the bank. He stated that this agreement had been carried out and that the deposits with the bank accordingly were insured by United States Bonds. At the conclusion of his report the unanimous ballot was cast by the Esquire for his reelection.

The program of education as developed by the Commissioner of Education, Judge William C. Hueston, was being conducted with increased momentum as a result of the work of the regional directors and the state directors. The contests during the year, he said, were largely attended and more vigorously contested than ever before and he knew this from the attendance which he himself had seen at most of these Oratorical Contests. He still felt the difficulties of operating on a reduced income and from the requests which were coming to him there was need for an increased budget to do the work of aiding students. He had devoted his time also as managing editor of the *Washington Eagle* and each month he had published the paper devoting its columns to news concerning the Order. The circulation had been confined to the lodges and temples and other subscribers who desired to take the paper. He was also of the opinion that the paper should be made a weekly and that the lodge should undertake to establish its own printing, badge and uniform plants. The rules were again suspended and the Grand Esquire cast the unanimous ballot for the reelection of William C. Hueston as Commissioner of Education for the ensuing term.

Realizing that the Negro population was not receiving its part in the National Recovery Program, the Grand Lodge through the Grand Trustees urged that Negro citizens be included in such a way that they might secure the prosperity which was proposed to be received through the National Recovery Program. They said that they asked no more and should be given no less than a just proportion of the expected prosperity. They endorsed the program of the Grand Exalted Ruler and the interest taken by him in securing employment for the Negro group and their integration into the program of the NRA in order that employment may come to them as to others irrespective of race or creed. The Grand Legal Adviser had been rendering opinions during the year to the lodges, although there was no case pending against the Order during this period, and had also devoted his time to the Department of Civil Liberties which has been transferred to his direction. He stressed the importance of this organization for said he, "you may have education, brotherly love, fidelity and even wealth, but if you are without civil liberties, you are all dressed up with nowhere to go." The Health Commission's report delivered by Dr. William J. Thompkins showed continuous endeavors to care for the instances of bad health which were numerous in Negro communities. The report was a very impressive one and was received with applause by the Grand Lodge. One of the proposals by the Health Commission was that every temple in the jurisdiction should have a health unit.

As a result of the pressures of the current crisis, the per capita taxation was reduced from twenty-five cents to twenty cents. It was also provided that the term of the Grand Exalted Ruler was to be for two years and that this term would begin with the 1933 session of the Grand Lodge. A committee with fraternal greetings from the Grand Temple made its visitation headed by Daughter Lethia Fleming, Daughter Ella G. Berry, Daughter Ida Cummings and others. Responses were made to the addresses which were delivered by these Daughter Elks. One of the actions of the Grand Lodge was the grant of authority to the Grand Exalted Ruler to appoint a committee to represent the

JAMES A. JACKSON, Grand Commissioner of Economies

REV. W. GEORGE AVANT, Grand Chaplain

ROY S. BOND, Grand Esteemed Loyal Knight

DR. MARCUS F. WHEATLAND, Grand Esteemed Loyal Knight; Grand Treasurer, 1946-

I.B.P.O.E. of W. on the Joint Committee on National Recovery as it engaged in the war against depression.

The Grand Lodge Officers for 1933-34 were: J. Finley Wilson, Grand Exalted Ruler, Washington, D. C.; Dr. S. H. George, Grand Esteemed Leading Knight, Paducah, Ky.; Roy S. Bond, Grand Esteemed Loyal Knight, Baltimore, Md.; Edward W. Simmons, Grand Esteemed Lecturing Knight, New York, N. Y.; James E. Kelley, Grand Secretary, Birmingham, Ala.; Edward W. Henry, Grand Treasurer, Philadelphia, Pa.; John Freeman, Grand Esquire, Philadelphia, Pa.; John F. Ross, Grand Inner Guard, Washington, D. C.; W. George Avant, Grand Chaplain, Durham, N. C.; Claude S. White, Grand Tiler, Indianapolis, Ind.; William C. Hueston, Commissioner of Education, Washington, D. C.; Perry W. Howard, Grand Legal Adviser, Washington, D. C.; Walter F. Weir, Grand Organist, Long Island, N. Y.; John T. Rhines, Director of Athletics, Washington, D. C.; W. T. Meade Grant, Jr., Director of Junior Elks, New Orleans, La.; W. W. Barnum, Chairman Publishing Board, Hagerstown, Md.; William H. Vodery, Grand Band Master, New York, N. Y.; F. King Watkins, Grand Organizer, Durham, N. C.

A regular feature of the Grand Lodge sessions had been instituted by the Department of Education. On Sunday speakers were sent to the various churches, on the following Monday morning, the Elks Alumni Scholarship Association held its annual meeting. The Daughter Elks gave a luncheon for the contestants and in the evening the annual Oratorical Contest was held. It was usual for enthusiastic crowds to attend and for a large chorus to render the music.

This was typical of the opening of the Thirty-fifth Annual Meeting of the Grand Lodge at Fitzgerald's Auditorium, Atlantic City, New Jersey, August 26-31, 1934. The Commissioner of Education planned these activities and they were conducted with marked success, with six capable contestants. The session opened with 192 lodges represented and 16 Past Grand Exalted Ruler Councils, who first heard the annual report of the Grand Exalted Ruler with the statement that the Order had been "through fire, earthquake and tidal wave during the past four years," and yet he stated that the Order was "a solvent corcorpation, substantial, good and solid," in spite of the national crisis. He had been determined to keep up the membership program and with Commissioner Hueston as Director of the membership drive, the campaign was continued. This was not a program of expansion but of internal development. The Proclamation of the Grand Exalted Ruler declaring that the Order should "increase our membership" was passed on to the lodges.

It was decided to concentrate efforts first in New York City. The Grand Exalted Ruler, the Grand Secretary and the Commissioner of Education visited lodges in December, 1933, January and February, 1934, and developed a spirit which had not been manifest since 1929. They also went into New Jersey to stimulate the lodges there.

There were forty-four lodges which had increased their membership one hundred per cent or more between 1933 and 1934. A prize had been offered for the lodge which had the largest increase. The award went to Manhattan Lodge No. 45 of New York City which had increased its membership from 1,000 in October, 1933 to 2,406 in July, 1934. Since there were five lodges in Manhattan the increase of Manhattan Lodge under these circumstances was the more remarkable.

The committees of the Grand Lodge continued their activities in advancing the external relations of the organization and these had direct relations internally also. The Civil Liberties Commission had devoted its attention to protests against the continued lynchings in the country, the Texas primaries, aid to governmental agencies in seeking to get what the committee called "a square deal under the New Deal" and the need for sane and sober leadership in all communities was called for in the report, which was given by Brother William H. Land as Director. The program of athletics directed by Brother John T. Rhines had manifested itself in the various leagues in which organizations were playing in the athletic field. There was a reorganization of the progam as it related itself to the state associations and the subordinate lodges and temples. The committee stated that its object was not only to have participation in these recreational and athletic activities but also to reduce the great amount of juvenile delinquency. The report of the Health Commission was again of marked interest to the organization as it indicated the work which needed to be done particularly in the field of tuberculosis and cancer, venereal diseases and diet.

The Grand Lodge Officers for 1934-35 were as follows: J. Finley Wilson, Grand Exalted Ruler, Washington, D. C.; Dr. S. H. George, Grand Esteemed Leading Knight, Paducah, Ky.; Roy S. Bond, Grand Esteemed Loyal Knight, Baltimore, Md.; Joseph A. Brown, Grand Esteemed Lecturing Knight, New York, N. Y.; James E. Kelley, Grand Secretary, Birmingham, Ala.; Edward W. Henry, Grand Treasurer, Philadelphia, Pa.; John Freeman, Grand Esquire, Philadelphia, Pa.; John F. Ross, Grand Inner Guard, Washington, D. C.; Claude S. White, Grand Tiler, Indianapolis, Ind.; William C. Hueston, Commissioner of Education, Washington, D. C.; Perry W. Howard, Grand Legal Ad-

Daughter Elizabeth Kimbrough, Grand Daughter Treasurer, 1933-1952.

viser, Washington, D. C.; W. George Avant, Grand Chaplain, Durham, N. C.; James A. Jackson, Grand Organist, New York, N. Y.; John T. Rhines, Director of Athletics, Washington, D. C.; Dr. Charles B. Fisher, Grand Medical Director, Washington, D. C.; W. T. Meade Grant, Jr., Director of Junior Elks, New Orleans, La., W. W. Barnum, Chairman Publishing Board, Hagerstown, Md.; James Miller, Grand Band Master, Washington, D. C.; F. King Watkins, Grand Organizer, Durham, N. C.; and four Grand Organizers in the respective areas of the nation.

The Daughter Elks facing the depression maintained their continuous advances in membership and the building of the traditions of the Order. In 1935 Memorial Day, May 30, was designated as a day for the special commemoration of the life of the Founder, Emma V. Kelley. It was authorized that annual pilgrimages would be made to the Calvary Cemetery at Norfolk, Virginia, where she was buried. A monument has been erected there and unveiled at the first Memorial service in 1934.

The growth of the work of the women leaders of Elkdom was demonstrated in not only 35,000 members and the large conventions held by them as the years passed, but also in the thousands of dollars raised for education and scholarships. During the administration of Grand Daughter Ruler Abbie Johnson and Daughter Buena V. Kelley, Second Grand Daughter Secretary, who undertook the secretarial work in 1932, the Past Grand Officers Council was organized, the first junior temple was set up, the idea of a national shrine for unfortunate women was adopted as a project and the organization of Ozalea Temple No. 628 in London, England gave an international character to the Daughter Elks. Emphasis was placed on Civil Liberties, anti-segregation, opposition to derogatory language on the radio and discourtesies to Negroes in travel. The Daughter Elks were parallelling the work of their brothers in the depression thirties and were also building solidly within their organization.

The movement to build internally for the Improved Benevolent and Protective Order of Elks of the World was continued as the Grand Lodge moved into the next year. When the Thirty-sixth Annual Meeting assembled at the Masonic Temple in Washington, D. C., August 26-31, 1935, there was one of the largest and most enthusiastic gatherings which assembled for the Educational and Economic Congress. This meeting was held at the Garnet-Patterson Junior High School with the Commissioner of Education, Judge W. C. Hueston, presiding. Its purpose was to study the problems and present their several aspects which affected the educational and economic status of the Negro and devise some ways for securing better facilities and opportunities.

DAUGHTER BUENA V. KELLEY, Second Grand Daughter Secretary, 1932-

The address which Brother Hueston gave stressed the urgent need of the schools to meet the challenges which were before them and the further need to assist qualified, capable boys and girls to complete their college and professional training. Other speakers included Dr. Gordon B. Hancock, Dr. Garnet C. Wilkinson, Brother Benjamin L. Gaskins, a member of the Board of Education of the District of Columbia, Dr. Ambrose Caliver of the United States Office of Education, the Grand Exalted Ruler, Dr. William H. Hastie, then of the Department of Interior and Dr. Robert C. Weaver, Lieutenant Lawrence A. Oxley from the Office of the U. S. Department of Labor, Dr. Sadie Mossell Alexander, Dr. Emmett J. Scott, Dean William E. Taylor of the Howard University Law School, Past Grand Exalted Ruler Harry H. Pace who was then Assistant Corporation Council of the State of Illinois, Miss Nannie Burroughs and the Grand Officers of the Order, including the Grand Secretary, James E. Kelley and the Grand Legal Adviser, Perry W. Howard.

The Baccalaureate address of the Department of Education was delivered at the Metropolitan African Methodist Episcopal Church on the following Sunday morning with a crowd of more than 3,000 persons present at the services. The Baccalaureate address was delivered by Dr. Charles H. Wesley, at that time Professor of History at Howard University, who used as his subject, "Vision and Response." The Alumni Association met at the Metropolitan Baptist Church with the address being delivered by Attorney Emory B. Smith and the student alumni address by Joseph Watty. The annual Oratorical Contest was held at the Metropolitan A.M.E. Church with the same interested audience and very capable speakers with Judge William C. Hueston presiding.

When the Grand Lodge met for its opening session, called to order by Grand Exalted Ruler J. Finley Wilson and the regular opening procedure had been followed, the Committee on Credentials made its report, with 234 lodges in attendance, nineteen Past Exalted Rulers Councils and ten state associations represented. This report represented a large increase over the attendance of the previous annual session, 1934. The first of the reports made was made by Grand Secretary James E. Kelley. This report showed that he believed not only that the organization should grow internally and continue to be what he called "the greatest fraternal organization," but he said that the greatest proof of an organization's right to live and grow was the service that it rendered mankind and he felt that there was a substantial increase in the services that were being offered by the Grand Lodge along all of its lines of endeavor. He added that

Edward W. Henry, Grand Treasurer, 1931-1946

there had been twelve new lodges instituted and sixty-one lodges which had formerly been unfinancial had been reinstated, all of which was due largely to the efforts of the Grand Officers to reactivate the lodges and to work internally for their advancement. This work was also advanced by the activity of the Deputies and Organizers in their respective districts who accomplished great work in the stimulation of activity. The Junior Elks were growing and there had been eight new herds organized. The reports from the Temples showed substantial increases in their membership and in the payment of taxes due the Grand Lodge. The Grand Secretary concluded his report with the statement that during the past year the officers had worked hard, "to lift high Elkdom's banner of progress." He received an ovation at the conclusion of his report and the motion was made to reelect him by acclamation and this was adopted by the Grand Lodge.

Notwithstanding the widespread complaints of depression in hard times, said Grand Treasurer Edward W. Henry in his annual report, "the members had stood solidly behind the Order and it was in a remarkably satisfactory condition." This was due, he said, primarily to the loyal support of the membership and the fine spirit of cooperation existing between the lodges and the Elk brotherhood. The total receipts for the year were $45,712.37 and the balance to the credit of all funds was listed as $13,502.22. The report of the Grand Legal Adviser showed that there had been two major difficulties with which he had dealt but none of them had been with outside groups. There had been internal differences developing over the session in Washington and the session in Indianapolis. He added that there was no contention on the outside.

The Grand Exalted Ruler's report gave emphasis to the report of the Grand Secretary concerning the growth of the Order, emphasizing the figures which he had given. He stated that there had been three lodges established in New York. The biggest lodge made during the year was National Capital No. 980 with nearly 500 members. There had also been a number of dedications of buildings occupied by lodges in several cities. These building programs had gone along in conjunction in several places with the membership drives. He congratulated the departments of educational and economic conferences, health, athletics, shrine, fidelity fund, Civil Liberties for the excellent work which they had been doing for the organization. At the conclusion of his address there was a presentation of a picture of the Grand Exalted Ruler as a gift from the Elks of the State of Florida. The Grand Exalted Ruler presented to the Grand Lodge Brother Jessie Owens and referred to his athletic successes while stating that some 500 Elks had been initiated into the Order in the State of Ohio. Brothers J. A. Mercer Burwell and Hobson Reynolds received great tributes from the Order for the work which they had done in the legislatures of New Jersey and Pennsylvania respectively. A picture was also presented of Judge William C. Hueston and was accepted by the Grand Lodge.

The Commissioner of Education's report presented the needs of the school populations in states showing the inequalities and the need for local lodges to be interested in the unequal situations in their respective communities and to begin to undertake efforts to remedy these situations. He said that the race needs educators and economists and that we should be endeavoring to support increasingly the program to develop these. He spoke of the graduates who were coming out this year with the support of the program of education maintained by the lodges and the temples. He regarded this as a very necessary work and stated that since the department had been started sixty-six young people had been graduated from college and some one hundred and forty-five students had been assisted. He described the work of the *Washington Eagle* in maintaining its place as the official organ and expressed the hope that at some time there would be a printing plant as well as a regalia house to furnish the lodge with the services of these two agencies. At the conclusion of his report he was reelected by acclamation, just as had been done in the case of the Grand Exalted Ruler.

The Committee on Resolutions offered one in which it expressed the consciousness of the unrest throughout the civilized world and the crisis through which the world was passing. It was their opinion that the call of Haile Selassie, Emperor of Ethiopia to the Christian world to bow in prayer for peace was a call which should be heeded by American Negroes. The resolutions said that the lone remaining black empire in Africa was being threatened with invasion and dissolution. The resolution recommended that the Grand Order of Elks through its Grand Exalted Ruler and Grand Officers take every step possible to aid in stopping the threatened war and to preserve the sovereignty of this last Negro empire. The motion was adopted by the Grand Lodge.

Another resolution, which was of historical significance, laid the basis for the expansion of the work in Civil Liberties. It was resolved that "the Director of Civil Liberties is hereby directed to secure and maintain a central office" and that ten dollars a month be appropriated for the use of the Civil Liberties Department. This motion was adopted and referred to the Grand Exalted Ruler.

The most significant development of the Grand Lodges of 1935-

36 was the interpretations and applications of the ideals of the fraternity to the situations affecting the race. At these sessions there were men who were thinking and planning for the people and endeavoring to discover ways by which they could improve their conditions. The keynote of the messages delivered by the speakers at the sessions and the reports of the Grand Officers were not only to build the fraternity within but also to insist upon service through its members and lodges to others on the outside. The confident opinion frequently expressed was, having

A History
—of The—
Founding-And-Workings
—of The—
Improved Benevolent, Protective Order
of Elks
of the World.

Sketches of the founder, Some
Outstanding Members, and all
Past Grand Exalted Rulers
of the Order

including
The Outstanding Proceedings
of the Grand Lodge Sessions
years. 1899 - 1933 inclusive.

—Foreword—

The following is a true account of the origin of the I.B.P.O.E. of W and also a true account of the Work and Sterling Events of past Grand Lodges.

The Material for this book was gathered after Much research and Travel by Jas. E. Kelley. G.S. of The I.B.P.O.E. of W.

Manuscript, Title and Foreword of Grand Secretary James E. Kelley's History of the I.B.P.O.E. of W. (First pencil copy of 16 pages).

strengthened the internal organization, the lodges could now make themselves into more effective instruments for service to a people who needed it. Their social program had been expanded and its services had been widened.

In spite of the fact that there were still effects of the changing economic conditions facing the Order, the Grand Officers seemed to be undaunted in carrying out the plan to conduct the work which had been so well planned. It was not strange accordingly to find the Grand Exalted Ruler reporting to the Thirty-seventh Meeting of the Grand Lodge which convened in the Elks Home at Brooklyn, New York, August 25-29, 1936, that this year had been a year of progress. He, with the Grand Organizer, had traveled extensively from Memphis to New Orleans through the Delta section, to the Atlantic Coast, covering Tennessee, Alabama, Georgia, Mississippi and Louisiana and then later into the Middle West, moving from this area into the Far West. The Grand Exalted Ruler was proud of the situation in which the Elks found themselves. He said that "it stands today as the most progressive organization in the whole racial setup of the world. Its membership standing is among the highest. Its principles are loftiest. Its ideals meet the answer of the lonely heart in the midst of the fast moving situation."

As an evidence of the fact that the Grand Lodge was becoming in reality a Grand Lodge of the Elks of the World, twenty Spanish speaking delegates entered the Hall and were presented to the Grand Lodge by Brother C. C. Valle, Grand Organizer. They were welcomed by the Grand Exalted Ruler and the interpretation was made by Brother Valle.

All of the reports showed increases in the various areas represented. The Committee on Credentials reported that there were 257 lodges represented, nineteen Past Exalted Rulers' Councils, seven herds, fourteen state associations and deputies to the number of thirty. Grand Secretary James E. Kelley in making his report stated that Brother Arthur J. Riggs who had passed on to the Great Beyond since the last Grand Lodge had sent him a brief summary of the birth of the Order. This created in Brother Kelley the desire to continue the research for other valuable information and when he made his report for 1936 and

Brief History of the Order

AND THE

Eighth Annual Report

OF

GRAND SECRETARY

James E. Kelley

TO THE

37TH ANNUAL MEETING

GRAND LODGE

IMPROVED BENEVOLENT AND PROTECTIVE ORDER OF ELKS OF THE WORLD

Brooklyn, New York

August, 1936

Brief History of the Order in the Eighth Annual Report of Grand Secretary James E. Kelley to the 37th Annual Meeting, Grand Lodge, Improved Benevolent and Protective Order of Elks of the World, 1936.

it was subsequently published, he placed in it a review in brief form of the past history of the Order. It was the first time that there had been a correct presentation and interpretation of the beginnings of the Improved Benevolent and Protective Order of Elks of the World.

His report stated that there had been fifteen new lodges instituted, forty-four lodges were reactivated. There were two new councils and twelve new herds. The records showed that the Order was growing steadily not only in the organization of lodges and their reactivation but also in the organization of new temples together with an increase in the temple membership. As to receipts, he found that the cash balance was somewhat larger than the balance last year and the receipts had surpassed this previous year. He found, however, that the income of the educational department had not been sufficient to carry on its work in order to meet the scholarship demands. The Commissioner of Education had often permitted his salary to go unpaid in order that the scholarship grants might be paid to the successful recipients.

The Grand Treasurer's report showed that there had been received since the last Grand Lodge a total of $48,094.17 and with a balance brought forward from the previous year, there was a total cash of $61,596.39. In addition to this amount there were special funds which had received amounts, such as the General Fund, $9,198.74; the Junior Elks Fund, $278.26; the Shrine Fund, $294.00; the Henry Lincoln Johnson Memorial Fund, $173.09; the Florida Storm Relief Fund, $225.54.

The Education Program had grown extensively according to the report of Commissioner Hueston, for when it was undertaken its object was to assist indigent young people of our group to improve their educational condition. Scholarships were established and oratorical plans were continued in operation through contests. He revealed some of the figures dealing with inequalities in the school situation. He referred to the 15 Southern and border states in which there are significant inequalities. He said that the per capita tax for high school students was $11.47 expended for whites and $2.11 for colored and he described the number of illiterates according to the census of the United States and declared that it was "absolutely impossible for the Negro race to advance to the degree desirable if handicapped by these conditions." He referred to this because it gave an opportunity for him to stress the importance of the Department of Education and the necessity for broadening its services. He stated that in order that this might be done it was necessary for every member to put himself squarely behind the educational program. He was encouraged by the large gatherings in attendance at the Educational Congresses held the night before the Grand Lodge sessions opened. In the case of this Grand Lodge the Educational Congress was held on August 21 and 22, 1936 and was addressed by the Grand Officers with reports coming from Committees on Findings, Ways and Means, the investigation of the postal telegraph. The Sunday morning service was taken over by the Department of Education and Rev. Emory B. Smith delivered the Baccalaureate sermon. Roscoe Conkling Bruce of New York City also gave an address at the Monday morning session. The Governor of the State of New York, Governor Lehman and Mayor La Guardia of New York City also delivered addresses. Mrs. Mary McLeod Bethune, President of the Bethune-Cookman College spoke at this session. The Oratorical Contest took place in the evening and was a spirited one with able contestants participating.

The year 1935-1936 had been a year of building within solidly in order to undertake a program without. The Brothers of the Improved Benevolent and Protective Order of Elks of the World were advancing as a united body confident of the value of their program of education, health, civil liberties and service to Negro life. They could realize by this convention of 1936 that the Elks did not form a group of clannish members who were associated for their own benefit, but a body of men moved by high ideals, confident of their service to the people who were looking to them for the leadership which they must have in order to raise their status in citizenship and economic life.

The Grand Officers for 1936-1937 were: J. Finley Wilson, Grand Exalted Ruler, Washington, D. C.; Roy S. Bond, Grand Esteemed Leading Knight, Baltimore, Md.; Joseph A. Brown, Grand Esteemed Loyal Knight, New York, N. Y.; Mark F. Wheatland, Grand Esteemed Lecturing Knight, Camden, N. J.; James E. Kelley, Grand Secretary, Birmingham, Ala.; Edward W. Henry, Grand Treasurer, Philadelphia, Pa.; Eugene Sorral, Grand Esquire, Los Angeles, Calif.; Lonnie S. Williams, Grand Inner Guard, Providence, R. I.; Claude C. White, Grand Tiler, Indianapolis, Ind.; William C. Hueston, Commissioner of Education, Washington, D. C.; Perry W. Howard, Grand Legal Adviser, Washington, D. C.; W. George Avant, Grand Chaplain, Durham, N. C.; Dr. Lawrence J. Davenport, Grand Organist, New York, N. Y.; John T. Rhines, Director of Athletics, Washington, D. C.; Dr. Charles B. Fisher, Grand Medical Director, Washington, D. C.; W. T. Meade Grant, Jr., Director of Junior Elks, New Orleans, La.; W. W. Barnum, Chairman Publishing Board, Hagerstown, Md.; Duke Ellington, Grand Band Master,

New York, N. Y.; Walter H. Land, Grand Master of Social Session, Norfolk, Va.; Charles McGill, Grand Lodge Reporter, Brooklyn, N. Y.; C. C. Valle, Grand Organizer, New York, N. Y.; Emerson H. Gray, Major General Antlered Guard, Atlantic City, N. J.

One of the important actions at this 1936 Grand Lodge was the increased emphasis placed upon civil liberties. The Committee on Civil Liberties composed of Brother W. H. Land, Henry Lincoln Johnson and Emory B. Smith, recommended the extension of efforts to organize civil liberties leagues in the local lodges and the defense of the civil liberties of Negroes in the United States. On the adoption of this motion, Brother Hobson R. Reynolds made that which was described by the minutes as "a wonderful speech on the advantages and needs of the Civil Liberties Commission." Ways and means of raising funds and organizing for this important work were discussed, with Grand Exalted Ruler Wilson taking the lead. One of the results of this discussion was the final appointment of Brother Hobson R. Reynolds as Director of the Civil Liberties Commission by Grand Exalted Ruler Wilson. This step presaged a modern development in this area of Elkdom's operations.

Chapter XV

Progress Despite the Continuing Crisis

The Negro population was among the first of the racial groups to be forced on relief by the continuing crisis. There were riots over the distribution of food in New York and there were dissatisfactions throughout the country, while several thousands of farm tenants were evicted in Arkansas, Missouri and Oklahoma. The severity of these conditions of crisis pressed so upon the Negro population of the South that there were rapid migrations to Northern and Western areas. Between 1930 and 1945 it had been estimated that more than 3,000 Negroes moved Northward and Westward. With the depression bearing down upon the Negro people, they became beneficiaries of relief, low rent housing and minimum wage laws. As a result of these movements the Negro people gained political power by participation in political parties and the exercise of the suffrage. Accordingly the vote was sought by politicians in these areas.

Without the government assistance which came in and through the agencies established there would have been more severe results. It was a common practice to hear of savings being wiped out and of men walking the streets seeking work. In spite of the economic crisis and the New Deal philosophy of social planning, the conditions continued to be bad. While there were few evidences of starvation, there were many evidences of malnutrition and distress. The national and local agencies aided in these relief situations. The government could offer for these situations direct relief, relief employment, research and writing positions, cheaper housing, low interest loans, social security, health benefits and minimum wage levels. In large cities there were Federal projects for housing known as Slum Clearance Projects. Negroes and whites gained better housing as result of these projects.

There were significant developments in the field of education during this period to which the Elks program of education through Judge William C. Hueston continued to call attention. In 1928 a report of the United States Bureau of Education had been made on a survey of Negro colleges. The survey revealed that Negro colleges were below the standards as maintained by American colleges and that steps should be taken to bring these institutions forward to the same places that had been held by the other institutions. As a result of this survey there was an increased interest and activity on the part of Boards and Foundations for support of the Negro college. The secondary schools, the library facilities and science laboratories began to see advances during the thirties.

It was in the midst of these trends in 1937 that the Thirty-eighth Annual meeting of the Grand Lodge of the Improved Benevolent and Protective Order of Elks of the World convened in the Shiloh Baptist Church, in Cleveland, Ohio on August 24-29. The keynote of this convention was struck by the Grand Exalted Ruler Wilson when he stated, "This American people is passing through a great crisis. The Constitution as the charter of our liberties is on trial. The reverence and respect for the judiciary as impartial renderer of justice for all quivers with apprehension. The Fletcher-Black Bill aiming to spend millions for schools without protecting our quota; the Black-Connery Wage and Hour Bill which seeks to take business out of the hands of its proprietors and regulate it by Federal employees; the Farm Tenancy Bill that would sell us land in the deep South but fails to guarantee us equal protection of the laws all make a picture of dangerous shifts in American principles tried and true." He then added, "I am suggesting that we command our entire legal machinery to get behind the responsible agencies of government and to plead our cause before the bar of public opinion through the power of the press. Let us go forward with our Civil Liberties program! Let us send our agencies into the darkest sections of America, preaching the doctrine of equal opportunities for all Americans in all the states."

The Grand Lodge undertook to carry forward the command of the Grand Exalted Ruler. Report after report reflected the messages which he had given in his annual address. The Commissioner of Education Hueston described the inequalities in per capita expenditures which were traditional and seemed to be growing worse instead of better through the years. He showed that in the elementary schools $44.31 was being spent on the white child and $12.57 on the Negro child, which represented 252.5 per cent more spent on the white child than on the Negro child in the same community in eleven of the Southern states. The same disparities existed in public high schools and in the amount of Federal funds spent in the land grant colleges for extension services and for the program of education. He described the manner in which the Harrison-Fletcher Black School Bill, The Wagner Housing Bill, the Black-Connery Wage and Hour Bills would affect and influence the status of the Negro people.

It is of interest to observe that a conference was called in

Washington in July of 1937 by the Grand Exalted Ruler and the Departments of Civil Liberties and Education. This group of assembled race representatives met for several days. There were 379 delegates. The findings of this conference were of importance in developing a consensus of opinion regarding the crisis as it affected the Negro population and the steps which should be taken to improve their status. The findings were printed and copies were sent to the President of the United States, the Senators and Representatives of Congress, Cabinet officers and other distinguished citizens. The delegates who came from ten states wanted their opinion known on the legislation pending in Congress which would directly affect the Negro. This was the first of the conferences called under the joint auspices of the Department of Education and the Department of Civil Liberties. However, there had been called since 1935 in the city of Washington an Elks' Educational and Economic Congress. For the past three years this Congress had been in session and its accomplishments were approved by the Grand Lodge.

The Department of Civil Liberties kept constantly on the job and the Grand Exalted Ruler, together with the Commissioner of Education were attending the hearings on these several school and Civil Rights Bills. Hobson R. Reynolds, the Director of the Department of Civil Liberties gave this first report of activity and of progress in this aspect of the Elks program. He recommended that a representative of the Order should be active in every community to keep the Director of Civil Liberties informed of the facts and to suggest any needs which may arise. He asked that these representatives serve as the eyes and ears of the Civil Liberties Department. He said that if this program would work that it would attract thousands to the Order because of the militant and progressive program represented. The lodges would increase their membership and as the struggle for improvement of the Negro population advanced through the lodges, the status of the lodge would be also advanced and its membership increased.

The Order showed substantial progress as a result of these activities. Leading and inspiring the work was the Grand Exalted Ruler who had not traveled in any year over more territory, or as he said, "performed more services, nor built the Order more substantially in public estimation," than he had in this year. Fifteen new lodges had been established and 40 lodges had been reinstated with 9 new herds instituted and 2 reinstated. Among the recommendations which he made was one that the committee of the Grand Lodge be appointed to arrange for the celebration of the Seventy-fifth Anniversary of both the Emancipation Proclamation on January 1, 1938 and the Constitutional Emancipation in the state on December 18, 1940. He urged this in order that, "the progress of the colored American be reviewed and that the failure to secure his full freedom and equal rights, civil, political and economic be noted by the several Civil Liberties Units throughout the Order."

It was reported by Grand Secretary Kelley that notwithstanding the depression through which they had been passing the Grand Exalted Ruler and his corps of officers had been able to organize 318 lodges, 15 Civil Liberties Leagues and 64 Junior Elks herds. He said that the Grand Lodge had not accumulated a fortune because in line with its principles of charity, funds had been passed out to those who needed them and he added that this was done, "believing that this kind of investment would pay larger and more lasting dividends than bond or bank deposits." He said that during the past eleven years, $10,900.00 had been paid out in pensions, including a pension to the widow of the late Past Grand Exalted Ruler and Founder, B. F. Howard, to the extent of $2,700 and that scholarships have been given to youths totaling $86,777.97. He called the year which had just closed in 1937 one of "definite progress." More lodges had been instituted and reinstated than in any year since 1929 and the receipts showed an increase of more than $5,000 over the previous year. Progress was one of the keynotes of this convention and the Grand Secretary stated, "We have done well, we must do better."

This opinion of the Grand Secretary was reaffirmed by the report of Grand Treasurer, Edward W. Henry, who stated that notwithstanding the financial depression from which they had suffered for the past few years and which had not entirely lifted, that the lodge was in a remarkably satisfactory condition and this he said was due to the fine spirit of cooperation and loyal support of the membership. He said that the funds had been deposited in the Citizens and Southern Bank and Trust Company in accordance with the previous years and that the officials deserved praise for the efficient way in which they had handled the business and expedited the transactions of the lodge. The receipts for the year were $53,399.44 and there was a balance of $15,403.07.

The Educational report was again regarded as an important part of the work of the Grand Lodge and as Commissioner Hueston read his report there was a new innovation presented to the Grand Lodge and that was, each delegate was given a printed copy of this report. At its conclusion there was thunderous applause. His consideration and presentation of education showed that his belief was that education was more than the awarding of degrees and the assistance of individual students to complete their college courses. He thought of the education of the public and also of making places for the educated after they had graduated from college. The last Grand Lodge had inaugurated the position of Grand Economic Commissioner and to this position James A. Jackson was appointed. Commissioner Hueston praised him for the program which he had inaugurated. Each of the reports of the Grand Officers was received with favorable applause and each was reelected by acclamation.

The Commissioner of Economics had a report along with that of the Commissioner of Education. He referred to the patronizing of Negro business wherever it was possible, the purchasing power of the Negro people, the wide contacts which the Elks have in making the story of the economic position of the Negro known and of developing means for improving it. He urged that each temple and lodge create a local Director of Economics who would also be a member of the Civil Liberties League and the Educational Department and a local program should be held annually just as would be the case for the Grand Lodge where the Educational and Economic Congress was held at the opening of the sessions. Brother Jackson was also re-elected by acclamation.

Civil Liberties continued to constitute one of the very important areas of the consideration of the Elks. This was a counterpart of the picture of Negro life in the United States as well as overseas. This was the period of the work of the dynamic Marcus Garvey. With the assault of Italy on Ethiopia in 1935, there was another outburst of racial feeling for during the thirties several hundred Negroes had gone to Ethiopia and in 1930 the Emperor had appointed Dr. John West as his personal physician and John Robinson of Chicago was his personal aviator. The rumors that Ethiopians were not Negroes were answered by a number of persons, among them J. A. Rogers who wrote a brochure under the title, "The Real Facts About Ethiopia." This was evidence, however, that Negroes in the United States were casting their lot with colored people in other parts of the world and the interest of the Elks showed that they were endeavoring to live up to the tenets of their title which described the Order as being, "of the World."

This was the period also of the movement of jobs for Negroes. In various large cities the movement got underway as a reaction to the unemployment situations in Negro life. Picketing and boycotts were common features of the movement to secure work for Negroes. Labor unions, the National Negro Business League, various organized community organizations were behind the movement. The discrimination and segregation which were taking place in Negro life were further causes for emphasis upon these continuations of un-Americanism affecting the Negro population. Commissioner Hobson Reynolds stated that he had attended the anti-lynching hearings along with the other Grand Officers located in Washington. He described the introduction of legislation in the States of New York and Pennsylvania and the manner in which opposition had been experienced in Congress to legislation which seemed to ignore the status of the Negro. He concluded with the statement that, "we propose to carry the fight on until every Negro enjoys the rights and protection the Constitution guarantees to us. We shall fight until the Negro is allowed to exercise his franchise in every state."

This period was also one in which the question of the admission of Negro students to publicly supported colleges and universities was under discussion. Commissioner Hueston had been giving attention to this problem also. In 1935 Donald G. Murray of Baltimore, Md., who was a graduate of Amherst College made application for admission to the School of Law of the University of Md. His application was rejected. Assistance was given to him by the Grand Lodge in finally obtaining admission. A similar case had been started at the University of Missouri. The applicant was Lloyd L. Gaines of St. Louis, Mo. He was a graduate of Lincoln University, Missouri, in 1935, and in the same year he applied for admission to the Law School of the University of Missouri. The Supreme Court of the United States in 1938 reversed the opinion of the lower court and Gaines was authorized to enter the Law School at the University of Missouri. The Scottsboro Case was another issue in which the Grand Lodge and local lodges were interested because it concerned the legal status of the Negro people also. Contributions of money and services were made to all of these causes as well as cooperation with the National Association for the Advancement of Colored People in its endeavors for equality and opportunity.

The Commission on Health, through Dr. Charles B. Fisher, and the Grand Legal Adviser, Perry W. Howard, made reports which caused the convention to give rising votes of thanks and appreciation as they too represented progress in each of their respective fields. Similar approval was given to the activities of the Grand Organizer who had traveled extensively through the country building up the Order in membership and in interest. It was through his work that stimulus had been given to new organizations and to the reinstatement of organizations. He proposed an extensive program of action for 1938.

An important part of this Grand Lodge session was given over

PETITION TO DISSOLVE INJUNCTION AGAINST ELKS IN THE CITY OF MEMPHIS AND THE STATE OF TENNESSEE

In The Chancery Court of Shelby County Tennessee —14-630-RD

GRAND LODGE, BENEVOLENT AND PROTECTIVE ORDER OF ELKS, et. al.,

Complainants
Filed July 26, 1937
Vs.

GRAND LODGE, IMPROVED BENEVOLENT AND PROTECTIVE ORDER OF ELKS OF THE WORLD, et. al.

Defendants

Petition to Dissolve Injunction

Defendants, Grand Lodge, Improved Benevolent and Protective Order of the Elks of the World, respectfully represent to this Honorable Court.

I.

That it is a body corporate, organized and existing under the laws of the State of New Jersey, and that the Grand Lodge, Benevolent and Protective Order of Elks, is a body corporate organized and existing under laws of the State of New York, and that Memphis Lodge No. 27, Benevolent and Protective Order of Elks is a corporation organized and existing under the laws of the State of Tennessee.

II.

Petitioners, defendants in the above styled cause aver that some time on or about Octboer 19, 1937, complainants in the above cause obtained a temporary restraining order or a preliminary injunction restraining petitioners. their agents, attorneys, confederates, etc., from using the name and title IMPROVED BENEVOLENT & PROTECTIVE ORDER OF ELKS OF THE WORLD, or any title similar or identical thereto and from using the ritualistic and other ceremonies, emblems, secrets, etc., (a copy of said preliminary injunction is hereto attached and marked Exhibit "A" hereto).

II.

That on about January 2nd, 1909 the said preliminary injunction was made permanent by a final decree entered in the cause, as the same appears in M. B. 132 at page 136 of the records of this Court. (A copy of said final decree is hereto attached and marked Exhibit "B")

III.

That this cause at the April term, 1909 of the Supreme Court of the State of Tennessee and the decree of this Court affirmed as the same appears in this cause, styled **ELK VS ELKS 122 Tenn., page 144,** et. seq.

That the said injunction in this cause is now full force and effect.

Petition to Dissolve Tennessee Injunction, 1937.

to the presentation of the so-called Tennessee Case in which an injunction had been issued in 1907 against the Improved Benevolent and Protective Order of Elks of the World enjoining this Order not to use the title or a similar name or the ritualistic ceremony, secrets, emblems and mystic words of the Benevolent and Protective Order of Elks of the United States of America or its badges or emblems. This injunction had been in existence and was recognized as permanent but under the leadership of Brother Robert R. Church who appeared in July, 1937, before the court, the request was made for the dissolution of the injunction. This request stated that the Grand Lodge of the Improved Benevolent and Protective Order of Elks of the World was a body corporate organized and existing under the laws of the State of New Jersey and that the Grand Lodge of the Benevolent and Protective Order of Elks of America was a corporation organized under the laws of the State of New York, and that Memphis Lodge No. 27, B.P.O.E. was a corporation organized under the laws of the State of Tennessee.

ROBERT R. CHURCH, Grand Trustee, Commission on Civil Liberties

It was also stated that on January 2, 1909, the preliminary injunction against the Improved Benevolent and Protective Order of Elks of the World had been made permanent. The several steps which had been taken by the B.P.O.E. of the U.S.A., leading to the cessation of any litigations against the I.B.P.O.E. of W., was set out in the request. The action of the court was the issuance of the consent decree with the Grand Lodge B.P.O of Elks and the Memphis Lodge No. 27 of the same Order requesting that the cause should be dissolved and that the two groups were consenting to the disillusion. This was so decreed by the Chancellery Court of Shelby County, Tennessee, on July 26, 1937.

The Grand Lodge officers for 1937-1938 were as follows: J. Finley Wilson, Grand Exalted Ruler, Washington, D. C.; Roy

S. Bond, Grand Esteemed Leading Knight, Baltimore, Md.; Joseph A. Brown, Grand Esteemed Loyal Knight, New York, N. Y.; Marcus F. Wheatland, Grand Esteemed Lecturing Knight, Camden, N. J.; James E. Kelley, Grand Secretary, Birmingham, Ala.; Edward W. Henry, Grand Treasurer, Philadelphia, Pa.; Eugene Sorrel, Grand Esquire, Los Angeles, Calif.; Lonnie S. Williams, Grand Inner Guard, Providence, R. I.; Claude C. White, Grand Tiler, Indianapolis, Ind.; William C. Hueston, Commissioner of Education, Washington, D. C.; Perry W. Howard, Grand Legal Adviser, Washington, D. C.; W. George Avant, Grand Chaplain, Durham, N. C.; Lawrence J. Davenport, Grand Organizer, New York, N. Y.; Charles B. Fisher, Grand Medical Director, Washington, D. C.; W. T. Meade Grant, Jr., Director of Junior Elks, New Orleans, La.; W. W. Barnum, Chairman of Publishing Board, Hagerstown, Md.; Duke Ellington, Grand Bandmaster, New York, N. Y.; Walter H. Land, Grand Master of Social Sessions, Norfolk, Va.; Charles McGill, Grand Lodge Reporter, Brooklyn, N. Y.; C. C. Valle, Grand Organizer, New York, N. Y.; Hobson R. Reynolds, Director of Civil Liberties Commission.

The continued interest in aid to Negro education was shown in the award of scholarships for the year 1937-1938 and the announcement of the graduation of these scholarship winners by Commissioner Hueston. They were: Miss Betty Frances of Washington, D. C., who graduated from the Miner Teacher's College; Miss Dorothy Goodwin of Atlantic City, who graduated from New York University; Miss Joan Neal Moore of Kansas City, Mo., who graduated from Wilberforce University; Miss Hazel Rogers of Clarksville, Tenn., from the Tennessee A. & I. College; Miss Sarah Eloise Usher of Denmark, S. C., from Spellman College. These five students added to the ninety-five graduates from colleges and universities during the life period of the Educational Department brought the total graduates to one hundred.

There were nine lodges organized during this period of 1937-1938 and their locations are of interest: Johannesburg, No. 1018, Johannesburg, South Africa; San Joaquin, No. 1016, Stockton, Calif.; Paramount No. 1020, Evanston, Ill.; Pride of Vandenburg, No. 1022, Evansville, Ind.; Coller City, No. 1015, Troy, N. Y.; Pride of Hoskin, N. C.; Campbell City, No. 1021, Winston-Salem, N. C.; John M. Marquess, No. 1017, Frankfort, Pa.; Mountain View, No. 1023, Uniontown, Pa.

Grand Exalted Ruler Wilson traveled extensively throughout this period and was received with enthusiasm wherever he went. He was constantly on the move. Month after month he traveled issuing proclamations concerning the building of the Order and the making of progress both for it and for the race group. Stopping at one place he suggested that there was renewed energy coming to him. "despite the fatigue involved in moving about so constantly. Elkdom is ablaze!" In New York City he spoke to a mammoth gathering on January 1, 1938, celebrating the Emancipation Proclamation. There were 2,000 people who were unable to attend this meeting and were accommodated outside and in a lower hall with loud speakers. In each of these places he conferred with government officials, with Major La Guardia in New York City, with Governor Harry Nice in Maryland and with state officials in every community into which he went. Dedications of homes and mortage burnings representing clearances of debt were occasions which called for his presence throughout various parts of the United States, extending as far West as Los Angeles, California and into the deep South at Atlanta, Waycross, Valdosta and other cities and towns.

He described his work returning from Colorado with these words, "Like a master weaver, I have gone about this country, up and down, back and forth, in and out, heartening and being uplifted by the sights and achievements and above all the growing spirit of fraternalism marching forward with solid tread through the corridors of time. Brothers it is an honor as well as a satisfying feeling of union with one's fellows to be an Elk of this Improved Benevolent and Protective Order of today, 1938." His travels in Georgia with John Wesley Dobbs, Director of Civil Liberties in that state carried him through twenty-five cities in which they reorganized seven lodges and made five new ones. He declared that it was "the greatest year ever seen in a peaceful forward progress of the people in that state." The Grand Organizer, C. C. Valle, referred to the Grand Exalted Ruler's movements as "like a streak of lightning," as he moves from point to point.

The *Washington Eagle* under the editorship of Commissioner of Education Hueston and with the cooperation in editing of the Grand Exalted Ruler continued to be the official organ of the Grand Lodge. It published the proclamations and directives of the Grand Exalted Ruler, information concerning happenings in the lodges and temples, letters from the members of these organizations and news concerning the advancement of Negroes in various parts of the world. It was read not only by members of the organization but by a large number of citizens in Washington, D. C., and other cities.

It could be understood, accordingly, when the Thirty-ninth Annual Meeting of the Grand Lodge convened in Bethel A.M.E. Church in Baltimore, Md., August 23-27, 1938, why there were

344 lodges represented with their 455 delegates, fourteen state associations, twenty-five Past Exalted Ruler's Councils and district Deputies from twelve states. The greatest enthuisiasm and the largest attendance of people who were not members of the lodge obviously came in the sessions of the Educational, Economic and Civil Liberties Congress which were held on Sunday and Monday prior to the opening of the Grand Lodge. The Annual Sermon was preached by Bishop David H. Sims of the A.M.E. Church. It was called a stirring address and concluded with the words, "we must be able to follow intelligent leadership if we would live notably. We as a group exhaust ourselves in fighting each other so that there is no strength left to pursue the things we should. Noble living means a contribution that goes to lift the masses and not just to lift one's self. Let us say in conclusion that solitude, fellowship, habitual thinking and self analysis are all essential for noble living." Addresses were also given by Commissioner James A. Jackson, Honorable J. Leroy Jordan of Elizabeth, N. J.; Charles Duke, Architect, who was also Technical Editor of the *Washington Eagle.*

The annual sermon was delivered by the Grand Chaplain, Rev. W. George Avant and President H. C. Trenholm of the Alabama State Teachers College, Montgomery, Ala., delivered an address on the subject, "Our Responsibility as Laymen In the Program of Education"; Governor Harry Nice of Maryland delivered an address under the title, "Education of the Youth of this Nation"; the Honorable J. Mercer Burrell spoke on civil liberties. Other speakers included Judge Dickinson of the Maryland Supreme Court, Judge Taylor of the same court, Judge Armond Scott of the Municipal Court, Washington, D. C.; Honorable Hubert Delaney, Commissioner of Taxes of New York City; and Mr. Charles Thomas of the Washington School System. The National Oratorical Contest was held with six contestants using the topic of the Negro and the Constitution. The assembly gave hearty applause to each contestant showing their appreciation and enjoyment of the orations. Roscoe Conkling Simmons delivered a talk at the close of the contest.

The Thirty-ninth session of the Grand Lodge got under way in its business sessions on Tuesday morning, August 23, with the Grand Exalted Ruler Wilson presiding. At the preliminaries the first report presented was that of the Grand Medical Director who described the various diseases which were prevalent during this period. The Grand Exalted Ruler gave his sixteenth report in which he referred to the passing year with the words, "in spite of national business recession and in the face of such obstacles as arise from the imperfections of human nature, we have organized more lodges, reinstated more defunct lodges, councils and herds than in any year since the great world-wide panic. We are here to describe, celebrate, and rejoice in a victorious year for Elkdom.'' There had been continous progress he said, for when he became Grand Exalted Ruler, sixteen years before, there were only 300 lodges, but in July, 1936, the one thousandth lodge was chartered and installed. He described Elkdom, and particularly the Improved Benevolent and Protective Order of Elks of the World as, ''the greatest national and international constructive organization of Negroes ever convened anywhere. It ranks with our great church organizations. Elkdom's program is diversified; is modern; involves men, women and youth without artificial distinctions as to rank or social position; uses the abilities of those at the top in prestige, position and talents for the leveling up always and service to those in need. Elkdom is Christianity made practical, workable, manifest in brotherhood of man, sisterhood of women and fostering direction of youth under the fatherhood of God in a civilized world.'' He reviewed briefly the work in education, health, economics and civil liberties, and then at the close of this part of his address, referred again to the fact that the command was forward and he used this poetic expression:

Sail on, Beloved Order strong and great!
A Race of men with all its fears,
With all its hope of future years,
Is standing breathless on its faith;
In spite of rack and tempest roar,
In spite of false lights on the shore,
Sail on, nor fear to breast the sea!
Our hearts, our hopes, are all with thee,
Our hearts, our hopes, our prayers, our tears
Our faith triumphant o'er our fears,
Are all with I.B.P.O.E. of W.

At the conclusion of the report the Grand Exalted Ruler received an ovation which lasted for several minutes and he was reelected by acclamation.

The annual visit of the Daughter Elks was then a part of the program. Grand Daughter Abbie M. Johnson and her cabinet were received. The Grand Daughter Ruler presented Daughter Theresa Robinson, who in turn presented Past Grand Daughter Ruler Ella G. Berry, and Daughter Berry presented a gold collar to the Grand Exalted Ruler. He requested Brother Oscar G. Suarez of New York to respond in his behalf. A delegation was appointed to visit the Grand Temple in session.

The Grand Secretary's report, James E. Kelley, and the Grand

Treasurer's report, Edward W. Henry, showed that the Grand Lodge had not wavered in its march forward. The total receipts were slightly less than the last Grand Lodge and the explanation was that this decrease in total amount received was due to the "unfortunate financial condition of many of our smaller lodges and the general depression prevalent in our country." This amount was $49,247.42, received for 1937-1938. At the conclusion of these reports there were motions made for the reelection of the Grand Officers by acclamation and the Grand Lodge gave its approval.

The thirteenth report of the Commissioner of Education was given by Commissioner Hueston. He described the work of the office, the restrictions upon finances due to limited income, the regional and state Oratorical Contests and the National Contest. He concluded his report with the words, "we have educated children and paid for it; we have taught them the Constitution and they have orated on it; we have petitioned the Congress and won advancement for human kind in the Order; we stand today strong, virile and in marching order."

The Civil Liberties report was given by the Director of Civil Liberties, Brother Hopson R. Reynolds whose report was approved in the motion with the recommendation to the Grand Exalted Ruler, "that he be reappointed to head the militant army of the I.B.P.O.E. of W.," and thereupon the Grand Exalted Ruler immediately appointed him to serve the ensuing term. The Grand Legal Adviser, Perry W. Howard gave a report showing that there were no external cases and only minor disputes which had arisen between lodges, upon which he had been called for decision. A report from the Antlered Guard was made by Major General Emerson H. Gray. He said that the department had grown since it was approved by the Grand Lodge of Elks at Philadelphia, on August 27, 1931, and that the demonstrations had been unique. He asked for continued cooperation in order that this agency of the Order might continue to maintain good parades and create better ones. A report from the Grand Director of Music was made at this Grand Lodge which was unique because no similar report had been made previously. This helped to give the Grand Lodge the importance of music in the sessions of the Grand Lodge as well as the local one. He urged the use of the musical salutation, "Salute the Grand" which was as follows:

Salute the Grand
My, what a man: praise to the powers that be:
Stand up and sing, let voices ring;
Send word o'er land and sea
For he is the one we love so well and for him we'll

Always stand;
For Charity, Justice and Brotherly Love
Let's all stand and raise our hands, we are here
We are here to salute the Grand.

The report was made by Brother Billy Fowler at the conclusion of which Brother John W. Dobbs moved that Duke Ellington's name as Grand Bandmaster be dropped and Brother Fowler was elected in the place of Duke Ellington.

The Grand Lodge Officers for 1938-1939 were: J. Finley Wilson, Grand Exalted Ruler, Washington, D. C.; Roy S. Bond, Grand Esteemed Leading Knight, Baltimore, Md.; Joseph A. Brown, Grand Esteemed Loyal Knight, New York, N. Y.; Marcus F. Wheatland, Grand Esteemed Lecturing Knight, Camden, N. J.; James E. Kelley, Grand Secretary, Birmingham, Ala.; Edward W. Henry, Grand Treasurer, Philadelphia, Pa.; Eugene Sorral, Grand Esquire, Los Angeles, Calif.; Lonnie S. Williams, Grand Inner Guard, Providence, R. I.; John McKims, Grand Tiler, Charleston, W. Va.; William C. Hueston, Commissioner of Education, Washington, D. C.; Perry W. Howard, Grand Legal Adviser, Washington, D. C.; W. George Avant, Grand Chaplain, Durham, N. C.; Lawrence J. Davenport, Grand Organist, New York, N. Y.; Charles B. Fisher, Grand Medical Director, Washington, D. C.; W. T. Meade, Jr., Grand Director, Junior Elks, New Orleans, La.; W. W. Barnum, Chairman of Publishing Board, Hagerstown, Md.; Billy Fowler, Grand Bandmaster, New York, N. Y.; Walter H. Land, Grand Master of Social Sessions, Norfolk, Va.; Charles McGill, Grand Lodge Reporter, Brooklyn, N. Y.; C. C. Valle, Grand Organizer, New York, N. Y.

Similar work was carried on by the Daughter Elks in their sessions. One of the significant actions of their 36th annual session at Sharpe Street, M. E. Church was the adoption of the name and a more comprehensive program for the "Emma V. Kelley National Elks Shrine." Contributions continued to be sent in for this cause as the years passed.

Progress and crisis were intertwined as the Improved Benevolent and Protective Order of Elks moved with the nation toward the year 1939. New York City was holding its famous spectacle of "The World of Tomorrow," in the pageantry of a World's Fair. With the Order planning to build a brotherhood composed of inhabitants of the world, it seemed very appropriate that these two, the World's Fair and the World's Lodge should be meeting at a common altar. The last Grand Lodge session had provided for its meeting in New York City.

Continued progress was manifested in the opening sessions which were held by the Educational and Economic Congress at the St. Mark's Methodist Episcopal Church with the Baccalaureate address being delivered by Dr. Emmett J. Scott of Washington, D. C. Dr. Scott praised the work of the Elks, especially in the field of education, and the help that it had been giving to develop educated persons. He urged that those who were developing would be educated in the sense of humility and of service. There were several distinguished persons who addressed this Congress: The Commissioner of Economics, J. A. Jackson; Charles Thomas of the Public School System, Washington, D. C.; Dr. Lorenzo H. King, who delivered the annual sermon at the Memorial meeting; Director Hobson R. Reynolds of the Civil Liberties Department; Dr. Mary McLeod Bethune and Samuel S. Lebowitz. It is of interest to observe that he said, "I am a member of the I.B.P.O.E. of W., and I talk as a Brother Elk and we are living in troubled times and I see the world as a gang of hold-up men, as a gang of robbers without compunction of conscience." He spoke of how Italy was invading Ethopia and Germany was taking indignities against Jews. He said there was danger to America if Negro and Jew remained apart and he urged minorities to work together, shoulder to shoulder in order to make the world a better place in which to live. Mrs. Crystal Bird Fausett, a representative in the Pennsylvania State Legislature was introduced, Grand Daughter Ruler Abbie M. Johnson, Daughter Lethia Fleming and Judge Miles A. Page.

Following the usual activities of opening the Grand Lodge, the first business before it was the report of the Grand Exalted Ruler. As the lodge convened in the Renaissance Building, New York City, on August 20-26, 1939, a story of continuous travel and activity all over the United States was again told by the Grand Exalted Ruler's report. He gave a complete picture of new lodges, reinstated lodges, celebrations of various types which he had made efforts to attend and he closed this part of his report with the statement, "such is Elkdom of 1939." Said he, "standing here, where the swelling uproar of the enrolled achievements of forty years read like a fairy tale and the inspiration from those forebearers of this great people in this great nation bids us press on to a world of tomorrow—I proudly subscribe to this record of the past twelve months since the last session of the Grand Lodge of the Improved Benevolent and Protective Order of Elks of the World, and bid you give concern to the program for the future."

For the first time a joint session of the Grand Lodge and Grand Temple of the I.B.P.O.E. of W. was held. The session was opened by Brother Perry W. Howard, Grand Legal Adviser who presented the Grand Exalted Ruler. The audience arose and sang the Elks' Ode. The guest speakers of the occasion were Governor

Harold G. Hoffman of New Jersey, Representative Bruce Barton of New York State, Mayor F. H. La Guardia and Colonel Arthur W. Little. Responses were made by Dr. Emmett Scott and the Grand Exalted Ruler.

The business session of the Grand Lodge was again opened with the report of the Grand Secretary who said that, "depressions, recessions and war clouds have kept the condition of the country and the minds of its people unsettled and those who control finance and industry have been reluctant to move forward less they take the wrong step and suffer heavy losses, but in spite of all this our grand old Order has not missed a single Grand Lodge session and most of our lodges have held their own in the face of many handicaps. We assemble today in annual convention a bulwark of stability and consistency growing and building through all of this crisis." He paid tribute to the leadership of the Order and also to the leaders of the Daughter Elks and congratulated them upon their growth, both numerically and financially, which he described as marvelous. He reported eleven new lodges, thirty-four reinstated lodges, four new Past Exalted Rulers' Councils, four reinstated councils, twelve new herds of Junior Elks, eight reinstated herds and fifteen civil liberties leagues. The report of the Grand Secretary and Grand Treasurer showed that there had been total receipts of $55,233.56, which represented an increase over the amount received for the previous year. He said that there had been an increase also in the membership. The report of the Credentials Committee for this Grand Lodge showed that there were 332 lodges represented with 513 delegates, seventeen herds with seventeen delegates, eleven from state associations, thirty from councils, making a total of 613. The report was received with a vote of confidence and a motion was made and adopted that Grand Secretary Kelley be reelected.

The Commissioner of Education stated that there had been scholarship aid granted to over 200 young men and women and that 106 had graduated from the leading colleges and universities. He said that the Grand Exalted Ruler and his administration should be congratulated for the progress which had been made through the administration of the affairs of the Order in this period of unemployment.

One of the new developments in the department was the establishment of Elks' Study Clubs. In order to aid this idea, lessons were provided for study free of cost. Six lessons were distributed, one each month from January to June: (1) Civil Liberties. What They Are and How They Shall Be Obtained by William C. Hueston; (2) Importance of Factual Information, by Charles Ed-

*** ELKS' EDUCATIONAL STUDY CLUBS ***

Under the Auspices of the
Elks' Educational Dept.
****
1915-14th street,N.W.
Washington, D.C.

W.C.Hueston
Commissioner of Education
****

It is our pleasure to present as the third lesson instructor, Charles H. Wesley, Ph.D., well known educator and Dean of the Graduate School of Howard University, Washington,D.C. Dr. Wesley has carefully laid his lesson for March, 1939, and we are fortunate indeed to present "The Status of Negro Education" by Dr. Wesley.

Lesson No. 3.

"THE STATUS OF NEGRO EDUCATION"

By Dr. Charles Wesley

The principles of Democracy suggest that educational opportunities should be open to all people. In the southern states of the nation, these opportunities on an equal basis are denied millions of people on account of race and color. Democracy's future in America is seriously challenged by this situation.

In many communities, educational facilities furnished to white children are not furnished to Negro children. Where the school populations of Negroes are largest, the schools are the fewest in number and the most limited in service. And yet, in spite of prejudice, discrimination and neglect, the Negro has moved forward under a courageous leadership. Where the schools were denied them, somehow an education has been obtained and the group has marched forward. When they were not permitted by circumstances to continue their formal schooling, they have yet devoted themselves to a self-educative process, which has raised the Negro population from a general illitercy towards its rightful status in American life.

With a total population of 12 millions, one-fifth of whom live in the north and west, Negroes form one of the important population groups on the nation. They are found in every state of the Union. The states of Georgia and Mississippi have more than a million each, while North Dakota has less than 500.

In every state of the south except Tennessee and Téxas, one out of every three or four persons is a Negro, and in the entire United States about one in every ten is a Negro.

Decade after decade, Negroes have made advances in education, in spite of the meager facilities available to them. In 1930, Negro illiteracy was reduced to 16.3 percent, and 93.6 percent of these illiterates were in the southern states. Nineteen of the 48 states of the nation provided by law for the segregation of the races in schools. Such segragation has meant superior facilities for white and inferior ones for Negroes.

Sixty-seven percent of the Negro population live in rural areas and yet they have only 39 percent of the four-year high schools. Two hundred and thirty counties in 15 states with 158,939 pupils had no high school facilities for Negroes, while there were high schools for whites in every county.

Lesson No. 3, Elks' Educational Clubs, Prepared by Dr. Charles H. Wesley, 1939.

ward Hall, Grand Statistician of Elks; (3) The Status of Negro Education, by Dr. Charles H. Wesley, Dean of Howard University Graduate School; (4) Know your Race, by Arthur Huff Faucet of Philadelphia; (5) Voting in the United States, by William C. Hueston; (6) How to Read a Newspaper, by Claude A. Barnett, Director of the Associated Negro Press. He reported that there were 86 Elk Study Clubs formed with members ranging from 5 to 100 and the reports show that these Clubs had been meeting with enthusiasm and regularity. At the conclusion of his report he was reelected for another year.

The Grand Legal Adviser, Perry W. Howard stated that there was no suit pending against the Order and the Order faced no litigation. He was reelected by unanimous ballot. The Commissioner of Civil Liberties, Hobson R. Reynolds, made a report stating that the Negro was passing through an economic era which made it very difficult for the minority group to keep pace with the times. He gave the purposes of the Civil Liberties Department as follows: (1) Full citizenship rights for every American citizen regardless of race, creed or color; (2) Equal opportunity of public and private employment for all citizens; (3) The ending of all legal discrimination against members of the colored race; (4) Fair and equitable distribution of public school funds in every state of the union; (5) Elimination of disfranchisement; (6) Elimination of residential segregation; (7) Elimination of segregation on common carriers engaged in interstate comerce; (8) Passage of a Federal Anti-lynching Bill and other measures to secure and safeguard Civil Liberties; (9) Equal opportunities for Negro men in both branches of the armed services; (10) The passing of a Federal law to prohibit unions from barring persons on account of race, creed or color. He stated that the unit organization of Civil Liberties Leagues was going forward and was a first line of defense. He gave several instances of the action of the Civil Liberties Department in cases where its services were needed. He urged, however, that this department was not a political organization. He was commended by vote of the Grand Lodge for the accomplishments of his department.

The Commissioner of Economics, J. A. (Billboard) Jackson stated that he had traveled extensively in the interest of the development of the economic status of the Negro, that jobs had been secured in a number of places and that he had given addresses to colleges and organizations in a number of towns and cities.

The Fraternal session of the Grand Temple, which occupied a prominent place in the Grand Lodge was opened by the Grand

Exalted Ruler with addresses by Daughter Pearl Brown, and Daughter Lucy Kimball who brought a delegation of sixty-two Daughters from Memphis, Tennessee. This was the Baby Temple of the South. Bishop Sara Butler and Daughter Lethia Fleming gave addresses pledging their support of the Grand Lodge, the Grand Exalted Ruler and the Grand Daughter Ruler. The Past Grand Exalted Ruler, T. Gillis Nutter of Charlestown, W. Virginia, responded to these greetings as also did Dr. Lorenzo King. The Director of Junior Elks, W. T. Meade Grand, Jr., made a report which was well received by the Order and pledged himself to renewed service in this area.

It was recommended that each lodge and temple would hold a celebration in honor of the Grand Exalted Ruler on the first Friday in August. The proceeds from this celebration were to be divided, sixty per cent to be retained by the subordinate lodge and temple and forty per cent of the gross receipts to be forwarded immediately to the Grand Secretary for the benefit of the Shrine and the Civil Liberties Departments, which were to share equally.

The report of the Health Commission was read by Dr. William J. Thompkins and T. T. Wendell. This was another of the comprehensive reports of this commission concerning diseases and living conditions among Negroes. Shortly afterwards the Grand Exalted Ruler appointed Brother Dr. Carter Marshall of New Haven, Connecticut as the Grand Medical Director.

With America becoming the arsenal of democracy, repealing its arms embargo, transferring destroyers and aiding Europe against the German threat under the leadership of Hitler, it was natural that the question of the Negro serving the armed forces should come to the front. An important resolution was therefore adopted resolving to request Congress in this period of preparation for national defense to consider the advisability of training and adding Negro aviators, Negro regiments to the regular Army and officering them with Negroes trained in the National Guard in colleges, Reserve Officers Training Corps, Citizens' Military Training Camps, and at West Point.

Another resolution stated that whereas the world had become, "an armed camp and countless millions have been made to mourn because of the spreading dictatorial, totalitarian complex: Be it resolved that the Grand Lodge, I.B.P.O.E. of W., extends its deepest sympathy to all Brothers in distress—Abyssinians, Albanians, Czechs, Chinese and Jews who have been spoliated, herded in ghettos and concentration camps and exiled and are unable because of the overwhelming flood of persecution to find a safe landing place and that we call upon all true Americans, proud of the land of liberty, the square deal in equal opportunity, to condemn in our beloved country, Jim-Crowism, segregation, civil and political suppression and lynching.'' It was also resolved that the Grand Lodge would create a section to be known as the Division of Historical Research and Investigation under the supervision of the Department of Education to develop Negro History Study Clubs in the lodges and temples and to create a central committee to present to educational authorities the claim that the history of the Negro be included in history textbooks and taught in the public schools. The sum of $100 was to be expended for this purpose, under the direction of the Department of Education or the Grand Exalted Ruler.

As one stood in 1939 and looked back over the forty years along which the Improved Benevolent and Protective Order of Elks had come along history's pathway, he could see that there had been dynamic leadership and loyal service on the part of the delegates to Grand Lodge Sessions and the regular meetings of the subordinate lodges in order that there might be developed this unique organization which could show such widespread fraternal development and service to the people. The addresses and the total picture given by this Fortieth Annual Meeting showed that there was present the vision to place Negro Elkdom in a larger place of opportunity and service as it faced the ensuing year.

The Grand Lodge Officers for 1939-1940 were: J. Finley Wilson, Grand Exalted Ruler, Washington, D. C.; Joseph A. Brown, Grand Esteemed Leading Knight, New York, N. Y.; Dr. Marcus F. Wheatland, Grand Esteemed Loyal Knight, Camden, N. J.; Hubert E. Jones, Grand Esteemed Lecturing Knight, Washington, D. C.; James E. Kelley, Grand Secretary, Birmingham, Ala.; Edward W. Henry, Grand Treasurer, Philadelphia, Pa.; Eugene Sorral, Grand Esquire, Los Angeles, Calif.; J. Marian Washington, Grand Inner Guard, Brooklyn, N. Y.; John McKims, Grand Tiler, Charleston, W. Va.; William C. Hueston, Commissioner of Education, Washington, D. C.; Perry W. Howard, Grand Legal Adviser, Washington, D. C.; Hobson R. Reynolds, Grand Director of Civil Liberties, Philadelphia, Pa.; W. George Avant, Grand Chaplain, Durham, N. C.; Lawrence J. Davenport, Grand Organist, New York, N. Y.; Dr. Carter L. Marshall, Grand Medical Director, New Haven, Conn.; W. T. Meade Grant, Jr., Director of Junior Elks, New Orleans, La.; W. W. Barnum, Chairman of Publishing Board, Hagerstown, Md.; Duke Ellington, Grand Bandmaster, New York, N. Y.; Walter H. Land, Grand Master of Social Session, Norfolk, Va.; Charles McGill, Grand Lodge Reporter, Brooklyn, N. Y.; C. C

Valle, Grand Organizer, New York, N. Y.; James A. Jackson, Commissioner of Economics, New York, N. Y.; William E. Fowler, Grand Director of Music, Akron, Ohio; Cumberland Posey, Director of Athletics, Homestead, Pa.; Emerson H. Gray, Major General, Antlered Guard, Atlantic City, N. J.

While the crisis was continuing there was progress being made by Negro-Americans and also by the Improved Benevolent and Protective Order of Elks of the World. The efforts to lead the nation out of its crisis appeared to be making some successful developments. The slogans, "The New Deal," and "No Forgotten Man" had made their appeals to the Negro people for it was well known that there was need for a new deal in all of the relationships of Negroes with whites in the United States. Negroes also knew that they had for too long a period been the forgotten people in American life. These slogans coming from an administration which had pledged its promise to provide relief, allotments and work were factors that could not be minimized. The humanitarian program of President Franklin D. Roosevelt under the alphabetically designated organizations, such as the PWA, WPA, AAA, NYA and others, made up a program which could not be minimized in its influences upon Negro life as well as American life as a whole. These temporary measures developed a progress for Negroes in raising their standards of living, and made it possible for them to succeed so that they could maintain membership in such organizations as the Elks. With the United States becoming the Arsenal of Democracy and the employment of Negroes in industries serving the national defense, it was inevitable that there should be some manifestation of progressive developments. There was progress among Negroes in spite of the continuing crisis.

Title Page to *Some Contributions by Negroes to American Life* by Harry H. Pace, Published by I.B.P.O.E. of W., Department of Education.

Chapter XVI
National Defense and Elkdom's Reaction

World events were moving rapidly toward a climax of war from 1937 to 1940 and the storm-clouds of war were gathering while the Grand Lodge of the Improved Benevolent and Protective Order of Elks of the World was meeting in annual sessions and building its services in the interests of its members and the nation. The Grand Lodge and subordinate lodges with the American people watched the swiftly moving events without being too greatly disturbed for the United States was a neutral in all of these happenings and was determined to maintain its neutrality. In 1937 Japan invaded China, and in 1938 Hitler moved into Austria. The next year, he occupied Czechoslovakia and attacked Poland after the alliance with Stalin. In 1940 Russia attacked Finland, and Norway and Denmark were seized by Hitler's troops and France was occupied. These events had moved at such an accelerated pace that the news from abroad shocked the people of the United States into the meaning of war.

The policy adopted by President Franklin D. Roosevelt and approved by Congress was to remain out of the war rumors and events of war. Neutrality acts had been adopted in 1935, 1936 and 1937. When war started in 1939 and Great Britain stood alone, the Neutrality Acts were modified to allow the sale of arms and munitions, and the President transferred guns and destroyers for British use. American sympathy increased for China and the American government loaned $70,000,000 to the Chinese Government for the purchase of supplies. With 1940, there was preparation for a national defense program. Consideration was given to the first conscription of men in peacetime in American history. After debate Congress provided in September, 1940, that all men between the ages of twenty-one and thirty-five were required to register. From these registrants, selections were made for military induction and training.

While these events were taking place on the national scene and the nation was being influenced to consider its national defense, the Improved Benevolent and Protective Order of Elks of the World was also called upon to defend itself against an attack which came from within its own borders. Eureka Lodge No. 5 of

Norfolk, Virginia, was suspended by the Grand Lodge of 1939 for the non-payment of taxes. Eureka Lodge then endeavored to operate as an independent lodge and sought to have its articles of incorporation amended so that it would be known as Eureka Lodge No. 5 Independent Elks. When Grand Exalted Ruler Wilson and other Grand Officers learned of this fact, Grand Legal Adviser Perry W. Howard filed a writ requesting that Eureka Lodge No. 5 be restrained from using any name with any part of the word "Elk" and from using the ritual, jewels or paraphernalia of the Grand Lodge, Improved Benevolent and Protective Order of Elks of the World. The case was tried in the District Court of the United States for the Eastern District of Virginia with Judge Luther B. Way presiding.

The decision by Judge Way decreed that the court perpetually enjoined "Eureka Lodge No. 5 Independent Elks" from using this name or any other name so similar which along or in conjunction with other writings or symbols had "a tendency to mislead or deceive the public into believing that the defendant organization is a subordinate lodge of or in connection with the plaintiff." However, the decision permitted the use of the words "Elks" and "Eureka Lodge," or all of these words as parts of the name of their Order and in connection with their fraternal activities, provided that reasonable effort was made to prevent confusion as to the two fraternal Orders, so far as prospective members and the public were concerned.

Grand Legal Adviser Howard, the Grand Exalted Ruler and other Grand Officers were of the opinion that this decision was so split between that which seemed to be good for the Grand Lodge and against its interests that it was decided to appeal from that part of the decree authorizing Eureka Lodge No. 5 to use a title with the word "Elk" in it. The U. S. Circuit Court of Appeals of the Fourth District heard the case on June 12, 1940, and rendered its decision on August 17, 1940. The case was known as "The Grand Lodge Improved Benevolent and Protective Order of Elks of the World, a corporation, appellant versus Eureka Lodge No. 5, Independent Elks, a corporation, Jerry O. Gilliam and Walter C. Fulford, appellees." William C. Hueston and Perry W. Howard, with W. W. Foreman, T. H. Reid, Walter H. Land and J. C. Robinson on the brief, represented the Grand Lodge and James G. Martin and E. S. Peters represented Eureka Lodge No. 5. Judge John J. Parker delivered the decision which reversed the decision of the lower court and stated that the Grand Lodge of the Improved Benevolent and Protective Order of Elks of the World was the only fraternal body or corporation

UNITED STATES CIRCUIT COURT OF APPEALS
FOURTH CIRCUIT

NO. 4650

THE GRAND LODGE IMPROVED, BENEVOLENT, PROTECTIVE ORDER OF ELKS OF THE WORLD, a corporation
Appellant

versus

Eureka Lodge No. 5, Independent Elks, a corporation, Jerry O. Gilliam, and Walter C. Fulford,
Appellees.

Appeal from the District Court of the United States for the Eastern District of Virginia, at Norfolk.
(Argued June 12, 1940. Decided August 17, 1940.)

Before Parker, Dobie and Northcott, Circuit Judges.

William C. Hueston and Perry W. Howard (W. W. Foreman, T. H. Reid, Walter H. Land and J. C. Robinson on brief) for Appellant, and James G. Martin and E. S. Peters for Appellees.

Parker, Circuit Judge:

Plaintiff is the Grand Lodge of the colored fraternal order which was before this court as plaintiff in the case of Grand Lodge of Improved, Benevolent and Protective Order of Elks of the World v. Grand Lodge, Improved, Benevolent and Protective Order of Elks of the World, Inc., et al., 4 Cir. 50 F. 2d 860. Prior to 1939, Eureka Lodge No. 5 was one of its local lodges at Norfolk, Va. As a result of a controversy, the connection between this local lodge and the plaintiff grand lodge was definitely severed in the Summer of 1939, plaintiff claiming that the charter of the local lodge was revoked and its members expelled from the order for failure to pay dues, and defendants claiming that it withdrew from the grand lodge because of mistreatment.

After the severance of the relationship between plaintiff and the local lodge, the latter, which had been incorporated under the laws of Virginia, amended its charter, changing its corporate name to "Eureka Lodge No. 5, Independent Elks", and under that name continued to function as an Elks Lodge. This suit was thereupon instituted by plaintiff against the local lodge and two of its officers, and a temporary injunction was obtained restraining them from using the word "Elks" or the ritual, emblems, insignia, or other paraphernalia of plaintiff. On final hearing, decree was entered enjoining defendants from using as the name of their organization "Eureka Lodge No. 5, Independent Elks" or "any other name so similar to the name of the plaintiff, which standing alone, or in conjunction with other writings or symbols, has a tendency to mislead or deceive the public into believing that the defendant

which could lawfully use a name with the word "Elk," as far as colored people were concerned.

Judge Parker said that the word "Elk" was the dominant word in the name and that "Improved," "Benevolent," "Protective" and "of the World" were mere surplusage. Accordingly, he said, "The decree appealed from should be modified so as to forbid defendants using the word "Elks" in their corporate name, or upon their stationery or literature, and to forbid their using the ritual, emblems, insignia or other paraphernalia of plaintiff order."

Eureka Lodge No. 5 was dissatisfied with this decision and appealed to the United States Supreme Court for a writ of certiorari asking that the Supreme Court review the records of the case. On December 9, 1940, this Court denied this petition. This decision is a historical milestone because it restrained any Negro organization except the Improved Benevolent and Protective Order of Elks of the World from using the word "Elk" in any such name.

Grand Exalted Ruler Wilson said that "the decision closed a dramatic fight which has intruded upon the peace of our Order since the split in 1906, which was not healed by the union of 1910, nor by the decision of Judge Parker and his associates 10 years ago. But now this modification by the Justices of the Circuit Court of Appeals as set forth has closed the case, the last of its kind to be closed by our administration."

These discussions were at their heights when the Grand Lodge convened in its Forty-First Annual Meeting in Castle Hall, St. Louis, Missouri, August 27-31, 1940. The Educational and Economic Congress preceded the Grand Lodge sessions. Among the picturesque moments of the Congress was the presentation of caps and gowns to distinguished Daughters and Bills who had contributed to the successful operation of the program of education during the year, 1939-1940. One of the speakers at the Civil Liberties session was Lawrence Oxley, of the Social Security Administration who said that there would be 75,000 Negro youths called to military duty and that action should be taken to see, "that these Negroes are properly integrated in the National Defense Program." He said that Negroes were being denied the privilege of training classes in defense industries and that action should be taken by the Elks to open these opportunities to them.

The Business Session was called to order on August 27 by Grand Exalted Ruler Wilson. The report of the Committee on Credentials stated that there were present 26 Grand Officers, 304 lodges with 408 delegates, 13 state associations, 25 Past Grand

Exalted Rulers Councils and 26 deputies making a total of 498 delegates. In his annual report the Grand Exalted Ruler urged the Order to "advance unafraid, ready for any eventuality, any fate—but always *Forward!*" Since the Grand Lodge was meeting in Missouri he contrasted the Dred Scott Case and the Gaines Case and said that the latter outcome should hearten further advancement.

The Grand Exalted Ruler gave an extensive resume of his travels and described his contacts with lodges, state associations and dedications of Elk homes, extending from the Atlantic to the Pacific Oceans and from the lakes to the Gulf. He listed the passing of Grand Daughter Ruler Abbie M. Johnson of Philadelphia, of whom, he said, "She never lost step during the depression, nor missed a single convention but showed progress each successive year." He asserted that she was "a Queen in her own right."

In speaking of the case involving Eureka Lodge No. 5, the Grand Exalted Ruler reported that he had been to Norfolk and had reinstated the lodge, the members of which had promised "to make Eureka bigger, better, and grander than ever before." He regarded this lodge as having suffered from the actions of misguided and rebellious brothers. Grand Legal Adviser Howard described this action as "one of the strongest attempts ever made to set up a rival organization ever encountered." He regarded this decision as "the last word on this question," and it made Elkdom "like the Christian Religion—One Lord, One Faith, One Fraternity."

Another incident caused the Grand Lodge to defend itself occurred when there was a rumor circulating to the effect that the Grand Daughter Ruler. Elizabeth Ross Gordon who succeeded Grand Daughter Ruler Abbie M. Johnson following her death in 1940 had been chosen through the influence and pressure of Grand Exalted Ruler Wilson. The Grand Exalted Ruler branded this statement as false and as cowardly and subsequently a committee was appointed to draw up resolutions condemning the rumor. The following resolution was drawn stating that "whereas these false and malicious rumors had been circulated among the members and delegates, that the investigation disclosed that there was not a scintilla of evidence to justify such a report and therefore the Grand Lodge went on record as denouncing and deploring the circulation of these rumors and reaffirmed its confidence in the integrity of the Grand Exalted Ruler and the Grand Daughter Ruler." The resolution was adopted unanimously by the Grand Lodge.

It was reported by Grand Secretary Kelley that the Order was still growing and that during the past year there had been organized and reinstated forty-seven lodges, seven Past Exalted Rulers Councils, fifteen herds and three Civil Liberties Leagues. The Grand Treasurer Henry made his report stating that progress had been made although the lodge had been passing through a world of change and that the integrity of the Order had been impugned and yet the Grand Lodge had not faltered in extending its helpfulness to its members and to others. He said that it had taken administrative ability of no mean degree to weather the storm of financial chaos that had threatened the credit of the Order but that the budget had been balanced, with the Citizen's and Southern Bank and Trust Company of Philadelphia continuing to be a safe depository for the funds of the Order. The receipts as of July 31, 1940 were $55,148.79.

There had been twenty-six students who had been assisted by the Department of Education according to the report of the Commissioner, William C. Hueston. However, owing to the hold-over and this year's class, there would be forty students who could be assisted with the budget of the past year. He said that during the fifteen years of the existence of the Department of Education, the Order had raised and expended more than $350,000 for education and this he regarded as a very splendid record. One of these graduates, Miss Dorothy Height, was the Executive Secretary of the Y.W.C.A. in Washington, D. C., and was named by a National Commission, representing the *Parent's Magazine* as the young person under thirty years of age who had rendered the greatest service to American youth during the year. He described the Oratorical Contest and the Study Clubs in History and stated that under his direction there had been worked out the study lessons which were published in the official organ, *The Washington Eagle*. He called attention to the Educational Week Conferences, and rendered a report on *The Washington Eagle*. He also referred to the newspaper articles which were calculated to bring confusion among the Grand Lodge officers and members of the fraternity and labeled all of these charges as false. He stated that while there were fraternal orders that had either folded up or reduced their activities, the Improved Benevolent and Protective Order of Elks of the World had been functioning fully. These Grand Officers who had given their reports were elected by unanimous vote with the suspension of the rules.

Since one of the most important questions was the relationship of the Negro to National Defense, the report of the Commissioner

Bulletin No. 4
EDUCATIONAL DEPARTMENT, I.B.P.O. ELKS of W.
1915 Fourteenth Street, N. W.
Washington, D. C.

To those not in possession of the facts, we present, that in response to what appeared to be a very present need, namely lack of opportunity for scholarship aid for colored youth, the Improved, Benevolent and Protective Order of Elks of the World established in 1925 what is known as the Elks' Department of Education and committed it to educational endeavors as follows:

1. The granting of scholarship aid at the college level.

2. The encouragement of the study of the Constitution of the United States.

3. The general educational improvement of the colored race.

In pursuance of the general object of the department to sustain it, the grand lodge, the governing body of the Elks, levied an annual assessment on each male member of the order. This assessment, plus voluntary contributions chiefly made by the female members of the order, has totaled more than $325,000. These figures do not include sums raised and expended by way of educational assistance to students by the various local Elk units.

A fair, but unchecked, estimate of the funds raised and expended by the Elks' order for education is $350,000. An average of $25,000 per annum since the establishment of the department in 1925.

Under item No. 2 above, the department, beginning in 1927, has conducted a nation-wide oratorical contest for high school students. The subjects of the orations always being to create a favorable interest in our government and thus aid in sustaining it rather than to develope good speakers.

In these contests there have participated, according to our reports, over 30,000 bonafide high school students. We are unable to give information on how many students studied for the contest and were eliminate by the school faculties before contests. We do know that several hundred thousand people have attended these contests and in this way have been informed and impressed with the soundness of our Democratic form of government.

Under item No. 3 -- The Department of Education has inaugurated and conducted, beginning with 1926, an annual Elks' Educational Week. The purpose being to increase the interest of adult America in the educational needs of our youth. Each lodge and temple being required to devote the entire week to educational pursuits. Many thousands of meetings have been held in the interest of education throughout the United States, the Isles of the Sea and Africa, participated in by innumerable people.

In 1935 the Department of Education established the Elks' Educational and Economic Congress for the purpose of studying the problems indicated in the name of the effort. These meetings have resulted in exhaustive examination of the educational and economics status of the colored people, particularly those in the United States.

Out of these meetings efforts have been made to better the condition of the colored citizer on these fronts. These efforts have taken the form of petitions to the Congress of the United States and various state legislatures seeking to widen and extend the opportunities of the colored citizen in these particulars.

The most recent endeavor of the Elks' Department of Education is the establishment of what is called the Elks' Study Club. The object of this effort is to afford the opprotunity to all who may be interested in the history, economics and civil liberties of the colored citizen of America.

The department has prepared and distributed, free of cost, literature presenting information in the form of printed

of Civil Liberties, Hobson R. Reynolds, was listened to with great attention. He had already in previous reports referred to the discrimination thrust upon young men by the Army, Navy and Air Corps and reported the approaches, contacts and letters which had been sent to these several departments protesting against inequities. He also urged the use of the ballot and that the members of the Order should appeal to Negroes in their respective communities to register and to vote in order that they might show their numerical strength.

The report of the Commissioner of Health dealt with health conditions, the observance of National Health Day and the exhaustive study of the health of Negroes which had been made as a cross-section of total health conditions among them. He noted deaths by suicide, homicide, the condition of teeth, cancer, its control and treatment and the need for an annual check-up. The report was concluded with the words "take care of your health; it is your first wealth." Dr. William J. Thompkins served as Committee Chairman and Dr. E. T. Belsaw as Executive Secretary. The report of the Commissioner of Economics described the work which he had carried on through the year, making addresses in different places, to churches, schools and other organizations as well as subordinate lodges. He advised that he had worked in creating cooperative stores in Rochester, New York and advising other cooperative organizations. He urged the support of Negro business and trade with white merchants employing Negroes in their business. The Grand Medical Director, Dr. Carter Marshall made his report stating that articles had been published in *The Washington Eagle* setting forth the report of his office, with guest columnists such as Dr. William J. Thompkins, Dr. E. T. Belsaw, Dr. James A. Megahy and Dr. R. Beecher Costa. He said that the current issue of *The Washington Eagle* carried a Purple Cross Bulletin and that the slogan for 1940-41 would be "a Purple Cross Unit in every Temple." He urged the support of Negro Health Week and the conduct of discussions on health in both the lodges and the temples. At the conclusion of his report the Grand Exalted Ruler reappointed Dr. Carter Marshall as Grand Medical Director.

The following motion was adopted and is of interest because it deals with the history of the Order.

> Whereas, Alpha Lodge, I.B.P.O.E. of W., being the Mother of all Elkdom, the birthplace of the greatest Negro organization on earth, namely the Improved Benevolent and Protective Order of Elks of the World and whereas she has tried to meet all of its obligations,

Therefore, be it resolved, that from this date, August 1940, throughout the ceaseless ages that Alpha Lodge No. 1, I.B.P.O.E. of W., be exempt from Grand Lodge taxes.

Respectfully submitted
Alpha Lodge No. 1
Joseph C. Taylor, Exalted Ruler
I. D. Kelley, Secretary
G. O. Gordon, Recorder

Another matter concerning the term of the Grand Exalted Ruler was decided by motion that, in view of the excellent service which had been rendered by the Grand Exalted Ruler, J. Finley Wilson, in the future he should be elected for a period of four years, which would give him the opportunity and privilege it was said, to carry out his objectives to "victorious conclusions," and it was provided that the Constitution be so amended that his election was to take place every four years beginning with the current year.

The Committee on Resolutions requested that the Negro should be called upon to do his full part in the matter of the defense of the land where his fathers had toiled, fought and died, and that he should be called upon to serve in every arm of the federal defense system, on land, in the air and at sea, and be fully recognized and have the same opportunity as others for training and developing efficient service. Another resolution opposed the Lily White Primaries, discriminatory practices in elections and urged that a program be inaugurated to eliminate such undemocratic practices.

There were present in the Grand Lodge 342 lodges with 501 delegates, sixteen state associations and thirty-three councils representing fifty deputies. The Grand Lodge representation seemed to be returning to its large delegations of other days in the six hundred delegates at this session.

Grand Director Hobson R. Reynolds closed his report with this statement, "In the Armed forces of America Jim-Crowism has been expanded and glorified. Negro soldiers are segregated in every department, or even inducted separately. Wherever colored youths serve the common flag, they serve it in separate barracks, separate areas, separate recreational facilities, etc. Negroes have a right to demand and we will demand that our youth be given equal and the same treatment under all circumstances. So, let us close ranks; let us inform the world that the Elks of Atlantic City in 1941 are determined to carry on an extended program for the betterment of our entire race."

By action and recommendation of the Grand Auditors, the next year, 1941-42, was to be known and dedicated as "Jubilee

Executive Board of the Grand Temple, August, 1940.

Victory Year." The report of the Department of Athletics showed that there had been several lodges which had presented baseball games. The Ohio Elk's Day in Cleveland, Ohio, had presented the Homestead Grays v. New York Yankees on Sunday, May 18, 1941, with Brother Perry B. Jackson as Chairman of the Day. Pennsylvania Elk's Day was presented in Pittsburgh, Pa., with the Homestead Grays v. the Havana Cubans on July 13, 1941; the Metropolitan New York District had presented at Yankee Stadium the Havana Cubans v. the Memphis Black Yanks on August 10, 1941, and at Columbus, Ohio the Homestead Grays v. the Newark Eagles were presented on August 17, 1941. Commendation was given to President Roosevelt upon his stand against sending United States military expeditions to Europe and for the executive order against discrimination in employment. It was urged that this order be rigidly enforced and the anti-discrimination policy applied to all federal departments.

A beauty contest was held at this convention on the Boardwalk at Missouri Avenue on Wednesday afternoon so that the Bronze Venus for 1941 could be selected. There were seven contestants and the first place went to Miss Jane Moses of Atlantic City; second place to Miss Lucile Clark of Charleston, W. Va.; and third place to Miss Marion Parker of Atlantic City.

In this year, 1941, the Daughter Elks set up their Reserve Department and their membership reached a total of 41,844 members. Their departments included the Child Welfare Department, Arts and Crafts, Purple Cross Units, Grant Temple Birthday Department. The year 1941 also witnessed the appointment of Grand Directress of Purple Cross Nurses Anna B. Jones by Grand Exalted Ruler Wilson and Grand Daughter Ruler Elizabeth Ross Gordon. The Civil Liberties Department of the Grand Lodge united the Grand Temple work on civil liberties with its work, and a cooperative endeavor resulted. Other functioning departments established were the Seniors Mothers' Council; the Arts and Crafts Department in 1928; the Athletic Department; the Good Will Circle in 1937; the Baby Contest Department also in 1937; the Emma V. Kelley National Elks Shrine in 1938; the Public Relations Department in 1942; Emergency Relief Department in 1939; Emma V. Kelley Helping Hand in 1949; the Child Welfare Department in 1927; Birthday Department in 1936; and the Four Square, Hospitality, Music, Rainbow Charity, Reserve Fund, Rainy Day, Ways and Means, and Retirement Departments. The Daughters were responding to the cause of National Defense. They were working in defense plants and taking the places of men called into active war service. A survey of

Daughter Elizabeth Ross Gordon, Seventh Grand Daughter Ruler, 1940 1951.

a section showed that there were over 3,000 Daughters in volunteer service. War bonds and war savings stamps were purchased by the temples and individual Daughters.

The Grand Lodge Officers for 1941-1942 were: J. Finley Wilson, Grand Exalted Ruler, Washington, D. C.; Joseph A. Brown, Grand Esteemed Leading Knight, New York, N. Y.; Marcus F. Wheatland, Grand Esteemed Loyal Knight, Camden, New Jersey; Herbert E. Jones, Grand Esteemed Lecturing Knight, Washington, D. C.; James E. Kelley, Grand Secretary, Birmingham, Ala.; Edward W. Henry, Grand Treasurer, Philadelphia, Pa.; Eugene Sorral, Grand Esquire, Los Angeles, Calif.; J. M. Washington, Grand Inner Guard, Brooklyn, N. Y.; Simpson A. Smith, Grand Tiler, Huntington, W. Va.; William Hueston, Commissioner of Education, Washington, D. C.; Perry W. Howard, Grand Legal Adviser, Washington, D. C.; Hobson R. Reynolds, Grand Director of Civil Liberties, Philadelphia, Pa; W. George Avant, Grand Chaplain, Durham, N. C.; Carter L. Marshall, Grand Medical Adviser, New Haven, Conn.; J. Mercer Burrell, Director of Junior Elks, Newark, N. J.; John U. Strother, Chairman of Publishing Boards, Augusta, Ga.; Duke Ellington, Grand Bandmaster, New York, N. Y.; George Hyder, Assistant Bandmaster, Philadelphia, Pa.; Walter H. Land, Grand Master of Social Session, Norfolk, Va.; Sam Scott, Co-Grand Master of Social Session, Charleston, W. Va.; John C. Minkins, Grand Lodge Reporter, Providence, R. I.; C. C. Valle, Grand Organizer, New York, New York; James A. Jackson, Commissioner of Economics, New York, N. Y.; Cumberland Posey, Director of Athletics, Homestead, Pa.

The status of the Negro population, the declaration of loyalty to the nation and the support of the National Defense Program were continued in the Forty-Third Annual Meeting of the Grand Lodge at Philadelphia, Pa., August 23-29, 1942, with O. V. Catto Lodge No. 20 serving as host. At the sixteenth annual meeting of the Department of Education at which Judge W. C. Hueston presided, there was considerable enthusiasm on the part of both the Elks and the Grand Daughter Elks. There were congratulations extended to Commissioner Hueston by both groups for maintaining the successful program of the Department. Daughter Carey Curtis of Michigan spoke of the fact that the Department was "the selling point of the Order." The annual Baccalaureate service was held at the McKinley Temple, Methodist Episcopal Church, with an over-flow audience present. The Baccalaureate sermon was delivered by Rev. H. H. Johnson, pastor of St. Mary's Parish. Remarks were made by Grand Exalted Ruler Wilson and Grand Daughter Ruler Elizabeth Ross

W. T. MEADE GRANT, JR., Grand Director, Junior Elks

J. MERCER BURRELL, Grand Director, Junior Elks

W. W. BARNUM, Chairman of Committee on Official Organ; Chairman, Publishing Board.

WALTER H. LAND, Grand Master of Social Sessions, Civil Liberties Commission.

Gordon. Dr. J. C. Austin, Pastor of Pilgrim Baptist Church, Chicago, Illinois preached the annual sermon at the annual memorial service with remarks by the Grand Officers.

The National Cap and Gown Breakfast was given in the O. V. Catto Grill Room with Judge William C. Hueston, Commissioner of Education presiding. Among the important points made by him was that leaders come from men and women who are trained to think. He deplored the fact that a large percentage of our youth who are inducted into the Army were illiterates. He said about 60 per cent were uneducated and that while 40 per cent of the whites were high school graduates only 4 per cent of the Negroes were high school graduates. A National Cap and Gown Club was organized and it was proposed that by-laws for its government should be made.

The educational meeting was held on Monday, August 25, when Daughter Gertrude Holland announced that there was seventy Cap and Gown Clubs in the states. The Civil Liberties program with Commissioner Hobson R. Reynolds of Civil Liberties presiding was conducted with Dr. Mary McLeod Bethune as one of the speakers. One of the significant statements made by Grand Legal Adviser Perry W. Howard was "it's all right to get education, to get refinement and culture, but unless you control your civil liberties, you are lost." He said further, "We are not fighting to preserve the American way of life, but to improve the American way of life for full citizenship for Negroes." Dr. Bethune said, in part, "the power of Elkdom because of great leadership has done much. Those in high, middle and low places must listen, you have much to hope for, you have made great contributions in the fields of education. The world needs to be proud of the youth educated by the Order." Judge Harry S. McDevitt of Philadelphia was introduced by Commissioner Reynolds. He declared that there was no color-line in defense. He paid tribute to the

Dt. Gertrude Holland, President, National Cap and Gown Club.

Civil Liberties program of the Order. He said that he asked for an opportunity to fight for democracy and that he had two boys in the Army, one of whom commanded a Negro regiment and he added "if he dies, he'll die in good company." The National Oratorical Contest again struck its high note. During the sessions Grand Exalted Ruler Wilson outlined the program of the Order to buy $100,000 worth of War Bonds.

The business session of the Grand Lodge was opened on Tuesday, August 26, in due ritualistic form after which the Committee on Credentials was appointed and their report showed that there were twenty-two Grand Lodge officers, 39 councils, 11 state associations, 340 lodges with 450 delegates and six herds represented, which made a total of 528 delegates present. The Grand Exalted Ruler made his annual report and a motion was made by Dr. Hudson J. Oliver that inasmuch as the report was voluminous that the Grand Exalted Ruler suspend the reading of the full report and only read the highlights. This motion was approved.

The Grand Exalted Ruler said that "We are here to put to the test whether or not we merit that right and the four freedoms which are accorded us in Elkdom." He referred in this instance to the decision in the Virginia Case which made it possible for the Grand Lodge to control the affairs of Elkdom throughout a world jurisdiction. He stated that he had appointed "the old Schoolmaster" Judge William C. Hueston, who was Grand Commissioner of Education, to head up the Bond Drive and he hoped that ultimately there would be a million dollar record purchase by Elks of this Grand Lodge. This was to represent the amount purchased both by the Grand Lodge and by members of all of the Elk lodges. He said that now was the time for fidelity and loyalty to the land that had given them birth and he said that while we are faithful to the American cause, they were demanding an evenhanded justice from the government of which they were a part. In his announcement of necrology, he announced the death of Chu John who was the first Chinese to become a Brother Elk. He said that he and George Wong organized a lodge in Canton, China with 2,000 members and he had served as Grand Traveling Deputy of the World.

He also said that the growth of the Order had been affected but not seriously by the war, that there were Brothers everywhere employed in war industries or in governmental activities. On the other hand many of them had been taken away from their lodges to other places and the lodges had accordingly lost much of their membership relations. However, new lodges had been added since the last convention to the number of fourteen and there had been nineteen lodges reinstated, four new councils, one herd and one new civil liberties unit. He said, we believe, universally in the four freedoms for all the peoples of the earth and that the war is a global affair, as much if not more a colored man's war than a white man's war. He added, it is our war and all of the freedoms which we now have or ever hope to gain depend on the defeat of the Axis.

The Grand Exalted Ruler added "consequently we have sought to rally the colored people of America through the Elk organization to a wholehearted support of all of our war effort. We have held patriotic mass meetings such as this convention. We have organized campaigns for the purpose of defense bonds and stamps. We have contributed books to the boys in camp through the Victory Book Campaign. We have assisted in drives for Allied War Relief, especially the Russians and more especially the China Relief. We have gone out to do far more for Uncle Sam than Joe Louis did for the Navy. We have thrown our Elk's Homes open to the government. We have tended our near 25,000 antlered guards and more than 5,000 Purple Cross nurses to serve our land. We have demonstrated to the peoples of the earth that we stand as we have always stood in every crisis from Crispus Attucks at Boston Commons to Dorey Miller at Pearl Harbor, loyal to our common country. We have unflinchingly battled for double victory at home and abroad."

A pamphlet with the title "Elks and National Defense" was published and distributed. This was issued in several editions and was over-subscribed beyond the expectation of the first issue. This was a statement of the position of the Elks. The Grand Exalted Ruler called attention to the work of all the colleagues who were working with him in the Grand Offices, Civil Liberties, the Health Commission, the Athletic Department, the Official Organ, the Junior Elks, the Economics Department, the Grand Legal Adviser, the Past Grand Exalted Rulers Councils. He recommended that Certified Public Accountants should be employed to examine the accounts of each lodge of more than one hundred membership once a year and that the Grand Lodge stood behind the President's Manpower Commission under Paul V. McNutt, Federal Security Administrator. Each lodge and temple was called on to organize a Bond Drive Committee and the organization of the Negro workers was urged when employment would be secured. whether through the Fair Employment Practices Committee or the manpower commission or otherwise.

At the conclusion of his address Dr. William J. Thompkins stated "nothing has been more constructive or more matchless than this report. For twenty years this little 'Giant' has lifted the Order above all other fraternities in the country. From him has come the inspiration to fight on. He is the greatest fraternal leader the nation has ever produced. He is the Father of Negro fraternities of the world."

Grand Secretary Kelley was as keenly aware of the dual opportunity of the Order as it related itself to national defense and to the status of the Negro population. He realized that the nation was at war, but he also added "the Negro is not only fighting for this country, but he is fighting for an opportunity to fight. He is fighting for an opportunity to prove to the world, and particularly to America that a man's worth is not measured by the color of his skin, but by the quality of his manhood." His records showed that there had been seventeen new lodges and thirty-two reinstated, nine new and reinstated councils, ten new civil liberties leagues and sixteen new and reinstated herds.

The total receipts received by the Grand Treasurer Henry were $99,729.10 and there was a balance in the Treasury of $36,277.37. The report of the Commissioner of Education read by Judge William C. Hueston, among other things urged that before the convention adjourned, a definite stand should be taken and sent to the President of the United States and the Congress concerning the hopes and desires of those who are represented in the lodge. He urged that the Elks register their insistent contention that they were Americans and that they should be represented as were other Americans in the war and industrial efforts. He described the work which had been done on the *Washington Eagle,* the official organ, and the Elk's Bond Buying Campaign The rules were suspended and at the conclusion of his address Brother Hueston was reelected by acclamation.

The report of the Grand Medical Director, Dr. Carter Marshall, described the wide-spread celebration of Negro Health Week by lodges and temples, and in referring to the Purple Cross Units, he said "never before in the history of our Health Department or in the history of our country has it been more important for the women of the nation to be prepared to defend themselves and be prepared to administer first-aid." He added that the first Purple Cross Nurses Unit was organized on July 12, 1925 by Daughter Mayme Hutchinson of Forrest Temple No. 9, Washington, D. C., and that since then the units had grown very extensively. He urged personal attention to health as well as the group attention through lodges and temples. He was recommended to succeed himself as Grand Medical Director on motion and approved by the Grand Lodge.

Negro National Freedom Day, February 1, was endorsed by the Grand Lodge following an address by Major R. R. Wright,

J. Finley Wilson, Grand Exalted Ruler, in uniform (1945).

President of the Citizen's and Southern Bank of Philadelphia. The Grand Director of Civil Liberties, Brother Hobson Reynolds, stated that his department had been battling on all fronts against segregation and discrimination. Individual cases had been taken up and fought through to conclusion. The departments had engaged in the activities of the Order in the purchase of war bonds and stamps.

The Daughter Elks showed their interest in the history of their work by giving the first performance in 1942 of their "Pageant Progress." This production describing the building of their organization from its earliest days, was written by Daughter Buena V. Kelley with the assistance of Daughter Mandonia Owens, Leonora Mumford and Fannie Mais. This play was presented at the Philadelphia convention in 1942. The result of this presentation was the addition of a Tam Pageant section in connection with the annual pageant presentation. A Department of Public Relations was also established with Daughter Rachael Corrothers as First Grand Directress in 1942. She was succeeded by Daughter Lethia Fleming of Cleveland, Ohio.

Resolutions were passed embracing loyalty to the nation and the advancement of the status of the Negro. The main resolution stated that "We resent from the depths of our hearts attempts to perpetuate inequality of life and opportunity, even while fighting professedly for the Four Freedoms, Democracy, Liberty, and Christianity," and it was declared that "confident in the strength of our sacred cause, American Negroes appeal to our President, our Congress and our fellow citizens to do as they would be done by, to wipe out everything that would tend to promote disunity and to march shoulder to shoulder—on the home front, on war fronts until the Cross of Christ triumphs over the heathen swastika and the enlightened democracy of the founding fathers replaces autocracy, absolutism, totalitarianism—at home and abroad."

The Grand Lodge Officers for 1942-1943 were: J. Finley Wilson, Grand Exalted Ruler, Washington, D. C.; Joseph A. Brown, Grand Esteemed Leading Knight, Camden, N. J.; Herbert E. Jones, Grand Esteemed Lecturing Knight, Washington, D. C.; James E. Kelley, Grand Secretary, Birmingham, Ala.; Edward W. Henry, Grand Treasurer, Philadelphia, Pa.; Eugene Sorral, Grand Esquire, Los Angeles, California; J. M. Washington, Grand Inner Guard, Brooklyn, N. Y.; Dr. Simpson A. Smith, Grand Tiler, Huntington, West Virginia; William C. Hueston, Commissioner of Education, Washington, D. C.; Perry W. Howard, Grand Legal Adviser. Washington, D. C.; Hobson R. Reynolds, Grand Director of Civil Liberties, Philadelphia, Pa.;

W. George Avant, Grand Chaplain, Durham, N. C.; Dr. Carter L. Marshall, Grand Medical Director, New Haven, Conn.; J. Mercer Burrell, Chairman of Publishing Board, Augusta, Ga.; Duke Ellington, Grand Bandmaster, New York, N. Y.; George Hyder, Assistant Bandmaster, Philadelphia, Pa.; Walter H. Land, Grand Master of Social Session, Norfolk, Va.; John C. Minkins, Grand Lodge Reporter, Providence, R. I.; C. C. Valle, Grand Organizer, New York, N. Y.; James A. Jackson, Grand Commissioner of Economics, New York, N. Y.

The work of aiding the National Defense Program and of pushing forward the status of the Negro in the United States was continued in the Grand Lodge session of 1943. This was the Forty-Fourth Annual Meeting of the Grand Lodge which convened in Central Baptist Church, Pittsburgh, Pennsylvania, August 22-27, 1943. This session opened with the Education and Economic Congress in which this keynote was continued in the Baccalaureate services at which Dr. J. C. Austin of Chicago delivered the sermon; the National Cap and Gown Club at which Commissioner Hueston and W. W. Saunders of Charleston, W. Va., were the main speakers; at the annual education meeting at which Mr. Phillip Jones of Pittsburgh spoke on "Negro Leadership in the Post-War World" and Judge Perry B. Jackson of the Municipal Court of Cleveland, Ohio spoke; at the annual program of the Elk's department of Civil Liberties at which R. F. Lewis, President of the *Pittsburgh Courier,* Attorney Homer S. Brown, Dr. Forester B. Washington were the main speakers and at the annual Oratorical Contest in which six contestants spoke upon the subject "The Negro and the Constitution."

The Grand Lodge was opened with the Grand Exalted Ruler J. Finley Wilson presiding and after the usual ritualistic service the Grand Secretary made his report. He directed attention to the fight on the military front in which the Brothers were participating in the struggle for democracy at home. He said that the Department of Education was assisting in the education of youth. The Civil Liberties Department was seeking to bring justice to the minority group fighting for the rights of Negroes even to serve the country with dignity and honor, and the Health, Athletic and Economic Departments were seeking to lift the band of physical and economic slavery. The Junior Elks Department was striving to build a sterling manhood for the world of tomorrow. He declared "Elkdom is meeting this new challenge to our way of life with steadfastness and courage." He reported that there were thirty-eight new and reinstated lodges, three new councils, one new civil liberties league and two reinstated leagues, seven new herds and there were fifty-three lodges which had become inactive since the last report in 1942.

In addition to giving a full report of the work of the Department of Education which was in its eighteenth year of service, Commissioner Hueston entered into the same discussion which characterized this period of the Grand Lodge. He added that the task before them was to fight and fight until we get every boy and girl in the United States exposed to a sustained education. He said, "We must fight to make ourselves acceptable to the civilization in which we live. We must be informed, healthy, self-sustaining and sanitary, in order to be acceptable in this life in which we find ourselves." He described the growth of the Cap and Gown Clubs and that some of them had become so consolidated in their endeavors that they were sending cash contributions to carry on the work of the Elk's Scholarship Fund. He spoke of the Study Clubs, the growth and service of the *Washington Eagle* as the official newspaper. Special mention was made of the Bond Campaign in which he had been the leading organizer. He gave consideration to the Athletic Department and suggested that it should be attached in a more direct way to the Department of Education.

The reports of the Grand Legal Adviser Perry W. Howard, the Grand Director of Economics, J. A. Jackson; the Commission on Health, including Dr. William J. Thompkins, Dr. E. T. Belsaw, Dr. Charles E. Hall and Dr. T. T. Wendell, divided their attention between preparation for defense on the home front and activity in the development of a program for the upbuilding of the status of the Negro.

The report of the Grand Director of the Department of Civil Liberties was devoted directly to victory at home and victory abroad. A description was made of the local activities of the department through the local lodges and of the central office and a picture was drawn of the program for the future, including juvenile delinquency, riots and unrest which were in the nation as they concerned the Negro people. Even the Grand Treasurer in a report which dealt mainly with finances called attention to the four freedoms, "enunciated in the Atlantic Charter in the history making meeting between the Prime Minister of England and President Roosevelt" and stated that through these, as well as the other basic documents of the United States, we must demand the inclusion of the 13,000,000 American Negroes and insist, he said, that no particular section of the population should ignore these documents, but that we might all live as Americans in national peace and prosperity. The receipts of the Order showed the support of his program for they had reached the large sum of $138,487.33 and there was a balance shown of $68,836.78.

Governor Edward Martin of Pennsylvania gave a prepared address centering around the contributions of the American Negro to the development of the nation and the need for winning the war. The reports of the Grand Director of Music, George Hyder and the Grand Director of Junior Elks, J. Mercer Burrell, were heartedly acclaimed by the Order in session.

The climax of the reports was the presentation of the report of the Grand Exalted Ruler J. Finley Wilson. He referred again and again to the "present world conflict, ever with an eye single to the double victory proclaimed at our last convention—victory here on the home front as well as victory abroad." He urged the buying of bonds by the lodges and individuals and stated that the Grand Exalted Ruler had purchased $5,000 worth of "E" Bonds also in 1943. He urged the loaning of money to the government on the bond plan by lodges, temples and individuals. He described the mortgage burnings and dedications of new homes which had taken place in various parts of the nation in which he had participated. He mentioned Harmony Lodge, Springfield, Massachusetts; Majestic Lodge, Hackensack, New Jersey; Commonwealth Lodge, Boston, Massachusetts; East Baltimore Lodge, Baltimore, Maryland; Monongahela Moore Lodge, Ironton, Ohio; Sam Scott Lodge, Beckley, W. Virginia and Frederick Allen Lodge, Saratoga Springs, New York.

One of the announcements at this Grand Lodge was the death of the wife of the founder of the Order, Mary Louise Howard. The Grand Exalted Ruler made the announcement and in describing her work he said that she helped her husband "steer the ship of state in the dark and bloody days of Elkdom's infancy and acted as the Grand Exalted Ruler's Secretary until James E. Mills succeeded him in Detroit in 1909." The Grand Lodge took charge of the funeral and carried out her instructions and the remains were deposited by the side of her husband, the first Grand Exalted Ruler and the Founder of the Order. A monument had been erected there and the Grand Exalted Ruler said that it would bear the name of "the great man and his devoted wife." It was of interest that the minister who officiated at the passing of the Founder, B. F. Howard, served again at the passing of his wife, Mary Louise Howard.

Notice was also given of the passing of the Rev. George Avant who had been Grand Chaplain for a quarter of a century and of the death of Harry H. Pace who was described as "truly one of God's noblemen." The Grand Exalted Ruler stated that he had handled his campaign in Washington, D. C. and when he was promoted from Secretary of the Atkins' faction to Secretary of the United Grand Lodge, and then as Grand Exalted Ruler following J. Frank Wheaton. He said that he was the only man to serve in both offices, "that of Grand Secretary and Grand Exalted Ruler."

There had been extensive travel by the Grand Exalted Ruler during the past year, not only in the United States, but in shifting backward and forward from the Atlantic to the Pacific, meeting with lodges and temples but he had also traveled to Panama, visiting the lodges and temples there and had set up a council and a state association. He said that his next overseas flight would be to the Pearl Harbor Lodge set up by Brother Deputy Henry Green in Honolulu. The total report of bond purchases as made by the Grand Lodge and individuals brought these purchases to $2,782, 569.55. The Grand Auditors certified to the correctness of the accounts as reported by the Grand Treasurer and the Grand Secretary. The travels of the Grand Exalted Ruler were paralleled by the Grand Organizer, C. C. Valle, who reported wonderful progress throughout the jurisdiction with lodges making substantial increase in membership and manifesting healthy financial conditions.

The Fraternal Greetings Committee from the Grand Temple was received by the Grand Lodge. The Committee was led by Daughter Margaret Stout and Daughter Gertrude Holland. They brought greetings from Grand Daughter Ruler Elizabeth Gordon. Daughter Rachel Carruthers as Grand Directress of Public Relations made her first annual report to the Grand Lodge and to the Temple. The report showed that one of their important projects on the national scene was to organize a cigarette project for the purpose of sending cigarettes to the boys in the service. They had associated themselves with the Civil Liberties Commission in a fight against the poll tax, discrimination in federal hospital construction, federal aid to education, the procural of signatures numbering 20,000 on the Union for Democratic Action petitions presented to the President and on other bills in the Congress. The sum of $520.50 had been collected for the Overseas Cigarette Fund.

An important resolution concerning the esteem held for Grand Exalted Ruler J. Finley Wilson was adopted by the Grand Lodge designating him as a delegate to any peace conference which might be held. This resolution was:

> "Whereas the national leadership of the Honorable J. Finley Wilson commends him as a statesman, worthy of international responsibility and trust, and,
>
> Whereas his service to the nation through minority leader-

ship warrants his representation in any matters affecting the good of the nation.

Resolved that this Grand Lodge hereby endorse the Honorable J. Finley Wilson for membership in the United States delegation to the Peace Conference following this World War II, and

Further that a copy of this resolution be forwarded to President Roosevelt and the Department of State.

The Grand Lodge Officers for 1943-1944 were: J. Finley Wilson, Grand Exalted Ruler, Washington, D. C.; Joseph A. Brown, Grand Esteemed Leading Knight, Dayton, Ohio; Dr. Marcus F. Wheatland, Grand Esteemed Loyal Knight, Camden, N. J.; Herbert E. Jones, Grand Esteemed Lecturing Knight, Washington, D. C.; James E. Kelley, Grand Secretary, Birmingham, Ala.; Edward W. Henry, Grand Treasurer, Philadelphia, Pa.; Eugene Sorral, Grand Esquire, Los Angeles, Calif.; S. A. Smith, Grand Inner Guard, Huntington, W. Va.; S. D. Holsey, Grand Tiler, Reading, Pa.; William C. Hueston, Grand Commissioner of Education, Washington, D. C.; Perry W. Howard, Grand Legal Adviser, Washington, D. C.; Hobson R. Reynolds, Grand Director of Civil Liberties, Philadelphia, Pa.; Dr. Carter L. Marshall, Grand Medical Director, New Haven, Conn.; J. Mercer Burrell, Director of Junior Elks, Newark, N. J.; John U. Strother, Chairman of Publishing Board, Augusta, Ga.; Duke Ellington, Grand Bandmaster, New York, N. Y.; George Hyder, Assistant Bandmaster, Philadelphia, Pa.; William H. Land, Grand Master of Social Session, Norfolk, Va.; Sam Scott, Co-Grand Master of Social Session, Charleston, W. Va.; John C. Minkins, Grand Lodge Reporter, Providence, R. I.; C. C. Valle, Grand Organizer, New York, N. Y.; James A. Jackson, Commissioner of Economics, New York, N. Y.; and Edward H. Gray, Major General Antlered Guard.

JOHN U. STROTHER, Chairman, Publishing Board, Grand Master of Social Sessions.

Elkdom's reactions to the National Defense Program were clearly demonstrated in the addresses and adopted actions of this 1944 Grand Lodge. The delegates were loyal, patriotic citizens who were demanding the right to join in the fight and shoulder all of the responsibilities of citizenship as others were doing. They were willing to devote their energies to victory at home and victory abroad.

Chapter XVII

War and Peace

With the dawn of 1944, war and peace were drawing into closer alliance, and Negro Elkdom was participating in both areas. The signs of prosperity were appearing in the United States and unemployment had almost disappeared. The war machine was in constant motion with prosperity as one of its products. Negroes being largely in low income groups found that they were receiving more income except where they were frozen in their jobs and their wages. This era of war prosperity gave them a considerable boost. Elks were also air-raid wardens, and airplane spotters. Daughter Elks were taking first-aid and functioning in Purple Cross units. The youths of Elkdom were in the Army and Navy uniforms. They looked forward to the termination of the war and participated in the typical post-war planning in the various communities. They were in war and peace as were other Americans. They were interested in the signing of the pact of the United Nations in Washington, D. C. in 1942, and in fact, they were active participants in the war in Europe and the Pacific.

As the Forty-fifth Annual meeting of the Grand Lodge convened in Forum Hall, Chicago, Illinois, August 22-26, 1944, the significance of the war and the approaching peace was impressed upon the delegates by the message of Dr. Adam Clayton Powell of New York's Abyssinian Baptist Church at the Annual Baccalaureate Service. His subject was "The Negro in the Post-War World." His appeal was eloquent and stirring for the Negro to prepare for the movement from war to peace. A similar impression was left by Dr. J. C. Austin whose subject was "God in these Times—God in this Revolution." A. Phillip Randolph at the Annual Education Meeting described the central social question of the current conflict as one of race and color. He said that the basis of power was organization, and urged that Negroes organize themselves in order to win their rights during the war instead of seeking them at the close of the war.

Other opening meetings were conducted by the Department of Economics, Civil Liberties and Education. Grand Commissioner of Economics, James A. Jackson at the annual meeting of the Department of Economics stressed the need for working and serving now and of curtailing useless spending during the war period, using these savings for the purchase of government bonds. The Annual Civil Liberties Program under the Grand Director, Hobson R. Reynolds embraced addresses on civil liberties in war time and in the post-war period. The Negro and the Constitution was again the subject used in the annual oratorical contest at Pilgrim Baptist Church at which Grand Commissioner of Education, William C. Hueston presided, with Daughter Pearl Brown, Assistant Directress of Education sharing with him.

The official attendance at this annual meeting in 1944 was reported by the committee on credentials as 35 Grand Lodge Officers, 60 Deputies, 200 lodges with 300 delegates, 20 state associations and 40 Past Grand Exalted Rulers' Council delegates. There were hundreds of visitors who crowded each of the sessions, manifesting interest, loyalty and enthusiasm.

The Grand Exalted Ruler's report was awaited with expectation by the delegates and audience of lodge members. A message was needed for war times and the period of peace. Grand Exalted Ruler Wilson did not disappoint them. He described the war emergency, the need for closing ranks in order to fight discrimination and support the directives of the Fair Employment Practices Committee, and said he, "We are here, our allegiance unquestioned, offering our prayers for peace, and for God's blessing on America, the Home of the Brave and the Free."

The Grand Exalted Ruler reported that he had engaged in bond drives, and that in the drive in New York City there had been $2,000,000 worth of bonds sold on September 22, the day of the announcement of the issuance of the Emancipation Proclamation effective on January 1, 1863. This drive was conducted with marked display of loyalty and patriotism. The Grand Exalted Ruler declared that this convention at Chicago was the climax of these efforts and that it was to be more of a patriotic meeting than a fraternal one, for every asset of Elkdom was to be placed at the disposal of the government.

Advancement had been made by the individual lodges. There were ninety mortgages which had been burned and eighty-five Elk homes had been dedicated. There was a combined evaluation in the cancelled mortgages of over $15,000,000. Chris J. Perry Lodge had purchased property for its home valued at over one million dollars. Lodges in Cleveland, Detroit and other places were building up their membership, burning mortgages, purchasing homes and bonds, and engaging in war efforts. Ten new lodges had been added to the rolls, twenty-one lodges had been reinstated, two new councils had been instituted, twenty-four new Herds and thirteen new civil liberties leagues. Upon the basis of this first year's record, the lodges were urged by the Grand Exalted Ruler to "march onward and upward in the light of our fine tradition, so that others may know and understand our eyes

THE ELK'S ATOMIC NATIONAL MEMBERSHIP CAMPAIGN
GRAND LODGE AND GRAND TEMPLE ASSIGNMENTS

Date ....

New York City, N. Y.

To the National Director, Elk's Atomic National Membership Campaign,
Professor C. C. **Vallee, Grand** Organizer
81 Morningside Avenue, Apt. 5-S, New York **27,** N. Y.

Dear Sir:

Please be advised that I shall participate in the Elk's Atomic **National Membership Campaign sponsored by the Grand Lodge and the Grand Temple.**

I will accept any assignment to be made by the Grand Exalted Ruler **and will collaborate and assist the following Lodges** ....

Temples .... **during drive.**

Name of Lodge and No.	Name of Temple and No.
1..	1..
2..	2..
3..	3..
4..	4..
5..	5..

City.. **State**..

Remarks ....

....

....

....

Respectfully submitted,

Signature ....

Membership Campaign Report, 1946-1947.

have seen the glory of the coming of the Lord.'' Following this report, the Grand Exalted Ruler was reelected by unanimous ballot.

Increases in membership were reported by Grand Secretary

Kelley in spite of the hundreds of members who had been called into the armed forces. With these resources and organization he believed that Elkdom should pledge itself to lead all Negro fraternities in preparing the race to meet its problems in this period and in the post-war era. Another evidence of a successful year was the large increase in total receipts of $134,341.26 and the cash balance of $122,577.48 as reported by Grand Treasurer Edward W. Henry. This was the largest cash balance in the history of the order. Both the Grand Secretary and the Grand Treasurer were re-elected by unanimous ballots following their submission of reports.

Nineteen years had passed since Grand Commissioner of Education William C. Hueston had undertaken the work of the Department of Education. He had already been named affectionately, "the old Schoolmaster." He regarded this year's report which he made in 1944 as "the most successful year the Elks Department of Education has ever had. There were nineteen undergraduates on Elks scholarships in colleges and universities. This number made a total of more than three hundred who had been graduated on full scholarships awarded by the order. While war had offered its handicaps in the calling of young men into war services, it had not overlooked a quota from the educational committees and state directors. He said that his work had continued, however, with effective service to the people. The oratorical contests had attracted attention to education and to the limitation of rights under the constitution. He reported that the joint Health and Education work had been conducted with cooperation from Dr. Carter L. Marshall, Grand Medical Director in 1944 as in 1943 when the joint effort was first undertaken. At the conclusion of his report, Commissioner Hueston was reelected by acclamation.

The Civil Liberties report was made by Grand Director Hobson R. Reynolds, who declared that his continued purpose was to carry on a campaign for equality along all lines for the Negro. He outlined a program for the subordinate lodges which should include (1) full citizenship rights for all regardless of race, creed or color; (2) the ending of all legal discrimination; (3) adequate federal laws passed to give all citizens the right to vote in every state; (4) elimination of all forms of segregation; (5) equal opportunities for Negro men and women in all branches of the armed forces without segregation; and (6) equal employment opportunities. He said that gains had been made through pressures on the War Manpower Commission and cooperation with the Fair Employment Practices Committee, the Office of War Information, government contracting agencies and labor unions.

ROBERT H. JOHNSON, Grand Commissioner of Transportation, Grand Esteemed Lecturing Knight, Grand Esteemed Leading Knight.

He declared, "We shall continue this fine work until the colored people of America in all parts of America, in all parts of the land receive all the rights and privileges guaranteed to them by the Constitution." At the conclusion of his report, unanimous action prevailed to recommend him to the Grand Exalted Ruler for reappointment.

The work of the Grand Lodge in Economics was reported by Grand Commissioner James A. Jackson. Music was surveyed by Brother George Hyder, and the Antlered Guard by Brother Emerson H. Gray. The work in Health was reported by Grand Medical Director Carter L. Marshall, who paid tribute to the pioneering efforts of Brother William T. Thompkins, deceased, as chairman of the Health Commission in the earlier years, and to the work of Daughter Anna B. Jones as Grand Directress of the Purple Cross Nurses. He said of Daughter Jones, "her genius and her dynamic, inspiring leadership are largely responsible for the growth and progress of this Department." The cooperative project of Elks Health Day with Education Week was reported as a most successful one and the efforts of the lodges in this endeavor were praised.

Since the war had occasioned such difficulties in transportation for the Grand Officers, the Grand Lodge and the lodge representatives, the office of Grand Commissioner of Transportation had assumed marked significance. Grand Commissioner Robert H. Johnson made his first report to the 1944 Grand Lodge and referred to the Order of the Office of Defense Transportation of the Federal Government forbidding the holding of conventions, although the right of assembly was protected by the Constitution, and suggesting that the cessation of conventions had to be a voluntary act. The Grand Commissioner stated that his wide correspondence with the lodges and his conferences with the Grand Officers and railroad representatives had facilitated the holding of this Grand Lodge session. The lodges, he said, had cooperated and plans had been made to hold a convention with as many Elks as would attend. He also declared that the purpose of this convention was to bring victory in war through the contributions of Elkdom and to aid America's post-war program. This declaration was verified when subscriptions with cash accompanying them were received for U. S. War Bonds in the total amount of $64,775.00 as reported by Brother George W. Lee, chairman of the Bond Drive Committee. Commendation was given to the report of Brother Johnson by vote of the Grand Lodge and Grand Exalted Ruler Wilson immediately reappointed him Grand Commissioner of Transportation for the ensuing year, as this office was vital to successful Grand Lodge sessions.

Herbert E. Jones, Grand Organizer, Grand Esteemed Loyal Knight

Joseph A. Brown, Grand Esteemed Leading Knight, Grand Esteemed Lecturing Knight

Emerson H. Gray, Major-General Antlered Guard

John C. Minikins, Grand Lodge Reporter

Greetings were brought from the Grand Temple by a Committee on Fraternal Greetings headed by Vice Grand Daughter Ruler, Lucy Dorsey. A birthday presentation was made to Grand Exalted Ruler Wilson and an address was made by Past Daughter Ruler Minetta Dobson. The Daughters had been making progress during the year. The Good Will Circle was adopted as a department in 1944 and the Purple Cross Department had its first graduation exercises at which 158 graduates were presented with diplomas.

There were thousands of Junior Elks in the Army, Navy, Marines, Coast Guard and Merchant Marines, according to the report of the Director of Junior Elks. He said that entire Herds had volunteered or had been inducted into the services. He said that some had carried their banners along side of the Star Spangled Banner. His objective for the future was "a victory of the Four Freedoms abroad and of fair play, justice and democracy for all American citizens at home, regardless of race, creed or color."

Resolutions were adopted providing for an Elks Bureau on Housing with informative and advisory functions; the encouragement of the establishment of business and recreational centers in connection with post-war adjustments; and the appointment of a Post-War Planning Board. When the proposal was made that the Grand Exalted Ruler be elected for four years, Grand Exalted Ruler Wilson said that personally he would decline the four year term, and no vote was taken.

The Grand Lodge Officers for 1944-1945 were: J. Finley Wilson, Grand Exalted Ruler, Washington, D. C.; Joseph A. Brown, Grand Esteemed Leading Knight, New York, N. Y.; Dr. Marcus F. Wheatland, Grand Esteemed Loyal Knight, Camden, N. J.; Herbert E. Jones, Grand Esteemed Lecturing Knight, Washington, D. C.; James E. Kelley, Grand Secretary, Birmingham, Alabama; Edward W. Henry, Grand Treasurer, Philadelphia, Pa.; Eugene Sorral, Grand Esquire, Los Angeles, Calif.; S. A. Smtih, Grand Inner Guard, Huntington, W. Va.; S. D. Holsey, Grand Tiler, Reading, Pa.; William C. Hueston, Grand Commissioner of Education, Washington, D. C.; Perry W. Howard, Grand Legal Adviser, Washington, D. C.; Hobson R. Reynolds, Grand Director of Civil Liberties, Philadelphia, Pa.; Dr. Carter L. Marshall, Grand Medical Director, New Haven, Conn.; J. Mercer Burrell, Director of Junior Elks, Newark, N. J.; John U. Strother, Chairman of Publishing Board, Augusta, Ga.; Duke Ellington, Grand Bandmaster, New York, N. Y.; George Hyder, Assistant Bandmaster, Philadelphia, Pa.; Walter H. Land, Grand Master of Social Session, Norfolk, Va.; Sam Scott, Co-Grand Master of

Social Session, Charleston, W. Va.; John C. Minkins, Grand Lodge Reporter, Providence, Rhode Island; C. C. Valle, Grand Organizer, New York, N. Y.; James A. Jackson, Commissioner of Economics, New York, N. Y.; Frank G. Ellis, Director of Athletics, Syracuse, N. Y.; Robert H. Johnson, Grand Commissioner of Transportation, Philadelphia, Pa.; Dr. Lawrence J. Davenport, Grand Organist, New York, N. Y.; C. Henri Lewis, Chairman Post-War Planning Committee, Detroit, Michigan; Emerson H. Gray, Antlered Guard, Adjutant General, Phialdelphia, Pa.; Brazil J. Bryant, Chairman, Grand Trustee, Detroit, Michigan; W. Gray Hoyt, Grand Trustee, Atlantic City, N. J.; John T. Freeman, Grand Trustee, Philadelphia, Pa.; C. Sylvester Jackson, Grand Trustee, Harrisburg, Pa.; Charles A. Oliver, Grand Trustee, Annapolis, Md.; James B. Allen, Grand Auditor, New York, N. Y.; James T. Copper, Grand Auditor, Chicago, Ill.; S. B. Mitchell, Grand Auditor, New York, N. Y.

During the remaining months of 1944 following the Grand Lodge, the war was carried into the enemy's camp. D-Day had come in the invasion of France on June 6, 1944, with General Dwight D. Eisenhower as Supreme Commander of the Allied Expeditionary Forces, and by August the allied armies had occupied Paris and parts of France. The Nazi drive against these forces was stopped in December. Iwo Jima was invaded by the United States Joints Expeditionary Force in February, 1945, and Okinawa, a principal Japanese base was invaded on April 1, 1945. Shortly thereafter the German armies began their surrender on May 4, 1945 and the unconditional surrender was signed on May 7. In the meantime, atomic research had been advancing, and the first atomic bomb in war was dropped on Hiroshima, August 6, 1945, and the second bomb on Nagasaki on August 9.

Earlier in this year plans were laid for a conference of the nations, with President Franklin D. Roosevelt among the leaders who called the conference. Although his death occured on April 12, 1945, the United Nations continued their plans for a conference at San Francisco, California on April 25. The representatives of forty-six nations assembled in the United Nations Conference on International Organization, with the United States, Great Britain, and Russia as the dominant powers. The charter was completed for a World Security Organization on June 26.

This conference drew the attention of the Improved Benevolent and Protective Order of Elks of the World, and as a world organization, Grand Exalted Ruler Wilson was determined that even indirect participation should be had by its representatives. Accordingly, he appointed as representatives of the Order associated with him and to be present at San Francisco, Grand Secretary James A. Kelley, Grand Legal adviser Perry W. Howard, Grand Daughter Secretary Buena V. Kelley, Grand Commissioner of Civil Liberties Hobson R. Reynolds, Grand Directress of Civil Liberties Theresa Lee Robinson and Post-War Committee Chairman C. Henri Lewis. Other organizations had also sent representatives to San Francisco. These representatives formed a group under the designation of Federated Organization of Colored People, with Dr. J. L. Horace of Chicago as chairman, Commissioner of Civil Liberties Hobson Reynolds as vice-chairman, Miss Lillian Jackson of Oakland, California, as Secretary, Grand Exalted Ruler Wilson as Treasurer and Grand Legal Advisor Perry W. Howard, Chairman of the Steering Committee and advisor to the Federation.

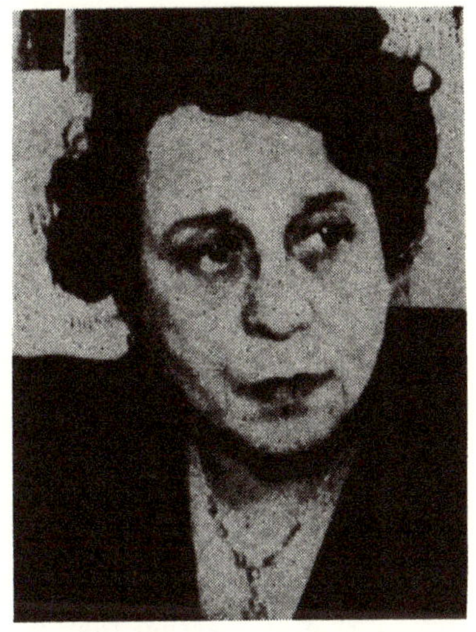

Dt. Theresa Lee Robinson, Grand Directress of Civil Liberties

This Federation was formed because Negroes throughout the world were concerned that pronouncements such as the Atlantic Charter and the agreement at Dumbarton Oaks were general and not sufficiently specific so as to include the peoples of color. An effort had been made by the Grand Exalted Ruler to have a Negro representative appointed as a member of the delegation representing the United States in the Conference, although three Negroes were appointed to serve as advisors to the conference. The Federation was an independent group of representatives who hoped to achieve their purpose even by indirect participation. Grand Director of Education Hueston thought that good would result even "if we had in the Conference City well dressed intelligent representatives of the race, walking up and down the street contacting the delegates from the world over, telling our story, presenting our cause and demanding our rights." For there was skepticism among Negroes concerning the sincerity of the conference as it related to them.

Negro newspapers manifested these opinions. Even the far-off

West African Pilot on the eve of the conference stated, "We are pessimistic because there is no new deal for the black man. We are worried about San Francisco because colonialism and economic enslavement of the African are to be maintained. We shall not be happy until the world is rescued from its half slavery and half freedom. God grant this miracle happens at San Francisco."

These representatives participated in the meetings arranged by the U. S. Department of State for consultants and advisors. They met and had discussions among themselves and adopted as their creed the following: "(1) that there should be freedom of worship, of speech, of religion and of civic association; (2) In order that these freedoms might obtain and these rights secured, there must be a guarantee of universal suffrage and free elections; (3) There should be representation in government based upon population; (4) Colonialism should be abolished, and autonomy given to all peoples; (5) That we believe that the darker peoples have been misled, exploited, under the pretense of spreading a civilization that is based upon power politics; (6) We believe that the basis of all war during the past 50 years has been from greed; (7) We believe that there can be no permanent peace as long as one group or one nation or one people subjugate or exploit another; (8) We further believe that as long as any nation, race or people take the position that they are superior socially, economically or otherwise by reason of color, there will never be universal realization of that brotherhood which is necessary for peace and goodwill; (9) and finally, so far as the darker races are concerned, nothing will be accomplished in their interest, unless there be a definite statement that the United Nations conference will look with disfavor upon any nation, however large or small it maybe, that discriminates by law, practice or custom, directly or indirectly against any segment of its population by reason of race, color or creed."

In addition to this creed, an International Association of the Colored People of the World was formed with Grand Exalted Ruler, J. Finley Wilson, as President. This organization grew out of a get-together at a banquet table of the representatives of China, the Philippines, Korea, Haiti, Liberia, India and Egypt. This organization was regarded by the Elk delegates as a parallel concept with their world organization of Negro Elkdom.

The echoes of this conference were reverberating in the memories of Elk leaders when they were called upon to assemble in the Forty-sixth annual meeting of the Grand Lodge in the Chris J. Perry Home, Philadelphia, Pa., August 28-31, 1945. This year was the 20th anniversary of the Department of Education and a membership badge with a portrait of Judge William C. Hueston was presented in honor of his leadership of the department. Dr. Marshall Shappard, Recorder of Deeds of the District of Columbia, in addressing the joint meeting of the Departments of Education and Economics declared that "the best that the war's end had brought is not peace, but the opportunity for the nations to build peace." The Grand Exalted Ruler, J. Finley Wilson, made a report on his attendance at the United Nations Conference at San Francisco, California. He said in this connection, "Without a doubt, our activities in connection with the San Francisco Conference, and the resultant publicity have placed the Improved Benevolent and Protective Order of Elks of the World fairly upon the pinnacle of world esteem."

In addressing the first business session, the Grand Exalted Ruler explained the war restrictions which limited the number of delegates in attendance and stated that the primary purpose of the convention was a Mammoth Bond Buying Rally. He said that he hoped that the Grand Lodge would purchase at least $100,000 in Victory Bonds and that the Grand Temple would purchase no less than $50,000 in bonds. Despite the limitations on attendance the Committee on Credentials reported that there were 615 delegates in attendance.

There were fifty lodges organized during the past year and forty lodges had been reinstated, according to the report of the Grand Exalted Ruler. He stated that there were one hundred and ten mortgages burned and ninety dedications since the last Grand Lodge in 1944. His report then dealt with the Antlered Guard, Housing, Fair Employment Practice, the Civil Liberties Department, Membership, Health, Necrology and Recommendations.

The Grand Parade took place on August 28. It was variously estimated at from three to five miles long. It was described in the following brief sentence, "the nattily tailored strollers, the women's and men's drill teams in smartly designed uniforms, the sport units, the mounted patrols, the snappily uniformed bands and bugle corps with their high stepping majorettes, the motor flects, the junior bands, the military service groups, the purple cross units, the elegant floats, the rhythm steppers, and the clever special features entrants all shared the approbation and generous applause of nearly a half million enthusiastic spectators who watched them pass." Prizes were awarded to the 14 best units selected by the Committee on Trophies and Awards.

Progress was presented in the reports of Grand Secretary James E. Kelley, Grand Commissioner of Education Hueston and Grand Commissioner of Economics Jackson. Grand Director Hobson Reynolds of the Civil Liberties Department struck a familiar keynote of this Grand Lodge, when he said, "Now that the war has been won, we should turn our attention to the winning of the peace." Grand Treasurer Edward W. Henry reported that "this has been a remarkable and satisfactory year in Our Grand Lodge history both because of the wonderful income that has come into our treasury and because of what our organization has accomplished under the tireless and indomitable courage of our Grand Exalted Ruler, because of our remarkable contribution to the war effort in money and manpower, for we have purchased millions of dollars worth of war bonds, thousands of our fathers, sons and brothers have counted in our armed forces, more thousands of our brothers and daughters have been enrolled in the manufacture of ammunition and implements of war, and finally, we had a powerful committee of members of our Order at San Francisco to help guide the world's statesmen in their deliberations and their final adoption of ways and means acceptable to all the allied nations of the world in their efforts to make this horrible war the world's last one." He gave the total receipts for the year as $169,033.43 and a cash balance of $193,-607.25. The Grand Auditors stated that they were enthused because of this increase in the cash balance, and they congratulated the Grand Temple on the increase in their affiliation taxes.

The Grand Commissioner of Transportation, Brother Robert H. Johnson, described the conditions which he faced in arranging for the transportation for the convention. He said that this was "a major undertaking of big proportions even in peace time," and that in war times with its overloaded and overtaxed railroad system it required "the ingenuity and resourcefulness of a master magician." The estimated attendance at this convention was placed at ten thousand from the various places in the United States. Commissioner Johnson sent letters requesting rates to 76 railroads, after securing the regulations from the Office of Defense Transportation. With the cooperation of Grand Exalted Ruler Wilson, the Commissioner reported that they were successful in making arrangements for transportation to the convention. At the conclusion of the report, the Grand Lodge gave Commissioner Johnson a rising vote of thanks and recommended unanimously that the Grand Exalted Ruler would reappoint him for another year.

Grand Exalted Ruler Wilson presented Major R. R. Wright with a check for $100,000 for the purchase of U. S. Government Bonds through the Citizens and Southern Bank of Philadelphia. It was also reported that the Grand Temple had purchased Bonds in the amount of $50,000. These purchases were continued evidences of the loyalty of the Grand Lodge, the Grand Temple and their memberships to the nation.

There were endorsements and approvals given to the support of National Freedom Day, the establishment of zones and zone health directors for the work of the Health Commission, an Elks Housing Bureau operative in various parts of the country, activity by all lodges in all post-war planning in their respective communities, the continuation of the plans for the National Shrine, the writing of the history of Elkdom and the investigation of civil service practices as they relate to Negroes.

The Grand Lodge Officers for 1945-1946 were: J. Finley Wilson, Grand Exalted Ruler, Washington, D. C.; Joseph A. Brown, Grand Esteemed Leading Knight, New York, N. Y.; Herbert E. Jones, Grand Esteemed Loyal Knight, Washington, D. C.; Robert H. Johnson, Grand Esteemed Lecturing Knight, Philadelphia, Pa.; James Kelley, Grand Secretary, Birmingham, Alabama; Dr. Marcus F. Wheatland, Grand Treasurer, Camden, N. J.; Eugene Sorral, Grand Esquire, Los Angeles, California; S. A. Smith, Grand Inner Guard, Huntington, W. Va.; S. D. Holsey, Grand Tiler, Reading, Pa.; William C. Hueston, Grand Commissioner of Education, Washington, D. C.; Perry W. Howard, Grand Legal Advisor, Washington, D. C.; Hobson R. Reynolds, Grand Director of Civil Liberties, Philadelphia, Pa.; Dr. Carter L. Marshall, Grand Medical Director, New Haven, Conn.; J. Mercer Burrell, Director of Junior Elks, Newark, N. J.; Edwin W. Burke, Chairman of Publishing Board, Savannah, Ga.; Duke Ellington, Grand Bandmaster, New York, N. Y.; George Hyder, Assistant Bandmaster, Philadelphia, Pa.; John U. Strother, Grand Master of Social Session, Augusta, Ga.; John C. Minkins, Grand Lodge Reporter, Rhode Island; C. C. Valle, Grand Organizer, New York, N. Y.; James A. Jackson, Commissioner of Economics, New York, N. Y.; Frank G. Ellis, Director of Athletics, Syracuse, N. Y.; Albert Reading, Grand Commissioner of Transportation, Chester, Pa.; Dr. Lawrence J. Davenport, Grand Organist, New York, N. Y.; C. Henri Lewis, Chairman Post-War Planning Committee, Detroit, Mich.; Emerson H. Gray, Antlered Guard, Major General, Eastern Division, Atlantic City, N. J.; Joseph T. Booker, Antlered Guard, Adjutant General, Philadelphia, Pa.; Roy Barnet, Antlered Guard, Western Division, Chicago, Ill.; Brazil J. Brant, Chairman, Grand Trustee, Detroit, Mich.; W. Grey Hoyt, Grand Trustee, Atlantic City, N. J.; John T. Freeman, Grand Trustee, Philadelphia, Pa.; Chas. A. Oliver, Grand Trustee, Annapolis, Md.; C. Sylvester Jackson, Grand Trustee, Harrisburg, Pa.; James T. Copper, Grand

Auditor, Chicago, Ill.; James B. Allen, Grand Auditor, New York, N. Y.; S. B. Mitchell, Grand Auditor, New York, N. Y.

Following this convention, the belief of many Elks was that the efforts of their representatives at the San Francisco Conference were contributory to its action on Human Rights. This conference had been presented a memorandum proposing the establishment of a committee, which was approved as a Committee on Human Rights of the United Nations with Mrs. Eleanor Roosevelt as chairman. It was with satisfaction that this action was received by the subordinate lodges after the 1945 session of the Grand Lodge.

On August 14, 1945, President Harry Truman announced that hostilities had ceased. This action followed the dropping of the first atomic bombs on Hiroshima and Nagasaki, which practically destroyed both cities. General Douglas MacArthur was named Supreme Allied Commander for Japan, and on August 29, the occupation of the Japanese Islands began. Three days afterward, the Japanese signed the documents of surrender on the battleship Missouri with representatives present of nine members of the United Nations. The war had come to an end.

The period of peace began with plans for international cooperation. By the close of 1945, fifty-one nations had signed the Charter of the United Nations. The first meeting of the General Assembly of the United Nations was held on January 10, 1946 in London. Special agencies of the United Nations were established and began operations. The League of Nations voted its own termination in Geneva, Switzerland, and turned over its assets to the United Nations on April 18, 1946. Subsequent meetings of the Security Council and the General Assembly in New York City revealed conflicts between the nations of the East and West over international relations.

Aware of the contributions made by the members of the Improved Benevolent and Protective Order of the Elks of the World in the winning of World War II, the leaders of the Order were determined to coordinate their efforts on the national scene and to make the nation a better place for its Negro citizens. Prosperity continued with wages and income remaining high, with Negroes sharing in these good times. Nevertheless, there was a rising tide of dissatisfaction among Negroes concerning the second-class citizenship existing for them.

Among the leaders who urged action against these conditions was Grand Exalted Ruler Wilson who declared that the poll tax was an "inhibition of human rights" and that a fight should be launched for a free and untrammeled ballot; that "lynching, dealing death without due process of law, is another inhibition which now more than ever rears its ugly head,'' and that better housing should be demanded, with a plan for the ''abolition of every Negro cabin, every Negro shack, every Negro shanty and every Negro slum.'' Grand Secretary Kelley seconded these efforts and urged that the brothers of Elkdom should redouble their efforts, their practices and procedures in order to secure the ballot for all people, for this, he believed was their ''most important weapon.'' Commissioner Hobson Reynolds said that his Department of Civil Liberties was ''more determined now than ever to wage a relentless fight against the forces of discrimination, segregation and prejudice that would, if not stopped, relegate the Negro to the Ghetto of Employment Insecurity, Economic Instability and Political Impotency.

Meanwhile the plans went forward for the session of the Grand Lodge of 1946. This session, the Forty-seventh Annual Meeting met in the Home of Frontier Lodge No. 1024, Buffalo, New York, August 27-31, 1946. The following official delegates constituted this Grand Lodge: 18 Grand Officers, 3 past Grand Exalted Rulers, 32 District and State Deputies, 360 lodges with 700 delegates, 59 Past Exalted Rulers Councils with 65 delegates, 15 State Associations and 2 Junior Herds, a total delegation of 835.

The growth of the Order was described by the Grand Exalted Ruler who said that during the past year there had been organized forty-one new lodges, twenty-six lodges had been reinstated, six new councils and two were reinstated, and twenty-two new civil liberties leagues. He reported that he had received a citation from the Treasury Department through its War Finance Division for the purchase of more than $30,000,000 worth of bonds. A citation had been received also from Selective Service for draft board service. He said that he had been designated by the Republican County Committee of the State of New York to run on the Republican ticket for the State Senate from the 23rd New York District. His recommendations were that the G. I. Bill of Rights be read aloud in the lodges, that the state associations develop health programs, that the fraternity should be ''as militant for our rights in 1946 as in 1776 and 1876, that every Brother and Daughter register and vote,'' and ''that we go all out to put down mob violence, lynching, and work for the destruction of the Ku Klux Klan, the development of FEPC legislation, and use of the ballot in Georgia, Alabama and Mississippi and in all states where we have been by subterfuge or otherwise deprived of the same.'' These recommendations were adopted and the rules were suspended and Grand Exalted Ruler Wilson was reelected to succeed himself for another term.

The receipts for the year were reported by General Secretary

Kelley of $190,300.36, and a cash balance of $173,083.08. The death of Judge Edward W. Henry, Grand Treasurer, on February 2, 1946, led Grand Exalted Ruler Wilson to appoint Grand Secretary Kelley to fulfill the duties of the Grand Treasurer. An audit showed that the books were in proper order and the funds were intact. The Grand Auditors stated that the present good condition of the Order was a fitting climax to the twenty-five years of constructive and progressive leadership of the Grand Exalted Ruler.

With the dawn of peace and the development of post-war plans the Grand Lodge officers undertook to continue the emphasis which had been placed on human rights, during the war, as in peace. As the plans developed for the 1947 Grand Lodge the slogan for the meeting had to be decided. It was finally agreed that the principle theme of the meeting would be "Human Rights and Citizenship." One of the important addresses at this meeting was made by A. Phillip Randolph of the Brotherhood of Sleeping Car Porters, co-chairman of the Counsel for a Permanent Fair Employment Practice Commission. He was joined by Dean William Pickens, of the U. S. Treasury Department whose main purpose was the purchase and holding of U. S. Treasury Bonds, Dr. Mary McLeod Bethune, Mayor Samuel of Philadelphia, Lee Pressman, General Council of the C. I. O., and all of the Grand Officers.

This 48th Annual Meeting of the Grand Lodge was convened in St. Charles Auditorium, Philadelphia, Pennsylvania, August 26-30, 1947. In the expressed opinion of the Grand Exalted Ruler, J. Finley Wilson, it was very fitting that the Grand Lodge should hold its sessions in the city of Brotherly Love, at a period when human rights were under consideration all over the world, and he declared that the Grand Lodge of Elkdom had assembled in this city again to crusade for liberty. His annual report to the Grand Lodge directed attention to the contacts which had been made with State Legislatures through the civil liberties chairman and his associates, and to a memorial which had been sent to the members of the 88th Congress. This memorial stated, "We, representing the Grand Lodge of the Improved Benevolent and Protective Order of Elks of the World, an organization with a membership of hundreds of thousands, and with branches reaching into every part of the world where there are members of the colored race, do petition you to pass and enact the following legislation: (1) An anti-lynching bill; (2) an anti-poll tax bill; (3) an FEPC bill; (4) a change of rules of voting so that a majority vote can shut off debate, and so that laws may be passed in the senate."

He stated that a check for $1,000 had been given to A. Phillip Randolph, through Elmer Henderson for the FEPC movement, a column in the *Washington Eagle* had vigorously approved and advocated the extension of civil liberties, the post-war planning committee had been directing attention along with the Department of Economics to the advancement of the economic status of colored peoples. The health program had been advanced and an iron lung had been given as a gift to the Provident Hospital, Chicago, Illinois.

Housing, voting and property rights were given presentation in the statement by the Grand Exalted Ruler. In conclusion he declared that there was a rising tide of color and in "Elkdom, therefore we of the Improved Benevolent Protective Order of Elks of the World must not only take care of the sick and bury the dead, we must not only eat, drink, and be merry, but also, as evidence of social maturity on our own, we must get into that tide and demonstrate our fitness for freedom." He also called attention to the approaching Golden Anniversary Convention in 1948. Following the reading of his address it was moved and approved that the Grand Exalted Ruler Wilson be designated the representative of the Improved Benevolent and Protective Order of Elks of the World, to the forthcoming World's Conference on Human Rights in Geneva, Switzerland, in November, 1947.

The Grand Secretary's report showed that there had been added to the rolls of the Grand Lodge, forty-nine new and reinstated lodges, two new past Exalted Ruler's Councils, thirty-four new and reinstated Civil Liberties Leagues, and twenty-seven new and reinstated Herds. The death of Grand Treasurer, Judge Edward W. Henry had made it necessary for Grand Secretary Kelley to act as Grand Treasurer and Grand Secretary for a part of the previous year and the current year. This made him operate with double duties thrust upon him but it was all accomplished to the satisfaction of the Grand Lodge when his report was rendered. He reported receipts of $190,217.83 and that there was a cash balance of $229,079.30. This represented the largest cash balance in the history of the Grand Lodge.

Progress was shown in the reports of the Grand Legal Advisor, Perry W. Howard, the Grand Commissioner of Economics, James A. Jackson, the Shrine Commission of which Brother George W. Lee was the chairman, the Health Commission, of which Dr. Carter L. Marshall was the chairman and Dr. E. T. Belsaw was the Executive Secretary, Major General Emerson H. Grey of the Antlered Guard, and the Grand Director of Junior

Hobson R. Reynolds, Director of Civil Liberties in 1947.

Elks, Brother J. Mercer Burrell. The first report of the Grand Director of Veterans' activities was made at this lodge by Brother Adolphos W. Anderson. Other reports included the Director of Public Relations, C. Henri Lewis, Jr.; the Grand Commissioner of Athletics, Brother Frank G. Ellis; and the report of the Grand Auditors with James T. Copper as Chairman.

An important report was made by Grand Director Hobson R. Reynolds of the Civil Liberties Department. It was one of the most comprehensive reports which marked the influence on any session in which Human Rights was a consideration. His report dealt with legislation in the state legislatures and in Congress, the publication of a souvenir convention-edition of the book *Black Justice Exposed,* with an annotated bibliography, the proposed legislation to abolish a jim-crow army and the resolution of the I.B.P.O.E. of W., stating its demands, anti-lynching legislation, FEPC, Public Housing, Public Health, Federal Aid to Education and the Federal Minimum Wage Law.

This session was highlighted by the Daughters' Anniversary Committee who were admitted to the session and made a presentation to Dr. J. Finley Wilson in recognition and appreciation of his 25 years of distinguished service as Grand Exalted Ruler. The acceptance for the Grand Exalted Ruler was made in an address by Colonel Roscoe C. Simmons. A duo of the Daughters sang songs, "Hello Bill" and "The Grand's Song" written in honor of and dedicated to the Grand Lodge, the Grand Exalted Ruler and the Grand Daughter Ruler.

The daughters reported considerable progress during this period. In 1946 they unveiled a picture of their founder, Mrs. Kelley, in the headquarters of the National Council of Negro Women in Washington, D. C. This picture was dedicated in a room beautifully furnished at these headquarters to be known as the Beuna V. Kelley Room. Daughter Rulers of the Temple had taken great interest in promoting the work of the Purple Cross nurses and had extended their activities beyond the temples to churches or other organizations and groups. It was during this period also, 1946 and 1947, that the temples worked on a program of education in the principles of the Order.

Eight new temples had been organized in this period, and there were several organized in Honduras and in Cuba. The outstanding deputies in many of the southern states who worked in this expansion were Daughters Hattie R. James, Marie White, Mattie Hollaway, Ruby Stamps Burton, Anna Thomas, Rhoena Brown, Nesby Armstrong and Edna L. Butler. Along with them and in the leadership were Grand Daughter Ruler Elizabeth Ross Gordon, Grand Daughter Secretary Beuna V. Kelley, and

THOMAS E. GREENE, Grand Treasurer, 1947-1951.

J. F. SIMMONS, Grand Trustee

J. FRANK ELLIS, Grand Director of Athletics

ROY E. BARNETT, Major General Antlered Guard

Grand Treasurer Elizabeth Kimbough who traveled throughout the nation encouraging and stimulating the Daughters in the expansion of their work. Their interest extended equally to the subject of human rights and the transition from war to peace. Under the leadership of these individuals, the Grand Daughter Ruler and the Grand Exalted Ruler Wilson, together with their associates, the Improved Benevolent and Protective Order of Elks of the World marched steadily forward from war to peace with confidence in the mission of our great brothers.

The Grand Lodge Officers for 1947-1948 were: J. Finley Wilson, Grand Exalted Ruler, Washington, D. C.; Joseph A. Brown, Grand Esteemed Leading Knight, New York, N. Y.; Herbert E. Jones, Grand Esteemed Loyal Knight, Washington, D. C.; Robert H. Johnson, Grand Esteemed Lecturing Knight, Philadelphia, Pa.; James E. Kelley, Grand Secretary, Birmingham, Alabama; Thomas E. Greene, Grand Treasurer, Akron, Ohio; J. Chavous, Grand Esquire, Seattle, Washington; Dr. S. A. Smith, Grand Inner-Guard, Huntington, West Virginia; S. D. Holsey, Grand Tiler, Reading, Pennsylvania; William C. Hueston, Grand Commissioner of Education, Washington, D. C.; Perry W. Howard, Grand Legal Advisor, Washington, D. C.; Hobson R. Reynolds, Grand Director of Civil Liberties, Philadelphia, Pennsylvania; Dr. Carter L. Marshall, Grand Medical Director, New Haven, Conn.; J. Mercer Burrell, Grand Director of Junior Elks, Newark, N. J.; Edwin W. Burke, Chairman of Publishing Board. Savannah, Georgia; Duke Ellington, Grand Band Master, New York, N. Y.; George Hyder, Assistant Band Master, Philadelphia, Pennsylvania; John U. Strother, Grand Master of Social Sessions, Augusta, Ga.; John C. Minkins, Grand Lodge Reporter. Providence, Rhode Island; James A. Jackson, Commissioner of Economics, New York, N. Y.; J. Frank Ellis, Director of Athletics, Syracuse, New York; Albert Reading, Grand Commissioner of Transportation, Chester, Pennsylvania; Dr. Lawrence J. Davenport, Grand Organist, New York, N. Y.; C. Henri Lewis, Chairman, Post-War Planning Committee, Detroit, Michigan; Emerson H. Gray, Antlered Guard, Major General Eastern Division, Atlantic City, N. J.; Joseph H. Booker, Adjutant General, Philadelphia, Pa.; Roy E. Barnett, Antlered Guard, Major General Western Division, Chicago, Illinois; Grand Trustees: Brazil J. Bryant, Detroit, Michigan; W. Grey Hoyt, Atlantic City, New Jersey; John T. Freeman, Philadelphia, Pennsylvania; Charles A. Oliver, Annapolis, Md. and C. Sylvester Jackson, Harrisburg, Pennsylvania. The Grand Auditors included James T. Copper, Chicago, Illinois: James B. Allen, New York, N. Y.; S. B. Mitchell, New York, New York.

The Order under the leadership of these men had moved from war to peace. Adjustment had been made to each of these periods and the activities of the Order had been conducted with marked success both during the periods of war and peace. The Grand Lodge and the subordinate lodges moved away from the period of Hitler and Mussolini into the prospect of increased democracy under their own chosen leadership, with the confidence that they were reaching a climax in their services to their members and their communities. Groups of brothers and daughters in all lodges were working for the application of the simple program to advance Elkdom among Negroes and around the world, with the confident belief that its way of fraternal life and organization would continue to attract the thousands.

Chapter XVIII
The Golden Anniversary Years

The years 1948 and 1949 were the Golden Anniversary years. They were the fiftieth anniversaries of the inception and permanent foundation of the Order. Fifty years before the assembly of the Grand Lodge of 1948, the Mother Lodge, Alpha Lodge No. 1, was founded in Cincinnati, Ohio. These Golden Jubilee occasions were milestones in the onward march of the organization, and its leadership was determined that these years would not pass without adequate consideration of them.

It was planned by the leaders of the Order that these years would be the occasion when a look backward and a look forward would be taken. The fact that fifty years had passed would be used as a basis to inspire and encourage the continuance of the work and to remind all that there would be greater service to be rendered in the advancement of the people whom the Order was serving. The plan was to pay tribute to the little band who had founded the Order fifty years before and to the legion of devoted leaders of subordinate lodges and temples who had rendered significant service throughout these years. It was well known that the unnumbered host of members in whose lives and hearts were written the ideals of the Order and whose support had undergirded its growth would remain unsung and unknown unless there was some marked emphasis made of this great historical event. It was during these golden anniversary years that emphasis was placed on the beginnings of the Order and that there was re-dedication to the high cause represented by it.

It was here in the Queen City of the Buckeye State that Benjamin Franklin Howard had experienced the vision of an Order of Elks for Negroes, and it was here that Arthur Riggs had started the plan to print the first copy of the ritual. With Frank Hunter they brought together the first men to form an Elks lodge. A year later they initiated the movement to hold the first Grand Lodge. They were intimidated, threatened, and forced underground, but they were faithful to their visions and dreams. As a result Negro Elkdom had its origin and its opportunity to grow and serve through its thousands of members and through them the millions of the Negro population.

The call was made by the Grand Exalted Ruler in his proclamation for the Grand Lodge and its delegates to assemble at the annual convention in Cincinnati, Ohio, from August 21 to

August 27, 1948. This call was repeated by the mother-lodge, Alpha Lodge No. 1, in the same spirit for attendance at this significant session. The occasion was to commemorate the Fiftieth Anniversary of the inception of the Order in this city in 1898. Thousands of Elks, Daughter Elks, their relatives, friends, and associates, assembled in the metropolis of the southwestern section of Ohio to pay tribute to the founding fathers who assembled to mark the beginning of the Order. They came to share in the celebration of this ''Golden Jubilee'' marking the half-century of its growth and fraternal service. The official hosts were Alpha Lodge No. 1 and Ettawah Temple No. 7. The session was planned as a great ''Homecoming'' and the welcomes were couched in terms of the fifty years of constructive achievement. These were manifested by the sentiments of Governor Thomas J. Herbert of Ohio and Mayor Albert D. Cash of the city of Cincinnati, and in the major address of Honorable Henry A. Wallace, who called for a goal of ''sixty-million jobs'' for all Americans.

In response to the Call of the Grand Exalted Ruler and the invitation of Alpha Lodge No. 1, the delegates of the Grand Lodge came in large numbers to the Forty-ninth Convention and Golden Jubilee Celebration in Cincinnati, Ohio, August 21-27, 1948. Each of these paid tribute to the founders of the Order and to the leaders who had followed in their footsteps. Other distinguished representatives of the Buckeye State participated in the program.

Dr. Charles H. Wesley, President of Central State College at Wilberforce, Ohio, delivered the annual baccalaureate address. The Annual Minutes state, ''The speaker held his hearers in gripped attention throughout the discourse, as he challenged the mighty and powerful organization of Elks to stronger growth and greater accomplishment through exercise of its vast influence in the spirit of the Master.''

The special prayer invoked at this time in memory of the founder of the Order, Benjamin Franklin Howard, was as follows:

> "Oh, God, Thou hast been the hope of Thy people in ages past, and Thou art also their hope for years to come. The experiences of life art sternly testing but Thou art all sustaining. This is the day of sacred memories in our Fraternal Order as we recall the deeds of our valiant forefathers and the great price which they paid for our freedom and unity. May we resolve to be worthy of their sacrifice. Hear us, O God of the Nations, as we pray that our people may remember the way in which they have been led and the deliverance Thou has

brought for them. May our youth cherish the spirit of fraternalism and learn the lesson of self-control. Greatly comfort, our Heavenly Father, the hearts that today are thinking of those dear to them and whom they have been called to mourn, through Jesus Christ our Lord. Amen."

The first meetings of this Grand Lodge drew large crowds; The Educational Congress; The Welcome Session; The Junior Program; The Health and Purple Cross Program; The National Shrine Program; The Memorial Program; The Cap and Gown Breakfast and Annual Meeting; The Department of Education Session and the Capping Ceremonies; The Departments of Economics and Civil Liberties; The National Oratorical Contest; and the National Program. The Grand Convention Parade was regarded as a great event together with the Grand Temple Pageant, and the sessions which were conducted for other special purposes during the afternoons and evenings were also so regarded. The Cincinnati Music Hall was crowded to capacity at each of these occasions.

The first report of the Credential Committee showed that there were present twenty-three Grand Lodge officers; seven Past Grand Exalted Rulers; sixty-three District and State Deputies; fifty delegates of Past Exalted Rulers Counsels; fourteen State Associations delegates, and five hundred and eighty-three delegates from three hundred and sixty-five lodges, making a total of seven hundred and forty delegates. This was a partial report and later reports showed that these delegates were over a thousand.

"This is a great homecoming," said Grand Exalted Ruler J. Finley Wilson in giving his address to the assembly. He also declared, "Today we have returned to the place where we were born. A half century has passed since first we came to this metropolis of the Ohio Valley."

The proposal for a National shrine received definitive action at this 1948 session. The convention in Philadelphia in 1947 had passed a resolution directing the Grand Exalted Ruler Wilson to visit several locations and examine their prospects. Accompanied by a joint committee, he visited all available places and decided that the best location was at the corner of 114th Street Manhattan and Morningside Avenues beside the triangle opposite Morningside Park and facing Columbia University. This committee consisted of Grand Exalted Ruler Wilson, Grand Secretary Kelley, Grand Treasurer Greene, Commissioner Hueston, Past Grand Exalted Ruler Nutter, the Grand Daughter Ruler, the Grand Daughter Secretary and the Grand Daughter Treasurer. This property was approved for purchase at a price of $150,000.00 with a payment of $75,000.00 cash. The building was seven stories with basement, thirty-nine apartments, with an income of more than $30,000.00 annually.

It was resolved by resolution that the Grand Legal Adviser was authorized and instructed immediately after the adjournment of the Grand Lodge to complete the transfer of the Shrine and the headquarters property, which had been purchased in the name of the Grand Exalted Ruler J. Finley Wilson, to the Grand Lodge of the Improved Benevolent and Protective Order of Elks of the World, and that all things that were right and proper were authorized to be done in this real estate transaction. This resolution was approved by motion of Brother Roscoe C. Simmons and seconded by Brother George W. Lee.

It was reported by the Grand Exalted Ruler that forty new Lodges had been made and that eight had been reinstated. There were also twenty-five new Herds made and ten had been reinstated. There were five Past Exalted Rulers Councils created and one had been reinstated along with the establishment of seventeen new civil liberties leagues and the reinstatement of two others. This record was regarded as very significant progress. In helping to develop this program of growth, Grand Exalted Ruler Wilson stated that he had traveled from one end of the country to the other attending state association meetings and developing the organization for these increased memberships and organizations.

Then turning his attention again to this historical occasion on which the Grand Lodge was meeting, the Grand Exalted Ruler said, "We have come back to Cincinnati, the city of our birth, where 'Daddy' Riggs and B. F. Howard and Frank Hunter set up the first Elk Lodge in our history. Some of the original charter members are here today. We are here in the cradle of Elkdom where Brother B. F. Howard reached down into the sea of nothingness and brought forth a bright and shining star of Elkdom back in 1898." At every opportunity throughout the convention, the Grand Exalted Ruler kept before the delegates of the Grand Lodge the fact of the Grand Jubilee celebration.

There had been participation in several cases involving civil rights by the Brothers of the Order, the primary case in South Carolina, the Covenant Case and the Oklahoma School Case. Opposition was also expressed to regional schools as proposed by Southern governors. The Grand Exalted Ruler took pride in calling attention to this activity by the members of the Improved Benevolent and Protective Order of Elks of the World. Grand Secretary Kelley also said that, "Today, as in other days, Elkdom can be justly proud of the fact that Civil Rights for all people have been the goal and ideal sought by the I.B.P.O.E. of W., and we hope it is soon to be realized.''

Closely associated with this program was the educational program under Grand Commissioner Hueston's direction. There were forty-nine students supported during the year by scholarships, the maximum grant being $250.00, in thirty-four colleges and universities. The oratorical contests were conducted by each of the Lodges, as the constitution required each Lodge located in a community with a high school to conduct an oratorical contest. From the local contests, the contestants moved to the regional ones and then to the nationals. These contests served to carry out the main objective of Elks, and that was ''to make all members of the colored race constitution conscious.'' There were one hundred and thirty-nine Lodges which sent donations for the educational fund. Illiteracy and adult education were problems which the department had attacked repeatedly before the Grand Lodge. Charts were shown and figures were presented. Teachers' manuals had been prepared, lessons and leaflets were distributed to each Lodge and Temple.

So impressed was Commissioner Hueston by the needs of education among Negroes that he called a Conference on Problems in Negro Education, at Washington, D. C., January 29-31, 1948. It was reported as ''the most effective yet held on these questions.'' Dr. Ambrose Caliver of the United States Department of Education took a prominent part in the organization and conduct of this conference and a committee of educators developed its findings. One of its findings called for the setting up of educational councils in communities composed of Elks, non-Elks, white and Negro persons. These councils were organized in many places.

Grand Director of Civil Liberties Hobson R. Reynolds reported activity by his department in connection with the abolition of Jim-Crow in the army and that a conference was held in 1948 in Washington for this purpose, with action against the poll tax, lynching, for FEPC, public housing, Federal Aid to Education, public health, Federal minimum wages and for changes in the Senate rules to prevent filibuster. He said that the Covenant Case was argued before the United States Supreme Court by Attorney George R. Vaughn and a brief was filed on behalf of the department.

The financial status of the Order was presented in the report of receipts for the year 1947-1948:

General Fund	$103,851.30
Educational Fund	35,112.33
Official Organ Fund	29,315.63

Civil Liberties Fund	18,623.91
Health Fund	3,145.45
Economic Fund	2,019.86
Junior Elk Fund	1,167.39
Shrine Fund	3,123.96
Total Receipts	$196,359.85
Balance Brought Forward	229,079.35
Total	$425,439.20
Less Deductions in Closed Banks	2,037.05
Grand Total	$423,402.15
Total Disbursements	168,089.61
Cash Balance (July 31, 1948)	$225,312.54

The net worth of the Order was $356,762.70, which included the cash balance of $225,312.54, $100,000.00 worth of government bonds, notes receivable of $600.00, and real estate valued at $850.16.

This was a long step historically from the first years of the Order. The first receipts and disbursements in 1901, 1902, and 1903 showed that Grand Secretary J. H. Bush had collected and turned over to Grand Treasurer J. C. Evans $251.00 and the disbursements were $262.50. From this period to 1928, a total of $404,610.89 was collected and the disbursements were $297,582.60. From 1928 when Grand Secretary James E. Kelley was in charge to 1948 there was collected $1,694,283.80, and the disbursements were $1,392,502.57.

The reports of the Grand Exalted Ruler J. Finley Wilson, Grand Secretary Kelley, Grand Treasurer Thomas E. Green, and Grand Commissioner of Education W. C. Hueston were received with praise and the regular rules were suspended and each was re-elected by acclamation by the Grand Lodge. It was moved later by Dr. Hudson J. Oliver that the regular rules of election be further suspended and that the following incumbents be re-elected by acclamation to succeed themselves: Joseph A. Brown as Grand Esteemed Leading Knight; Herbert E. Jones, Grand Esteemed Loyal Knight; Robert H. Johnson, Grand Esteemed Lecturing Knight; J. A. Chavis, Grand Esquire; Simpson A. Smith, Grand Inner Guard and Samuel D. Holsey, Grand Tiler. Further nominations were called for by the Grand Exalted Ruler and none being proposed, there was a unanimous standing vote in favor of the motion. The Grand Trustees elected were Charles A. Oliver, John T. Freeman, C. Sylvester Jackson, J. F. Sim-

LEROY JORDAN, Grand Trustee

CHARLES A. OLIVER, Grand Trustee

C. SYLVESTER JACKSON, Grand Trustee

SAMUEL B. MITCHELL, Grand Auditor

mons, Leroy Jordon and the Grand Auditors were James T. Copper, Samuel B. Mitchell and Harry St. Clair.

The Grand Legal Advisor, Perry W. Howard had rendered a long list of opinions for lodges and had saved many from court procedures. Grand Director of Economics, James A. Jackson, reported continued activity on the economic front, especially in the extension of knowledge among lodges, institutions and people about the right use of income and savings. He also offered his resignation from his office effective at the close of the session. Grand Commissioner of Transportation Albert A. Reading stated that his task had been difficult in providing for the travel of the host of delegates and visitors to this Golden Jubilee Convention, but that success had attended his efforts. Grand Director of Veteran Activities Adolphus W. Anderson described his work in reaching veterans and urging them to take advantage of the benefits extended to them by the Federal Government.

Dr. E. T. Belsaw, Executive Secretary of the Health Commission, with Dr. Carter L. Marshall as chairman, read the report showing the donation of an Iron Lung for the Flint Goodrich Hospital at New Orleans, Louisiana, the publication of health articles, the organization of Purple Cross Nursing units by Daughter Anna B. Jones, Directress, assistance in the establishment of a Blood Bank at Baltimore, Maryland, the addition of Dr. Roscoe C. Brown of the United States Department of Public Health to the Elks Health Commission and the cooperation of a committee from the National Medical Association. The report advocated that the lodges and temples with their thousands of members in all parts of the nation in all professions and vocations, should accept the challenge to improve the health and living conditions of the Negro, as an individual, as a member of the home and family and as a resident of the community.

The Golden Jubilee Parade and Pageant were great demonstrations of this significant historical event presented by the Grand Lodge and the Grand Temple. The description of the committee on Trophies and Awards began with, "First came the B. F. Howard Float in costumes of 1898, followed by the present Grand Lodge Float with our Grand Secretary 'Smiling' Jim Kelly. Next we saw the Educational Float with our Grand Commissioner Judge Hueston and his co-worker Daughter Charleston, followed by the Grand Temple officers in costumes of 1898, then came our Queen of Elkdom, Grand Daughter Ruler Elizabeth Ross Gordon on her throne." There were over 200 units, 31 bands, with drum and bugle corps in the parade. In marking the Golden Milestone, the Committee on Resolutions declared "the fifty years which have intervened between our birth in 1898

Dr. Carter L. Marshall, Grand Medical Director

Dr. E. T. Belsaw, Member of Health Commission

Dr. T. T. Wendell, Member of Health Commission

Dr. Anna B. Jones, Grand Directress Purple Cross Nurses

and the historic year in which we now meet are as rich in achievements and in heroic struggles against oppression and slavery as any period recorded by the pen of time."

Similar references to the Golden Anniversary were made in each of the reports. One of these, the Grand Auditor's report, will suffice to mention: "Fifty years ago marked the prophetic birth of this the Greatest Fraternal Organization of modern times. Twenty-six years ago we elevated Dr. J. Finley Wilson to the office of Grand Exalted Ruler. You have assisted his personal appointment by electing to office capable assistants. Under the leadership of Dr. Wilson, the Improved Benevolent and Protective Order of Elks of the World has reached the greatest Fraternal height. It has proven the marvel of the century. It had done the unprecedented. Its fame and influence are nation wide. It is respected from within, feared from without and membership therein is a source of great pride and ambition." While it is easily recognizable that these were words of extravagant praise of the Order, and some may be bold enough to say that they are exaggerations, but when these are toned down, it must also be acknowledged that there are elements of truth in these estimations, for the Order was a great one and it had an especially qualified leadership.

This leadership had grown in great measure since the time of B. F. Howard, the Founder, whose name was heard repeatedly throughout the convention. Reverence for his memory was evidenced further by the pilgrimage of Elks and Daughters to the cemetery in Covington, Kentucky, in which the remains of the Founder were interred. The Grand Exalted Ruler led the delegates in a motorcade to the Founder's grave, on which a wreath was placed by him. Tribute was also paid to Brother E. G. Gaithers, the only surviving member of Alpha Lodge, Number 1. Brother Sidney Thompson then moved that the honorary degree of Past Grand Exalted Ruler be conferred upon Brother Gaithers. This resolution was adopted unanimously and the honor was conferred by Grand Exalted Ruler Wilson.

While the Golden Jubilee Year of 1948 was highlighted by organization of the first Lodge of Elks among Negroes in the city of Cincinnati and was celebrated by the Grand Lodge Session in this city, the Golden Jubilee idea continued to be present in the minds and hearts of the hundreds of thousands of Elks scattered throughout the world. As the year 1949 approached, it was fifty years before this event that the First Grand Lodge also under the leadership of B. F. Howard had assembled in Cincinnati where Brother Howard acted and was elected the first Grand Exalted Ruler. This event seemed also to be an occasion for a

Golden Jubilee celebration. Throughout the period following the close of the 1948 Grand Lodge into the next year 1949, the concept of the Golden Jubilee was kept alive. There were celebrations, parades, field events, athletic contests, social events, under Elks auspices, which reached the public and gave demonstration of the confidence which Negro Elks had in their long time historical tradition.

One of these events was represented in the assembly by the Grand Exalted Ruler of a conference in the city of Washington in 1949. Recalling that he had been made president of an organization planned to unite the races of the world involving all religions and colors and that the principals of Elkdom embraced similar groupings of people, he issued a Call and planned a national meeting at the Metropolitan Baptist Church in Washington, D. C. He invited to this conference representatives of all political parties, Republicans, Democrats, Progressives and representatives of all organizations fraternal and non-fraternal. These representatives assembled on February 11-12, 1949. This assembly was regarded by Grand Director of Civil Liberties Hobson Reynolds as "a history making occasion." It was said by the Grand Exalted Ruler that there was a common purpose in the session concerning the whole matter of the rights of the people, which had brought the group together.

The sessions were largely attended and it was said that there were at least two thousand people in regular attendance. Reports were presented on Federal Regulation of Employment Practice, a Ban on Lynching, the Abolition of the Poll Tax, the Exercise of the Suffrage, Federal Aid to Education, the Anti-Lynching Bill, the Right to Work, Discrimination and Segregation in various fields. The Grand Exalted Ruler said that while there were various shades of opinions represented, "Where the Communistic line would protrude itself or dogma seek to take over our Fraternal program, we were alert to prevent any one organization to seem to dominate or take the rights of others." This meeting came at an opportune moment when there was no discussion in the Congress of the United States concerning equality and the rights of mankind, and it was timed well to serve a definite need. It also brought to the attention of the representatives of the National Government the lot of the peoples of color in the United States and elsewhere.

Another event of historical moment in the year 1949 was the decision to purchase the John Brown Farm near Harper's Ferry. This was a 235 acre farm surrounded by the memories of the Battle of Antietam and the Civil War, the traditions of John Brown and his farmhouse near which he drilled his small group, and from which he led them to an attack on the Harper's Ferry Arsenal. It seemed to be a great event for the Elks to acquire this farm and turn it into a Shrine of historical significance so that it would serve as an inspiration to youth as they recalled the life of John Brown.

During the Spring of the year 1949 Grand Exalted Ruler Wilson and Grand Commissioner of Education Hueston with a committee inspected the farm and decided to recommend its purchase to the Grand Lodge of 1949. In connection with this recommendation they published a brochure entitled *The John Brown Reader*. This brochure by Judge William C. Hueston and Grand Exalted Ruler J. Finley Wilson gave in detail the salient facts of the life of John Brown and endeavored to show the high rank which he held among American immortals. In addition to chapters on the life and work of John Brown, there was an opening chapter on the "Grand Lodge History of I.B.P.O.E.W.," a chapter on "Grand Temple daughters of the I.B.P.O.E.W." and a final chapter on the "Meaning of Freedom." Representatives of the Grand Temple became interested in the John Brown project and sent representatives also to participate in its inspection and to report so that its decision might be reached to cooperate in its purchase.

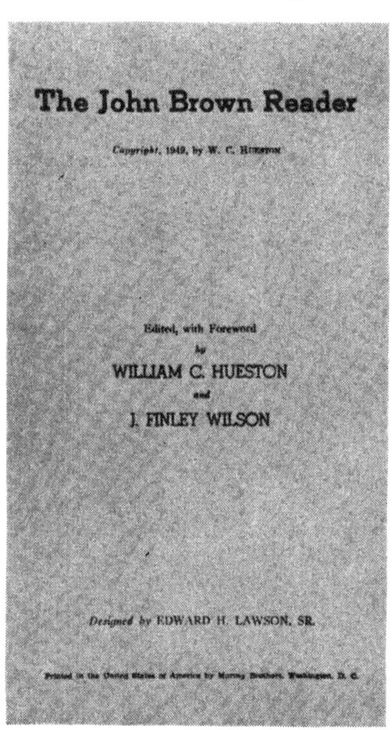

The John Brown Reader

Copyright, 1949, by W. C. HUESTON

Edited, with Foreword
by
WILLIAM C. HUESTON
and
J. FINLEY WILSON

Designed by EDWARD H. LAWSON, SR.

Printed in the United States of America by Murray Brothers, Washington, D. C.

The Title Page, *The John Brown Reader*, 1949.

The Golden Jubilee Grand Lodge, the Fiftieth Annual Session of the Grand Lodge of the Improved Benevolent and Protective Order of Elks of the World assembled in Commandery Hall, San Francisco, California, August 23-26, 1949, with Grand Exalted Ruler J. Finley Wilson presiding and Grand Secretary James E. Kelley as Grand Secretary. The Grand Lodge was preceded by the Twenty-fourth Annual Congress of the Department of Education which met on Saturday, August 20, the Annual Baccalaureate Service on Sunday, August 21, with the sermon being preached by the Reverend Paul E. Davis, Grand Chaplain, who spoke from the theme "Vision." The Annual Health Meeting and the Capping Ceremony of the Purple Cross were held in the afternoon of the same day and in the evening the program of the Shrine Department and the Annual Memorial Service were held. The National Cap and Gown Club assembled on Monday, August 22, and held its services followed by the Annual Meeting of the Department of Education, the Department of Civil Liberties, and in the evening the Annual Oratorical Contest with Judge William C. Hueston Grand Commissioner of Education presiding.

The business meetings of this Fiftieth Grand Lodge began with a call to order by Honorable J. Finley Wilson Grand Exalted Ruler. Following the ritualistic ceremonies and the announcements with the reading of the minutes of the previous session, the report of the Credentials Committee was heard as a preliminary one, showing that at this opening session there were twenty-four Grand Lodge Officers, six Past Grand Exalted Rulers, forty-two Deputies, five hundred and eight delegates from three hundred and ninety-one Lodges, fifty-six delegates from fifty-five Past Exalted Ruler's Councils and sixteen from sixteen State Associations.

The Grand Exalted Ruler's address directed attention to the State of California and the implications of the meeting in this far western state. He described the turnover of funds following the deaths of Grand Treasurer Edward W. Henry and Grand Treasurer Marcus F. Wheatland to the new Grand Treasurer Thomas A. Greene; the cases which had to be adjudicated by him involving the lodges; the dispensations issued; the dedications of new buildings, the mortgage burnings, the Thanksgivings and memorials; the growth of the Order, the state associations; Civil Liberties, economics, education, health, the rise of the Order in public estimation, and the National Shrine; all of which indicated that there was excellent spirit and work among the Lodges of Elkdom.

The Golden Jubilee Idea was again presented in the report of Grand Secretary Kelley. He said in opening his report, "According to our records, our first Grand Lodge Session was held in 1899, in a small room in Cincinnati, Ohio, with representatives of five Lodges present. A half century has passed since that memorable occasion and today we gather in this great city of the Far West in a beautiful and spacious building with representatives from more than one thousand Lodges and Auxiliaries. We not only point with pride to our success in numerical growth,

Calendar Announcement of the Golden Convocation Year, 1949.

but we take even pride in the service we have been able to render through the various departments of the Order." There had been, during the year closed, thirty-nine Lodges organized and reinstated along with six Past Exalted Ruler's Councils, thirteen Herds and sixteen Civil Liberties Leagues.

A report of all funds showed that there was a total of $396,735.90 with an actual cash balance of $56,787.24. As Grand Secretary Kelley presented this report he stated that he had a measure of pride in this program of service rendered by the Order through its various departments, for this type of service was not rendered by any other organization, and he felt that every member of the Order should be proud that he could consider himself a link in a great chain that formed the jurisdiction of Elkdom. He concluded his report with, "Through the help of God, the Father of all, and the united efforts of the membership, we have fifty years of achievements not dreamed of in 1899, and with a leadership that combines mental brilliancy, honesty, loyalty, aggressiveness and progressiveness supported by this continuing growing army of loyal members, we pledge to each other and the world that through our cardinal principles of charity unlimited, justice impartial, brotherly love unrestrained, and fidelity unwaivering, we shall continue to serve mankind and shall leave forever a monument to those who have passed on as an inspiration to all that follow them."

The Grand Commissioner of Education Judge W. C. Hueston began his report with reminiscences of the beginning of this department, its origins in 1924, its legislation in 1925, the establishment of the oratorical contest in 1926, the establishment of the Department of Economics as part of the Department of Education in 1935, cooperation in 1946 with the United States Department of Education, the endeavor to overcome functional illiteracy among Negroes, and a continuing grant of scholarships through these years. He reported that there would be over sixty in the school year 1949-1950, to whom commitments had been made for scholarships. He described the John Brown Elks Memorial Farm, the action which had been taken toward its purchase, and the recommendation that the Lodge make its decision at this convention. The rules were then suspended following the reading of his report and Judge William C. Hueston was reelected by acclamation, and it was carried unanimously.

In a similar vein the Grand Director of Civil Liberties, Hobson R. Reynolds, presented his report stating in the historical way that the Civil Liberties Department had been organized in Cleveland, Ohio, at the 1926 convention and that in 1936 the Grand

Exalted Ruler honored him with appointing him to head the department and the next year in 1937, he made his first report. He stated that the observations he made at that time were still true and that the Civil Liberties Department was spearheading in many instances movements which would give to the Negroes of America rights which had been denied to them, and that this department was cooperating with organizations local and national on all fronts toward these objectives. He described the endeavors to secure Civil Rights provisions for adoption in the platforms of the three major political parties. He described his appearance before one of the Congressional sub-committees on education and labor and presented a summary of his presentation on this occasion. He called for the organization of more civil liberties leagues. He said that there should be a league in each community to take cognizance of all forms of injustice against Negroes. He regarded the John Brown Farm project as a symbol of the objectives of the Civil Liberties Department and urged that Elks should support this great movement. When he had concluded his report, a recommendation was unanimously approved for his re-appointment as Grand Director of Civil Liberties for the ensuing Grand Lodge term. Similar action was taken on the report of the Grand Treasurer, Thomas E. Greene, and he, too, was reelected unanimously by acclamation.

One of the significant innovations in the long trip across the country, was reported by Grand Commissioner of Transportation, Albert A. Reading, who stated that there had been set up the J. Finley Wilson Special Train which made provision for a scenic ride across this country with stopovers at various places to and from San Francisco. He said that he planned to make this type of program for each convention city. He was recommended for re-appointment for the next term.

A period in the Grand Lodge was taken to call attention to the achievements of the administration of Grand Exalted Ruler J. Finley Wilson. It was noted by Brother Ernest Copeland of O. V. Catto Lodge No. 20 of Philadelphia that Brother Wilson had given twenty-seven years of continuous service, that this year marked his twenty-fifth wedding anniversary and his sixty-ninth birthday. In consideration of the fact that he was not in such good health, and of the fact that he had not taken time out for vacations during this period, he moved that the Grand Lodge appropriate the sum of $5,000 from its general funds and authorize that it be given as a gift to the Grand Exalted Ruler, "in token of the highest esteem in which he had held by the members of the Order." This motion was seconded by Dr. Hudson J. Oliver and was passed unanimously in a standing demonstration of confidence and a moment of jubilant expression of esteem.

The annual parade of the Grand Lodge was described as, "one of the gayest ever staged." There were costumed marchers, sixteen shiny new cars carrying Grand Lodge officers and their staffs, four bands and four drum and bugle corps, a motorcade of eighty cars followed by three elaborately decorated floats. Pride was taken by the committee on awards in offering the prizes granted for participation in this exhibition. The Grand Medical Director, Dr. Carter L. Marshall, described the work of his department during the year, the mass X-ray project which was started in Philadelphia 1947, conducted in Cincinnati in 1948, and continued at this session, the work of the Purple Units, the articles in the *Washington Eagle,* the Baltimore Blood Bank, the health bulletins and exhibits, Health Day, the iron lung program, and the organization of twenty-five additional nurse units for 1948 and 1949.

A major portion of the convention period was taken up with the discussion of the acquirement of the John Brown Farm. The property was valued at approximately $30,000.00 which would include all fees and expenses incident to the transfer. Following the full discussion of the subject, Brother Truly Hatchett moved that immediate steps be taken to negotiate for the purchase of the approximately two hundred and thirty-five acres known as the John Brown Farm by the Grand Lodge. The motion was seconded by Brother F. C. Jones and carried unanimously by a standing vote. Representatives of the Grand Temple were present at this time and assured the Grand Lodge of their cooperation with the project of the Grand Exalted Ruler.

A unanimous ballot for all offices elected by acclamation during the session was ordered. The following offices were included: Joseph A. Brown, Grand Esteemed Leading Knight; Herbert E. Jones, Grand Esteemed Loyal Knight; Robert H. Johnson, Grand Esteemed Lecturing Knight; James E. Kelley, Grand Secretary; Thomas E. Greene, Grand Treasurer; A. E. Bradley, Grand Esquire; Simpson A. Smith, Grand Inner-Guard; Samuel D. Holsey, Grand Tiler; William C. Hueston, Grand Commissioner of Education; C. Sylvester Jackson, Grand Trustee; J. F. Simmons, Grand Trustee; J. Leroy Jordan, Grand Trustee.

One of the resolutions adopted provided that the book, "The John Brown Reader," as compiled by the Grand Exalted Ruler and the Grand Commissioner of Education shall be included in the approval of the sale and transfer of the John Brown Farm, provided that the author and producers shall be allowed ten cents on the sale of each reader and which shall be sold for not more than one dollar per copy. Provision was also made for the award of the Annual Elijah P. Loyjoy Medal which was to be presented to that person regardless of race or color judged most distinguished for service rendered humanity during the previous year. The Grand Exalted Ruler was to appoint a committee of which he would be chairman to provide the medal and select the person to whom the award was to be made. Roscoe Conkling Simmons was among the Elk leaders who were interested in this project.

The reports of the Grand Director of Junior Elks, J. Mercer Burrell, the Grand Director of Golf, Peter Dillard, the Public Relations Department with Grand Commissioner of Public Relations Charles P. McClane rendering the report, were all received with acclaim by the Grand Lodge. The session closed with confidence in the minds of the delegates as they left for their homes with the evident determination to carry forward the approaching year of 1950 with continuing success for the Grand Order.

The Golden Anniversary of the Daughters of Improved Benevolent and Protective Order of Elks of the World was also celebrated in 1952. A Golden Jubilee Year Book dedicated to Mrs. Emma V. Kelley, the Founder and Supreme Mother was published to commemorate this Golden Year. A Golden Jubilee Celebration Committee was appointed consisting of Buena V. Kelley, Grand Daughter Secretary who was General Chairman, Grand Daughter Ruler Nettie Carter Jackson, Elizabeth Ross Gordon, Elizabeth Kimbough, Georgianna Henry, Grace Bryant, Lelia Fultz, Mattie L. Hollowell, Reaba A. Jefferson, Ada A. Jones, Fannie Lee Mais, Mandonia Porter Owens, Katye H. Steele and Vivian C. Mason, Editor.

Grand Daughter Secretary Buena V. Kelley made the following significant comment in connection with this event:

Fifty Years and After

> The Golden Jubilee Celebration of the Daughters of Elks is an appropriate time to assess the past and thoughtfully contemplate the future. It is perhaps helpful to reflect upon the beginnings of the organization with thirteen eager women who without previous experience or knowledge determined to establish an organization which through the years has grown to the astonishing number of sixty-five thousand. There is one aspect of the establishment and subsequent growth that always holds considerable interest for us today. That point of interest is the basis for the organization and its program. It is essential to understand both of these very thoroughly in order to determine whether or not we shall continue in the same way in the future or if program emphasis will take another slant. The basic

Golden Jubilee Year Book, 1902-1952, published by the Grand Temple I.B.P.O.E. of W.

principle which had such an immediate appeal for women was the principle of charity as expressed by the Founder, Emma V. Kelley. She contemplated that the daughters of Elks would be devoted to a program largely of giving—giving of friendship and love, of opportunity to others, of warm personal friendships. That was basic in her thinking, underlying the whole philosophy of the organization. To the Daughters of Elks there can be no more beautiful or vital principle of life than just this.

The other interesting aspect of the early beginnings of the organization was the program. This program has been elaborated upon as the temples have multiplied, but the hard core of the beginning of the program is still there. This basic program incorporated the development of the temples as a fraternal body with all the meaningful ritualistic ceremonies and services. Step by step the Daughetrs progressed in the organization from one station of service to another, each step having its own particular recognition symbols. Departments were added to meet the growth of the orgnization until here, in 1952, there are twenty-five flourishing sections, each created to meet some unmet need.

The extension of the program to meet growing and serious needs of this second half of the twentieth century requires a broadening of the program scope of the Daughters of Elks and a more intensive system of relating ourselves to the local and national scene. It requires the development of many interests in temple activities, but most of all it brings a large opportunity to develop women to be more competent citizens in their community and more able homemakers and mothers.

Many organizations are specializing in certain phases of community life such as the Parent-Teachers Association, concerned with school needs; athletic association and similiar organizations concerned with recreational problems; voters' leagues, working on the political education of citizens; foreign policy groups, concerned with problems of international relations and peace; child welfare commissions and organizations working to extend protective legislation, and enforce current legislation for the protection of children; civil rights groups such as the National Association for the Advancement of Colored People and National Council of Negro Women, making a tremendous struggle to lift Negroes from second class to first class citizenship. These are all in need of support, financial and moral. The Daughters of Elks belong to many of these organizations but could more effectively cooperate with them. Membership is a necessary step, active participation in the program is a second more important method of cooperation. Many of these organizations have programs which can be utilized in the departments in the Daughters of Elks.

Changes have taken place in American life in the past dec-

Dt. Mandonia Porter Owens, Grand Organist

Dt. Leah F. Wilson, Widow of Deceased Grand Exalted Ruler J. Finley Wilson, Grand Organizer

Dt. Katye Steele, Grand Recorder, Grand Temple; State Directress of Education.

Dt. Vivian C. Mason, Editor, Golden Jubilee Yearbook

ade which affect the Negro people most profoundly. Universities in southern states have opened their doors to Negro youth. Employment opportunities unheard of and undreamed of a half-century ago have been made available to Negro people. There has been encouraging participation in the national life of our country by many individuals and groups. More opportunities will be obtained, greater educational opportunities made available, and wider participation in many aspects of American life will be forthcoming in this half-century. The Daughters of Elks can make a distinguished contribution to this new area of development of American Negroes. They can initiate and advance a definite program to prepare Negro women to more competently participate in all aspects of American life. Some of the lessons which we must learn are elemental. They are lessons in personal appearance and group behavior, in knowledge of current events, in the ability to discuss intelligently the happenings in the world today. The Daughters of Elks must encourage Negro women to become really thoughtful citizens who are prepared by training and culture to meet the crisis of each day. Many hard lessons will have to be taught and learned but with passionate zeal for unified action the Daughters of Elks exemplify, we have every reason to believe that the future will find this organization moving forward in a new direction—towards new horizons of human welfare.

A poem by PDR Viola Adams of American Temple, No. 258, Paterson, New Jersey, in connection with the Golden Anniversary of the Daughter Elks was awarded the first prize for the most unique ideas expressed in verse concerning this Golden Year:

Fifty Years of Building

Fifty years of building
Plans laid by pioneers,
Spanning the golden brink of time
For many anxious years.
Dreaming the dream to show the world
The best there is in man,
Shaping and moulding this lodge of Elks
Tightening every span.

Fifty years of building,
Through the night and heat of the day.
In town, hamlet or country,
With faith, not fear or dismay.
Their book of law was the Word of God
Their precepts and virtues too,
Was the foundation for all that's good
In the work they strove to do.

Fifty years of building
And God sure heard their prayer,
For from all corners of the earth
You'll find Elks everywhere.
Continuing to build, in arts and education
Religion, culture, citizenship.
Shouldering the burdens of the nation.

Fifty years, time marches on
And there still is work to do.
The caravan is moving fast
For Elks like you and you.
So gather seeds and plant them
Do your building too.

The stalwart women gone ahead
Are looking down today,
Sending the message "Keep building,
Our plan is there to stay."
The progress of these golden years
Kept the spirit of Elkdom strong,
And the memory of our pioneers
Can be made a happy song.
Build on, Build on, Elks of the world,
In all you do or say.
Build on, with banners high, unfurled,
Live on, live on alway.

Chapter XIX
The Climax of an Era

The qualities of leadership exhibited by the Grand Exalted Rulers of the Improved Benevolent and Protective Order of Elks of the World are evidences of their individual capacities and of the strength of the organization in the awakening and exercise of their powers. All of the Grand Exalted Rulers made distinctive and special contributions to the Order in their times. The long time leadership of J. Finley Wilson as Grand Exalted Ruler was productive of unusual results for the growth and expansion of the organization in periods of history when it was greatly needed. He came upon the scene in 1922 at a period of organizational development when the stage was set for his type of service. He led the Order from the valley of small things to the heights of great accomplishment. He carried it on high levels through depression, panic, deflation, inflation, a world war, and the periods in which social and economic processes were in disorder. Through these times he exercised his knowledge of the theory and practice of organization and the masterly control of groups and of individuals not only through emotion but also by intelligence, skill and experience. He manifested energy and talent bordering upon a genius for leadership, and always commanded respect, honor and even reverence.

This leadership of Grand Exalted Ruler Wilson was to reach its climax in the years 1950-1952. This was the climax of an era —the Wilsonian Era. These would be years of great endeavors but they would be periods also of his decline in physical ways. He would refuse with his accustomed determination to seek release from any of his duties, and yet it was apparent to close observers that he could not work for long periods with his usual efficiency. Since the last Grand Lodge, he had been hospitalized at Johns Hopkins Hospital, St. Mary's Hospital at Rochester, Minnesota, and at the Cleveland Clinic, Cleveland, Ohio. After weeks at these hospitals, he was permitted to return to his home in Washington, D. C. Efforts were made at the sessions of the Grand Lodge to assist him in the costs of medical attention. At one Grand Lodge, a gift of five thousand dollars was made to him. He was not required to read his report in its entirety because of the exhaustion which occasioned its reading and since it would be published in the minutes of the Grand Lodge sessions.

Every effort was made to conserve the health of the leader who was honored, revered and followed by Elkdom.

It was due to this fact that there was the large attendance at the fifty-first Convention of the Grand Lodge at the DuSable High School auditorium, Chicago, Illinois, August 22-24, 1950. The Grand Temple convened at the Bethesda Baptist Church. The minutes of this session state: "In great measure this convergence of Elks from across the nation was a testimonial of honor and felicitation to Doctor J. Finley Wilson, Esteemed leader of the Antlered Herd and for more than a quarter-century the Grand Exalted Ruler. Convalescing from illness and hospital confinement over most of the year, the Grand Exalted Ruler returned to awaken the convention to a new spirit of faith and aspiration. His presence inspired courage and confidence and occasioned numerous manifestations for fraternal devotion."

The Convention program began with the Pre-Convention Department Meetings in which the Grand Lodge and the Grand Temple representatives participated. There were also Elks Day at the Chicago Fair, J. Finley Wilson Handicap Day at the Washington Park Races, the Antlered Guard Dance, Elk's Night at Chicago White Sox Ball Park, the National Parade, the National Bathing Beauty Contest, Birthday celebration and Testimonial of Appreciation honoring the Grand Exalted Ruler.

At the pre-convention session of the Department of Civil Liberties, the Elijah Lovejoy Award of the Improved Benevolent and Protective Order of Elks of the World was presented to Governor Alfred E. Driscoll, Governor of the State of New Jersey in recognition of the distinguished public service rendered by him in the area of civil rights in his state. Grand Commissioner Hobson Reynolds presented Colonel Roscoe Conkling Simmons who eulogized Governor Driscoll and the Grand Exalted Ruler read the citation and made the award. The Governor responded pledging the continuation of his endeavors for the equality of opportunity for all peoples.

A resolution of this Department addressed to the President, the Congress and People of the United States was adopted. This resolution called for the achievement of the promise of the Fourteenth Amendment, for Negro citizens were denied the rights and blessings of American citizenship. It was proposed that the President create an Equal Economic Opportunities Commission, that each cabinet officer utilize his authority to eliminate segregation and discrimination, that a Congress be chosen pledged to support and adopt a Fair Employment Practice Act, an Anti-Lynching Act, a Civil Rights Act for the District of Columbia and the prohibition of segregation on inter-

J. T. WITBECK, Director of Economics

HENRY BERTH, Major General Antlered Guard

DR. L. W. WILLIAMS, Chairman of Publishing Board; Grand Trustee; State President of Georgia

DR. SIMPSON A. SMITH, Grand Director of Awards

state carriers, that the President call a conference on the elimination of racial and religious discrimination, that the governors and state officials take similar steps and that the American people stand together in a true unity for the American way of life.

After the first session opened with the usual ceremonies, there was a period of felicitation, in which representatives of the Grand Temple participated complimenting the Grand Exalted Ruler "on his recovery from the illness which beset him over the past year."

In beginning his report, Grand Exalted Ruler Wilson said that, "Over a half million Elks have made this favorite trek to the Windy City, at the South bend of Lake Michigan to attend this convention of the era. We have swept across the continent from the Atlantic, the Pacific, the Border and the Gulf, to a bigger and better convention and jamboree than Chicago saw in 1944, or at any previous convention. This shall be the greatest fraternal convention brought to the Midwest with a constructive program for all branches of the Order."

The report had reference to the John Brown Farm and a program of education there, the promotion of the purchase of United States Savings Bonds and the expansion of the Grand Lodge services in Health, Civil Liberties, the exercise of the vote, the Youth program and the Twenty-fifth Anniversary of the Department of Education. The call was made for the union of the free peoples of the world against Communism and the prophecy was made that unless the United States follows the leadership having the capacity of making it the moral center of the world as it is the economic and political center, "it is headed for collapse before a Rising Tide of Color more fatal than destruction by the Atom or Hydrogen Bomb."

With the termination of the address there was a demonstration of acclaim which was described as "tumultuous." Brother George W. Lee of the Shrine Commissioner finally gained the floor and after an eloquent and heart-warming tribute to Grand Exalted Ruler Wilson moved that the rules be suspended and that the Grand Esquire cast a unanimous ballot for the reelection of the Grand Exalted Ruler to succeed himself for the ensuing two year term. Grand Esteemed Loyal Knight Herbert E. Jones seconded the motion, and it was adopted unanimously. As additional evidence of the spirit of sympathy of the Grand Lodge, Brother Ernest Copeland addressed the delegates voicing his sentiments in sincere words. Afterwards he made a motion which was severally seconded that "a gift in the sum of Ten Thousand Dollars be made to Brother J. Finley Wilson from general funds of the Grand Lodge not otherwise obligated—the same to be considered by Brother Wilson as a token of appreciation and esteem which may serve to recompense in part the necessary costs of his medical and hospital care.'' This motion was carried by unanimous standing vote, and it represents a kind of index of the love and esteem held by his brothers in Elkdom.

In describing the illness of the Grand Exalted Ruler, Grand Secretary Kelley said, ''The band of affliction has been upon our 'Grand' during the greater part of the year, and a part of the time he has been unable to leave his bed. But through his great determination to live, the fine and expert services of the doctors and nurses and your prayers to Almighty God for his recovery, he is with us today and we thank God for his presence.''

There had been continuing growth in the Order according to the Grand Secretary. There had been added thousands of new and reinstated members, thirty-five new and reinstated lodges, six Past Exalted Rulers Councils, ten Civil Liberties Leagues, and twelve Junior Elks Herds. He said that the state associations were functioning one hundred per cent and many of them had sent delegates to this Grand Lodge. He reported also that the Grand Temple and the Subordinate Temple with their Daughter Elks' programs were keeping pace with their brothers in growth and in progress.

A strong stand was proposed by him against anti-democratic tendencies in the nation. He urged the necessity for united action of all forces within the country and the defense of the four freedoms. He added, ''We must not permit Communism nor any other evil force to enter our ranks. We must hold high always the principles for which we stand, proving to the world that the Improved Benevolent and Protective Order of the Elks of the World is like the Rock of Gibraltar, a solid unit of American manhood and womanhood holding high a beacon that will light the way for future generations.'' Following the report after sentiments of appreciation had been made the rules were suspended and Brother Kelley was reelected by acclamation to succeed himself in the Office of Grand Secretary for the ensuing term. The Lodge was then addressed by Honorable Martin H. Kennelley, the Mayor of the City of Chicago; Alderman George D. Kells, Alderman Archibald J. Carey, and responses were made by Colonel Roscoe Conkling Simmons on behalf of the Convention.

The Grand Commissioner of Education, Judge Hueston, delivered his twenty-fifth report as Commissioner of Education. He called attention to the milestones along the pathway which he had traveled in the development of the Department. He stated that during the present year there were fifty-four students in the various colleges and universities and that eleven had recently graduated as a result of the support by scholarships of the Grand Lodge. In connection with the admission to the Oratorical Contest, he said that there had been applications from white students to enter the contest and that there had been opposition from some of the members of lodges concerning such admissions. He said that it should be remembered that our youth were being accepted in the contest conducted by the American Legion, the Pepsi-Cola Company and other organizations and that we could not afford to draw the color line ourselves. He said, "We are contending for our place in the sun and we must accord an equal opportunity to all in anything we offer by way of competition and then bend over backwards to see to it that they get a square deal when they appear in our contests as participants." He said that the *Washington Eagle* was supporting the cause of the Order as the official organ and that he wanted to call attention again to the need for a publishing house and urged a consideration of his earlier recommendations on this project. The John Brown Farm was described in its progress and the developments there as a farm and the proposal for it as a shrine was developed by the Commissioner of Education. When the reading was completed he was reelected by acclamation of the Convention to succeed himself for the ensuing Grand Lodge year.

The report of the Grand Treasurer, Thomas E. Green, showed that there had been total receipts in all funds of $38,717.11. There had been receipts during the year of $230,881.37 and when the amount brought forward of $157,835.74 was added there was the above grand total. He reported $100,000.00 in the United States Government Bonds and a grand total balance on hand of $282,627.06. At the conclusion of his report addresses were made and a motion was offered by Brother Perry B. Jackson, and unanimously adopted to reelect the Grand Treasurer, Thomas E. Green, for the ensuing Grand Lodge year.

An Appreciation Hour was held, during which the Committee on Birthday Testimonial and the Grand Temple representatives made presentations to Grand Exalted Ruler Wilson. Responses of acceptance were made at his request by Brother C. Henri Lewis, Luther Sylvan and George W. F. McMechen. Further evidence of the esteem in which J. Finley Wilson was held was demonstrated when a representative of *The Afro-American*, George B. Murphy, Jr., presented the Grand Exalted Ruler with "a plaque especially designed to honor him for conspicuous leadership in the fields of journalism and human relations."

Expressions of loyalty were made in a resolution supporting

the President of the United States and the nation in all steps which were taken to support the principles of the United Nations and calling upon the Grand Lodge to appoint a permanent standing committee on Fraternal Conferences to confer with leaders of all other fraternal organizations for the purpose of working toward the bringing in of a just and lasting peace and of improving the democratic way of life for all peoples of each of the nations of the world.

This resolution was followed by the report of the Grand Director of Civil Liberties, Hobson R. Reynolds, who described the work which had been accomplished by his department since the last Grand Lodge, and said that the Grand Lodge had been represented in all of these fights and in the struggle for an FEPC Bill on the national level and integration in the armed forces, which had been making steady progress. He urged registration and voting on the part of Negroes in all sections of the country as there was continuous evidence of the value of the vote. Following his report the Convention recommended to the Grand Exalted Ruler the reappointment of Commissioner Hobson R. Reynolds to serve another term as Grand Director of Civil Liberties. This motion was unanimously approved.

Grand Legal Adviser Perry W. Howard in making his report gave a summary of the historical contributions of his department. These were of interest and value in gaining a view of this work. These accomplishments were as follows: (1) The reconstruction of the constitution and by-laws; (2) The lessening of confusion with respect to the application and interpretation of laws; (3) Providing for the restoration of lodge property from closed corporations back to the lodges; (4) Creating a Civil Liberties Department as an offspring from the Law Department; (5) Recodifying and simplifying the laws; (6) Settling through diplomacy as well as law the control of our lodges under the government of other countries from the Canadian borders to the Bahamas; (7) Working out the medium of exchange of currency so that we could collect the dues of members of foreign lodges; (8) Recodifying and simplifying the laws of the Grand Temple and the Temples; (9) Working out a uniformity between the Grand Lodge laws and the Temple laws; (10) Definitely settling the procedures in the matter of charges, trials, and appeals.

Following the reading of this report it was observed that this year 1950 completed the twenty-fifth year of continuous service that Grand Legal Adviser Howard had given to the Grand Lodge. It was then moved that he should be recommended for reappointment as Grand Legal Adviser and that a substantial monetary contribution from unobligated funds be made to him as "a token of recognition and appreciation of outstanding services rendered." The motion was agreed to by a standing vote.

The report of the Health Commission, with Dr. Carter L. Marshall Chairman and Grand Medical Director, was made under the following headings; (1) The Health of Our Grand Exalted Ruler; (2) Health Activities at the San Francisco Convention, The X-Ray Project, The First Aid Room, The Purple Cross and Health Meeting; (3) Articles in *The Washington Eagle*; (4) Iron Lung Program; (5) Health Bulletins and Exhibits; (6) First Aid Rooms; (7) The Health Commission; (8) John Brown Farm; (9) Insurance Program; (10) Purple Cross Activities; (11) Baltimore Blood Bank; (12) Elk's Health Day. In conclusion the report called for continued cooperation and support and added that with these the Health Department could become "a vital force for the welfare of our Order, our race, and our country." It was then recommended that the Commission be recommended to the Grand Exalted Ruler for reappointment to their respective positions, and this was adopted.

The reports followed of the Grand Commissioner of Transportation, Albert A. Reading; the Grand Lodge Reporter, John C. Minkins; the Press Committee with E. H. Lawson as Chairman and the Committee on Resolutions; the Committee on Awards; Grand Director of Golf, Peter Dillard; the Department of Athletics presented trophies to be permanently maintained at the John Brown Shrine; the Grand Trustees made their report concerning all of the funds and property of the organization; the Charity Committee, the Antlered Guard Department, the Law and Revision Committee, the Shrine Department, the Committee on Appeals and Grievances, and the Grand Auditor. The final report of the Committee on Credentials showed that there had been accredited participation in the 1950 Grand Lodge of 829 accredited members.

The sense of climax to an era was manifested not only by the physical disability which had come down upon the Grand Exalted Ruler and the indication that he was not as active physically as he had been in earlier years and by the excellent reports which had been made concerning the increasingly healthful condition of The Improved Benevolent and Protective Order of Elks of the World, but it was also apparent in the passing of Grand Secretary James E. Kelley who had served as Grand Secretary from 1928 until 1951. He had served also as Secretary and Exalted Ruler of Jones Valley Lodge, Birmingham, Alabama, from 1903 until the day of his death, a period of approximately forty-eight years. He had accomplished a superior task in the organization of the office of Secretary and had stood solidly with the "Grand" in all of the progressive accomplishments. Finley Wilson, Bill Hueston and Jim Kelley were the "three musketeers" of modern Elkdom as Howard, Riggs and Hunter were in early Elkdom.

The Grand Officers elected at this grand lodge Session of 1950 were: J. Finley Wilson, Grand Exalted Ruler, Washington, D. C.; Joseph A. Brown, Grand Esteemed Leading Knight, New York, N. Y.; Herbert E. Jones, Grand Esteemed Loyal Knight, Washington, D. C.; Robert H. Johnson, Grand Esteemed Lecturing Knight, Philadelphia, Pa.; James E. Kelley, Grand Secretary, Birmingham, Ala.; Thomas E. Greene, Grand Treasurer, Akron, Ohio; Paul E. Davis, Grand Chaplain, Charlotte, N. C.; Dr. Simpson A. Smith, Grand Inner Guard, Huntington, W. Va.; A. E. Bradley, Grand Esquire, Long Beach, Calif.; S. D. Holsey, Grand Tiler, Reading, Pa.; William C. Hueston, Grand Commissioner of Education, Washington, D. C.; Perry W. Howard, Grand Legal Adviser, Washington, D. C.; Perry B. Jackson, Assistant Grand Legal Adviser, Cleveland, Ohio; Hobson R. Reynolds, Grand Director of Civil Liberties, Philadelphia Pa.; Dr. Carter L. Marshall, Grand Medical Director, New Haven, Conn.; Dr. E. T. Belsaw, Executive Secretary, Health Commission, Mobile, Alabama; A. William Hill, Grand Director of Junior Elks, Lancaster, Pa.; Dr. L. W. Williams, Chairman of Publishing Board, Valdosta, Georgia; Lionel Hampton, Grand Bandmaster, New York City; St. Clair Cobb, Grand Band Director, Knoxville, Tennessee; George Hyder, Assistant Bandmaster, Philadelphia, Pa.; John U. Strother, Grand Master of Social Session, Augusta, Ga.; John C. Minkins, Grand Lodge Reporter, Providence, Rhode Island; J. T. Whitbeck, Director of Economics, Cleveland, Ohio; Dr. J. B. Martin, Director of Athletics, Chicago, Illinois; Charles P. McClane, Sr., Director of Public Relations, Steelton, Pa.; Albert Reading, Grand Master of Transportation, Chester, Pennsylvania; Dr. Lawrence J. Davenport, Grand Organist, New York, New York; C. Henri Lewis, Chairman Post-War Planning Committee, Detroit, Michigan; Antlered Guard: John H. Graves, Lt. General Eastern Division, Pittsburgh, Pennsylvania; Henry Berth, Philadelphia; Roy E. Barnett, Major General Western Division, Chicago, Illinois; Grand Trustees: John T. Freeman, Chairman, Philadelphia, Pennsylvania; Charles A. Oliver, Annapolis, Maryland; C. Sylvester Jackson, Harrisburg, Pennsylvania; J. F. Simmons, Norfolk, Virginia; J. LeRoy Jordan, Elizabeth, New Jersey; Grand Auditors: James T. Copper, Chicago, Illinois; S. B. Mitchell, New York, New York; Harry St. Clair, East Chicago, Illinois; Health Commission: Dr. Carter L. Marshall, Chairman, New Haven, Conn.; Dr. T. T. Wendell, Lexington, Kentucky; Dr.

E. T. Belsaw, Executive Secretary, Mobile, Alabama; Charles E. Hall, Statistician, Washington, D. C.; Dr. J. A. Megahy, Chicago, Illinois; Dr. Leslie E. Howell, St. Louis, Missouri; Shrine Commission: George W. Lee, Chairman, Memphis, Tennessee; Ernest M. Thomas, Secretary, New Orleans, La.

This climax was also manifested in the passing during the period following the Grand Lodge of the Grand Treasurer, Thomas E. Green, a member of Rubber City Lodge formerly Delta City Lodge of Akron, Ohio and who was Past Exalted Ruler of Delta Lodge. While his years of service were not as lengthy as those of Grand Secretary Kelley, he had served with efficiency in his office and had been a member of the Executive Group who had carried the order to the great heights represented in its membership, its holdings and the services rendered to its members, lodges, and communities. There was also the passing of the Lieutenant General John H. Graves who had built the Antlered Guard into one of the colorful military organizations of Elkdom. The passing of these outstanding leaders of the Order and the two years of personal illness of Grand Exalted Ruler Wilson seemed to indicate clearly that an era was approaching its climax. Nevertheless, with definite spirit Grand Exalted Ruler Wilson urged the Order to "close ranks and carry on!"

In his annual report to the Fifty-Second Annual Meeting of the Grand Lodge which convened in Technical High School, Buffalo, New York, August 25-31, 1951, the Grand Exalted Ruler called on "every loyal Elk, every Past Exalted Rulers Council, every state association, together with our Grand Temple and all of our departments, to move forward and follow through with that same determination bolder than ever to snatch victory out of the jaws of defeat." He was proud of the fact that the Elks throughout the jurisdiction had brought over thirty million dollars worth of Defense Bonds and that this was an indication that they intended to defend American faith and liberty. He said that they had survived the question of their leadership in the meetings of the Negro Congress and that they moved forward with faith and looked ahead with confidence. He said that there would be "street block" volunteers who would spearhead the movement to bring out the vote and to have the people register so that they could vote. The lodges were called upon, with every brother Elk and every daughter Elk regardless of race, color or creed, to qualify and vote somewhere on election day. He added, "Now let us all close ranks. Help register and vote. We want the thousands of Negroes who have failed to exercise their American birthright throughout the forty-eight states to register in the coming campaign and vote on election day."

The James E. Kelley Membership Drive had been sponsored by the Grand Exalted Ruler immediately after the news of Brother James E. Kelley's death had reached him. He selected this project because of Brother Kelley's interest in such a movement. He reported that there had been very unusual developments from this drive. There were thousands of members brought into Elkdom. Although the Grand Exalted Ruler had been upon his bed of affliction, his associates had aided and cooperated in the development of the program. He said that his administration had organized over one thousand new lodges and for practically every new lodge a temple and that together they were headed for the second thousand. In this respect the basis was being laid by him for another era of development of The Improved Benevolent and Protective Order of Elks of the World.

There had been a total amount of cash on deposit in the banks at the close of the fiscal year 1951 of $181,390.31, according to the report of Grand Treasurer Perry B. Jackson, who made his first report to the Grand Lodge at this session. He paid tribute to his predecessor, "the beloved Thomas A. Greene."

Grand Treasurer Jackson had been requested by Grand Exalted Ruler Wilson to act as Grand Treasurer in the interim of the Grand Lodges of 1950 and 1951 as a result of the death of the former Grand Treasurer Thomas E. Greene, Jr. The transfer of funds had been made with the smallest possible amount of effort and the Grand Auditors had approved the details of the transfer.

The net worth of the organization was represented by the following:

Cash in bank	$181,390.31
United States Government Bonds	100,000.00
Shrine Building, New York	137,000.00
John Brown Farm (purchase price)	30,000.00
Vacant lots in Savannah, Georgia	850.16
Notes receivable	1,050.00
Total	$450,290.47

Tributes were paid to Brother Perry B. Jackson for the excellent service which he had rendered; and he was elected by acclamation to the office of Grand Treasurer.

The Acting Grand Secretary, William C. Hueston, described his experiences with Grand Exalted Ruler Wilson during his illness. Said he, "I have seen J. Finley Wilson suffer as few men have suffered, and still come up smiling. I have listened to the doctors tell him that if he wanted to live they must take his leg off, and I have heard Finley say, 'No, I came into this world with two legs, and I am going out with all that I have now.' And I

JAMES E. KELLEY, Grand Secretary, 1928-1951

have thought that Finley was making a mistake, for the best authority in the world was making the decision. This was at Mayo's. I have seen the leg heal until it was no longer a handicap that he could go on doing his work—answering his mail and doing all things that his office required, just as any man in the best of health could do. Truly, he is a miracle man. So he is here today, and we say, 'Thank God, he is alive.' "

Referring to the death of Grand Secretary James E. Kelley, and Colonel Roscoe Conkling Simmons, editor of *The Washington Eagle,* Dr. Hueston said that "the hand of affliction has been upon us." In describing the excellent work of Grand Secretary Kelley, Dr. Hueston said, "Then we are remembering him in 1928. He was elected Grand Secretary amid much excitement and enthusiasm. From that time down to the day of his death, no Brother ever offered to take his place. For twenty-two years he was the Grand Secretary without opposition. In this office he was the beloved brother of every member of this order, always kindly, ever attentive."

However, these sad happenings represented only one side of the picture. The work of these men had been so well done that he reported that the Order was growing and that thousands of new members had been added to the roles. There were thirty-six new and reinstated lodges, two Past Exalted Rulers Councils, five new and reinstated Civil Liberties Leagues and ten Junior Elk Herds. The Daughter Elks were said to be keeping pace with the Brothers in growth and progress. At the conclusion of acting Secretary Hueston's report he was elected Grand Secretary by acclamation.

A dual report was necessary from Brother William C. Hueston who had not only served as Grand Secretary but also as Commissioner of Education. His educational report stated that he was giving a report for the twenty-sixth year of service in the Department of Education. He described the scholarships which had been offered to students during the year and the institutions to which they had been admitted for study, the list of graduates for the year 1951 with the assistance of the Improved Benevolent and Protective Order of Elks of the World. The emphasis was made by him upon the program to reduce illiteracy which had been conducted in past years and was being conducted again by the representatives of the Grand Lodge and the Department of Education. An arrangement had been made with Storer College to offer a course of instruction but only two persons had signified their desires to join in this study during the previous year. In the second year of the program only one had entered the course.

Perry B. Jackson, Grand Treasurer, 1951-

Judge Hueston urged the lodges and temples to begin to pay attention to this aspect of the program as a result of the facilities which could be had at the John Brown Farm in cooperation with Storer College at Harpers Ferry. Here too, he said, was an opportunity for adult education through which a school for the education of indigent adults could also be conducted.

Further emphasis was placed upon the John Brown Shrine by the Acting Commissioner of Education George W. Lee, who had also served as chairman of the Shrine Commission. He emphasized the life of John Brown and its meaning to the present generation. He said, "The Shrine at Harper's Ferry will be a glorious pattern revealing a startling picture of what Brown and Lincoln saw deep beneath the surface of the Abject Black Man for whom they fought and gave their lives." At the conclusion of his report Brother George W. Lee was elected by acclamation to the office of Grand Commissioner of Education.

A further expression of the appreciation of the Grand Lodge for the great work which had been accomplished by Grand Exalted Ruler J. Finley Wilson was demonstrated in the adoption of the resolution by unanimous vote providing for a gift of $10,000.00 to the Grand Exalted Ruler to be appropriated from Grand Lodge funds. This was done, "in manifestation of appreciation by the members of the Order for the extraordinary accomplishments on the part of Brother J. Finley Wilson in spite of handicapping circumstances." The Grand Exalted Ruler accepted on behalf of the Grand Lodge a certificate of appreciation from the National Foundation for Infantile Paralysis in acknowledgement of interest and support of the Elks in the Foundation's March of Dimes Campaign.

When the offices were opened for election, the following were elected: J. Finley Wilson, Grand Exalted Ruler, Washington, D. C.; Robert H. Johnson, Grand Esteemed Lecturing Knight, was promoted by acclamation to the office of Grand Esteemed Leading Knight; Brother Bertram V. Gregory was elected Grand Esteemed Loyal Knight; Brother Bernard Harris was elected the Grand Esteemed Lecturing Knight succeeded by Harvey L. Harris; Brother Henry Davis was elected the Grand Esquire; Brother Samuel R. Houchins, the Grand Inner Guard; Brother L. W. Williams, Grand Tiler. The other officers were as follows: W. C. Hueston, Grand Secretary, Washington, D. C.; Perry B. Jackson, Grand Treasurer, Cleveland, Ohio; Rev. R. H. Collins Lee, Grand Chaplain, Chicago, Illinois; Lt. George W. Lee, Grand Commissioner of Education, Memphis, Tennessee; Perry W. Howard, Grand Legal Advisor, Washington, D. C.; Hobson

R. Reynolds, Grand Director of Civil Liberties, Philadelpha, Pa; Dr. Carter L. Marshall, Grand Medical Director, New Haven, Connecticut; Dr. E. T. Belsaw, Executive Secretary, Health Commission, Mobile, Alabama; A. William Hill, Grand Director of Junior Elks, Lancaster, Pennsylvania; Lionel Hampton, Grand Bandmaster, New York City; St. Clair Cobb, Grand Band Director, Knoxville, Tennessee; George W. Hyder, Assistant Bandmaster, Philadelphia, Pennsylvania; John C. Minkins, Grand Lodge Reporter, Providence Rhode Island; Dr. J. B. Martin, Director of Athletics, Chicago, Illinois; Charles P. McClane, Director of Public Relations, Steelton, Pennsylvania; Albert Reading, Grand Master of Transportation, Chester, Pa.; Dr. Lawrence J. Davenport, Grand Organist, New York; Antlered Guard; Henry Berth, Major General Eastern Division, Philadelphia, Pa.; Roy E. Barnett, Major General Western Division, Chicago, Illinois; Grand Trustees: John T. Freeman, Philadelphia, Pa.; Charles A. Oliver, Annapolis, Md.; C. Sylvester Jackson, Harrisburg, Pa.; J. F. Simmons, Norfolk, Va.; J. LeRoy Jordan, Elizabeth, N. J.; Grand Auditors: James T. Copper, Chicago, Ill.; Samuel B. Mitchell, New York City; Harry St. Clair, East Chicago, Ind.; William H. Walker, Washington, D. C.; Health Commission: Dr. Carter L. Marshall, Chairman, New Haven, Conn.; Dr. T. T. Wendell, Lexington, Ky.; Dr. E. T. Belsaw, Executive Secretary, Mobile, Ala.; Charles E. Hall, Statistician, Washington, D. C.; Dr. J. A. Megahy, Chicago, Ill.; Dr. Leslie B. Howell, St. Louis, Mo.; Shrine Commission: Ernest M. Thomas, Secretary, New Orleans, Louisiana.

The Committee on awards reported that the annual parade of the Grand Lodge was one of the best ever staged by the Order during its long history. There were in the parade line, two hundred and sixty-three units, thirty bands, ten drum and bugle corps, sixty-five cars, and ten floats headed by the Grand Exalted Ruler. The committee commended the entire group and made awards to those selected by its judges.

When the report of the Grand Medical Director and Health Commission was made, the hope was expressed that Grand Exalted Ruler Wilson would conserve his strength in the administration of his office wherever possible and they called upon the brotherhood of the lodges to make every effort to spare the Grand Exalted Ruler and thus contribute to his recovery. There was considerable endeavor concerning health manifested by the lodges and temples on the Health Day Program the second Sunday in April. Free chest x-rays were offered to the membership and the public during the period of the Grand Lodge. Health exhibits and posters were set up in the lobby where the Grand Lodge was in session. It was reported by Dr. Marshall that the *Washington Eagle* had carried articles on some phase of health in all of its issues and that there was a first-aid room in each of the meeting halls under the supervision of Daughter Anna B. Jones and the Purple Cross Nurses.

The subject of civil liberties was discussed by Grand Director, Department of Civil Liberties, Hobson R. Reynolds. He said that throughout 1950-1951, the Department had continued an unrelenting crusade for the establishment of equality among all citizens. He and his colleagues had cooperated with organizations and individuals in the struggle to achieve civil rights for Negroes in the United States.

He described decisions rendered by the United States Supreme Court on various phases of civil rights which were most encouraging to the members of the Grand Lodge. One of these cases was the Henderson Case. This decision was made during this year. While the Supreme Court did not rule on the Separate but Equal Doctrine, a mandate of the Court eliminated the reserve table and the curtain which were used in a dining car. The Court declared, "The right to be free from unreasonable discriminations belongs to each particular person. Where a dining car is available to passengers holding tickets entitling them to use it, each such passenger is equally entitled to its facilities in accordance with reasonable regulations. The denial of dining service to any such passenger by the rules before us subjects him to a prohibited disadvantage—the curtain, which serves only to call attention to a racial classification of passengers holding identical tickets and using the same public dining facilities." A second victory during this year was gained when the United States Supreme Court dendered its decision in connection with the two cases of Heman Sweatt in seeking admission to the University of Texas and G. W. McLaurin to the University of Oklahoma. The decision in these cases opened these two institutions to Negro applicants and brought the whole question of the admission of Negro students to southern institutions of higher education squarely into the open so far as Negro applicants were concerned, and brought consummation to the Gaines Case of 1938.

The fight against segregation in the Armed Forces had been undertaken by the Elks several years ago, according to Brother Hobson R. Reynolds, in their appearances before Congressional Committees and their contacts with members of Congress. Said he, "Today, we can say that we see some results in this field also. However, the disagreeable situation still exists very strongly in the army. The Air Force and the Navy have shown more disposition to do away with segregation than the army, but we shall not let our boys down. If our boys are good enough to fight and die for this country, they are good enough to fight and die on an equal basis and as first class citizens. We want nothing more and we shall expect nothing less.'' Segregation in the nation's captial, education, an FEPC bill, the exercise of the ballot and action on local levels by lodges and temples were presented. Grand Director Reynolds by vote of the Grand Lodge was recommended for reappointment.

Representatives of the Grand Temple were then admitted to the Grand Lodge sessions: Daughter Buena V. Kelley, Grand Secretary; Daughter Carrie Chapman, Educational Directress of Tennessee; Daughter Lethia Fleming, Grand Directress of Public Relations; and Daughter of Berth McKanlass, Grand Directress of the Shrine. Each of these Daughters addressed the Grand Lodge bringing the greetings of the Grand Temple and feliciting the Grand Exalted Ruler on his birthday. Later a delegation of twenty-two Daughters headed by Vice Grand Daughter Ruler Nettie Carter Jackson brought greetings from the Grand Temple. Musical selections were rendered by them in honor of the Grand Exalted Ruler.

Among the resolutions adopted by the Grand Lodge were the following referring to Christianity as the only remedy, the Korean War, the United Nations, the end of the Jim Crow Army, America must practice what she preaches, Asiatic Propaganda, Diplomatic Service, Department of Justice, Fair Employment Practice and Civil Rights Laws, the District of Columbia, the conspiracy to keep the Negro down, Housing, Cloture, the Get-out-the-vote Campaign, Dixiecrats and the Purchase of the Grand Lodge Office Building.

There were two of these resolutions which rank in importance above the others. They show that the Elks were in the vanguard of progress for democracy. One of these was on Jim-Crow schools. It said, ''we call for and urge forceful action by the United States Congress, the President and State Legislatures to accomplish the elimination of the separate schools, both public and tax favored, that exist in many places in the North and throughout the South.'' The second resolution authorized the appropriation of one thousand dollars for the Grand Exalted Ruler ''to expend as in his wisdom he shall see fit for investigation, study and research on the Civil Rights of the Negro in the South, said study and research report or thesis when completed shall be filed with the General Secretary and shall then be and become the property of the Grand Lodge of I.B.P.O.E. of W., to be used as a compendium and guide by the Fraternal Order.'' Another of the definitive actions of the Grand Lodge was the creation of the position of Grand Traveling Auditor who was to audit the accounts of the local lodges and auxiliaries, whenever he was so directed by the Grand Exalted Ruler.

This Grand Lodge was one of the largest in the history of the Order. There were 1,105 delegates in attendance including thirty-three Grand Lodge Officers, twenty-six Past Grand Exalted Rulers, seventy-six District and State Deputies, eight hundred and twenty-five Lodge Delegates, one hundred and seven Past

1952 Calendar Announcement

Exalted Rulers Councils, and thirty-eight state associations. These delegates were urged to come to Buffalo with the John Brown Memorial theme ranking high in their minds. The Souvenir Program for this convention carried an article with the title ''John Brown, Abolitionist,'' with pictures of the John Brown Memorial Farm, and also declared, ''Elkdom moves to heights unvisioned as J. Finley Wilson's spirited leadership abounds.'' The convention was addressed by Rev. Archibald J. Carey, and Jesse O. Thomas. Dr. Ralph J. Bunche addressed the Champions of Human Rights Breakfast and was awarded the 1951 Lovejoy Medal in recognition of his outstanding contribution to human progress.

Following the closing of the Fifty-Second Grand Lodge held in Buffalo, New York, Grand Exalted Ruler J. Finley Wilson led a post convention tour of Canada and New England under the leadership of the Grand Director of Transportation, Albert Reading. During this trip there was not only the pleasure of the trip involved, but the Grand Exalted Ruler used it also as a means of increasing the membership and initiating a program to establish lodges and temples of the Order. He was accompanied on this trip, as usual, by his wife who was known affectionately in the Order as "Mrs. Finley," his secretaries, and the Grand Lodge Officers and selected members. He visited the Canadian National Exposition and delivered an address. When the group had returned from this convention, a meeting was called at the Royal York Hotel in Toronto and after a review of the events of the day the following resolution was adopted:

> "Be it resolved, that this Grand Lodge of The Improved Benevolent and Protective Order of Elks of the World do hereby authorize and instruct all of its officers having power and authority pertaining thereto to immediately proceed to the program of reviving all existing lodges, temples and shrines and increase the membership thereof, and establish new lodges, temples and shrines throughout the Dominion of Canada, in Mexico, Central and South America, the Caribbean area, in Africa and Europe, throughout Asia, the Pacific Ocean area and other parts of the world, in full and strict compliance with the Constitution, By-Laws and Ritual of The Improved Benevolent and Protective Order of Elks of the World.
>
> Be it further resolved, that this program of action is one of prime importance to our nation and to the world which needs the true spirit of brotherhood to bring peace and prosperity to all nations and peoples of the world."

Visits were then made to Montreal and other places in Canada and thence to New England. Shortly thereafter a meeting of the General Committee for the 1952 Grand Lodge Convention was called by the Grand Exalted Ruler at Atlantic City. On September 22, more than 2,000 Grand Lodge officers, brothers, daughters and friends from lodges and temples throughout the country assembled at the historic John Brown Farm near Harper's Ferry, West Virginia to dedicate this national shrine in a two day celebration. The purpose of this meeting was to proclaim the fact that Negroes had not forgotten and were now on the march to bring in the fulfillment of what was termed as the "Holy Mission of John Brown, that of human equality of all men." Outstanding personages were present and participated in the program with the assembled brothers and daughters coming in more than 500 private cars and 20 buses. They saw the John Brown Home completely renovated, a renovated barn with a veranda running

Dr. Nettie Carter Jackson, Eighth Grand Daughter Ruler, 1951-

its entire length and seating about 200 persons, a new large auditorium fully equipped for meetings and a sample cottage with bath. At the entrance of the National Shrine a 14 foot arch had been erected and a new picket fence had been constructed. The lawn was graded and picnic tables placed in the shady orchard. It was on this occasion that Grand Exalted Ruler Wilson said, "If this farm shall prove to our Junior Elks in the years to come the inspiration which we have hoped for, we shall not have wrought in vain." The travels of the Grand Exalted Ruler were continued through the months of October and November as he attended stated occasions of lodges and temples, testimonials, dedications and official visits.

Throughout all this period he continued to be in poor health and yet no sacrifice in health and home life was too great for him to make in order to carry out his ambitions for the Order, for the Order was his life. He had joined it in 1903 and in 1904 he came as a delegate to Atlantic City from Denver, Colorado. He became a Deputy in 1913, an Organizer in 1919, and in 1922 was elected the Grand Exalted Ruler. The Fifty-Second Convention was the closing convention in his great career in building one of the great fraternal organizations of the world. He passed into the great beyond on February 19, 1952. This was on the eve of his thirtieth year in office. He died as he had lived, working constantly until the end came. He was survived by his widow, Mrs. Leah Belle Farrar Wilson whom he had married in 1924.

Shortly after the close of the convention of 1951, the news came of the passing of Grand Daughter Ruler Elizabth Ross Gordon, Seventh Grand Daughter Ruler. Although in failing health, she carried out her duties with unfaltering courage in this final year of her life and left a great example of devotion to duty. She had come up from the ranks, serving as Grand Chaplain, Grand Assistant Daughter Ruler, Grand Vice-Daughter Ruler and in 1940 was elected Grand Daughter Ruler to succeed Grand Daughter Ruler Abbie M. Johnson. Under the administration of Grand Daughter Ruler Gordon, the organization grew, new departments were established and a new spirit was infused through her leadership in the conventions, state associations and temples. Her death also marked the passing of an era in the history of the Grand Temple.

It has been well said that the election of Grand Daughter Ruler Nettie Carter Jackson "opened the doors of Elkdom to a new era." She came to this work of leadership with foundation experiences as a charter member of Raritan Temple No. 218, services as Daughter Ruler, District Deputy, Senior Mother, Financial Secretary, Recording Secretary of Past Daughter Rulers

Council, State Recorder of New York State Association, Vice Grand Daughter Ruler and activities in many areas of Temple life and organization. Her election brought new hope for the future and definitely announced the beginning of a new era for the organization of which she was the leader. The first report of Grand Daughter Ruler Nettie Carter Jackson to the Grand Temple stated, "I am happy to say that although we have suffered keen losses through the death of our key officers of this Grand Order yet the work has progressed. New temples, councils and juvenile and junior classes were organized within the ten months of my administration. Some of the temples were reinstated. The Daughters who revived them informed me that these temples had taken on new life and seemed anxious to work. I am sure that you will note the increase in membership."

This in reality was the climax of an era for the Order. The termination of life and work for J. Finley Wilson, James E. Kelley, Thomas E. Greene and Elizabeth Ross Gordon closed a chapter in The History of the Improved Benevolent and Protective Order of Elks of the World. The new day dawned with new leadership for men and women in Elkdom.

Chapter XX
A Master-Administrator Begins a New Era

The close of the administration of J. Finley Wilson, Grand Exalted Ruler, affectionately known as "The Grand," terminated an era of growth and expansion which had produced marked developments in the history of one of the great fraternal organizations in American life. The influence of the Order had become so extensive that it was described by Brother Charles P. McClane, Director of Public Relations, as "the greatest Negro organization in the world." It had withstood the shocks of two world wars, which threatened the existence of the nation without the omission of a single annual session, and it had come through the depression of the thirties with its banks failures, unemployment and reduced income, and had grown continuously in stature. Its programs of service had become more realistic and constructive as the years passed.

The necessity for change in administration was brought about by the death of Grand Exalted Ruler Wilson on February 19, 1952 at Washington, D. C. This was not entirely unexpected because of the well-known state of his health for the past two years. However, when the expected event came, the I.B.P.O.E.W. was unprepared for it. His funeral services at the Metropolitan Baptist Church, Washington, D. C. were attended by overflow crowds who attested the affection and high esteem in which he was held. The testimonies of his associates given on this occasion were from the hearts of those who revered and appreciated his services as their leader. The newspapers carried tributes and commentaries on his life and work.

The Journal of Negro History for July, 1952, said of Grand Exalted Ruler Wilson, "There was statesmanship in the leadership of J. Finley Wilson as he looked beyond fraternalism. He realized the necessity of preparing his followers for a tomorrow of greater responsibility as he maintained close touch with the world about him. Most observers will remember him best, perhaps, from the glamour of the annual Elk parades in various great cities. These events meant much in opportunity for expression among masses born, nurtured, and subjected from the cradle to the grave in segregation. But Mr. Wilson saw infinitely farther and always had some distinguished spokesman like Bunche, DuBois and Wesley bring an annual message of hope and inspiration about colored people. He demonstrated by precept and example that great leadership must stem from the people who are led and that any imposed by outsiders is doomed to fail. James Finley Wilson's tribe of genuine colored leaders should increase and may his mantle rest on worthy shoulders.''

Inevitably the reins of government of the Order would fall into the hands of a qualified successor. In the traditional words of empire, ''the king is dead, long live the king.'' The work had to be carried on although the Grand Exalted Ruler had passed to the Great Beyond. In this spirit and with a keen sense of sorrow, Robert H. Johnson took up the work and carried on with a faith and determination which soon made for him a distinctive place in the annals of the fraternity. The growth of the Order was to continue under his wise leadership.

The new leader of the Improved Benevolent and Protective Order of Elks of the World was Robert H. Johnson of Philadelphia, Pennsylvania, who was Grand Esteemed Leading Knight. He was educated in the public schools of Philadelphia and at Delaware State College and was subsequently awarded the degree of Doctor of Laws by Bethune-Cookman College. He was a veteran of World War I. He had come up from the ranks and had proved himself in all offices which had been held by him in local and national circles. He had risen step by step and his services as Exalted Ruler of his lodge, Commissioner of Transportation, Grand Esteemed Lecturing Knight and Grand Esteemed Leading Knight, demonstrated efficiences which were distinctive and in many respects superior to some of his predecessors in these offices. J. Finley Wilson saw these superior qualities in Robert H. Johnson and placed him in the position where he could demonstrate his capacities for leadership. It was through this foresight that Brother Johnson was advanced from the office of Grand Esteemed Lecturing Knight to Grand Esteemed Leading Knight, so that the executive mantle fell upon him when his hour had come.

When this time arrived through the passing of Grand Exalted Ruler Wilson, the transition was made with the smallest break in succession which could have possibly occurred. The mantle fell from the shoulders of ''The Grand'' and was accepted by a worthy successor who rapidly also became ''The Grand'' in his own right. He did not attempt to be another J. Finley Wilson, for he wanted to be himself, and had no desire to make himself a slavish imitation of his predecessor. He knew confidently that each had his own abilities and qualifications. He believed

Dr. Robert H. Johnson, Grand Exalted Ruler, 1951-

also that God has a way of choosing men for historic occasions and uses them in His own way. When J. Finley Wilson passed into the Great Beyond, many within and outside of the Order were dubious about a worthy successor. Those who knew "Bob" Johnson had no such misgivings. He accepted the mantle with its tremendous responsibilities and immediately demonstrated the qualities which were to make him into another great Grand Exalted Ruler of Elkdom.

The work of Robert H. Johnson was not only to continue the growth of the Order but to give to it the administration and the maturity which the Order needed. Its widespread growth had been at the same time its strength and its weakness. This challenge was accepted by the new Grand Exalted Ruler and good results were manifest even before the session of the Grand Lodge of 1952, the first Grand Lodge over which he was to preside. His judicial and court experiences were invaluable aids to him in immediate and complete adjustments to the new office and in continuing a high degree of efficiency as an administrator. The Order needed a builder and an administrator and it was not long before it was being said that while J. Finley Wilson was the "Master-Builder," Robert H. Johnson was the "Master-Administrator," who also continued the process of building.

The first Grand Lodge presided over by Grand Exalted Ruler Robert H. Johnson assembled at Atlantic City in the National Guard Armory, August 23-29, 1952. The pre-convention sessions were conducted with great success, the Educational Congress presided over by Brother George W. Lee of Memphis, Tennessee, the Grand Commissioner of Education; the annual baccalaureate service addressed by Grand Daughter Ruler Nettie Carter Jackson of New York who spoke on "The Golden Jubilee Dedication" in honor of the founder of the Grand Temple, Emma B. Kelly; and also Mrs. Robert L. Vann, widow of the late Robert L. Vann, publisher of the *Pittsburgh Courier;* the Shrine Service in which John Brown was eulogized by the Grand Director of Public Relations Charles P. McClane and Brother Hugh McBeth of California; the graduation exercises of the Purple Cross Nurses presided over by Daughter Anna B. Jones, Grand Directress of the Purple Cross Nurses; the Annual Memorial Service with the Honorable Robert H. Johnson Grand Exalted Ruler and Mrs. Nettie Carter Jackson Grand Daughter Ruler presiding with Rev. R. H. Collins Lee officiating as Grand Chaplain; the Annual Champions of Human Rights Breakfast at which tribute was paid to the general manager of the Pittsburgh Baseball Club of the National Baseball League, Branch Rickey who was awarded the 1952 Lovejoy Award of the Improved Benevolent Protective

Order of Elks of the World in recognition of outstanding contributions to human progress; the Annual Meeting of the National Cap and Gown Club which was presided over by the National President, Daughter Gertrude S. Holland and addressed by Past Grand Exalted Ruler Armond W. Scott, and the National Oratorical Contest in which there were seven participants speaking upon the Constitution and the Negro.

When the award was made to Branch Rickey, Grand Exalted Ruler Robert H. Johnson delivered the address hailing Rickey as the Grand Champion of Human Rights in 1952 and decorating him with the Lovejoy Medal. In his acceptance address Mr. Rickey stated, "Advancement in racial problems had doubtless seemed slow to contemporaries in all ages. It has been difficult to understand why progress from human slavery to full equality of opportunity to work has seemed beset by delay and opposition. The American public is more concerned with the ease and power of the second baseman's swing at bat, the dexterity of his slide, the gracefulness of his fielding and the great speed of his rhythmical legs and whether he is out or safe, than it is with the pigmentation of his skin or the last syllable of his name." When the address had been completed, Brother Perry W. Howard made the motion that 10,000 copies of Mr. Rickey's address be printed and distributed to all Elks throughout the country and the motion was carried.

The business sessions were called to order by the Honorable Robert H. Johnson, Grand Exalted Ruler, who presided over the ritualistic ceremonies and the business sessions. The report of the Credentials Committee submitted as a partial one, showed that there were nine hundred and sixty-five accredited delegates present at the opening session. A subsequent report revealed the fact that there were thirty-nine Grand Lodge Officers, thirty-five Past Grand Officers, six hundred and seventy-seven delegates from four hundred and sixty-eight Lodges, eighty-four representatives of state associations, two hundred and twenty-eight commissioned officers, making a grand total of one thousand one hundred thirty-seven official delegates. There were large numbers of members of the lodges and temples in attendance.

The Annual Report of Grand Exalted Ruler Robert H. Johnson was read by him to the Grand Lodge. He began with terming the past year as the saddest year of the long existence of the Improved Benevolent Protective Order of Elks of the World and that among those who had passed was the "Dearly beloved Grand Exalted Ruler, Dr. J. Finley Wilson." He urged that in reverence "to that great man I ask this body to stand, face West with heads bowed for one minute of absolute silence." In referring to the selection of the next Grand Exalted Ruler to succeed Dr. Wilson, Grand Exalted Ruler Johnson said, "It is my hope and prayer that God will give to his successor the determination and understanding to carry on—and expand—this great order to even greater heights; that he will bring to the organization more credit and praise, through the inspiration passed on to all of us by the untiring efforts and determined leadership of the grandest of all leaders, Dr. J. Finley Wilson." He urged that the Grand Lodge and all of the Orders and Temples should close ranks, forget their personal animosities and individual ambitions and carry the flag of the Order onward and upward to greater heights.

One of the first evidences of his interest in improving the Order's administration was the issuance of his order to have a detailed audit of the funds of the Grand Lodge. He engaged for this assignment, Brother William H. Walker who was an experienced accountant and tax consultant. As a result of this audit, as of February 1952, the total cash on hand was reported as $165,918.21, plus United States Government Bonds totaling $100,000.00 which made a grand total of $265,918.21 The details of this report were included in the reports of the Grand Secretary and Grand Treasurer. The Grand Exalted Ruler listed the number of cases that had been adjudicated, the dispensations granted in 1952, the necrology including Grand Exalted Ruler Wilson and Grand Daughter Ruler Elizabeth Ross Gordon, who also had been called from labor to reward. In referring to her, the Grand Exalted Ruler said, "She rose from the ranks and gave to the temple one of the most progressive administrations in its history." He also referred to the passing of Daughter Elizabeth Kimbrough, Grand Treasurer of the Daughters, and described the total growth of the Order during the past year.

His recommendations included that the Grand Exalted Ruler should not serve more than two year terms with election every two years; that the Civil Liberties Department be placed on a full-time basis and be given the authority to process and investigate all matters pertaining to civil rights; that the Athletic Department be allotted two assistants to work out a solution to the youth program; that an additional major-general of the Antler Guard should be appointed for the southern division, and finally that a Grand Historian should be appointed for the Grand Lodge to bring the record of the Grand Lodge from its institution to date. The latter was a great step in the development of the Order for it showed that the Grand Exalted Ruler was specifically interested in the development of a history of the Order. While it would take two years for this consummation to be brought again before the Grand Lodge for complete adoption, it was a step in the right direction and showed that the Grand Exalted Ruler was seriously interested in a historical project for the I.B.P.O.E. of W.

This report of the Grand Exalted Ruler was concluded with the following statement of sincerity and confident hope which looked toward the past and again toward the future. Said he, "As we gather here at the convention from every corner of the United States and the Islands, let us thank God for the glorious history that is ours. Let us be thankful for the blessings which have made our present program possible; and let us resolve anew to spread the virtues of charity by our daily acts and deeds, ever mindful of Him whose guiding hand brought final triumph to our bewildered forebearers in the long ago. They trusted Him and He did not fail them. He shall not fail us now; for He giveth power to the faint, and to them who hath not might; He increases strength; those that wait upon the Lord shall run and not be weary and they shall walk and not faint."

When the report had been concluded and assigned to the committee, the name of Robert H. Johnson was placed in nomination for Grand Exalted Ruler. When further nominations were called for Brother Herbert Jones and Brother Leroy Johnson proceeded to withdraw their candidacy. On motion, Brother Robert H. Johnson was elected unanimously to the office of Grand Exalted Ruler for the ensuing term of two years and the motion was unanimously carried.

The report of the Grand Secretary, Judge William Hueston called attention to the action of the Grand Lodge authorizing a gift of $10,000.00 to the late Grand Exalted Ruler J. Finley Wilson in 1951. He stated that after the Grand Lodge he had called attention to the fact that a similar appropriation of this amount had been made in 1950. He approached the Grand Exalted Ruler J. Finley Wilson concerning this second payment and he was informed that he should wait awhile for the payment. In December of 1951 and again in January of 1952 he approached him about the matter and was informed on the later date that this sum should be kept until the next Grand Lodge and "he would tell the boys that he wanted it used for the John Brown Farm." The gift had not been paid prior to the death of Past Grand Exalted Ruler J. Finley Wilson. Whereupon there were those in the Lodge who thought that this constituted a debt which should be paid to his estate. Both the Grand Secretary and Past Grand Exalted Ruler T. Gillis Nutter, and also Past Exalted Ruler Austin Ficklin conferred on the matter and it was their agreement generally that the Grand Lodge would have to

Judge William C. Hueston, Grand Secretary, 1951-

pass a specific act donating this sum to the Wilson Estate and particularly to Mrs. Wilson since there was no act of the Grand Lodge authorizing the officers to pay the claim.

This opinion was supported by the legal evidences which were quoted that in order to be effectual as a gift, the action had to be fully executed by the Grand Lodge and for the reason that there was no consideration in this case, no action could develop to enforce the payment of the gift. No affirmative action by the Grand Lodge was taken on this proposal. However, the original proposal indicates the high regard in which Grand Exalted Ruler Wilson was held and the desire of the Grand Lodge to assist him in every way in taking care of the tremendous expenses which were associated with his continuing hospitalization and illness requiring the services of expensive specialists at hospitals.

Grand Secretary Hueston reported that there were during the year twenty-five new lodges organized and that there were eight reinstated lodges, one new council and one reinstated council, seven new herds, three reinstated herds, eight new civil liberties leagues and thousands of new memberships. When the report was completed, the rules were suspended and Brother William C. Hueston was re-elected to the office of General Secretary for the ensuing term.

The report of Grand Treasurer Perry B. Jackson paid tribute to J. Finley Wilson for the great work which he had done and praised Grand Exalted Ruler Robert H. Johnson, who had "carried on in the same fine tradition of the late J. Finley Wilson." He said further, "He is in every way worthy of the high office of Grand Exalted Ruler." One of the recommendations of the Grand Treasurer was that a Budget Committee be appointed to prepare a yearly budget. At the conclusion of this report, the motion was adopted for the re-election of Grand Treasurer Perry B. Jackson. This was accomplished by acclamation.

There were forty-eight scholarship students in colleges and universities in 1952, according to the report of the Grand Commissioner of Education, George W. Lee. The problem of illiteracy was still causing the department considerable concern, and to aid in its solution a five point program for illiterates was developed: (1) to learn to read the Bible; (2) to learn to read the Constitution; (3) to learn to write one's name; (4) to know how to vote; (5) to learn faith and pride in ourselves. He urged that a School of Fundamentals in Education should be set up in every Elk Lodge, with volunteer teachers and prepared lessons from the Office of the Grand Commissioner. The Grand Commissioner said that Brother G. W. C. Brown, of Virginia State College at

George W. Lee, Grand Commissioner of Education, 1915

Norfolk, the State Director of Virginia, had been working on this problem and that he had pursued graduate work in adult education at Columbia University. A bill known as the Reece-Kilgore Bill was introduced in Congress through the endeavors of Grand Commissioner Lee, Brother Brown, Congressman Reece, Senator Kilgore and others to appropriate funds to the United States Department of Education for a widespread attack on illiteracy. An advisory committee of persons interested in adult education was appointed.

Upon the basis of this plan, Grand Commissioner Lee declared, "We are beginning here in Atlantic City the second chapter in a book which Finley Wilson began more than a quarter of a century ago. The Little Napoleon of Elkdom made the first chapter of this book come true when he gave fraternalism a new meaning. With the echoes of his command rising like wind music through eternity we shall march on—we shall march on under the leadership of Bob Johnson and meet the guidance of the Eternal God who tempers the winds to the showing lamb and mindeth the fall of the sparrow." Brother Lee was re-elected by acclamation following the submission of his report.

The prophecy and fact that the new Grand Exalted Ruler, Robert H. Johnson, had given and would give the Grand Lodge, the lodges and temples an excellent administration was declared frequently during the Grand Lodge sessions. One of these declarations was made by Grand Legal Advisor Perry B. Howard who said, "Grand Exalted Ruler Johnson, like Grand Exalted Ruler Wilson, had been a reasonable, practical and hardworking official, always with the interest of the order at heart." He also added, "His sincerity of manner and bearing, his common sense approach to problems, his agreeable personality, his long experience as an executive of his great lodge have all combined to make his a most successful administration and make of him an experienced administrator and executive."

Similar sentiments were expressed by Grand Director of Civil Liberties Hobson R. Reynolds. After referring to the contributions of the late Grand Exalted Ruler J. Finley Wilson to the civil liberties program, Grand Director Reynolds praised the encouragement and leadership given by Grand Exalted Ruler Johnson to this program and his purpose to make the department "a real live working organization for the advancement of minority groups." Director Reynolds described cases taken to the courts by the lodges and the department, the fight to end segregation in the armed forces, the right to vote, segregation in Washington and local problems of the lodges. Expressions of loyalty and cooperative action as well as reports of the successful administration of their respective assignments were made by Grand Organizer Herbert E. Jones, Grand Director of Public Relations Charles P. McClane; Lieutenant General Henry Berth of the Antlered Guard; Grand Medical Director Carter L. Marshall; A. William Hill, Jr., Grand Director Junior Elks Department; the Charity Committee with R. H. Collins, Jr., as chairman; the Grand Trustees; the Commissioner of Transportation Albert A. Reading; the Shrine Commissioners: Joseph A. Brown, Ernest M. Thomas, Samuel D. Holsey and R. T. Robertson; the Grand Auditors: S. B. Mitchell, Henry St. Clair, James T. Copper; the Committee on Awards with Dr. S. A. Smith as chairman and the Committee on Appeals and Grievances with E. H. Copeland as chairman.

Resolutions were adopted expressing sincere regret over the passing of Grand Exalted Ruler J. Finley Wilson and Grand Daughter Ruler Elizabeth Ross Gordon; commendation of the work of Grand Exalted Ruler Robert H. Johnson who had carried forward his work with honor and distinction; the return of peace and the speedy end of the Korean War; approval of the United Nations; the termination of segregation; a wider use of men and women of color in our diplomatic service; the enforcement of civil rights legislation and the investigation of violations; adequate housing; elimination of segregated schools; termination of the filibuster in the United States Senate; and action concerning details of operation and administration of the Order.

An additional proof of the high regard for the administrative work of Grand Exalted Ruler Robert H. Johnson was given in the report adopted, unanimously by the Grand Lodge, of the Committee on Grand Lodge Officers and Departments. This report stated of the Grand Exalted Ruler, ''having examined carefully his report, we have no hesitancy in saying to you that we, the committee, are happy to say that our Grand Exalted Ruler has exemplified unusual administrative ability, qualifications and integrity.'' This was another of the tributes to the Grand Exalted Ruler's administration during the remainder of the year following the death of his predecessor, Grand Exalted Ruler J. Finley Wilson. In spite of the high esteem that was held for Grand Exalted Ruler Johnson, there was a general opinion in the Grand Lodge that a Grand Exalted Ruler's term of office should be reduced, and this was a reaction to the continuous long terms of Grand Exalted Ruler J. Finley Wilson. Action was approved that the Grand Exalted Ruler should not serve more than two consecutive full terms. Congressman William L. Dawson addressed the Grand Lodge, paid tribute to the Late Grand Exalted Ruler J. Finley Wilson, congratulated the Order on its new outlook for the future and expressed pride in being a member of the Order.

A first report to the Grand Lodge for the State Presidents' Council was made by Dr. H. W. Hunter of Cleveland, Ohio, who was also the first president of this council of state presidents. The various presidents were mutually helpful to one another through their exchange of ideas and programs. Through this cooperation, it was reported that great good would come to the local lodges, the district councils and the state associations.

Dr. H. W. Hunter, President of the State Presidents' Council

The Grand Temple's Shrine representatives under the leadership of Daughter Bertha McKanlass, Grand Directress of the Shrine Department, reported $13,305.50, from Gemsco $3,540.00 and from the Grand Secretary, $9,765.60 which had been received from the Temples. The fraternal Greetings Committee of the Grand Temple visited the Grand Lodge including Daughter Lucille Ellett, Grand Vice Daughter Ruler; Daughter Isabelle Fultz-Hyder, Past Grand Daughter Ruler Secretary of Arts and Crafts, who brought greetings from the Grand Temple; Daughter Willa B. Lucas, Grand Temple Trustee; Daughter Gertrude S. Holland, National President of Cap and Gown Club; Daughter Barker Terry, District Regional Organizer of Civil Liberties; Daughter Lillian Archer, District Deputy of Nassau, Bahamas; Daughter Mary Ingraham, Chairman of Delegation of Nassau, Bahamas; Past Grand Daughter Rulers Maggie Hill, Margaret K. Kelson, Harriet D. Jackson, Daughter Violet R. Green, Grand Assistant Escort; and Grand Trustees Daughters Edith Davis and Nellie Bees. Magnificent work had been accomplished by the Daughters under the able leadership of Grand Daughter Ruler Nettie Carter Jackson and her associates. Mrs.

DT. REABA A. JEFFERSON, Grand Assistant Daughter Ruler

DT. ETHEL CHARLESTON, Grand Directress, Educational Department

DT. PEARL BROWN, Grand Daughter Treasurer

DT. REITA CORNELL, Grand Assistant Daughter Ruler

Leah F. Wilson, widow of Past Grand Exalted Ruler Wilson presented the Grand Lodge with a report of the activities of the Late Grand Exalted Ruler to the period of his passing, February 19, 1952.

The officers for the period, 1952-1953, were as follows: Robert H. Johnson, Grand Exalted Ruler, Philadelphia, Pennsylvania; William C. Hueston, Grand Secretary, Washington, D. C.; James T. Copper, Assistant General Secretary, Chicago, Illinois; Harry H. Eddicks, Grand Recorder, Philadelpha, Pennsylvania; Perry B. Jackson, Grand Treasurer, Cleveland, Ohio; B. V. Gregory, Grand Esteemed Leading Knight, Detroit, Michigan; Harvey L. Harris, Grand Esteemed Loyal Knight, Mt. Vernon, New York; K. P. Battles, Grand Esteemed Lecturing Knight, Rocky Mount, North Carolina; L. W. Williams, Grand Tiler, Valdosta, Georgia; Benjamin T. Butler, Grand Inner Guard, Brooklyn, New York; Henry W. Davis, Grand Esquire, Los Angeles, California; Perry W. Howard, Grand Legal Advisor, Washington, D. C.; Grand Trustees: John T. Freeman, Philadelphia, Pennsylvania; Charles A. Oliver, Annapolis, Maryland; C. Sylvester Jackson, Harrisburg, Pennsylvania; J. F. Simmons, Norfolk, Virginia; Lloyd Randolph, Baltimore, Maryland; Grand Auditors Samuel B. Mitchell, New York, N. Y., Harry St. Clair, Chicago, Illinois and J. B. Yearwood, New York, N. Y.; George W. Lee, Commissioner of Education, Memphis, Tenn.; Hobson R. Reynolds, Director of Civil Liberties, Philadelpha, Pa.; R. H. Collins Lee, Grand Chaplain, Chicago, Ill.; W. Franklin Hoxter, Grand Director of Music, Philadelphia, Pennsylvania; Lionel Hampton, Grand Bandmaster, New York, N. Y.; George W. Hyder, Assistant Grand Bandmaster, Philadelphia, Pennsylvania; A. William Hill, Jr., Director of Junior Elks, Lancaster, Pennsylvania; Charles P. McClane, Director of Public Relations, Steelton, Pennsylvania; Milton S. J. Wright, Director of Economics, Wilberforce, Ohio; John Minkins, Grand Reporter, Providence, Rhode Island; Ike Styker, Grand Organist, Princeton, New Jersey; Albert A. Reading, Commissioner of Transportation, Chester, Pennsylvania; Paul K. Holt, Grand Historian, Detroit, Michigan; Herbert E. Jones, Grand Organizer, Washington, D. C.; Albert A. Bethume, Southern States and Bahamas, Daytona Beach, Florida; Douglas Simpson, Western States, San Francisco, California; Henry Berth, Lt. General Antlered Guard, Philadelphia, Pennsylvania; Charles Donaway, Major General Antlered Guard, Atlantic City, New Jersey; J. B. Martin, Director of Athletics, Chicago, Illinois; James H. Fultz, Director Bathing Beauty Contest, Newark, New Jersey; Simpson A. Smith, Director of Awards, Huntington, West Virginia.

Dt. Lucille Ellett, Grand Vice Daughter Ruler

Dt. Isabella Fultz-Hyder, Past Grand Daughter Ruler; Secretary of Arts and Crafts

Dt. Bertha McKanlass, Grand Directress of the Shrine

Dt. Alice Nichols, Grand Directress of Civil Liberties

In the wake of the Grand Lodge, there were thankgsgivings, mortgage burnings, celebrations, state associations, parades, birthday parties, public meetings sponsoring the programs of the Grand Lodge and the regular sessions of the subordinate lodges. On July 4, 1953, a large and enthusiastic crowd assembled at the National Shrine, the John Brown Farm, Harper's Ferry, West Virginia. The program was under the direction of Brother Charles P. McClane, Director of Public Relations and Grand Commissioner of the John Brown Shrine. Among the speakers were Robert H. Johnson, Grand Exalted Ruler; Perry W. Howard, Grand Legal Advisor; Herbert Jones, Grand Organizer; K. P. Battle, Grand Esteemed Lecturing Knight; Dr. Adolphus Anderson, State President of Pennsylvania; Oscar Price, District Deputy Grand Exalted Ruler of Pennsylvania; Daughter Nettie Carter Jackson, Grand Daughter Ruler; Daughter Anna Perrine, Grand Directress of Athletics; and Daughter Isabelle Fultz-Hyder, Secretary of Arts and Crafts.

A feature of the program of the Department of Education approved by Grand Exalted Ruler Johnson, was the conduct of a night school for illiterates in Memphis, Tennessee. Grand Commissioner of Education George Lee had requested that night schools be set up in each lodge and temple to teach people in their communities to read and write. The Memphis school was to be a model and an experiment. Newspaper and radio announcements were used. On February 1, 1953, the classes started. The enrollment was so large that the classes had to be held not only at the Elk's Rest but also at the Atlanta Life Insurance Company and the Union Protective Assurance Company. There were five volunteer teachers for these classes. The experiment showed that the night school program was workable. Brother Lee said that "what is being done in Memphis can be done in every city where there is an Elk Lodge or Temple."

The Memphis Press Scimitar stated, "Memphis Negro Elks have opened a night school for adult Negroes. The first sessions this week were swamped. The four teachers were not enough. The aim of the school is to reduce illiteracy in the adult Negro population. The Elks hope suitable quarters, such as Booker T. Washington High School, may be obtained. The city will never have a more sensible request for use of city property. We hope the city readily consents and offers full cooperation in this worthy project."

As Commissioner Lee said, this was more than a program of wiping out illiteracy. As he said, it was "to teach Negro-Americans how to live sane, healthy lives in decent homes, how to find and hold occupations that will enable them to enjoy the finest

James T. Copper, Assistant Grand Secretary

Bertram V. Gregory, Grand Esteemed Leading Knight

Harvey L. Harris, Grand Esteemed Loyal Knight

K. P. Battle, Grand Esteemed Lecturing Knight

things of life, and how to participate in the community intelligently as voting citizens.''

All of this was to be launched under the leadership of Grand Exalted Ruler Johnson. The genius of ''Bob'' Johnson for leadership in the situations which faced him in Elkdom was again demonstrated in the Grand Lodge sessions of 1953. This Grand Lodge assembled in its furthest southern convention city, Atlanta, Georgia, August 22-28, 1953. There were various predictions about what would happen to the Brothers and Daughters who would come together for this Grand Lodge in Georgia. There were the critics who alleged that the conduct and decorum of Negro Elks would be such that race relations would be affected by convention activities. Others thought that there would be undesirable reactions of various types from this convention, which would affect the status of the Negro.

All of these fears proved to be groundless. The Fifty-fourth Annual Meeting of the Grand Lodge of the Improved Benevolent and Protective Order of Elks of the World at Atlanta, Georgia, August 22-28, 1953, was one of the best attended and organized of recent periods. Directions were given by Grand Exalted Ruler Johnson concerning undesirable types of activity and such guidance was given that the results were most favorable for the Order. Newspapers and public opinion were favorable in their attitudes and commendatory in their expressions from the opening to the closing periods.

The sessions preliminary to the Grand Lodge Business sessions were conducted with the usual success. With Grand Commissioner George W. Lee presiding, the Educational Congress got under way. The main address was given on adult education by Dr. G. W. C. Brown, Assistant Grand Commissioner of Education. The Baccalaureate Service convened at Big Bethel A.M.E. Church with Grand Exalted Ruler Johnson presenting the Grand Lodge officers and the Grand Daughter Ruler who in turn presented the Grand Temple officers. The sermon was delivered by Rev. Blair T. Hunt of Memphis, Tennessee, Principal of the Booker T. Washington High School who used the subject, ''All God's Children Got Wings.''

The Grand Exalted Ruler addressed the delegates sounding a spiritual note when he said, ''Never before have our people had greater need for Divine guidance in making decisions which they now face. We need spiritual aid, not only in our relations with other nations, but also in our domestic affairs. We need to get closer to God. . . . As your Grand Exalted Ruler, I am calling on you to lead the way in your community throughout the country in bringing together all elements of our population to go to Church. . . . The Elks can render no greater service than to contribute the vast resources of its manpower to this movement to make religion the guiding factor in our daily decisions."

The graduation exercise of the Purple Cross Nurses was directed by Dr. Carter Marshall and Daughter Anna B. Jones. The Honorable Perry B. Jackson, Grand Treasurer, was the principal speaker for the occasion. The Shrine service under Brother Charles P. McClane, the Memorial Service with Grand Exalted Ruler Johnson and Grand Daughter Ruler Nettie Carter Jackson presiding, the Annual Meeting of the National Cap and Gown Club under Daughter Gertrude Holland, the Annual Champion of Human Rights Breakfast with Grand Director of Civil Liberties Hobson R. Reynolds presiding, the National Oratorical Contest with Grand Commissioner of Education George W. Lee presiding were largely attended and the enthusiasm was high at each of these sessions.

A highlight of these sessions was the presentation of the Lovejoy Medal at a meeting of the Department of Civil Liberties under the direction of Grand Director Reynolds and Grand Directress of Civil Liberties Daughter Alice Nichols. Chairman Reynolds introduced the Grand Exalted Ruler to present to Dr. Mary McLeod Bethune, the fourth annual Lovejoy Medal Award. Following a fitting address, Grand Exalted Ruler Johnson presented the medal. A response of appreciation was made by Dr. Bethune who praised the Order for its contributions to education, health, civil liberties and the advancement of the status of the people.

The Grand Lodge business session was called to order by the Honorable Robert H. Johnson, Grand Exalted Ruler. There was then the singing of the National Anthem followed by the Ritualistic Ceremonies. The final report of the Committee on Credentials showed that there were present thirty-three Grand Lodge officers, twenty-nine Past Grand Exalted Rulers, two hundred and forty-six district and state deputies, seven hundred and fifty-one delegates from lodges, sixty-three Past Exalted Rulers Councils and twenty-four state association representatives, making a total delegated session of one thousand one hundred and forty-six.

A new note in the annual addresses of Grand Exalted Rulers was struck in the report of Grand Exalted Ruler Robert H. Johnson. He directed attention to three words which were interwoven throughout parts of his address. These words were courage, ideals and integrity. They were to be thought of in terms of American citizenship and their relationships to one another. He stated that this was no time for mere survival but a period for activity in terms of these qualities. A large number of cases had been adjudicated by him and a considerable number of dispensations were granted. He had traveled extensively attending meetings and elections throughout the nation. State association conventions saw him present, mortgage burnings and thanksgiving occasions witnessed his presence. Sixteen new lodges had been instituted and four had been reinstated. There were seventeen new herds, five reinstated herds, four new civil liberties leagues and one reinstated league.

His recommendations were for the establishment of the Department of Veterans Affairs with the appointment of a Grand Commissioner by the Grand Exalted Ruler, a permanent Police Department to supervise the National Conventions, a committee to consolidate the Junior Herd and the Athletic Department and to work out a youth program, and a Committee on Budget to be appointed to work out a program for submission to a later Grand Lodge. The report was closed by the Grand Exalted Ruler on a note of patriotism and loyalty to American principles, on the part of its citizens. The appeal became very personal when the Grand Exalted Ruler said, "I want each of you to help me demonstrate how much we can do to preserve for our children the heritage that has been handed down to us by our forefathers." This appeal referred both to Elkdom and to the American heritage. The Grand Exalted Ruler was determined to remain loyal to the founding fathers of the Improved Benevolent and Protective Order of Elks of the World and to carry it forward. At the conclusion of the report the Grand Lodge went on record as endorsing the program of the Grand Exalted Ruler as outlined by him and pledging full cooperation.

The Grand Secretary's report rendered by Brother William C. Hueston described the visits which he had made to various parts of Elkdom in company with the Grand Exalted Ruler and the Grand Commissioner of Civil Liberties together with Brother Herbert Jones, the Grand Organizer. He said that this swing through the country had taught them "that Elkdom today is in the best condition it has known since the establishment of the State Associations." He said further that he had the "greatest satisfaction to report that in both membership and financial strength our great Order is showing a sound and vigorous growth which is a tribute to our Brothers and Daughters of the Improved Benevolent and Protective Order of Elks of the World throughout the length and breadth of this country and the islands of the sea in which this Order has taken root." The *Washington Eagle* continued to be the fraternal channel through which news was distributed to the Order and was its official organ. The report showed that there were total general fund receipts of $118,299.46 and total general fund expenditures during the year of $104,210.08, leaving a balance in the general fund, as of July 31, 1953, of $14,098.38. The net worth statement showed the following:

Cost	$169,893.19
United States Government Bonds	100,000.00
Shrine Building, New York	137,000.00
Cost, John Brown Farm	30,000.00
John Brown Farm Improvement	30,000.00
John Brown Farm Equipment	5,500.00
Other real estate	1,000.00
Furniture and fixtures, inventory of supplies, etc.	7,654.75
Total	$490,848.94

The recommendations included an increase in the Grand Lodge per capita tax to take care of the increased expenditures voted by the Grand Lodge, the sale of the New York property owned by the Grand Lodge at the first opportunity provided that there could be received what had been paid for it; and the reason for this sale was that the Charter of the Grand Lodge does not permit it to hold property for profit.

The Grand Treasurer, Perry B. Jackson, made a report which gave similar figures to those of the Grand Secretary. One of the recommendations which he stressed again as last year, was the approval of the creation of a Budget Committee. At the conclusion of both reports, Grand Secretary William C. Hueston and Grand Treasurer Perry B. Jackson were re-elected by acclamation to succeed themselves in their respective offices with the Grand Esquire casting the ballot of the convention.

The Grand Legal Adviser, Perry W. Howard, described the good administration of Grand Exalted Ruler Johnson in solving one of the difficult cases through his patience and tact and in placing the Puget Sound Lodge on a sound footing with peace reigning once more. He also referred to the effort on the part of the group in Chicago to set up a rival Grand Lodge. He said that the matter was being taken care of under the Supreme Court decision in the case at Norfolk in which the Supreme Court made it clear in a very lucid decision that the Grand Lodge of The Improved Benevolent and Protective Order of Elks of the World had the exclusive right to the name "Elks," wherever Negroes sought to be Elks. In this case in Chicago the correspondence and citations to the cases were not sufficient. It was necessary for the Grand Legal Adviser to go into the United States District Court of Illinois and obtain a writ of injunction against the group enjoining them from using the word Elks and ordering them dissolved. He said that from the legal and judical point of view the Grand Lodge was in better shape than it had been for many years and assured them that he was continuing to serve to his best ability.

The Grand Commissioner of Education, George W. Lee, gave his annual report showing the philosophy on which the department had been working and that he had been dealing with two of the weaknesses of the Negro, namely the influence of segregation and the mis-education of the poor school system in certain areas and these two weaknesses were being corrected through the program of adult education. One of the significant sentences in his report stated that "long after F.E.P.C. has been written into the law, long after the Supreme Court has nullified segregated school houses in the United States, we will still have to educate Jim Crow out of our own minds." He reported on the Adult Education School in Memphis, Tennessee, and the conduct of schools and programs in various areas of the nation under the individual grand lodges. He said that his assistant, Brother G. W. C. Brown had just finished a study project under the title "How to Find and Train Volunteers to Teach Illiterates," and that this had been carried on in part through the cooperation of the Department of Education. The scholarships granted to students were listed in the school to which they were to go and the assistance given to a young man who sought to enter the University of Tennessee was described and the proposal for another to enter the University of Georgia was mentioned. Brother Lee was re-elected by acclamation at the conclusion of his report.

The Grand Director of the Department of Civil Liberties called attention to the fact that the Grand Lodge was meeting in the South. Said he, "We are meeting here in Atlanta for the first time in the history of our Order—in the deep South. Traveling here from all parts of the country covering many many thousands of miles we have had an opportunity to think and plan for our future. I am glad we are meeting in the deep South because it is from here many of us started and it is my opinion if the race problem in America is to be solved at all it must be solved in the South as well as elsewhere. So, we have a great job to do while here and let us attack our problem with sincerity." Civil rights cases in several communities were investigated by this department, in Detroit, Michigan: Springfield, Illinois; Cario, Illinois, and the state of Florida. North and South individual cases had been followed and carried into court by the department. Such conditions as bias in employment, school integration, railroad discrimination, segregation in Washington were also discussed.

One of the important sections of the report dealt with the trip taken by Grand Commissioner Hobson Reynolds to Germany and other countries in Europe in order to survey the development of integration in the Armed Forces. His attention had been called, he stated, at an earlier period to the condition of "Brown Babies" in Germany. He said that statistics showed that there were approximately no less than 95,000 illegitimate children by occupational troops in Germany and that less than 10,000 were colored boys and girls. Their situation was regarded as unfortunate and he thought that some steps should be taken to improve their status. He suggested that the Elks would raise a fund in order to make some definite contribution for the solution of the problem and that perhaps some adoptions of the children could be made here in the United States. The recommendation of the reappointment of Brother Hobson R. Reynolds to succeed himself as Grand Director of Civil Liberties was approved by the Grand Lodge.

Other reports showing considerable progress were made by Henry Berth, Grand Lt. General of the Antlered Guard; Albert A. Reading, Grand Commissioner of Transportation; Milton S. J. Wright, Grand Director of Economics who stated that Brother Crawford McGerald, Jr., had been commissioned by the Grand Exalted Ruler as Secretary of the department. He stated in his report that following a conference with the Grand Exalted Ruler the important project to the Department of Economics was the proposed Elks Foundation. The details of the project were presented to a special committee of Grand Lodge officers which met in Atlanta in January 1953. A Business and Economic Clinic Exhibit was held during the convention. He also proposed as had been done through the years the development of a central cooperating purchasing program for Elks' uniforms and regalia.

Reports showing progress came from Grand Medical Director of the Health Department and Health Commission Carter L. Marshall with Dr. Roscoe C. Brown as Executive Secretary; The Grand Director of Music W. Franklin Hoxter; the Grand Trustees; Brother Peter Dillard, the Grand Director of Gold; William Hill, Jr., Grand Director of Junior Elks; Trezzvant W. Anderson, Chairman of the Grand Lodge Press Committee; Dr. Simpson Smith, Chairman of the Awards and Trophy Committee. The Grand Organizer Herbert E. Jones described the presentation of prizes to the lodges, the J. Finley Wilson Plaque for one hundred or more members, the J. E. Kelley Plaque for fifty or more members and the Marcus Wheatland Plaque for twenty-five or more members. He said that his plan for the next

ALBERT A. READING, Grand Commissioner of Transportation

J. B. YEARWOOD, Grand Auditor

DR. MILTON S. J. WRIGHT, Director of Economics

DR. ROSCOE C. BROWN, Executive Secretary, Health Commission

year was an increase in membership to 10,000 new members. The program was to be known as the Memorial Membership Drive.

Charles P. McClane, Grand Commissioner of Public Relations reported that so far as public relations were concerned this was evidently one of the most prosperous years in the history of the Order. He said that the Grand Exalted Ruler had given rare leadership and manifested vision in working out the program for the Order. He described the progress in the development of the national Shrine and stated that the Pennsylvania State Association had chosen its cabin location and was near ready to break ground and that the Grand Daughter Ruler Nettie Carter Jackson and Daughter Bertha McKanlass Grand Directress of the Shrine were working on the details for a juvenile recreation room.

CHARLES P. McCLANE, Grand Director of Public Relations

Commissioner of Education George W. Lee described the plan for an education department dinner meeting to be held on February 1, 1954, at Howard University where the winner of the National Oratorical Contest would be presented to the President of the United States. He regarded this as a history making event in the field of education and it would be known as National Education for Citizenship Day.

A large number of resolutions were adopted concerning national and international affairs directing the attention of the membership of the lodges and temples to liberal policies and practices between peoples commending the President of the United States and Congress upon these actions which manifested the development of democratic principles.

Proposals were adopted to permit the establishment of new Elk lodges in any city with a population of 10,000; the creation of a Department of Veteran Activities, the director to be appointed by the Grand Exalted Ruler; the appointment of such police assistance from among the members of the Order as the occasion may justify; the amendment of the constitution to permit the appointment by the Grand Exalted Ruler of an Assistant Grand Secretary; the increase of Subordinate Lodge taxes; that twenty-five per cent of all monies turned in by the Antlered Guard be allocated to the use of the department; the deferment until the Mid-winter Conference of a proposal to establish the J. Finley Wilson Memorial Foundation as a non-profit corporation for the support of the programs of the Order, the Grand

Entrance to John Brown Farm, National Shrine, I.B.P.O.E. of W.

Exalted Ruler, Robert H. Johnson to be the director of the foundation to serve a life term.

As to the John Brown Farm, the Grand Auditors stated that its slow development had been giving them some concern and that the state associations and lodges should begin their parts of the program for the erection of bungalows and of conducting excursions and attending celebrations on special days. After Walter White had spoken to the Grand Lodge, Grand Commissioner Reynolds said that he hoped that it would be possible for the N.A.A.C.P. and the Department of Civil Liberties in the future to work in close unison as their combined efforts would be more effective in achieving the desired goal. A motion prevailed that the Director of Civil Liberties was authorized to combine the efforts of his department with the N.A.A.C.P., and work jointly in all matters concerning the interests of the group.

The list of elected and appointed officers included the following: Robert H. Johnson, Grand Exalted Ruler, Philadelphia, Pennsylvania; B. V. Gregory, Grand Esteemed Leading Knight, Detroit, Michigan; Harvey L. Harris, Grand Esteemed Loyal Knight, Mt. Vernon, New York; K. P. Battle, Grand Esteemed Lecturing Knight, Rocky Mount, North Carolina; William C. Hueston, Grand Secretary, Washington, D. C.; James T. Copper, Assistant Grand Secretary, Chicago, Illinois; Harvey D. Eddicks, Grand Recorder; Perry B. Jackson, Grand Treasurer, Cleveland, Ohio; Herbert Fernanders, Grand Tiler, New Haven, Connecticut; Benjamin T. Butler, Jr., Grand Inner Guard, Brooklyn, New York; Henry W. Davis, Grand Esquire, Los Angeles, California; Perry W. Howard, Grand Legal Advisor; Hobson R. Reynolds, Grand Commissioner of Civil Liberties, Philadelphia, Pennsylvania, George W. Lee, Grand Commissioner of Education, Memphis, Tennessee; Charles P. McClane, Director of Public Relations, Steelton, Pennsylvania; Milton S. J. Wright, Grand Director of Economics, Wilberforce, Ohio; A. W. Hill, Grand Director of Junior Elks, Lancaster, Pennsylvania; John Minkins, Grand Lodge Reporter, Providence, R. I.; S. R. Houchins, Grand Master Social Sessions, Norfolk, Virginia; Dr. Carter L. Marshall, Grand Medical Director, New Haven, Connecticut; Dr. Adolphus W. Anderson, Grand Director of Veterans Affairs, Philadelphia, Pennsylvania; Dr. Roscoe C. Brown, Executive Secretary of Health Commission, Washington, D. C.; Captain Milton Smith, Police Commission, Philadelphia, Pennsylvania; Rev. R. H. Collins Lee, Grand Chaplain, Chicago, Illinois; Ike Styker, Grand Organist, Princeton, New Jersey: Rev. Charles W. Peters, Grand Historian, Atlanta, Georgia; Lionel Hampton, Grand Bandmaster, New York, N. Y.; Grand Trustees: John T. Freeman, C. Sylvester Jackson, Joseph F. Simmons, Lloyd Randolph and L. W. Williams; Grand Auditors: Henry St. Clair, Samuel B. Mitchell and J. B. Yearwood; William H. Walker, Grand Traveling Auditor, Washington, D. C.; Lloyd O. Garriest, Grand Commissioner of Transportation, Philadelphia, Pennsylvania; J. B. Martin, Grand Director of Athletics, Chicago, Illinois; Charles Donoway, Major-General, Atlantic City, New Jersey; James H. Fultz, Grand Director, Bathing Beauty Contest, Newark, New Jersey.

An important program adopted at this Grand Lodge was the creation of the Department of Veteran Affairs. This department was the realization of one of the dreams of Grand Exalted Ruler Robert H. Johnson, who was a veteran of World War I, and

Henry W. Davis, Grand Esquire

S. R. Houchins, Grand Master of Social Sessions

Herbert C. Fernanders, Grand Tiler

Henry St. Clair, Grand Auditor

knew from personal experience of the problems of veterans. He had proposed, at the Grand Lodge of 1927, that a Legion of Honor be established composed of ex-service men. He appointed Dr. Adolphus W. Anderson of Philadelphia as Grand Commissioner of Veteran Affairs. Dr. Anderson had been active in veteran affairs, having served since World War I as an accredited service officer and on committees of the Pennsylvania Veterans of Foreign Wars and the Veterans of Foreign Wars of the United States. Additional staff was appointed, consisting of George L. Holland, an assistant to the United States Administrator of Veteran Affairs; Albert L. Dunlap, specialist in employment and American Legion official; Dennis C. White, National Claims officer; James McDaniels, National Rehabilitation officer; Dr. Vernon Collins, National Medical Consultant; Thomas M. Dent, National Insurance officer and Dr. Franklin Potter, National Field officer. Through the work of the officials, hundreds of claims were successfully adjudicated, scores of flags were presented and thousands of cigarettes were sent to hospitalized veterans.

The plans for the National Citizenship Dinner began to materialize with definite steps in January, 1954. Commissioner Lee stated that it would be "a day in which Grand Exalted Ruler Robert H. Johnson and our Department of Education will write another chapter in the book which J. Finley Wilson and Judge W. C. Hueston began nearly one half a century ago." The winner of the oratorical contest of 1953, Huey Shepherd, would present a bound copy of his speech on "The Constitution and the Negro" to President Eisenhower. Under the caption "Mr. Shepherd goes to Washington," the celebration began to take form. It was planned to take place on February 1, the date on which President Lincoln had signed the bill authorizing the Thirteenth Amendment adopted by Congress the previous day, January 31, 1865. The Grand Exalted Ruler gave his full support to the development of this program.

The travels of Grand Exalted Ruler Johnson about the country in response to invitations from the lodges and the temples were summarized by him in a column in the *Washington Eagle* under the caption, "Rolling with the Grand." Day by day accounts of his contacts were read with great interest by members of the Order, as the Grand Exalted Ruler remained constantly on the move to state association meetings, subordinate lodge sessions and to celebrations, breakfasts, luncheons, dinners and special occasions. Aside from the direct descriptions, there were comments from others. Dr. A. W. Anderson, President of the Pennsylvania Association and Grand Commissioner of the De-

Lloyd Randolph, Grand Trustee

Harry H. Eddicks, Grand Recorder

William H. Walker, Grand Traveling Deputy

Dr. Adolphus W. Anderson, Grand Director Veteran Affairs

partment of Veterans Affairs, wrote in a section "Veterans Bandwagon:" "The Grand Exalted Ruler has been constantly on the move covering the various state conventions; beginning in Florida and continuing up until the other day, he presided at the Ohio State Convention at Youngstown." The honor accorded the Grand Exalted Ruler and Mrs. Johnson in New York City was one of the great demonstrations in Elk history.

These messages of the Grand Exalted Ruler were not only descriptions of his travels and honors received but there were notes of administrative admonition and sound advice which were sounded. In one of these, he advised that the Exalted Rulers and Daughter Rulers give attention to the development of "harmonious, eventful and satisfactory administration," to lay the ground work for their meetings, to select their committees carefully and to realize that the success of the Order depends on the conduct of the various subordinate lodges and temples. He called attention to the 1954 Revision of the Laws which were issued on March 1, and the need for the study of them. These expressions of advice were of value coming from the Grand Exalted Ruler and they demonstrated his interest in good administration for Elkdom. In this same spirit, Grand Secretary Hueston called for a solid growth in 1954, awareness of every move that means progress and readiness to throw weight intelligently behind it, for the building for the future of the Order.

With the approval of the Grand Exalted Ruler, Grand Organizer Herbert E. Jones announced a membership drive for 1954 honoring the three Grand Masters, T. Gillis Nutter, Armond W. Scott and George W. F. McMechen. This announcement stated, "adding another milestone in his inspirational leadership in the rise of Elkdom, Robert H. Johnson, Grand Exalted Ruler, cites the three living Past Grand Exalted Rulers for their worthy contributions to this great organization. This is the year of progress, 1954."

The night of February 1, witnessed the assembly at Howard University of five hundred guests and leaders of Elkdom under the leadership of Grand Exalted Ruler Johnson and Grand Daughter Ruler Nettie Carter Jackson. At the speakers table, there were Joseph W. Martin, Speaker of the House of Representatives, Congressman M. Carroll Reese of Tennessee, Grand Secretary Hueston, Grand Commissioner George W. Lee, Dr. Mordecai W. Johnson and others. Huey Shepherd presented his oration to President Eisenhower at the White House and was heartily congratulated by him. Grand Exalted Ruler Johnson said that Grand Commissioner Lee was "to be complimented on his foresight in establishing this day, which we intend to celebrate annually.'' Grand Commissioner Lee announced that in 1954 the educational program would be expanded to include not only scholarships, oratorical contests and illiteracy, but also education in citizenship to include registration and voting.

The Mid-Year Conference of Grand Lodge and Grand Temple Officers had assembled on January 28-30, 1954 with Grand Exalted Ruler, Brother Robert H. Johnson presiding. Reports were presented from the Grand Officers of the Grand Lodge and the Grand Temple. Panel discussions were held at a later period to stimulate the work of the departments. Discussions were held concerning the John Brown Memorial Foundation and reference was had especially to a rural health program with a mobile unit under the direction of the Grand Medical Director Dr. Carter Marshall. Adult Education occupied another part of the session, together with the Regalia Project and the Economics Program. The Grand Exalted Ruler in reporting the history project stated, ''The history of the I.B.P.O.E. of W., was submitted by Dr. Charles Wesley, who is a brother Elk, educator and one of America's outstanding orators. As we have never had a complete history written for a number of years, I, as Grand Exalted Ruler of the I.B.P.O.E. of W., by the power vested in me, have authorized a committee to work with Brother Wesley to bring our history up to date from 1898 to 1953.'' Grand Lodge committees were appointed by the Grand Exalted Ruler for the 1954 session.

Several honors came to Grand Exalted Ruler Johnson. One of these was the appointment by President Eisenhower to the National Conference on Highway Safety which he attended, February 16-20. Another honor was the award of the honorary degree of Doctor of Laws on March 17, 1954 by Bethune-Cookman College, Daytona Beach, Florida. He was honored along with Jackie Robinson of the Brooklyn Dodgers and Rev. Chester McCoughlin of the Methodist Church. These awards were evidences of the high esteem in which the Grand Exalted Ruler was held by Elks and by educators. By June, 1950, all states had unanimously endorsed the Grand Exalted Ruler with many citations of commendations concerning his administration.

The Grand Exalted Ruler was fulfilling the duties of citizenship in his native state during this period and was accorded a high place of leadership. He was chosen as Chairman of the Negro Division of the Pennsylvania Republican State Committee. He had been a member of the Republican Executive Committee of the 30th Ward in Philadelphia for thirty years and for fourteen years he had been the chairman of this committee. During the campaign of 1954, he urged all citizens to vote and appealed "to all people to recognize the great administration under President Eisenhower's leadership that we have enjoyed particularly as a race. Not since the Civil War have Negroes received the opportunity to become free in the world of education. This equals a second emancipation."

There were members of the Order who were active in the councils of the national government as well as their state governments. They were prominent in the field of Negro leadership in politics and civic life. Among these were such prominent figures as Representative Adam Clayton Powell, Representative William L. Dawson and Representative Charles C. Diggs, Jr., the three Negro Representatives in the House of Representatives. All three of these men were members of the Improved Benevolent and Protective Order of Elks of the World. They had come up through their local lodges and had participated in the Grand Lodge Sessions. They had delivered addresses to the Grand Lodges and had manifested their loyalties to the principles of the Order. In turn, they were supported by their brothers.

Representative Adam Clayton Powell had served over the years as the popular and talented minister of the Abyssinian Baptist Church in New York City, which was the largest church for Negroes in this city. He had been a leader in community welfare work and a member of the New York City Council. Since becoming a member of the House of Representatives, these activities by Representative Powell had reached national proportions. His foreign travels have given him additional background materials on the world's problem of the color line. His determination to attend the Asian-African Conference in Indonesia in 1955 was another manifestation of his continuing interest in improvements in the status of the black and brown peoples in the Twentieth Century.

Another outstanding example of the leadership of an Elk in the councils of the United States Government was the Congressman from Illinois, Honorable William L. Dawson. He was recognized as a top American statesman and politician. He was the first Negro to head a regular congressional committee when he became Chairman of the Government Operations Committee. He served also as Vice-chairman of the Democratic National Committee.

A third member of this trio, Honorable Charles C. Diggs, Jr., of Detroit, Michigan, was the first Negro to represent the state of Michgan in the United States Congress. He was an active Elk and served as its State Director of Civil Liberties. He was in attendance at the Grand Lodge of 1954, just prior to his successful campaign for Congress. He was devoutly loyal to his Elk lodge and his state association.

Among the State Representatives who were active Elks were two who were making notable contributions in 1954 to political life. They were Brothers Truly Hatchett and Harry Cole who were the first Negroes to hold membership in the legislature of Maryland. This accomplishment was the more significant because of its border state location and the dominance of Southern traditions of Negro inferiority among its citizens.

These individual leaders in politics were sources of great strength to the Order, whose membership included large numbers of the Negro population, the learned, the unlearned, the proud, the humble, the men and women of competent means and those with less of the world's goods. There were others of Elk origins who were named and appointed to political offices in national, state and city governments. These individual leaders such as Dawson, Powell, Diggs, and many others were made possible by the activity, interest, and loyal support of the Elk membership. Their participation with many thousands of others in political activities led to the election of representative leaders from their number to Congress, state legislature and city councils. The successes of their representatives gave a feeling of security and of belonging to their followers and supporters, and their appearances were received with hearty welcomes by their brothers and sisters in Elkdom.

Education continued to be one of the goals of the I.B.P.O.E. of W. The project of the Curtis Candy Company to give seven scholarships of $1,000 each to boys or girls in each of seven regions had been approved. The sale of candy was to be promoted by the lodges and temples and the profits were to be divided between the Department of Education and the local lodge or temple. In May, 1954, there were fifty-six students on Elk scholarships in the universities and colleges of the nation. The first summer session of the National Workshop for Training Adult Leaders and Teachers was held at Camp Young, Norfolk, Virginia, June 14-24. This project was under the co-sponsorship of the I.B.P.O.E. of W., and the Division of Adult Education of the Norfolk Division of Virginia State College.

The United States Supreme Court Decision on May 17, 1954, was an occasion for calm rejoicing among Elks and Daughters. They had been fighting segregation in all its forms and among these was segregation by race in the public schools. They had been contributing their funds and their representatives had been taking the initiative and cooperating with the officials of the N.A.A.C.P., in its campaign to end segregation. *The Washington*

Eagle stated, "The N.A.A.C.P. is to be congratulated and other groups who helped. The Elks shared as they stood by through our Grand Lodge and subordinate lodges under the leadership of our Grand Exalted Ruler Robert H. Johnson." Elks were proud also of their Thurgood Marshall, who was called by a Federal Judge, "our greatest civil rights lawyer." He was both a loyal Elk and one of the most important leaders of his day in the fight against racial discrimination. His addresses and relationships with the Elk's Civil Liberties Commission and with Negro Elks were stimulating and influential in their fight for full citizenship as Americans. This victory against school segregation was one of the successful steps in the march toward this goal. Perry W. Howard, Grand Legal Adviser observed that when he heard the news of the decision he was "irresistably driven to recall that no agency, no institution, no individual has ever expounded the question of Civil Rights and the adherence to our Federal Constitution than the oratorical contests of the I.B.P.O.E. of W., with the exception of the N.A.A.C.P., which is an institution for that purpose." He stressed the educational contributions of his friend, Bill Hueston as Commissioner of Education, through the oratorical contests in which the contestants and people who heard them were educated on constitutional matters related to the citizenship of Negro-Americans. Then turning to the years of his service, the Grand Legal Adviser said, "Bill, you have wrought well, and those who think that you are too old have little mental failings of their own."

While pausing to make judgments upon past contributions, there was plenty of evidence that the I.B.P.O.E. of W., was looking to the future. An editorial in the *Washington Eagle* stated that with their Grand Exalted Ruler, the lodges and temples forming the great fraternal organization of Elkdom and representing over a half million members stood ready to help work out the details tending to assist the national and state governments to bring unity into the field. Grand Commissioner of Education George W. Lee declared that with the approval of Grand Exalted Ruler Robert H. Johnson the fall and winter of 1954 had been proclaimed as "a period to achieve favorable reaction north and south towards the Supreme Court decision on racial segregation in education in educational institutions." The call, he said, was for the development of Sunday evening forums continuing through the Fall and Winter on racial tensions in the schools and culminating in a National Citizenship Dinner at Howard University on January 31, 1955, with the theme "Human Freedom."

The July 4th celebration at the John Brown Farm was an un-

Past Grand Daughter Ruler Mary M. Johnson, Wife of Grand Exalted Ruler Robert H. Johnson

usual success. A record crowd of over 3,000 was in attendance, coming by automobiles, bus and train. Addresses were delivered by Grand Exalted Ruler Johnson, Grand Secretary Hueston, with Grand Director of Civil Liberties, Hobson R. Reynolds serving as Master of Ceremonies. The Grand Exalted Rulers Degree was conferred by the Grand Exalted Ruler upon Daughter Bertha McKanlass. This was the first time this award had been awarded to a woman by the Order. The first state association cottage — that of Pennsylvania—was dedicated. Dr. Adolphus Anderson was the President of the Pennsylvania Association. A cottage was erected during the year for the Grand Daughter Ruler, Nettie Carter Jackson. Funds for this cottage were raised through a national campaign by the Daughter Elks under the leadership of Past Grand Daughter Ruler Mary M. Johnson, wife of the Grand Exalted Ruler, who was chairman of the project. As the month of August approached, all eyes were turned toward the Grand Lodge session in Chicago.

SATURDAY-JULY 4th!
10 A.M. Till Midnite
John Brown Farm
NATIONAL SHRINE
I. B. P. O. E. W.
Direct from Club 421 N. Y. City
MARGE AND HER MAJORS BAND
DANCING AND ENTERTAINMENT
Special Program 2 p. m.
Evening Dance - 8 p.m. $1.25
Also
BIG DAY SUNDAY, JULY 5th
Don't Miss This Two Day Event!

Poster of John Brown Farm Social Events

The Fifty-fifth Grand Lodge Session assembled, August 22-27, 1954, at the Corpus Christi Center. The pre-convention activities were conducted by the Departments of Education, the Baccalaureate Service, the Shrine and Public Relations, the Junior Herd, the Memorial Service, The Annual Cap and Gown Breakfast, the Civil Liberties Breakfast and the Oratorical Contest. One of the highlights of the convention was the parade through the South side before a crowd estimated by the police at 350,000 to 600,000. Railroad officials estimated that 25,000 delegates and visitors had been transported while bus lines and private transportation had carried other thousands. Other events of dramatic types were the Bathing Beauty Contest, the Musical and the Grand Ball. The Elijah Lovejoy Award was presented to Thurgood Marshall for his successful endeavors in the cases against segregated education before the United States Supreme Court.

This was significant because this award was made in the state of Illinois where the Martyrdom of Elijah Lovejoy had occurred 117 years before this session.

Grand Exalted Ruler Johnson said on this occasion, "we are here today to honor another great American, a very learned, distinguished lawyer in the person of Attorney Thurgood L. Marshall, who was responsible for the great victory achieved by our people in the school segregation case. He led the fight with other lawyers in the Supreme Court to give our people victory." Four persons had previously received this award, Governor Alfred Driscoll of New Jersey, Branch Rickey, Ralph Bunche and Mary McLeod Bethune. In accepting the Lovejoy Award, Mr. Marshall said, "this medal which I have just received from the Grand Exalted Ruler means more to me than money which I receive in my legal practice. It gives me a sense of feeling that I must be right." Referring to the progress of desegregation, he said, "It will take time, but the majority of local boards will discover that they cannot escape responsibility which is placed upon them to carry out the law. These school boards will desegregate their schools one way or another. Some school boards will try delaying, evasionary tactics to try and circumvent the Supreme Court decision. Others will refuse to act at all, and will defy our government. So, therefore, here is where you as an individual and an American have an opportunity to shape policy."

He expressed appreciation for the check of $2,000 which the Grand Lodge had given to him through Bob Johnson and Hobson Reynolds. He said that $40,000 had been contributed to fight these cases by Negroes and that $9,000 of this amount was raised by white friends. A resolution was adopted extending thanks to Attorney Marshall and his staff for their brilliant victory resulting in the Supreme Court's decision outlawing segregation in the public schools.

The report of the Credential Committee showed that there were present at this Grand Lodge session 50 Grand Lodge officers, 29 Past Grand Exalted Rulers, 303 District and State Deputies, 706 Lodge Delegates, 327 Lodges, 62 Past Exalted Rulers Councils, 27 State Associations, making a grand total of 1,883 delegates.

The highlight of the convention's opening was the address and report of the Grand Exalted Ruler, Honorable Robert H. Johnson. His report covered every phase of the program of the Order, the adjudication of lodge matters, financial interests and an account of his continuous travels whose details had also been given in his column in the *Washington Eagle* entitled "Rolling With the Grand.'' Emphasis was placed by the Grand Exalted Ruler on the Elk Foundation, youth, expansion of the Order, education, health, dispensations, state associations, civil liberties, loans and mortgages. He announced that a Chinese Lodge in New York City had been organized and given a charter. In referring to expansion, the Grand Exalted Ruler stated that plans would be made for the expansion and setting up of new lodges in Europe and Africa. He also said that ''Dr. Charles H. Wesley, Central State College President and Historian had been engaged to prepare a history of our great Order for distribution to our brothers and daughters throughout the entire Elk jurisdiction.'' The recommendations were (1) the adoption of a Foundation in order to perpetuate the programs and any other program of advancement for all peoples not contrary to the Grand Lodge and functions of said Foundation; (2) a definite program for expansion in foreign lands; (3) a program for the youth of the Order, their entertainment as well as educational development.

It is significant that prior to this report, the movement had arisen spontaneously for the re-election of Grand Exalted Ruler Robert H. Johnson, with Past Grand Exalted Ruler T. Gillis Nutter presiding. Brother Sylvester Sylvahn of New York prefaced the motion to elect with a commendatory address eulogizing the Grand Exalted Ruler ''as a great leader of progress and a man who had demonstrated his administrative ability.'' The motion to suspend the rules and re-elect the Grand Exalted Ruler for the next two terms was seconded by Dr. Walter Cholmondely and Brother Herbert Jones, Grand Organizer, who led the assembly in a demonstration terminating in the unanimous approval of the motion. This action brought into reality the convention slogan, ''Year of Progress, Onward and Forward Behind the Great Leadership of Bob Johnson.'' Presentations were made to the Grand Exalted Ruler of a portrait of himself with Brother Perry W. Howard, Grand Legal Advisor, accepting the portrait for him and a Gold Badge was also presented to him by the newly created Police Department members.

The second session of the Grand Lodge was opened with the report of the Grand Secretary, Judge William C. Hueston, who said that he was presenting his twenty-ninth Grand Lodge report, up to 1950 as Commissioner of Education and since then as Grand Secretary. He began this report by expressing gratitude to the Grand Exalted Ruler for his cooperation, kindness and his leadership in conserving the Order's rich tradition. After memorial references, attention was directed to the New York property, the apartment house at 351 West 114th Street, and was followed with the recommendation that this property be sold since it cannot be controlled wholly by its owners and was the occasion for court appearances, and as the report stated "the tenants have everything in their favor." It was recommended also that the proceeds from the sale be placed in a foundation or in government bonds. This recommendation was approved later by the Grand Lodge.

Membership was emphasized by the Grand Secretary, its meaning and its increase. He said that there should be 100 per cent increase in membership in 1954-1955. The improvements at the National Shrine, the John Brown Farm, were described. The total original cost was $30,000 and it was reported by Grand Secretary Hueston that less than $10,000 was against it for improvements. The goal for the future, he said, was "to enlarge, beautify and extend the usefulness of this National Shrine for ourselves and our children, preserving in our memories a man who stands as a sainted leader of men, who fought for the freedom of American Negroes, in their struggles for a decent, just, equal place in the sun."

The cost of the Grand Lodge, he reported, had nearly tripled in the last several meetings. The increased expenses had been paid previously out of surplus accumulated over the years, but that "the bottom had been reached" and "there is no more." He said that the delegates would have to depend on what had been set aside for them by their subordinate lodges. An increased assessment, he added, would have to be made.

Other subjects presented were Department of Education, contributions of subordinate lodges and temples, functional illiteracy, workshops and the oratorical contest. In regard to the latter, the Grand Secretary said that over six million hearers had heard 70,000 declamations and that over the years an intelligent climate had been created, which had helped in laying the ground work for the Supreme Court decision on May 17, 1954.

The statistics showed a balance brought forward on August 1, 1953 of $11,292.71. The total Grand Fund Receipts were $118,-136.83 and the expenditures were $97,609.19, United States Government Bonds of $100,000.00, the Shrine Building at $137,000.-00, the John Brown Farm at $100,000.00 and other holdings. There were reported thirty-one new lodges, twelve reinstated lodges, fifteen new junior herds and six reinstated herds, six new civil rights leagues, two reinstated leagues and one new council. There had been 540 deaths during the year.

After extolling the virtues of Grand Secretary Hueston and congratulating him on his report, Brother Ernest Copeland in a brilliant speech moved that the rules be suspended and Brother Hueston be re-elected by acclamation to succeed himself as Grand

Secretary, and that the Grand Esquire be empowered to cast the unanimous ballot. The motion was seconded by Brothers Robert Jackson and Truly Hatchett and others and was unanimously adopted, with Past Grand Exalted Ruler Nutter presiding.

The financial report of Grand Treasurer Perry B. Jackson was presented by him. It concurred with the report of the Grand Secretary. He again stressed the necessity for the adoption of a budget for Grand Lodge operations and proposed the creation of a Budget Committee. His report was referred by motion of Brother Charles Freeman. Dr. H. W. Hunter then commended Brother Jackson for the conduct of his office and moved that the rules be suspended and that he be re-elected for the ensuing term, with the Grand Esquire casting the unanimous ballot for his re-election. The motion was seconded by Brothers Sylvester Sylvahn and Ernest Wright, and was carried unanimously.

The work of the Civil Liberties Department was reported by Grand Director Hobson R. Reynolds who had traveled with the Grand Exalted Ruler into every state in order to make the people civil rights conscious. He outlined the main objectives of the department as the formulation of plans for the desegregation of the public school system, to urge participation in voting, to fight segregation in all its forms, to organize civil liberties leagues, and to cooperate with the other departments and with labor organizations in opposing discrimination on account of race and color. Brother George W. Lee moved that the report be received and referred to the committee on Grand Officers Reports. By motion of Brother G. Winsmore Mason the rules were suspended and Brother Reynolds was re-elected. The motion was seconded by the Grand Exalted Ruler who called attention to the fine work performed by Brother Reynolds and by Brother Herbert E. Jones, Grand Organizer. Grand Esquire Henry Davis then cast the unanimous ballot for re-election amid the enthusiasm of the Grand Lodge.

The Grand Commissioner of Education, Brother George W. Lee then rendered his report. Calling attention to the history making Supreme Court decisions, Grand Commissioner Lee said that the lodges and temples should help to create the attitudes for the practice of desegregation. One of these methods was the encouragement and development of Sunday Forums in which good conduct, manners, fair play, self-confidence and self-pride could be stressed. He described the banquet at Howard University and the "Mr. Shephard-Goes-To-Washington Program," the oratorical contests, the Curtiss Candy campaign and student scholarships. At the conclusion of his report, a motion was made by Brother Walter Cholmondely and duly seconded that Grand

Hobson R. Reynolds, Grand Commissioner of Civil Liberties

Commissioner Lee be re-elected as a result of his fine work, and with the suspension of the rules, the Grand Esquire cast the unanimous ballot for him.

The Grand Exalted Ruler, Brother Robert H. Johnson taking the chair previously held during this session by Past Grand Exalted Ruler Nutter introduced Dr. Charles H. Wesley to give a report on the progress of the preparation of the history of the Order. The minutes state, "Addressing the body, Dr. Wesley told the delegates, Grand Lodge officers assembled that he had been appointed by the Grand Exalted Ruler to write, compile a History of the Improved Benevolent and Protective Order of Elks of the World for distribution and sale to members of the I.B.P.O.E. of W., Elk lodges and temples. He stated that at the present 16 chapters had been completed and that he hoped to have the history completed by 1955. He stated that the book would have pictures of leaders and builders of the Elks organization, living and dead, also information about the Grand Past Exalted Rulers who served the chair and who headed the organization in years gone by, as well as Past Grand Secretaries and other Grand Lodge officers who served in various capacities our Great Order. The history would contain valuable information and its leaders from 1898 to 1954. The book will contain illustrations, also 400 pages. All brothers and daughters who had historical material dealing with the history of Elkdom were requested to send this material to the author of the history."

At the conclusion of this report, Hobson R. Reynolds, Grand Commissioner of Civil Liberties moved that the Grand Lodge authorize the publication of the history and that the Grand Exalted Ruler be empowered to appoint a committee to work out all financial details in connection with the work to be done and that the necessary money stand appropriated for the publishing of the history. The motion was seconded by Brother Milton S. J. Wright and was adopted unanimously. The committee on Grand Lodge reports commended the historian "for the painstaking efforts he had put forth to compile a factual history of the progress of the largest, strongest and most serviceable Negro fraternal organization in the world." The committee recommended "that Dr. Wesley under the leadership of the Grand Exalted Ruler be given full responsibility to prepare this history for publication as rapidly as facts can be gathered."

An important action by the Grand Lodge was a resolution adopted unanimously creating an Elk's foundation "to perpetuate and expand the program of the Elks' organization with reference to health, economics, education and other programs for the advancement of all peoples not contrary to the Grand Lodge laws or functions of said foundation to be hereinafter known as the Elks' Foundation of the Improved Benevolent and Protective Order of Elks of the World, said Foundation to be a nonprofit foundation which does not contemplate profit for its members; also to be directed by seven trustees, the majority to consist of the Grand Exalted Ruler and Grand Lodge officers and non-Elks.'' It was unanimously approved by the Grand Lodge delegates as the Committee on Law and Revision recommended. In order to create an immediate fund, the financial officers were authorized with the approval of the Grand Exalted Ruler to appropriate and transfer an initial amount not to exceed $100,000.00 nor less than $50,-000.00 from such Grand Lodge funds as may be available. The Foundation was also advised to raise funds through any Grand Lodge channels.

DR. J. B. MARTIN, Chairman of Publishing Board, Director of Athletics

The Grand Temple session was reported as a very constructive one and in keeping with the programs of the Grand Lodge by Brother Sylvester Sylvahn, Chairman of the Committee on Fraternal Greetings. He said that he was cordially received by Grand Daughter Ruler, Daughter Nettie Carter Jackson.

An outstanding event of the Annual Session of Daughters at Chicago in 1954 was the presentation of their second annual award to Grand Daughter Secretary Buena V. Kelley. Mrs. Edith Sampson, former alternate delegate to the United Nations, was the speaker for the occasion. Miss Etta Moten sang a group of songs. Grand Daughter Ruler Nettie C. Jackson made the presentation to Grand Daughter Secretary Kelley, and traced the development of the Daughters until they had organized 1,000 temples, describing the patience, skill and devotion of Miss Kelley in contributing to this result. In referring to her cooperation as Grand Daughter Ruler with Grand Exalted Ruler Johnson, Mrs. Jackson said, ''we have walked side by side in the affairs of this Order.'' Grand Exalted Ruler Robert H. Johnson, Grand Secretary W. C. Hueston, Grand Organizer Herbert K.

Jones, Mrs. Inez H. Jefferson, Mrs. Lola A. Bentley, Mrs. Alice Cordall and Mrs. Marion Campbell were among the participants on the program.

The Shrine committee reported through Brother Charles P. McClane who stated that progress was being made at the John Brown Farm, that several cabins had been erected, namely the Grand Daughter Ruler's Cabin, the Pennsylvania State Association Cabin, and that a new cabin was in process of formulation for the Grand Exalted Ruler. Grand Legal Adviser, Perry W. Howard, stated in his report, which was his twenty-ninth, that there had been organized a helpful legal program to aid all lodges and temples. Dr. Carter L. Marshall, Grand Medical Director,

PAST GRAND EXALTED RULER
ARMOND W. SCOTT

PAST GRAND EXALTED RULER
T. G. NUTTER

described the clinics for the benefit of delegates and members and introduced Dr. Roscoe C. Brown, Executive Secretary of the Health Commission who read a voluminous report on health activities. Grand Organizer Herbert E. Jones reported that he had traveled 10,000 miles through the United States and Canada and had found a finer and greater spirit among the members. He said that he had set a goal of 50,000 members for the next year.

Three Past Grand Exalted Rulers were honored at a joint meeting of delegates of lodges and temples. Addressing the meeting, Brother Herbert Jones stated that the purpose of the occasion was to honor Past Grand Exalted Rulers T. Gillis Nutter, Armond

W. Scott and George W. F. McMechen who was absent on account of illness. Judge Hueston was introduced and gave a historical summary of the accomplishments of these leaders in Elkdom.

The citations were as follows:

> "The Honorable T. Gillis Nutter—West Virginia's Noted Lawyer—Past Grand Exalted Ruler

T. Gillis Nutter, noted lawyer, assistant to the Grand Exalted Ruler and at present presiding over Grand Lodge Sessions, served as Grand Exalted Ruler of I.B.P.O.E. of W., from 1913 to 1916. During his administration, fraternal relationships were improved with the white Elks, a new charter was adopted and the Grand Lodge report showed 144 lodges with a membership of more than 10,000."

> "The Honorable Judge Armond W. Scott, Judge of the Municipal Court, Washington, D. C., Noted Lawyer and Judge (for over 18 years).

Past Grand Exalted Ruler, Armond W. Scott, Washington, D. C., noted jurist, Judge of the Municipal Court served as the head of our great organization from 1916 to 1919 During his administration it was mutually agreed between colored and white Elks that all litigation over the use of the name Elks would be discontinued. Past Grand Exalted Rulers Councils were established for the first time and $10,000.00 worth of liberty bonds were purchased. In view of his great leadership as head of the Elks organization he was honored as being named the first Grand Patriarch of the Grand Temple."

> "Brother George W. F. McMechen, Past Grand Exalted Ruler

Past Grand Exalted Ruler George W. F. McMechen, Baltimore, Maryland, served as head of the I.B.P.O.E. of W., from 1919 to 1921. During his administration the membership

GRAND EXALTED RULER GEORGE W. F. MCMECHEN

GRAND COMMISSIONER ADOLPHUS ANDERSON of Veteran Affairs presents First Registration Card to Grand Exalted Ruler Robert H. Johnson.

grew to 217 lodges and 29,143 members and the treasury report was $29,150.00 in cash; $1,866.00 was raised to aid the victims of the Tulsa, Oklahoma riot. State Associations were also legalized and 62 new lodges were set up which was the largest number organized in two years up to that time.''

Awards of $150.00 cash were presented to Grand Exalted Rulers T. Gills Nutter and George W. F. McMechen. Grand Exalted Ruler Armond W. Scott was the recipient of a wrist watch, a cane, an Elk Charm and cuff links formerly worn by the late John T. Scott. They expressed their appreciation for the honors and gifts. Past Grand Exalted Ruler George W. F. McMechen sent a telegram of appreciation and best wishes for continued success under the leadership of Grand Exatled Ruler Robert H. Johnson.

Dr. Adolphus Anderson, Grand Commissioner of Veterans Affairs read his report. He acknowledged the support to his work by the Grand Exalted Ruler and the sources of specialists in veterans affairs. Statistics, advice to veterans and the ''Veterans Band Wagon'' in the *Washington Eagle* were parts of the report. The report of the Grand Director of Economics, Dr. Milton S. J. Wright, described the functions of the Department of Economics and its planning for the economic future of the people.

The Joint Birthday Party for Grand Exalted Ruler Robert H. Johnson and Grand Daughter Ruler Nettie Carter Jackson was an evidence of unity which was given commendation by all who were present. The report of Daughter Bertha McKanlass. Grand Directress of the Shrine Committee showed that there were receipts of $13,700.58 and a balance in August, 1954 of $2,001.50.

Grand Traveling Auditor William H. Walker made a report giving a complete account of his work with the individual lodges. More than two hundred lodges had been visited by him in the last three years. He proposed that a study be made of the sick benefit payments of the subordinate lodges. The report of the Grand Director of Junior Elks was commended by the Committee on Grand Lodge Reports for emphasis upon plans for the future based upon the slogan, ''Youth of Today Are Elks of Tomorrow.''

The following officers were elected for the next ensuing term of office: Brothers Robert H. Johnson, Grand Exalted Ruler (2 years); Bertram V. Gregory, Grand Esteemed Leading Knight (1 year); Harvey L. Harris, Grand Esteemed Loyal Knight; K. P. Battle, Grand Esteemed Lecturing Knight; Judge William C. Hueston, Grand Secretary; Judge Perry B. Jackson, Grand Treasurer; Patrick Taylor, Grand Esquire; Benjamin Butler, Grand Inner Guard; Herbert Fernanders, Grand Tiler; Dr. L. W. Williams, Grand Trustee (3 year term); John T. Freeman,

J. Amos Harris, Grand Lodge Inspector

Captain Milton S. Smith, Police Commission

Ernest M. Thomas, Shrine Commission

S. D. Holsey, Grand Tiler

JAMES H. FULTZ, Past State President, New Jersey Grand Director Bathing Beauty Department

CHARLES H. DONAWAY, Major General, Eastern Division

WILFORD E. LEWIN, Grand Organizer, New England and Islands of the Sea

DOUGLAS SIMPSON, Grand Organizer Western States

(1) year term, Grand Trustee; Henry Davis, (1) year term, Grand Trustee; John D. Cooper (1) year Grand Auditor; Perry W. Howard, Grand Legal Advisor; Hobson R. Reynolds, Grand Commissioner of Civil Liberties.

The officers appointed by the Grand Exalted Ruler for the next ensuing term of office were: James T. Copper, Assistant Grand Secretary; Harry H. Eddicks, Grand Recorder; Ike Styker, Grand Organist; Rev. R. H. Collins Lee, Grand Chaplain; Charles P. McClane, Grand Director of Public Relations; Dr. Milton S. J. Wright, Grand Director of Economics; A. William Hill, Grand Director of Junior Elks; John Minkins, Grand Lodge Reporter; Joseph Walker, Grand Master of Social Sessions; Dr. Carter L. Marshall, Grand Medical Director; Dr. Adolphus W. Anderson, Grand Director Veterans Affairs Department; Dr. Roscoe C. Brown, Executive Secretary of Health Commission; Herbert E. Jones, Grand Organizer; Albert A. Bethune, Grand Organizer; James Stewart, Grand Organizer; Oscar Pride, Grand Organizer; Henry Berth, Lieutenant General of Antlered Guard; George B. Hunt, Grand Adjutant General Antlered Guard; Paschall Todd, Major General of Western District Antlered Guard; Hillman Hanley, Major General of Antlered Guard; J. B. Martin, Grand Director of Athletics; Dr. Simpson A. Smith, Grand Director of Awards; W. Franklin Hoxter, Grand Director of Music; Ernest M. Thomas, Grand Secretary of Shrine; Dr. Leslie B. Howell, Health Commission; Dr. W. H. M. Pitts, Health Commission; Dr. Albert P. Johnson, Health Commission; Lionel Hampton, Grand Band Master.

Under the leadership of the Grand Exalted Ruler, Dr. Robert H. Johnson, the Improved Benevolent and Protective Order of Elks of the World had reached the number of 1,400 lodges and with the guidance of Dr. Robert H. Johnson as Grand Patriarch, the temples reached the number of 1,000. Under the direct leadership of Grand Daughter Ruler Nettie Carter Jackson, the membership of the Daughters was over a quarter of a million members. New projects were announced. One of these was care for dependent children, which has grown in value through the years.

A membership drive was also launced for 1954 by Grand Exalted Ruler Johnson. It was planned to carry Elkdom into Liberia, the Gold Coast of Africa, the West Indies and to give it an international membership, so that its designation "of the world" should become a factual attainment. The Order looked forward to the future with optimism and the confident belief that there

THE

Washington Eagle

OFFICIAL PUBLICATION OF THE ELKS AND DAUGHTER ELKS OF I. B. P. O. E. OF THE WORLD

VOL. 50 — No. 3 WASHINGTON, D. C. OCTOBER, 1954

Bob Johnson, Entire Cabinet Re-Elected; Program Approved

CHICAGO—(ANP)—With the reelection of Dr. Robert H. Johnson and his entire cabinet, and with approval of his program by the 1,300 delegates representing lodges from this country and from abroad, the 55th annual convention of the IBPOEW, reached its climax last week. Chicago, with its broad streets, lakeshore drives, shady parks and its mid-western hospitality, proved a gracious host.

Strangely enough, the Elks received no official welcome to the city. Mayor Martin H. Kennelly who was to attend the sessions on Monday, in a telegram said he could not appear.

Highlight of the convention, for the citizens of Chicago, occurred Tuesday afternoon, when the Elks annual parade was held through the streets of the city's teeming last weekend and were housed in the big loop hotels, in [illegible] hotels on the Southside and in the homes of citizens.

By Tuesday morning buses and trains, carrying gay Elk pennants, had arrived from every section of the country. Railroad officials estimated that they had carried at least 25,000 delegates and visitors into the city, while the bus lines and private transportation accounted for another 15,000 to 20,000 people.

Among the highlights of the convention were the annual East-West game, played before more than 10,000 people; the presenting of the Elijah Lovejoy Award to Thurgood Marshall of the NAACP, the musical Sunday night at Corpus Christi center; the Elks Oratorical Contest Monday; the Bathing Beauty

Johnson To Head GOP State Drive

Robert H Johnson, Grand Exalted Ruler of the Elks has been [illegible] chairman of Negro Activities [illegible] the Republican State Committee for the forthcoming campaign.

ROBERT H. JOHNSON

The selection was made at a meeting in the Republican City Committee's headquarters attend-

Delegates Re-Elect Judge W. C. Hueston By Acclamation

CHICAGO—(ANP)—Judge William C. Hueston, Elkdom's revered sage, now in his 31st year of service to the order, was re-elected without opposition as Grand Secretary of the Order Wednesday morning.

The action of the cheering delegates thus snuffed out an incipient rebellion which had been hinted earlier.

Following the Grand Secretary's reading of his annual report, the rules were suspended and he was elected by acclamation. Following a demonstration lasting several minutes, delegates from all sections of the country pressed forward to congratulate the beloved Elk official.

Judge Hueston's report, filled with the sharp darts of praise and criticism, revealed that the net worth of the Order, as of July 31 rial farm.

Hueston, who served as the 1st Commissioner of Education, held the former office for 23 years before being elected Grand Secretary in this city in 1930.

In his report, Judge Hueston recommended to the delegates the sale of the New York property, provided the lodge can get out of the property the amount they invested; he also commented on membership of the Order, insisting that the lodges launch a '54-55 campaign to increase membership.

In discussing the John Brown Farm, Judge Hueston revealed that the national shrine is today valued at $70,000, without improvements. Already erected at the shrine are a modern recreation hall, an improved barn, with every facility; five cabins equipped

The Washington Eagle, October, 1954.

would be greater opportunities of service to the people, an increasing membership for the subordinate lodges and a richer spiritual life for all Elkdom. The deep spiritual beliefs of the Grand Exalted Ruler, observed in his addresses and in his personal life, were basic to the successes of the Grand Lodge and the spread of good will among the brothers and daughters. Unity was a factor of importance under this master-administrator. Competition for office was of lesser importance than the continuance of the good servants of the Grand Lodge. Elkdom's members had confidence in their leader and manifested greater desires to follow his leadership in whatever ways he manifested it. The lodges and temples wanted him to visit them, and their delegates voted to increase his traveling expenses. They saw that honors were bestowed upon him on every possible special occasion. In turn the Grand Exalted Ruler extended himself in the details of the administration of his office as the executive of the largest fraternal order serving a predominantly Negro membership for more than a half century.

Together, the Grand Exalted Ruler and his followers looked backward on a glorious history from whose pinnacle Elkdom looked forward to a future in which greater deeds would be performed than the past had known. Elks stood, with the Daughters at their side, on the mountain peak of fifty-six years of pressing forward and upward towards the better life. They could now see their gains, and in counting the costs and the sacrifices, they knew that these achievements were worth all of their endeavors. Elkdom under Negro leadership had arrived and was now girding itself in 1955 for the greater victories of the future.

The Appendix

I

GRAND LODGE SESSIONS

Date	*Place*
1899	Cincinnati, Ohio
1901	Norfolk, Virginia
1902	Washington, Pennsylvania
1903	Hampton, Virginia
1904	Atlantic City, New Jersey
1905	Washington, D. C.
1906	Columbus, Ohio (Howard); Brooklyn, New York (Atkins)
1907	Reading, Pennsylvania (Howard); Chicago, Ill. (Atkins)
1908	St. Louis, Missouri (Howard); St. Paul, Minnesota (Atkins)
1909	Detroit, Michigan
1910	Washington, D. C.
1911	Boston, Massachusetts
1912	Dayton, Ohio
1913	Atlantic City, New Jersey
1914	Norfolk, Virginia
1915	Chicago, Illinois
1916	Philadelphia, Pennsylvania
1917	Cleveland, Ohio
1918	Baltimore, Maryland
1919	Atlantic City, New Jersey
1920	Kansas City, Missouri
1921	Boston, Massachusetts
1922	Newark, New Jersey
1923	Chicago, Illinois
1924	Pittsburgh, Pennsylvania
1925	Richmond, Virginia

Date	*Place*
1926	Cleveland, Ohio
1927	New York, New York
1928	Chicago, Illinois
1929	Atlantic City, New Jersey
1930	Detroit, Michigan
1931	Philadelphia, Pennsylvania
1932	Atlantic City, New Jersey
1933	Indianapolis, Indiana
1934	Atlantic City, New Jersey
1935	Washington, D. C.
1936	Brooklyn, New York
1937	Cleveland, Ohio
1938	Baltimore, Maryland
1939	New York, New York
1940	St. Louis, Missouri
1941	Atlantic City, New Jersey
1942	Philadelphia, Pennsylvania
1943	Pittsburgh, Pennsylvania
1944	Chicago, Illinois
1945	Philadelphia, Pennsylvania
1946	Buffalo, New York
1947	Philadelphia, Pennsylvania
1948	Cincinnati, Ohio
1949	San Francisco, California
1950	Chicago, Illinois
1951	Buffalo, New York
1952	Atlantic City, New Jersey
1953	Atlanta, Georgia
1954	Chicago, Illinois

II

THE GRAND EXALTED RULERS

1. Benjamin Franklin Howard, Alpha Lodge No. 1, Cincinnati, Ohio 1899–1909
2. William E. Atkins, Excelsior Lodge, No. 4, Hampton, Virginia 1907–1910
3. James E. Mills, Eureka Lodge, No. 5, Norfolk, Virginia 1909–1910
4. Frank J. Wheaton, Manhattan Lodge, No. 45, New York, New York 1910–1911
5. Harry H. Pace, Memphis Lodge, No. 96, Memphis, Tennessee 1911–1913
6. T. Gillis Nutter, Kanawha Lodge, No. 130, Charleston, West Virginia 1913–1916
7. Armond W. Scott, Morning Star Lodge, No. 40, Washington, D. C. 1916–1919
8. George W. F. McMechen, Monumental Lodge, No. 3, Baltimore, Maryland 1919–1921

9. George F. Wibecan, Brooklyn Lodge, No. 32, Brooklyn, New York 1921–1922
10. J. Finley Wilson, Columbia Lodge, No. 85, Washington, D. C. 1922–1952
11. Robert H. Johnson, O. V. Catto Lodge, No. 20, Philadelphia, Pennsylvania 1952–

III

THE HONORARY PAST GRAND EXALTED RULERS

Arthur J. Riggs, Detroit, Mich.
Frank H. Hunter, St. Louis, Mo.
George E. Bates, Newark, N. J.
J. T. Brandy, Washington, Pa.
Dr. M. R. Bibb, Chicago, Ill.
William H. McFarland, Brooklyn, N. Y.
Stewart A. Hoyt, Boston, Mass.
C. Clay Lewis, Atlantic City, N. J.
William H. Lewis, Baltimore, Md.
William H. Shands, Philadelphia, Pa.
Samuel E. Jones, Washington, D. C.
James C. Avery, Philadelphia, Pa.
W. George Avant, Durham, N. C.
John F. Ross, Washington, D. C.
Carey Wheaton, Richmond, Va.
R. R. Church, Memphis, Tenn.
John A. Bailey, Norfolk, Va.
William P. Burrell, Sr., Newark, N. J.
Louis E. Williams, New York, N. Y.
Thomas F. Harper, Washington, D. C.
A. J. Gaskins, Washington, D. C.
Dr. J. W. Ames, Detroit, Mich.
Major R. R. Wright, Philadelphia, Pa.
Guy U. Blaine, Indianapolis, Ind.
Albert O. Avant, Petersburg, Va.
C. Henri Lewis, Detroit, Mich.
Mark Cooper, New York, N. Y.
James T. Copper, Chicago, Ill.
W. C. Hueston, Washington, D. C.
James E. Kelley, Birmingham, Ala.
Perry W. Howard, Washington, D. C.
John Powell, Jacksonville, Fla.
W. Gray Hoyt, Atlantic City, N. J.
Pope Billups, New York, N. Y.
Perry B. Jackson, Cleveland, Ohio
Samuel B. Mitchell, New York, N. Y.
Lawrence J. Davenport, New York, N. Y.
T. T. Wendell, Lexington, Ky.
Thomas L. Higgins, Brooklyn, N. Y.
John T. Freeman, Philadelphia, Pa.
A. A. Roundtree, Portsmouth, Va.
E. G. Gaither, Cincinnati, Ohio
Henry Lincoln Johnson, Atlanta, Ga.
William J. Thompkins, Kansas City, Mo.
Walter L. Land, Norfolk, Va.
A. E. Pullam, Kansas City, Mo.
George A. Jackson, Los Angeles, Calif.
Tom English, Chicago, Ill.
Dr. L. W. Williams, Valdosta, Ga.
E. L. Johnson, Indianapolis, Ind.
John B. Williams, Norfolk, Va.
Steve Ball, Cleveland, Ohio
Robert D. Addison, Bremerton, Wash.
Ham Jenkins, Denver, Colo.
F. W. Malloy, Charleston, S. C.
Ed. Carvest, Macon, Ga.
William F. Maxwell
Joseph Snowden, Chicago, Ill.
Hobson Reynolds, Philadelphia, Pa.
Wallace Williams, Detroit, Mich.

Tecumseh H. Bradshaw, Washington, D. C.
John U. Strother, Augusta, Ga.
Albert Bethune, Daytona Beach, Fla.
Ernest Copeland, Philadelphia, Pa.
Lt. George W. Lee, Memphis, Tenn.
Dr. Carter L. Marshall, New Haven, Conn.
Dr. E. T. Belsaw, Mobile, Ala.
Samuel D. Holsey, Reading, Pa.
Simpson A. Smith, Huntington, W. Va.
Claude C. White, Indianapolis, Ind.
Hugh McBeth, San Francisco, Calif.
Charles Gray, Cleveland, Ohio
Oscar Price, Pittsburgh, Pa.
Herbert E. Jones, Washington, D. C.
Dr. James A. Megahy, Chicago, Ill.
Harry Eddicks, Philadelphia, Pa.
Edward W. Simmons, New York, N. Y.
Dr. Henry W. Hunter, Cleveland, Ohio
Ernest M. Thomas, New Orleans, La.
Dr. J. B. Key, St. Louis, Mo.
N. E. Tillman, Des Moines, Iowa
Dr. C. Morris Cain, Atlantic City, N. J.

IV

THE GRAND SECRETARIES

G. F. Bowles, Natchez Lodge, Natchez, Mississippi 1899–1901
J. H. Bush, Alpha Lodge No. 1, Cincinnati, Ohio 1901–1906
Dr. Welcome T. Jones, Pandora Lodge No. 2, Newport News, La. 1906–1907
Dr. James W. Ames, Wolverine Lodge No. 72, Detroit, Michigan 1907–1908
W. T. Anderson (Acting), Alpha Lodge No. 1, Cincinnati, Ohio 1907–
R. M. S. Brown, Excelsior Lodge No. 4, Hampton, Va. 1907–
J. Welford Holmes, Keystone Lodge No. 6, Washington, Pa. 1907–1908
Harry H. Pace, Bluff City Lodge No. 96, Memphis, Tenn. 1908–1911
George E. Bates, Pride of Newark Lodge No. 93, Newark, N. J. 1911–1928
James E. Kelley, Jones Valley Lodge No. 14, Birmingham, Alabama 1928–1950
William C. Hueston, Morning Star Lodge No. 40, Washington, D. C. 1950–

V

THE GRAND TREASURERS

Dr. James C. Erwin, Alpha Lodge No. 1, Cincinnati, Ohio 1899–1902
J. F. Brandy, Keystone Lodge No. 6, Washington, Pa. 1902–1906
Wesley Raney, Pandora Lodge, Newport News, Virginia 1906–1907
J. F. Brandy, Keystone Lodge No. 6, Washington, Pa. 1906–1910
Dr. W. T. Jones, Pandora Lodge No. 2, Newport News, Va. 1907–1910

Henry Stevenson, Excelsior Lodge No. 4, Hampton, Va. 1907–
William E. Gales, Columbia Lodge No. 85, Washington, D. C. 1910–1913
R. N. Hyde, Acting Treasurer 1913–
James T. Carter, Williams Lodge No. 11, Chicago, Ill. 1913–1928
Henry S. Warner, Imperial Lodge No. 127, New York 1929–1931
Edward W. Henry, O. V. Catto Lodge, No. 20, Philadelphia, Pa. 1931–1946
Marcus F. Wheatland, Pride of Camden Lodge, No. 83, Camden, N. J. 1946–
Thomas E. Greene, Rubber City Lodge No. 233, Akron, Ohio 1947–1951
Perry B. Jackson, Cleveland, Ohio 1951–

VI

THE GRAND LEGAL ADVISERS

Prior to 1913 there was no formal appointment of a Grand Legal Adviser. There were attorneys who aided and directed the legal action and defense of the Order. Among these were E. Burton Ceruti, of New York City, who was also known as National Receiver of Defense Funds; L. Melendez King, Washington, D. C.; Benjamin L. Gaskins, Washington, D. C.; T. Gillis Nutter, Charleston, W. Va.

Armond W. Scott 1913–1914
William H. Stanton 1914–1917
George W. F. McMechen 1917–1919
C. Henri Lewis 1919–1921
Thomas W. Fleming 1921–1922
Henry Lincoln Johnson 1922–1925
Perry W. Howard 1925–

VII

THE GRAND DAUGHTER RULERS
(The Grand Temple)

1. Dt. Mary P. Barnes, Norfolk Temple No. 1A, Norfolk, Va. 1903–1906
2. Dt. Mamie E. Hodge, True Light Temple No. 5, Hampton, Va. 1906–1923
3. Dt. Nora E. Taylor, Warden Temple No. 16, Chicago, Ill. 1923–
4. Dt. Laura E. Williams, Eureka Temple No. 22, New York, N. Y. 1923–1926
5. Dt. Ella G. Berry, Warden Temple No. 16, Chicago, Ill. 1926–1929
6. Dt. Abbie M. Johnson, Quaker City Temple No. 73, Philadelphia, Pa. 1929–1940
7. Dt. Elizabeth Ross Gordon, Forest Temple No. 9, Washington, D. C. 1940–1951
8. Dt. Nettie Carter Jackson, Raritan Temple No. 218, Staten Island, N. Y. 1951–

VIII

THE GRAND SECRETARIES

(The Grand Temple)

1. Dr. Emma V. Kelley, Norfolk Temple No. 1A, Norfolk, Va. 1903–1932
2. Dt. Buena V. Kelley, Norfolk Temple No. 1A, Norfolk, Va. 1932–

IX

THE GRAND TREASURERS

(The Grand Temple)

1. Dt. Annie Spencer, Norfolk Temple No. 1, Norfolk, Va. 1903–1906
2. Dt. Frances Young, Truelight No. 5, Hampton, Va........ 1906–1933
3. Dt. Elizabeth Kimbough, Excelsior Temple No. 35, Brooklyn, N. Y........ 1933–1952
4. Dt. Pearl Brown, Great Southern No. 30, Baltimore, Maryland 1952–

X

INCORPORATION IN THE DISTRICT OF COLUMBIA

CERTIFICATE OF INCORPORATION GRAND LODGE OF IMPROVED BENEVOLENT AND PROTECTIVE ORDER OF ELKS OF THE WORLD

KNOW ALL MEN BY THESE PRESENTS, That we, the undersigned, William E. Atkins, of Hampton, Virginia, J. Welfred Holmes and John A. Brown, both of Pittsburgh, Pa., all being citizens of the United States and of full age, and L. Melendez King, Harry J. Williams, A. B. Rice and Samuel E. Jones, all of whom are citizens of the United States and residents of the District of Columbia, and being also persons of full age, pursuant to and in conformity with sub-chapter three (3) of the incorporation laws of the District of Columbia, enacted by Congress and approved by the President of the United States, do hereby associate ourselves together for benevolent and charitable purposes and for mutual improvement and we do hereby certify:

FIRST: That the corporate name of this organization shall be the "GRAND LODGE OF IMPROVED BENEVOLENT AND PROTECTIVE ORDER OF ELKS OF THE WORLD."

SECOND: That the term of its existence shall be perpetual.

THIRD: That its objects shall be and are benevolent, social and altruistic, to promote and encourage manly friendship and kindly intercourse; and to aid, protect and assist its members and their families and to do and perform every lawful act and thing necessary or expedient to be done, or performed for the efficient and profitable conducting of said business is authorized by the laws of Congress, and to have and to exercise all the powers conferred by the laws of the District of Columbia upon corporations organized under the aforesaid sub-chapter three (3).

FOURTH: That the number of trustees shall be seven (7), viz: William E. Atkins, J. Welfred Holmes, John A. Brown, H. Strawbridge, J. Woolridge, L. Melendez King and Thomas F. Harper, and they shall hold office during the first year of its existence, or until their successors are elected. And the said organization by said name may have and use a common seal, and may meet annually or oftener at such times and places and in such manner as may be specified in the By-laws.

This corporation reserves the right to amend, alter or change any provision contained in this Certificate of Incorporation in any manner prescribed by statute.

IN TESTIMONY WHEREOF We have hereunto set our hands and seals this 14th day of December, A.D., 1907.

William E. Atkins
J. Welfred Holmes
John A. Brown
L. Melendez King
Harry J. Williams
A. B. Rice
Samuel E. Jones

UNITED STATES OF AMERICA

DISTRICT OF COLUMBIA, TO WIT:

I, SAMUEL E. LACY, a Notary Public in and for the District aforesaid do hereby certify that L. Melendez King, Harry J. Williams, A. B. Rice, Samuel E. Jones, parties to the annexed CERTIFICATE OF INCORPORATION of the GRAND LODGE OF IMPROVED BENEVOLENT AND PROTECTIVE ORDER OF ELKS OF THE WORLD, bearing date on the 14th day of December 1907, personally appeared before me in said District, the said L. Melendez King, Harry J. Williams, A. B. Rice, Samuel E. Jones being personally well known to me to be the persons who made and signed the said Certificate and acknowledged the same to be their act and deed, for the purposes therein set forth.

WITNESS my hand and seal this 17th day of January, 1908.
(Seal)

Samuel E. Lacy
Notary Public, D. C.

UNITED STATES OF AMERICA

STATE OF VIRGINIA, } SS:
COUNTY OF Elizabeth City }

I, J. Henry Diggs a Notary Public in and for the State and County aforesaid do hereby certify that William E. Atkins party to the annexed CERTIFICATE OF INCORPORATION OF THE GRAND

LODGE OF IMPROVED BENEVOLENT AND PROTECTIVE ORDER OF ELKS OF THE WORLD, bearing date on the 14th day of December 1907, personally appeared before me in the State and County aforesaid, the said William E. Atkins, being personally well known to me as the person who made and signed the said certificate and acknowledged the same to be his act and deed for the purposes therein set forth.

WITNESS my hand and seal this 14th day of December 1907.

J. Henry Diggs
Notary Public.

(Seal)

My commission expires
October 18, 1911.

UNITED STATES OF AMERICA

STATE OF PENNSYLVANIA, } SS:
County . . . Allegheny }

I, S. G. Barnes, a Notary Public in and for the State and County aforesaid do hereby certify that John A. Brown and J. Welfred Holmes parties to the annexed Certificate of Incorporation of the GRAND LODGE OF IMPROVED BENEVOLENT AND PROTECTIVE ORDER OF ELKS OF THE WORLD, bearing date on the 14th day of December, 1907, personally appeared before me in the State and County aforesaid, the said John A. Brown and J. Welfred Holmes being personally well known to me as the persons who made and signed the said Certificate and acknowledged the same to be their act and deed for the purposes therein set forth.

WITNESS my hand and seal this 9th day of January, 1908.
(Seal)

S. G. Barnes
Notary Public.

My Commission Expires
January 21st, 1911.

LODGES OF I.B.P.O.E.W.

Name	*No.*	*Location*
ALABAMA		
Jones Valley	14	Birmingham
Gulf City	244	Mobile
Shell Bayou	361	Plateau
Southern Pride	431	Montgomery
Coosa Valley	715	Gadsden
Tuxedo	750	Fairfield
Booker T. Washington	762	Tuskegee Institute
W. R. Pettiford	770	Anniston
Tennessee Valley	808	Decatur
Wire Glass	810	Dothan

Name	No.	Location
Oak City	816	Tuscaloosa
Shades Valley	884	Bessemer
Pride of Alabama	1170	Selma
College City	1171	Talladega
Black Belt	1297	Demopolis
Peanut Pride	1322	Enterprise
James E. Kelley	1328	Eufaula
Spirit Andalusia	1369	Andalusia
James C. Dooley Sr.	1384	Brewton
ALASKA		
Forty Ninth State	1357	Anchorage
Yukon	1365	Fairbanks
Eklutna Dam	1373	Anchorage
ARIZONA		
Bert Williams	335	Douglas
William H. Patterson	477	Phoenix
Pilgrim Rest	601	Tucson
Western Empire	1151	Yuma
Pride of Flagstaff	1184	Flagstaff
Desert Scene	1267	Winslow
ARKANSAS		
Vapor City	379	Hot Springs
Wonder State	478	Little Rock
McGehee	546	Rockydondia
Oil City	548	Camden
Gusher	560	El Dorado
Scipio Jones	1103	Eudora
W. M. Townsend	1149	Pine Bluff
Alpha-Omega	1355	Helena
BAHAMAS		
Eureka	11411-B	Nassau
Curfew	1162	Nassau
Hercules	1202	Nassau
Guiding Star	1374	Bimini
Pride of Andros	1376	Fresh Creek
Conchshell	1383	Fresh Creek
Morning Star	1414	Mastic Point
CALIFORNIA		
Athens	70	Oakland
Golden West	86	Los Angeles
Shasta	254	San Francisco
Peninsula	320	Redwood City
Good Will	325	Bakersfield
Harmony	481	Santa Barbara

Name	*No.*	*Location*
Clementine McDuff	598	San Diego
Salton Sea	627	El Centro
Golden Sun	634	Santa Monica
Mt. Shasta	866	Weed
Arrowhead	896	San Bernardino
Ocean View	903	Long Beach
20th Century	988	Fresno
J. B. Bass	1004	Watts
San Joaquin	1016	Stockton
Braxton B. Berkley	1074	Tulare
Pearless	1146	Berkeley
Capital City	1147	Sacramento
Victory	1185	Richmond
Hooker Oak	1197	Oroville
Sunset	1198	Pasadena
Navy City	1268	Vallejo
Warren McCree	1285	Pittsburg
Mount Rubidoux	1306	Riverside
James A. Coleman	1313	Merced
Citadel	1320	Monterey
Sands of the Desert	1339	Victorville
Pacific Coast	1350	Los Angeles
Lake Ellis	1351	Marysville
James Hicks	1356	San Jose
James Finley Wilson	1403	Oxnard
Mount Helix	1405	San Diego
Calico	1411	Bartow
La Cienega	1419	Compton
CANADA		
Menelik	528	Winnipeg
Pride of Montreal	678	Montreal
John Henry Valentine	740	Toronto
Victory	1088	Montreal
Pride of Sydney	1421	Nova Scotia
COLORADO		
Mountain	39	Denver
Pikes Peak Region	473	Colorado Springs
CONNECTICUT		
Charter Oak	67	Hartford
New Nutmeg	67	Hartford
East Rock	141	New Haven
New Era	290	Bridgeport
Shining Star	303	Stamford
Copper City	666	Ansonia
Victory	1096	New London
Goodwill	1325	Waterbury

Name	*No.*	*Location*
CUBA		
El Morro Nimrod	525	Havana
Maceo Immortal	1065	Havana
DELAWARE		
Paul Lawrence Dunbar	106	Wilmington
Pride of Delaware	349	Newark
Alexander Dumas	378	Milford
Pride of Dover	1125	Dover
Benjamin Butler	1348	Wyoming
DISTRICT OF COLUMBIA		
Morning Star	40	Washington
Columbia	85	Washington
National Capitol	980	Washington
Greater Deanwood	1093	Washington
J. Finley Wilson Memorial	1371	Anacostia
FLORIDA		
Maceo	8	Jacksonville
Sunshine City	255	St. Petersburg
Bay City	268	Tampa
Atlas	308	Miami
Rose Height	318	Lakeland
Royal Palm	439	Orlando
Peninsula City	503	Daytona Beach
Paramount	526	West Palm Beach
Celery City	542	Sanford
Palm City	577	Fort Myers
Springtime	592	Clear Water
Pride of Leon	594	Tallahassee
Coral City	610	Key West
Fountain of Youth	649	St. Augustine
Pride of Ft. Lauderdale	652	Ft. Lauderdale
J. A. Nottage	660	Palatka
Sunny South	671	Delray Beach
Indian River	692	Cocoa
Deep Water City	751	Pensacola
Poinsetta	777	Eustis
Carillon	880	Lake Wales
Manatee River	883	Bradenton
Liberty	1052	Miami
Overseas	1078	Homestead
Oak City	1083	Bartow
Non Pareil	1092	Panama City
Dan Laramore	1097	Florence Villa
Pride of Sarasota	1098	Sarasota
Peace River	1099	Arcadia

Name	*No.*	*Location*
Greater Miami	1113	Miami
Royal Poincianna	1116	Sebring
Senator Coleman	1175	Deland
Pride of Saint Lucy	1189	Ft. Pierce
Indian Mound	1205	Ft. Walton
University City	1218	Gainesville
Frederick Kelley	1270	Brooksville
Everglade	1323	Belle Glade
O. W. Bannerman	1380	Perrine
Ocean Front	1410	Fernandina Beach
Pride of Port St. Joe	1415	Port St. Joe
GEORGIA		
Weldon	26	Savannah
Gate City	54	Atlanta
Non Pariel	506	Columbus
Garden City	537	Augusta
Melba	555	Macon
Lincoln Johnson	633	Albany
Utopia	650	Waycross
G. W. F. Phillips	691	Americus
Henry McNeil Turner	719	Atlanta
Pride of Cordele	727	Cordele
N. G. McCall	730	Dublin
Golden Leaf	736	Valdosta
Pride of Brunswick	745	Brunswick
Pride of Vidalia	746	Vidalia
Ebenezer	956	Thomasville
George Washington Carver	1121	Macon
Blue Ribbon	1279	Meridian
A. W. Cummings	1287	Savannah
Meritt Wallace	1334	Millen
Granite City	1343	Elberton
William James	1346	Statesboro
J. Finley Wilson	1364	Rome
Boston Rushing	1381	Metter
Pride of Monroe	1406	Monroe
Packer City	1418	Moultrie
SPANISH HONDURAS, C. A.		
Central Star	612	Tela
IDAHO		
Portneuf	558	Pocatello
ILLINOIS		
Great Lakes	43	Chicago
Hercules	90	East St. Louis
Illinois	147	Danville

Name	*No.*	*Location*
Fort Erie	167	Joliet
Lovejoy	250	Lovejoy
Protective	346	Madison
Greater Fort Dearborn	444	Chicago
Peter H. Clarke	483	Peoria
Pride of Centralia	599	Centralia
University	619	Champaign
Black Hawk	921	Rockford
Greater Chicago	954	Chicago
Lakeview	1132	Decatur
Capital City	1160	Springfield
Robert S. Abbott	1252	Chicago Heights
Greater Robbins	1272	Robbins
E. H. Wright	1327	Chicago
Little Fort	1359	Waukegan
John Wesley Harris	1387	Chicago
INDIANA		
Indiana	104	Indianapolis
Lake City	182	Gary
Wabash	283	Terre Haute
La Salle Landing	298	Southbend
Harbor Light	405	East Chicago
Hametic	428	Fort Wayne
Pride of Kokomo	429	Kokomo
Onyx	479	Richmond
Blue Valley	488	Connersville
Two Rivers	557	Logansport
Fort Harrison	709	Indianapolis
Pride of Anderson	772	Anderson
Oak City	1075	Marion
Michiana Shoals	1091	Mich. City
Greater Indianapolis	1233	Indianapolis
B. G. Pollard	1242	Bloomington
Deroloc	1269	Evansville
Golden Jubilee	1273	Hammond
Eltonia	1362	Elkhart
Greater Marion	1420	Marion
IOWA		
Hawkeye	160	Des Moines
Highland	327	Fort Dodge
Savoy	373	Sioux City
Cedar Valley	426	Waterloo
Fidelity	1058	Cedar Rapids
KANSAS		
Sunflower	204	Kansas City
Peerless Princess	243	Wichita

Name	*No.*	*Location*
KENTUCKY		
Lexington	27	Lexington
Ira	37	Covington
Shackelford	66	Winchester
Blue Grass	292	Louisville
Diamond	309	Richmond
Attucks	475	Henderson
Banneker	582	Danville
Park City	1062	Ashland
Robert Russa Moton	1134	Middlesboro
Rising Sun	1142	Lynch
Frazier	1237	Hopkinsville
J. W. Pitts	1248	Guthrie
Howard Walker	1282	Bowling Green
James E. Kelley	1341	Owensboro
Pride of East End	1385	Louisville
Tuckyanna	1386	Louisville
LOUISIANA		
Crescent City	299	New Orleans
P. B. S. Pinchback	377	Scotlandville
D. C. Hill	522	Monroe
Winter Capitol	595	New Orleans
Judge C. C. Valle	620	Lake Providence
Hub City	646	Alexandria
W. H. Ennis	700	Morgan City
St. Benedict	835	Opelousas
Starr	953	Tallulah
Capital City	993	Baton Rouge
Golden Gate	999	Algiers
R. B. Chapman	1108	Houma
Shafter Gordon	1191	Jennings
Israel Walker	1228	Napoleonville
Samuel J. Sparks	1258	Gretna
Acme	1294	Shreveport
MARYLAND		
Monumental	3	Baltimore
Ancient City	175	Annapolis
Fort Cumberland	176	Cumberland
Crisfield Pride	194	Crisfield
Dorchester	223	Cambridge
Pride of Hagerstown	278	Hagerstown
Chesapeake	314	Havre De Grace
Pride of Montgomery	347	Rockville
Crescent	355	Catonsville
W. Bruce Evans	380	Fairmont Heights
Mountain City	382	Frederick
Pride of Talbot	383	Saint Michael

Name	*No.*	*Location*
Pride of Bladensburg	514	Bladensburg
Pride of Baltimore	713	Baltimore
Sidney Mudd	748	Upper Marlboro
Pride of Towson	842	Towson
Pride of Southern Maryland	968	Bryans Road
Samuel T. Hemsley	974	Easton
W. Sampson Brooks	981	Baltimore
Pride of Prince George	1003	Aquasco
East Baltimore	1043	Baltimore
Queen City	1051	Salisbury
W. A. C. Hughes	1053	Wayside
Spirit of Chesapeake	1107	Baltimore
Pride of Saint Mary's	1120	Valley Lee
Pride of Patapsco	1344	Elkridge
Thomas R. Smith	1404	Baltimore
MASSACHUSETTS		
Commonwealth	19	Boston
Massasoit	129	Cambridge
Harmony	140	Springfield
Quinsigamond	173	Worchester
William H. Carney	200	New Bedford
Bunker-Attucks	1275	Boston
MICHIGAN		
Pratt	322	Ann Arbor
Reeds	354	Port Huron
Silverleaf	534	Lansing
Epicurean	674	Saginaw
Sylvanlake	723	Pontiac
Pride of Michigan	875	Detroit
Motor City	962	Detroit
Golden Gate	973	Inkster
Heart of Detroit	1014	Detroit
Victory	1029	Grand Rapids
Vehicle City	1036	Flint
Robert Settle	1112	Detroit
Nordet	1145	North Detroit
Lake Erie	1164	River Rouge
George Washington Carver	1173	Detroit
Eureka	1231	Hamtramck
Brazil J. Bryant	1311	Battle Creek
J. W. Johnson	1319	Kalamazoo
Timber	1367	Benton Harbor
Charity	1397	Muskegon
MINNESOTA		
Gopher	105	Saint Paul
Ames	106	Minneapolis

Name	*No.*	*Location*
MISSISSIPPI		
Fidelity	507	Vicksburg
L. K. Atwood	518	Jackson
Metropolitan	551	Meridian
H. W. Nichols	556	Clarksdale
Serene	567	Greenville
Vernon Gilbert	576	Biloxi
Hart	640	Greenwood
I. T. Montgomery	664	Mound Bayou
Paul D. Jones	714	Hattiesburg
A. J. Oakes	767	Yazoo City
Henry Hampton	782	Tupelo
Hill	811	Belzoni
Pride of West Point	812	West Point
Pride of Starkville	823	Starkville
Excelsior	834	Canton
McComb Independent	846	McComb
Friendship	923	Brookhaven
Cyrus	1124	Pass Christian
J. T. Jeffry	1141	West Jackson
A. M. Snowden	1203	Cleveland
Pride of Gulfport	1288	Gulfport
Simmons	1338	Hollandale
Magnolia	1354	Moss Point
Tom Richardson	1382	Port Gibson
Winston McGuire	1408	Natchez
MISSOURI		
Heart of America	149	Kansas City
Oriental	976	St. Louis
Greater St. Louis	1012	Saint Louis
Pride of Central Missouri	1028	Jefferson City
Mid West	1122	Saint Louis
Hidalgo	1212	Lexington
Frank H. Hunter	1309	Saint Louis
New Greater St. Louis	1372	St. Louis
MONTANA		
Jackson	881	Billings
NEBRASKA		
Iroquois	92	Omaha
Cornhusker	579	Lincoln
NEVADA		
Silver State	1158	Las Vegas
Sierra	1243	Reno

Name	*No.*	*Location*
NEW JERSEY		
Lighthouse	9	Atlantic City
Pride of Jersey	22	Jersey City
Pride of Camden	83	Camden
Pride of Newark	93	Newark
Monmouth	122	Asbury Park
Ultra	130	Orange
Majestic	153	Hackensack
Witherspoon	178	Princeton
Nehemiah	192	Wildwood
Lackawanna	202	Newark
H. H. Garnett	209	Montclair
Superior	215	New Brunswick
Bates	220	Red Bank
Wayman	231	Salem
Absequam	300	Pleasantville
Mohawk	307	Plainfield
American	333	Paterson
Pride of Burlington	372	Burlington
Centennial	400	Westfield
Pride of Bayonne	461	Bayonne
Ideal	470	Englewood
Greater Woodbury	541	Woodbury
Greater Paulsboro	575	Paulsboro
John Johnston	587	Eatontown
R. H. Terrell	661	South Orange
George R. Carter	696	Mount Holly
Pride of Ocean City	757	Ocean City
George E. Cannon	858	Vaux Hall
Greater Newark	963	Newark
Samuel J. Roberts	979	Bridgeton
Joseph T. Newman	998	Neptune
Hillcrest	1002	Summitt
Pride of Morris	1032	Morristown
Pride of Elizabeth	1117	Elizabeth
Pride of Trenton	1118	Trenton
Pride of Scotch Plains	1168	Scotch Plains
James Elms	1180	Passaic
Pride of Perth Amboy	1183	Perth Amboy
Pride of Swedesboro	1206	Swedesboro
Pride of Lakewood	1225	Lakewood
Columbus Wright	1326	Linden
Pride of Penns Grove	1342	Penns Grove
Walter J. Conley	1379	Freehold
Charles H. Little	1395	Camden
Samuel S. Dadde	1400	Trenton

Name	*No.*	*Location*
NEW MEXICO		
Navajo	863	Albuquerque
Hillie Y. Moton	864	Roswell
NEW YORK		
Brooklyn	32	Brooklyn
Monarch	45	New York
Flower City	91	Rochester
Westchester	116	Tarrytown
Elite	119	Buffalo
Imperial	127	New York
Greater Manhattan	145	New York
Queen City	174	Elmira
Forest City	180	Ithaca
Empire	216	New Rochelle
Pride of Jamaica	217	Jamaica
Electric City	259	Schenectady
Sunset	295	Niagara Falls
Pride of Flushing	302	Flushing
Continental	319	Staten Island
Blossom Heath	348	Mount Vernon
Ferncliff	367	White Plains
Enterprise	401	Corona
Rockland	424	Nyack
Pride of Hudson	466	Poughkeepsie
Antler	494	Binghamton
Rockaway	532	Far Rockaway
Frederick Allen	609	Saratoga Springs
Henry Lincoln Johnson	630	New York
Gerrit Smith	690	Utica
Chadakoin	718	Jamestown
Colonial City	733	Kingston
Neptune	743	New York
William E. Atkins	822	Newburgh
Industry	889	New York
Sunset	894	Freeport
Rose of Sharon	972	Brooklyn
David McDaniel	982	Mamaroneck
Antler	985	Huntington
Queens	1001	Jamaica
Pride of Tuckahoe	1006	Tuckahoe
Pride of the Bronx	1007	Bronx
Frontier	1024	Buffalo
Pride of Syracuse	1104	Syracuse
Commando	1105	Albany
I. P. Turner	1111	Lackawanna
Woodstock	1114	Bronx

Name	*No.*	*Location*
New Home	1123	Hempstead
George E. Bates	1216	Troy
Finger Lakes	1259	Auburn
Bison City	1409	Buffalo
Dragon	1413	New York
NORTH CAROLINA		
Zeno	23	Newbern
Old North State	87	Greensboro
Golden Leaf	142	Elizabeth City
Philanthropin	193	Washington
Eclipse	230	Badin
Pitt	234	Greenville
Midway	241	Reidsville
Riverview	242	Tarboro
Golden Crown	253	Plymouth
Twin County	257	Rocky Mount
Pride of East	261	Goldsboro
Leading	263	Wilmington
Pisgah	266	Charlotte
Calumet	273	Farmville
Eclectic	274	Belhaven
Pride of Orange	276	Chapel Hill
Fidelity	277	Raleigh
Furniture City	282	High Point
Marshall	297	Wilson
Skyland Banner	316	Statesville
Bull City	317	Durham
White Lily	326	Ahoskie
Elwood	331	Albemarle
Fawndale	363	Asheville
Mountain Laurel	406	Hendersonville
Pride of Hickory	425	Hickory
Moloch	468	Gastonia
Star of Rockingham	487	Leaksville
Starr	495	Pinetops
Eastern Pride	512	Kinston
Mount Eagle	535	Lenior
Pilot	626	Monroe
Thermopylae	644	Mt. Airy
Security	688	Sanford
Reciprocity	693	Shelby
Mercury	712	Williamston
George W. Lee	756	Windsor
Solomon Reddick	798	Robersonville
Essex	862	Scotland Neck
Peace	868	Enfield
Cape Fear	995	Wilmington

Name	*No.*	*Location*
Camel City	1021	Winston-Salem
Triangle	1044	Mooresville
Pride of Beaufort	1101	Beaufort
New River	1109	Jacksonville
Warren County	1128	Warrenton
Clarence Carters	1140	Clinton
Garden Spot of the East	1169	Lagrange
New Columbus	1186	Chadbourn
Ocean Breeze	1188	Moorehead City
Long Park	1211	Rockingham
James Harris	1255	Oxford
Civil Rights	1260	Maxton
Pride of Vance	1263	Henderson
Everad	1265	Rutherfordton
Progressive	1280	Seaboard
Trent River	1283	Trenton
Ernest Carver	1312	Fayetteville
Blue Ridge	1324	Tryon
James E. Kelley	1353	Mount Olive
Albright	1401	Smithfield

OHIO

Name	*No.*	*Location*
Alpha	1	Cincinnati
Spirit of Ohio	52	Cleveland
Buckeye	73	Youngstown
Waldorf	76	Dayton
Muskingum Valley	82	Zanesville
Golden Rule	129	Toledo
Champion City	177	Cleveland
Franklin	203	Columbus
Louis Mitchell	222	Warren
Prince Albert	232	Steubenville
Rubber City	233	Akron
Victory	287	Canton
Lake Erie	362	Lorain
King Tut	389	Cleveland
Leroy	414	Portsmouth
Starlight	433	Painesville
A. L. Moore	442	Ironton
Silver Leaf	456	Middletown
Olentangy	521	Columbus
Pure Gold	591	Hamilton
Richland Valley	614	Mansfield
Iola	617	Xenia
Tuscarawas	632	Massillon
Montgomery	789	Sandusky
Moundbuilders	821	Newark
Mi-Ty Majestic	934	Cleveland

Name	*No.*	*Location*
Loco City	1056	Lima
Pride of Ohio	1057	Dayton
Pride of Cincinnati	1061	Cincinnati
Kokosing	1085	Mount Vernon
Tri-City	1150	Troy
Arthur J. Riggs	1153	Springfield
Cedar City	1165	Lebanon
Robinson-Fletcher	1192	Urbana
Longhorn	1209	Lockland
Highpoint	1214	Bellfontaine
George W. Carver	1245	Dover
Scioto	1264	Circleville
Mound City	1277	Chillicothe
George W. Rideout	1293	Liverpool
Sidney Thompson	1318	Glenville, Cleveland
Orr	1390	Orrville
Charles Helvey	1398	Springfield
OKLAHOMA		
Cosmopolitan	247	Tulsa
Victory	248	Oklahoma City
James E. Kelley	1332	Oklahoma City
Roscoe Conklin Simmons	1363	Muskogee
OREGON		
Billy Webb	1050	Portland
PANAMA		
Aurora	523	Colon City
Eyrie	530	Silver City
Mount Olympus	559	Panama City
United American	704	Panama, Republic of
Justice	832	La Boca, Canal Zone
Libertad	933	Colon
Unity	1084	Paraiso, Canal Zone
PENNSYLVANIA		
Keystone	6	Washington
Iron City	17	Pittsburgh
Lawrence	18	New Castle
O. V. Catto	20	Philadelphia
Berks	47	Reading
Anthracite	57	Scranton
Unity	71	Harrisburg
Greater Pittsburgh	115	Pittsburgh
Summit	115	Uniontown
Northside	124	Pittsburgh
Laurel	133	Chambersburg

Name	*No.*	*Location*
Conestoga	140	Lancaster
Mount Vernon	151	Coatesville
Captain Levi M. Hood	159	West Chester
Cyrene	169	Steelton
Arandale	184	Altoona
Canon	186	Canonsburg
Twin City	187	Farrell
Pride of the West	196	McDonald
Clinton J. Lewis	201	Bristol
Edgar A. Still	207	Williamsport
Monongahela Valley	208	Donora
Dunlap	214	Brownsville
Booker T. Washington	218	McKeesport
Brighton Pioneer	219	Beaver Falls
John A. Watts	224	Chester
Brotherly Love	228	York
Essex Reed	236	Ardmore
Mount Odin	284	Greensburg
Valley	294	New Kensington
Gem City	328	Erie
Dauphin	359	Middletown
Flood City	371	Johnstown
Elmwood	438	Norristown
Monroe	513	Stroudsburg
Tri-Boro	515	Rankin
B. F. Howard	580	Media
Triple City	694	Meadville
Oaky	697	Monessen
Juaniata	702	Mount Union
Quaker City	720	Philadelphia
William E. Burrell	737	North Hills
Maple View	780	Elizabeth
Robinson Welburn	794	Berwyn
John F. Moreland	801	Aliquippa
Twin County	838	Vandergrift
Magnet City	849	Midland
Chris J. Perry	965	Philadelphia
Mansfield Valley	966	Carnegie
Leonard C. Irvin	994	Philadelphia
John M. Marquess	1017	Frankford
City of Progress	1031	Clairton
J. T. Brandy	1047	Duquesne
Cora Steel	1064	Coraopolis
Chevy Chase	1133	Indiana
Edward W. Henry	1235	Germantown, Philadelphia
Montgomery	1271	Pottstown
Bethal	1284	Bethlehem

Name	*No.*	*Location*
Harry Matthew Dorsey	1345	Columbia
Glass City	1347	Ford City
RHODE ISLAND		
Trinity	183	Newport
Otha Boon	931	Providence
SOUTH CAROLINA		
Emanuel	339	Charleston
Palmetto	342	Columbia
Sterling	344	Rock Hill
Benjamin Banneker	364	Greenville
Union	430	Mullins
Ajax	443	Darlington
Richard Allen	472	Newberry
Pee Dee	505	Cheraw
McAdams	561	York
Wisteria	569	Summerville
Hill City	570	Chester
Henry McGowen	583	Anderson
S. J. Banfield	584	Beaufort
Fort Sumter	628	Charleston
Pride of South Carolina	793	Timmonsville
Pride of Union	1041	Union
Pride of Gaffney	1046	Gaffney
Ebenezer	1187	Clover
Birnies	1195	Sumter
Carver	1226	Walterboro
Progressive	1249	Mt. Pleasant
Living Water	1262	Myrtle Beach
Pineview	1337	Hyman
The Royal Sons	1393	Georgetown
Julius Thompson	1407	Anderson
TENNESSEE		
Bluff City	96	Memphis
Armistice	440	Chattanooga
Rose of Sharon	448	Greenville
General A. Boyd	457	Clarksville
Pinnacle	511	Etowah
Clinch Mountain	531	Kingsport
Pride of Tennessee	1102	Nashville
E. A. Davis	1138	Murfreesboro
Tennessee Valley	1152	Knoxville
Harlan Flippin	1155	Columbia
Pride of Franklin	1289	Franklin
W. J. O. Lee	1290	Humbolt
Atomic	1301	Oak Ridge

Name	*No.*	*Location*
Orange Mound	1361	Memphis
Aluminum City	1389	Alcoa
Knox	1391	Cleveland
J. Finley Wilson	1396	Dickson
Wautauga	1402	Morristown
TEXAS		
Trinity	480	Dallas
Mission	499	San Antonio
Gibraltar	500	Houston
Oleander	550	Galveston
Neches	593	Beaumont
Security	625	Port Arthur
Gateway	855	El Paso
Greater Houston	1039	Houston
Pride of Orange	1137	Orange
Northwest	1217	Wichita Falls
Pride of Amarilla	1292	Amarillo
West Texas	1298	Odessa
Ocean Wave	1303	Corpus Christi
UTAH		
Wasatch	51	Ogden
Bee Hive	407	Salt Lake City
VIRGINIA		
Pandora	2	Newport News
Excelsior	4	Hampton
Eureka	5	Norfolk
Capital City	11-A	Richmond
Williams	11-B	Richmond
Berkley	12	Berkley-Norfolk
Beacon Light	34	Portsmouth
Alexandria	48	Alexandria
Smithfield	65	Smithfield
Royal	77	Petersburg
Greater Norfolk	132	Norfolk
Evening Star	151	Covington
Lily of the Valley	171	Staunton
Old Dominion	181	Lynchburg
Morning Star	189	Danville
Mizpah	191	Phoebus
Rivanna	195	Charlottesville
Greater Suffolk	206	Suffolk
Evergreen	213	Capeville
Rappahannock	229	Fredericksburg
Tidewater	262	Windsor
Prince Edward	269	Farmville
Saint Luke	279	Franklin

Name	*No.*	*Location*
Blue Ridge	281	Roanoke
Pride of Arlington	384	Arlington
Patrick Henry	390	Martinsville
Roy Scott	391	Pocahontas
Tenneva	395	Bristol
Gregory Hayes	399	South Boston
Daniel Farrar	458	Winchester
Pride of Warren	486	Front Royal
Pride of Warrenton	510	Warrenton
Chihuahua	519	Pulaski
James H. Hayes	529	Vienna
Old Capitol	629	Williamsburg
Bull Run	698	Manassas
Prophet Elijah	701	Crews
Pride of Gloucester	837	Gloucester
T. T. Brown	859	Berryville
South Anna	874	Ashland
Star of Bethlehem	958	Gum Springs
Rock of Surry	975	Surry
Greater Deep Creek	1033	Deep Creek
Banner	1110	Chase City
Victory	1179	Emporia
Pride of Bedford	1368	Bedford
Greater Eastern Shore	1375	Parksley
J. Finley Wilson	1388	Radford
Pioneer	1412	Virginia Beach

WASHINGTON

Name	No.	Location
Puget Sound	109	Seattle
Mount Tacoma	142	Tacoma
Yakima Gem	353	Yakima
Olympic	1139	Bremerton
Columbia River	1222	Pasco
Cascade	1416	Seattle

JAMAICA, B.W.I.

Name	No.	Location
Pride of St. Lucia	1086	St. Lucia
Pearl of Antilles	1316	Kingston
J. A. G. Smith	1349	St. Andrews
Wm. Berchell Knibb	1378	Spanish Town, St. Catherine

WEST VIRGINIA

Name	No.	Location
Gate City	33	Bluefield
Pan Handle	74	Wheeling
Mountain State	117	Clarksburg
Pride of West Virginia	130	Charleston
Kanawha	130	Charleston
Eureka	131	Huntington

Name	*No.*	*Location*
Monongahela	148	Fairmont
Tug Valley	360	Williamson
Black Diamond	396	Eckman
Pride of Berkley	402	Martinsburg
Kings Creek	616	Weirton
John Brown	841	Charlestown
Short Creek	957	Power
Rhododendron	1034	Parkersburg
Coal Valley	1068	Osage
John Scott	1070	Beckley
George E. Turner	1080	Triadelphia
Progress	1207	Caretta
W. W. Sanders	1257	Morgantown
Dan Cole	1310	Northfork
John Cobb	1394	Moorefield

WISCONSIN

Badger State	1115	Milwaukee

WYOMING

Frontier	285	Cheyenne

TEMPLE ROSTER FOR THE IMPROVED BENEVOLENT AND PROTECTIVE ORDER OF ELKS OF THE WORLD

ALABAMA

Jones Valley	145	Birmingham
Gulf City	307	Mobile
Shell Bayou	337	Prichard
Coosa Valley	554	Gadsden
Wire Grass	566	Dothan
Oak City	626	Tuscaloosa
Southern Temple	644	Montgomery
Shades Valley	685	Bessemer
Tuxedo	771	Fairfield
College City	823	Talladega
W. R. Pettiford	845	Anniston
Pride of Alabama	919	Selma
Cosmopolitan	924	Tuskegee Institute
Peanut Pride	990	Enterprise
Black Belt	1016	Demopolis

ARIZONA

Nora F. Taylor	241	Bisbee
Grand Canyon	437	Phoenix
Pilgrim Rest	477	Tucson
Annie Kelley	813	Yuma

Name	*No.*	*Location*
Twin Peaks	838	Flagstaff
Meteor Crater	920	Winslow
ARKANSAS		
Derrick City	352	El Dorado
Rose City	379	Little Rock
Silver Leaf	797	Camden
Pine City	841	Pine Bluff
Rice Belt	928	McGhee
Mayhall	929	Warren
BAHAMAS		
Excelsior	37	Nassau
Curfew	816	Nassau
Alpha	909	Nassau
Guiding Star	1008	Bimini
Golden Gate	1027	Andros
Sacred Heart	1028	Andros
B. W. INDIES		
Rose of Antille	952	Kingston, Jamaica
CALIFORNIA		
Mizpah	18	Oakland
Hiawatha	91	Los Angeles
Guiding Star	181	San Francisco
Nautilus	436	San Diego
Cherry Blossom	515	San Mateo
Ne Plus Ultra	522	Bakersfield
Phyllis Wheatley	526	Calexico
Victoria	609	Long Beach
Campanile	630	Berkeley
Arrowhead	665	San Bernardino
Sunshine	681	Los Angeles
Mary D. Logan	706	Fresno
Carnation	734	Stockton
Lottie Augustus	796	Los Angeles
Camelia	831	Sacramento
Mamie Hicks	833	Richmond
Rose Garden	847	Altadena
Gem City	861	Duarte
Aquilla	892	Oroville
Adele B. Ashford	903	Vallejo
Rosebud	921	Tulare
Magnolia	943	Pittsburgh
Lily of the Valley	953	Merced
Kismet	966	Pebble Beach
Catherine Keith	983	Los Angeles
Elizabeth Ross Gordon	991	San Jose
Golden Poppy	994	Yuba City

Name	*No.*	*Location*
CANADA		
Queen Victoria	456	Winnipeg, Manitoba
Beaver	578	Montreal
Eastern	779	Montreal
Queen City	1003	Toronto
CANAL ZONE		
Eureka	309	Ancon
Jasmine	323	Cristobal
Eyrie	450	Cristobal
Narcisse	658	Balboa
COLORADO		
Mountain	174	Denver
Queen of the West	541	Pueblo
CONNECTICUT		
Pocahontas	55	New Haven
Alpha	83	Hartford
Excelsior	144	New London
Juanita	169	Bridgeport
Phyllis Wheatley	179	Stamford
Lily of the Valley	406	Ansonia
Trellis	663	Hartford
Clock City	895	Waterbury
CUBA		
La Havana	303	Havana
DELAWARE		
Pocahontas	60	Wilmington
Hester Dutton	235	Milford
Elizabeth Boulden	269	Newark
Pride of Dover	784	Dover
Julia E. Gibbs	981	Wyoming
DISTRICT OF COLUMBIA		
Forest	9	Washington
Columbia	422	Washington
National Capitol	659	Washington
Greater Deanwood	872	Washington
Elizabeth Ross Gordon	1011	Washington
FLORIDA		
Antlers	39	Miami
Paramount	48	West Palm Beach
Bay City	158	Tampa
Sunshine	168	St. Petersburg
Pride of Maceo	186	Jacksonville

Name	*No.*	*Location*
Highland City	217	Lakeland
Evergreen	321	Sanford
Peninsula	329	Daytona Beach
Tranquillo	350	Fort Myers
Pride of Ft. Lauderdale	395	Ft. Lauderdale
Coral City	400	Key West
Pride of Leon	411	Tallahassee
Pride of Fountain of Youth	413	St. Augustine
Magnolia	441	Cocoa
Nottage	484	Palatka
Unique	488	Ocala
Manatee River	612	Bradentown
Orange Blossom	661	Pensacola
Progressive	697	Eustis
Liberty	724	Miami
Oak City	743	Bartow
Pride of Oversea	745	Homestead
Laramore	752	Florenceville
George W. Carver	754	Panama City
Pride of Sarasota	756	Sarasota
Peace River	758	Arcadia
Pride of Greater Miami	769	Miami
Ridge	777	Sebring
Sunny South	819	Delray Beach
Carillion	821	Lake Wales
Carnation	834	Deland
Pride of St. Lucie	853	Fort Pierce
Booker Washington	862	Fort Walton
Royal Palm	890	Orlando
University	900	Gainesville
Emma V. Kelley	965	Belle Glades
Kelley's	1004	Brooksville
O. W. Bannerman	1018	Perrine
Pride of St. Joe	1040	Port of St. Joe

GEORGIA

Name	*No.*	*Location*
Gate City	43	Atlanta
Elite	71	Savannah
Electric City	407	Augusta
Eliza Turner	432	Atlanta
Melba	445	Macon
E. G. McCall	453	Dublin
Violet	457	Valdosta
Non Pariel	464	Columbus
Sunshine	470	Waycross
Ocean Breeze	474	Brunswick
Toombs	772	Lyons
Altamaha	974	Meridian

Name	*No.*	*Location*
G. W. Carver	993	Macon
Phoebe Floyd	1002	Statesboro
Kelley Rose	1005	Thomasville
G. W. F. Phillips	1020	Americus
Georgia Washburn	1023	Atlanta
Bomber City	1037	Atlanta
ILLINOIS		
Unique	15	Chicago
Warden	16	Chicago
Elmira	21	Chicago
Liberty	22	Chicago
Heliotrope	26	Chicago
Pride of Chicago	74	Chicago
Purple	126	Lovejoy
Tri-City	209	Madison
Macbeth	216	Joliet
Millie Willie	221	Metropolis
Golden Rod	234	E. St. Louis
Nora F. Taylor	270	Peoria
Ella Berry	359	Chicago
Golden Leaf	365	Centralia
Victory	530	Champaign
Vermillion	601	Danville
Daughters of Honor	622	Chicago
Greater Egyptian	732	Cairo
Macon	793	Decatur
Capital City	818	Springfield
Emma V. Kelley	901	Chicago Heights
Pride of Robbins	915	Robbins
Ida B. Wells	973	Chicago
Friendship	1021	Chicago
Venus	1042	East St. Louis
INDIANA		
Halcyon	127	Indianapolis
Emma L. Cherry	135	Gary
Bethany	171	Terra Haute
Carnation	253	Muncie
Pride of South Bend	264	South Bend
Ray of Light	305	Richmond
Morning Star	346	Fort Wayne
Rose of Sharon	404	Indianapolis
Mt. Calm	562	Indianapolis
Rose of Anderson	563	Anderson
Oak City	753	Marion
Eureka	791	Indiana Harbor
Greater Indianapolis	899	Indianapolis

Name	*No.*	*Location*
Calumet	906	Hammond
Clara E. Webster	926	Evansville
Royal Tower	937	Kokomo
Georgia Clemons	950	Bloomington
Evening Star	996	Elkhart
IDAHO		
Kingport	603	Pocatello
IOWA		
Rose	33	Des Moines
Melrose	277	Waterloo
Eureka	314	Sioux City
Emma V. Kelley	726	Fort Dodge
Padmore	729	Cedar Rapids
KANSAS		
Princess	557	Wichita
Sunflower	1019	Kansas City
KENTUCKY		
Blue Grass	72	Lexington
Golden Link	123	Winchester
Paramount	175	Louisville
Horace	333	Henderson
Phyllis Wheatley	371	Danville
Madison	392	Richmond
Silver Crest	728	Ashland
Meadowlark	731	Covington
Rising Sun	808	Lynch
Victory	809	Middlesboro
Rose Garrett	910	Earlington
Hattie Wolfe	933	Bowling Green
Cora	962	Hopkinsville
Yancy Payne	968	Guthrie
Katie Prather	980	Owensboro
Tuckyette	1034	Louisville
Mary E. Merrit	1035	Louisville
LOUISIANA		
Crescent City	185	New Orleans
Winter Capitol	427	New Orleans
Judge C. C. Valle	454	Lake Providence
C. J. Walker	460	Monroe
W. H. Ennis	527	Morgan City
Teche	540	Lafayette
C. J. Walker	648	Tallulah
Mary Howell	679	Newellton
Golden Gate	740	New Orleans

Name	*No.*	*Location*
R. B. Chapman	767	Houma
Israel Walker	885	Napoleonville
Larfargues	888	Alexandria
Emanuel Cooper	912	Gretna
Capital City	978	Baton Rouge
St. Benedict	1013	Opelousas
MARYLAND		
Great Southern	30	Baltimore
Pride of Annapolis	76	Annapolis
Light of Crisfield	86	Crisfield
Mountain City	136	Cumberland
Success	154	Salisbury
Sharon	160	Hagerstown
Susquehanna	196	Havre de Grace
Progress of Dorchester	224	Cambridge
Bright Hope	233	St. Michaels
Love	255	Fairmont Heights
Harmony	349	College Park
Emma Williams	358	Catonsville
Frances Ellen Watkins Harper	429	Baltimore
Golden Rod	430	Rockville
American Beauty	476	Upper Marlboro
C. J. Walker	509	Frederick
Esther Progressive	586	Towson
Pride of Southern Maryland	651	Bryans Road
W. Sampson Brooks	682	Baltimore
Loyal Ladies	712	Brandywine
Zorah Elliott	717	Baltimore
Abbie M. Johnson	718	Newburg
Spirit of Chesapeake	761	Baltimore
St. Mary's	782	Valley Lee
Pride and Joy	814	Easton
Elizabeth Ross Gordon	1041	Baltimore
MASSACHUSETTS		
Phyllis Wheatley	22	Wollaston
Juanita	31	Cambridge
Nokomis	36	Worcester
Susan Sullivan	94	New Bedford
Harriet Tubman	122	Boston
Forget-me-not	302	Springfield
Parthenia	905	Boston
MICHIGAN		
Florence Ames	17	Detroit
Daisy Chain	212	Ann Arbor
St. Clair	296	Port Huron
Capitol City	308	Lansing

Name	*No.*	*Location*
Golden Seal	334	Grand Rapids
Crystal	435	Pontiac
Charlotee Ray	549	Saginaw
Genessee	550	Flint
Beulahland	569	Detroit
Emma V. Kelley	650	Detroit
Lady Camile	755	Detroit
Cornetta	802	Detroit
Victory	807	Detroit
Silver Star	826	River Rouge
Grace	865	Detroit
Sunset	925	Inkster
Golden Star	951	Battle Creek
Buena V	971	Kalamazoo
Royal	1009	Benton Harbor
Ruth	1012	Hamtramck
Grace	1025	Detroit
MINNESOTA		
Como	128	St. Paul
Minnehaha	129	Minneapolis
MISSISSIPPI		
Gulf Coast	471	Biloxi
Hart	513	Greenwood
Grace Jones	639	Jackson
Twentieth Century	652	Greenville
Bettie Woolfolk	669	Yazoo City
Kissia Clifton	671	Tupelo
Martha Mongomery	674	Mound Bayou
Friendship	698	Brookhaven
Eureka	737	Vicksburg
R. B. Matthews	739	Meridian
Hill	783	Belzoni
Virginia Webb	795	Jackson
Minnie Cox	843	Indianola
Sarah Douglas	870	Cleveland
Anna Washington	932	Gulfport
Estelle Anderson	967	Canton
Mary Love	979	Long Beach
Boyd's	985	Hollandale
Emma V. Kelley	995	Moss Point
Pride of Marks	999	Marks
MISSOURI		
White	19	St. Louis
Polar Wave	87	St. Louis
Great Western	118	St. Louis
Heart of America	120	Kansas City

Name	*No.*	*Location*
Washington	131	St. Louis
Phoebe's Pride	132	St. Louis
Clover Leaf	141	St. Louis
Greater St. Louis	688	St. Louis
Midwest	850	St. Louis
Hidalgo	878	Richmond
Rocketta	1017	St. Louis
MONTANA		
Yellowstone	959	Billings
NEBRASKA		
Cherokee	223	Omaha
Golden Rod	390	Lincoln
NEVADA		
Desert Sands	824	Las Vegas
Tahoe	883	Reno
NEW JERSEY		
Ocean	13	Atlantic City
Essex	42	Newark
Amaranth	53	Orange
Fannie J. Coppin	57	Camden
Pride of Asbury	64	Asbury Park
Lily Belle	82	Wildwood
Pride of Jersey	98	Jersey City
Mt. Salem	114	Salem
Rising Sun	119	Princeton
Pride of Atlantic	121	Atlantic City
Artlu	147	E. Orange
Phyllis Wheatley	149	Montclair
Sunbeam	164	New Brunswick
Wenonah	165	Bridgeton
Mohawk	191	Plainfield
Acme	198	Morristown
Bayview	199	Pleasantville
Magnolia	207	Cape May
Lackawanna	208	Newark
Majestic	215	Hackensack
R. J. Walton	238	Burlington
Centennial	246	Westfield
American	258	Paterson
Pride of Bayonne	266	Bayonne
Phyllis Wheatley	276	Fair Haven
Watchung	289	Somerville
Ideal	290	Englewood
Sea Coast	326	Atlantic Highlands

Name	*No.*	*Location*
Greater Woodbury	341	Woodbury
Blossom of Maxwell	345	Eatontown
C. J. Walker	353	Paulsboro
Geranium	469	Ocean City
Friendship	479	Boonton
Pride of Mt. Holly	491	Mt. Holly
Greater Newark	503	Newark
Anita	564	South Orange
Bethune	572	Vaux Hall
Elizabeth Bunn	677	Neptune
Pride of Elizabeth	77	Elizabeth
Pride of Trenton	774	Trenton
Sojourner Truth	839	Passaic
Greater Swedesboro	844	Swedesboro
Octavia Washington	868	Lakewood
Hillcrest	947	Summit
Victoria	964	Roselle
Margaret Smith	976	Pennsgrove
Lee Gibson	1014	Freehold
Minnie Harding	1022	Camden
Golden Beryl	1026	Perth Amboy
Alice M. Shorter	1029	Trenton
NEW YORK		
Eureka	22-A	New York
Eureka	22-B	New York
Eldorado	32	Rochester
Excelsior	35	Brooklyn
Pyramid	45	New Rochelle
Cayuga	54	Ithaca
Sleepy Hollow	58	Tarrytown
Invincible	77	New York
Progressive	79	Brooklyn
Manhattan	93-A	New York
Manhattan	93-B	New York
Liberty	97	Jamaica
Cayadotta	113	Syracuse
Elite	143	Buffalo
Queen City	146	Elmira
Loyal	148	Albany
Pride of Flushing	163	East Elmhurst
Golden Eagle	183	Schenectady
Sunshine	187	Niagara Falls
Sunset	211	Yonkers
Raritan	218	Staten Island
Celestial	225	Mt. Vernon
North Shore	226	Glen Cove
Enterprise	240	East Elmhurst

Name	*No.*	*Location*
Rockland	261	Nyack
Sarah Allen	274	Binghamton
Queen of Hudson	293	Poughkeepsie
Rosebud	297	White Plains
Pride of Far Rockaway	320	Inwood
Mary A. Carter	362	Saratoga Springs
Apex	387	New York
Harriet Tubman	421	Utica
Progressive	475	Newburgh
Suffolk	478	Quoque
Chautauqua	542	Jamestown
Industry	576	New York
Sunrise	503	Freeport
Unity	617	Kingston
Lottie C. Kennedy	642	New York
Rose of Sharon	655	Brooklyn
Forget-Me-Not	667	Huntington
Queens	678	Jamaica
Pride of West Chester	683	Tuckahoe
Pride of the Bronx	699	Bronx
Emma V. Kelley	700	Buffalo
Queensboro	742	Corona
I. P. Turner	770	Lackawanna
Woodstock	780	Bronx
New Hope	786	Glen Cove
Laura E. Williams	787	Mamaroneck
Monarch	815	Bronx
Amity	882	Amityville
Victory	893	Troy
Owasco	896	Auburn
Elizabeth Ross Gordon	1000	New York
Elizabeth Kimbrough	1015	Hudson

NORTH CAROLINA

Silver Leaf	111	Elizabeth City
Old North State	142	Greensboro
Love and Union	150	Plymouth
Magnolia	151	Washington
Zeno	166	New Bern
Leading Light	178	Wilmington
Star of Orient	203	Tarboro
Lily of the Valley	204	Belhaven
Ark of the Covenant	214	Wilson
Garden of Iris	220	Winston-Salem
Truelight	222	Farmville
Pisgah	228	Charlotte
Piedmont	229	High Point
Mizpah	265	Rocky Mount

Name	*No.*	*Location*
Capitol City	310	Raleigh
Golden Rod	368	Greenville
Guiding Star	373	Pinetops
Evening Star	382	Hickory
Fidelity	434	Williamston
Sunbeam	447	Goldsboro
Dunbar	463	Reidsville
Eureka	521	Ahoskie
Golden Light	556	Robersonville
Rhododendron	573	Asheville
Rose Hill	580	Roper
Gloria	602	Kinston
Morning Star	615	Sanford
Cape Fear	668	Wilmington
Skyland Banner	670	Statesville
Excelsior	692	Windsor
Queen Esther	696	Chapel Hill
Salome	704	Durham
Emma V. Kelley	748	Kings Mountan
Essex	764	Scotland Neck
Social Elite	766	Beaufort
Guiding Light	768	Jacksonville
Aluminum	775	Badin
Jerusalem	799	Warrenton
Mountain Laurel	811	Hendersonville
Imperial	825	Chadbourn
Thermopylae	828	Mt. Airy
Mosettic	829	Clinton
Golden Star	849	La Grange
Rosebud	851	Albemarle
Triangle	869	Mooresville
Prosperity	887	Enfield
Macedonia	911	Burlington
Unity	914	Margarettsville
Ivey	916	Rockingham
Orchid	923	Gastonia
Gardenia	935	Rutherfordton
Mimoso	936	Lenoir
Ernest Carver	957	Fayettesville
Blue Ridge	963	Tryon
Utopia	969	Morehead City
York Jones	970	Charlotte
Mamie S. Hicks	982	Mt. Olive
Trent River	1031	Polloksville

OHIO

Etta-Wah	7	Cincinnati
Glenara	21	Cleveland

Name	*No.*	*Location*
Royal	41	Dayton
Mary Exalted	95	Akron
Naomi	124	Youngstown
Esther	176	Canton
Jeptha	195	Warren
Capital City	231	Columbus
Peerless	236	Loraine
Mary Talbert	257	Cleveland
Minnehaha		Middleton
Nora F. Taylor	272	Portsmouth
Alpha	351	Painesville
Golden Leaf	377	Hamilton
Jefferson	391	Steubenville
Sonora	396	Springfield
June	409	Mansfield
Grace	424	Toledo
Aurora	433	Xenia
Pride of Mound Builder	551	Newark
Pride of Muskigum	627	Zaneville
Mollie DeBraun	686	Cleveland
Abbie Johnson	722	Dayton
Jennie Porter	727	Cincinnati
Phyllis Wheatley	741	Lima
Queen Mary	778	Massilon
Roosevelt	803	Piqua
Emma V. Kelley	836	Urbana
Lily of the Valley	855	Lockland
Queen Esther	873	Bellefontaine
Sojourner Truth	881	Cleveland
Wallace Grimes	884	Lebanon
Pride of Sandusky	902	Sandusky
Logan Elm	918	Circleville
China Center	934	East Liverpool
Mary LaSantee	946	Dover
Frances E. W. Harper	958	Cleveland
Rose City	1032	Springfield
Elizabeth Ross Gordon	1033	Orrville
OKLAHOMA		
Cosmopolitan	133	Tulsa
Victoria	189	Oklahoma City
Oil City	714	Tulsa
R. C. Simmons	1010	Muskogee
OREGON		
Dahlia	202	Portland
PANAMA		
Libertad	649	Colon

Name	No.	Location
PENNSYLVANIA		
Western Star	3	Washington
Mosiwidael	38	Pittsburgh
Bon Ami	49	Pittsburgh
Chester Valley	50	Coatesville
Phyllis Wheatley	51	Philadelphia
Northampton	52	Easton
Unity	61	Harrisburg
Zylphia	66	Farrell
Quaker City	73	Philadelphia
Cyrenus	75	Steelton
Evening Star	85	Connellsville
Keystone	92	Donora
Oak Leaf	96	Brownsville
Sheba	99	Houston
Susan Shands	103	Chester
Queen Esther	105	York
Twilight	106	Bristol
Mary Alice	108	Reading
Ruth	116	Pittsburgh
Queen of Sheba	137	Lancaster
Ula Lee	156	Philadelphia
Valley	167	New Castle
Rising Star	177	McDonald
Keystone	197	Beaver Falls
Dauphin	227	Middletown
Montgomery	250	Norristown
Violet	260	Altoona
Carnation	267	Adamsburg
Mecca	294	Johnstown
Oziel	317	Erie
McKea	322	McKeesport
Rose of Sharon	357	East Stroudsburg
Elite	428	Monessen
Keystone	448	Philadelphia
Flotilla	455	North Apollo
Oceola	468	Ambler
Riverside	473	Rankin
Pride of West Chester	487	West Chester
Charlotte Hall	494	Media
Lily of the Valley	500	Elizabeth
Florence Mills	518	Wayne
Laurel	519	Chambersburg
Magnolia	532	Aliquippa
Good Luck	555	Midland
Ken-Ton-Ion	631	New Kensington
Laverta	653	Philadelphia
Pride of No. Philadelphia	657	Philadelphia

Name	*No.*	*Location*
Carolyn D. Irvin	673	Philadelphia
Pride of North East	689	Philadelphia
El Clairtonia	707	Clairton
Pocahontas	719	Mt. Union
M. V. Prillerman	715	Duquesne
SoJourner Truth	723	Verona
Abbie M. Johnson	725	Corapolis
Victory	805	Ernest
Queen Allona	827	Meadville
Pride of Germantown	875	Philadelphia
Mary Esther	917	Pottstown
Anthracite	927	Scranton
Lehigh	930	Bethlehem
Glass-ette	975	Ford City
Martha Dorsey	992	Columbia
Nancy W. Wilson	1036	Williamsport
RHODE ISLAND		
Harriet Tubman	88	Newport
Harriet Tillman	59	Providence
SOUTH CAROLINA		
Blue Ridge	219	Charleston
Sea Breeze	381	Charleston
Imperial	405	Chester
Sunshine	444	York
Eureka	590	Mullins
Primrose	611	Columbia
Living Beauty	709	Rock Hill
Union	711	Union
Electric City	716	Anderson
Piedmont	746	Greenville
Golden Hour	776	Bennettsville
Excelsior	790	Darlington
Liberty	800	Florence
Sacred Heart	835	Sumter
Azalea	877	Summerville
Phyllis Wheatley	907	Walterboro
Monticello City	944	Mt. Pleasant
Daughters of Liberty	948	Crecent Beach
Faithful Few	956	Timmonsville
Rose	986	Clover
Bon Filla	998	Hyman
Jasmine	1001	Beaufort
TENNESSEE		
Dunbar	344	Kingsport
Rose of Sharon	355	Greenville

Name	*No.*	*Location*
Lucy Ligon	356	Clarksville
Armistice	364	Chattanooga
Anna S. Church	695	Memphis
Spencer Jackson	763	Nashville
Rebecca Carney	798	Murfreesboro
Amarse	810	Knoxville
Callie Morton	817	Columbia
Lula Cliffe	938	Franklin
W. J. O. Lee	949	Humboldt
Atomic	960	Oak Ridge
Orange Mound	997	Memphis
Lena Thompson	1024	Dickson
Emma V. Kelley	1038	Etowah
Watauga	1043	Morristown
TEXAS		
Madonna Temple	423	Galveston
Tulip	581	Port Arthur
Western Star	634	El Paso
El Tex	636	Houston
Sunrise	751	Dallas
Gateway	822	Orange
Alpha	840	Beaumont
Daughters of Alamo	871	San Antonio
Faith	880	Wichita Falls
Unity	897	Texas City
White Orchid	931	Houston
Ever Ready	954	Amarillo
Ocean Wave	1030	Corpus Christi
UTAH		
Timpanogus	483	Salt Lake City
Zion	908	Ogden
VIRGINIA		
Norfolk	1-A	Norfolk
Norfolk	1-B	Norfolk
Beulah	4	Norfolk
Truelight	5	Hampton
Benjamin	20	Richmond
Beauty of the World	40	Portsmouth
Phyllis Wheatley	62	Phoebus
Blue Ridge	67	Charlottesville
Queen Esther	70	Richmond
Capeville	78	Cape Charles
Pride of Lynchburg	81	Lynchburg
White Rose Beauty	89	Newport News
Golden Gate	90	Suffolk
Venus	107	Fredericksburg

Name	*No.*	*Location*
Majestic	109	Petersburg
Eureka	112	Norfolk
Israel	138	Alexandria
St. Mary	152	Franklin
Manhattan	184	Farmville
Dorcas	243	Arlington
Silver Leaf	330	Windsor
Pride of Blue Ridge	372	Warrenton
Fidelity	384	Vienna
South River	420	Front Royal
Lily of Virginia	213	Staunton
Wisteria	545	Smithfield
Pride of Gloucester	560	Gloucester
Independence	575	Crewe
M. E. Wood	592	Pocahontas
Emma V. Kelley	660	Spring Grove
Octavious	666	Berryville
Gardenia	720	Deep Creek
Maggie F. Dismond	760	Winchester
Keene Memorial	788	Danville
Olivia Washington	830	Roanoke
Georgia P. Kelley	863	Emporia
Gardenia	864	Martinsville
Jennie Dean	987	Manassas
WASHINGTON		
Evergreen	157	Seattle
Lily of the West	180	Tacoma
Mt. Rainer	804	Bremerton
Valley of the Sun	852	Yakima
Rhododendron	866	Pasco
WEST VIRGINIA		
Deborah	125	Wheeling
Marion	153	Fairmount
Mountain City	159	Clarksburg
Alpha	248	Cora
Prodigal Guide	316	Williamson
Eureka	339	Bluefield
Twilight	452	Weirton
Kanawha	498	Charleston
Florence Mills	524	Montgomery
Golden Star	534	Huntington
Pride of Dorkey	635	Power
Rhododendron	710	Parkersburg
Coal Valley	733	Osage
Guiding Light	735	Triadelphia
Maggie L. Walker	738	East Beckley

Coles	765	Northfork
Ruth	848	Valls Creek
Pride of Raleigh	858	Raleigh
Shenandoah	913	Martinsburg
Monogalia	922	Morgantown
Queens	955	Northfork
WISCONSIN		
Juenau Fidelity	247	Milwaukee
Pioneer	641	Cheyenne

Index

H

I

J

K

N

Q

R

T

U

V

W

X

Y

www.ingramcontent.com/pod-product-compliance
Lightning Source LLC
Chambersburg PA
CBHW020458100426
42812CB00024B/2701

* 9 7 8 0 9 7 6 8 1 1 1 3 8 *